CHAPELS OF THE CYNON VALLEY.

CAPELI CWM CYNON

Photograph opposite:
   Hen Dy Cwrdd, Unitarian Chapel Trecynon, the
   oldest Nonconformist Chapel in the Cynon Valley.
   Founded 1751; Rebuilt 1862.
   Photograph taken circa 1900.

CHAPELS
OF THE
CYNON VALLEY

CAPELI CWM CYNON

ALAN VERNON JONES, M.R.I.C.S.

CYNON VALLEY HISTORY SOCIETY
2004

First Impression – 2004

ISBN 0 9531076 1 2

© Alan Vernon Jones & Cynon Valley History Society. 2004.

Printed in Wales at
Gomer Press, Llandysul, Ceredigion SA44 4JL

This Book is dedicated
to the Founders and Pioneers
of Nonconformity in
The Cynon Valley

ACKNOWLEDGEMENTS

My appreciation is due to the Committee Members of the Cynon Valley History Society for their contribution in providing some of the historical details and several photographs. My thanks also to the Society for publishing and allowing me the opportunity to write this book. My special thanks to Eric Rose and his wife Christine for their untiring effort in typing the manuscripts, and to Hywel Vaughan for kindly proof-reading the draft copies and for making helpful suggestions and observations. I am grateful to a fellow chapel historian, Professor Anthony Jones, C.B.E., President of The Art Institute of Chicago for writing the Foreword, and for his kind help over the past twenty years. Professor A. Jones is author of "Welsh Chapels", published 1984 and 1996, and has family connections at Mountain Ash, Merthyr Tydfil and Anglesey.

My gratitude is extended to the following groups and organisations for their assistance:-
  Ministers, Deacons and various officers for providing information and allowing me access to their chapels. The staff of Aberdare Central Library; Cynon Valley Museum; Glamorgan Record Office, Cardiff; CADW, and the Planning Department of the former Mid. Glamorgan County Council. The many individuals who have assisted in compiling historical notes and other information are acknowledged throughout this book. My gratitude also to Jonathan Lewis and staff of Gomer Press, Llandysul, Ceredigion, for their helpful suggestions and guidance throughout the printing process. Those who have allowed photographs from their collection to be used, are credited with the accompanying captions. Last but not least, I thank my lovely wife Judith for her understanding and encouragement throughout the writing and preparation of this book over many years.

Alan Vernon Jones.
Autumn 2004.

CONTENTS

FOREWORD   By Professor Anthony Jones, C.B.E.   xi
President of the Art Institute of Chicago.

INTRODUCTION   By Alan Vernon Jones, M.R.I.C.S.   xiii
Chairman of the Cynon Valley History Society.

CHAPTER 1   Chapel histories, drawings and photographs.   1

CHAPTER 2   History of Nonconformity and Dissent in the   181
Cynon Valley 1642 to 1920.

CHAPTER 3   An architectural study.   192

CHAPTER 4   The chapels – internally.   221

CHAPTER 5   The chapels – externally.   235

CHAPTER 6   Chapel – A way of life.   260

CHAPTER 7   Religious Revivals.   291

CHAPTER 8   Recreation and entertainment.   335

CHAPTER 9   The chapels in a time of change.   356

CHAPTER 10   A collection of tales, poems and facts.   381

APPENDIX A   Map of Cynon Valley.   399

APPENDIX B   Schedule of locations and towns.   400

APPENDIX C   List of the 180 chapels in alphabetical order.   401

APPENDIX D   Schedule of the chapels in each town.   406

APPENDIX E   Abbreviations used to denote denominations.   410

APPENDIX F   Religious denominations – a brief description.   411

APPENDIX G   Bibliography and further recommended reading.   414

INDEX   417

FOREWORD

Alan Vernon Jones has done us all a great service in publishing his work on 'Chapels of the Cynon Valley'. Anyone who is interested in what these buildings signify today, and what they meant in the past, will enjoy and learn from his research, because here they all are. Big and small, gaudy and dull, some with modest exteriors but fabulous interiors.

Chapels are those big boxes with no chimneys that dot the valley-scape from Ynysybwl to Penderyn. They are unmistakable shapes in the towns and villages, some crammed onto tiny plots of land, others with spacious front yards. Every street has one – sometimes two or three!

And every one of them has a story to tell. And in the telling they unveil the valleys past, reveal the lives of its population, showing us the transition of the Cynon Valley from its bucolic agricultural and forested past to the birthplace of modern industry it became. They tell us how its indigenous rural workers were overwhelmed by immigrants from all over Wales, whose work was to strip the cover off the hills and valleys, to get at the ores that lay beneath that cover. The population exploded, not only in Cynon, but also its sister valleys to east and west. The farming life that had been, literally, the meat-and-potatoes of the place was pushed north to the heads of those valleys. The brute force of industry fell on the cwms of Rhondda, Merthyr and Cynon, shredding the landscape and transforming the valleys into the shapes we see today. Foundries, factories, collieries, all produced the spoil, mine-tailings and huge tips that are still to be seen as a legacy of the industrial revolution. Individual hamlets and villages grew into continuous ribbons of housing and commerce, clinging to the valley sides, with homes in service to the pits and manufactories that sprang up close to the rivers.

Industry converted the valleys to iron and steel providers, coal was the energy source. But there was a different kind of conversion going on at the same time – the conversion of men's souls. Tiny Nonconformist congregations had lived in the Cynon and neighbouring valleys, forming simple chapels. As industry, population, and relative wealth increased, these congregations began to grow. Their chapels were inadequate. They were enlarged or, more often pulled down and rebuilt. And even those chapels were themselves demolished and replaced by others. Successive religious revivals sprang up with preachers pointing out the evil work of the Satan in the lethal outbreaks of cholera, but hope and the healing of the Lord was to be found in the chapels and churches. The revivals drew thousands into the chapels; in the Cynon Valley in the middle of the nineteenth century a large proportion of the population were attending a chapel, and the numbers shot even higher as the century wore on.

And the chapel buildings themselves were undergoing conversion and revival. As they were converted from small to immense, their architectural appearance began to revive styles from architectural history. They changed from modest barn-like buildings to Gothic and Classical temples, depending on whether a congregation could raise the funds for increasingly grand buildings. Building Fund-drives took donations from the poorest members, and from the mine-owners and industrial barons. They organised choral concerts – even raffles – and created the phenomenon of vast social events known as the 'te-parti mawr'. And teams of ministers would arrive as 'kings of the pulpit' for endless preaching marathons. Money came, chapels grew. By the onset of the First World War around 6,700 to 7,000 chapels had been built in Wales, the vast majority in the industrial south. But by the end of that war, chapel building had come to a virtual dead stop.

Since then, time and tide have been hard on chapels. Congregations have dwindled from the thousands to the dozens, and sometimes even smaller. Few could afford the upkeep of these great big draughty boxes. Chapels fell into disarray and disrepair, crumbled and collapsed. Disuse and vandalism became partners. Structures became unsafe, demolition followed. The valleys proud heritage of the tight relationship between industry and Nonconformity collapsed together, as South Wales de-industrialized and religion faded as a central social concern.

Ironically, as more-and-more chapels disappear from the valley landscape, more-and-more people have become interested in them. Fortunately, a few good people like Alan Vernon Jones became interested in the chapels before they disappeared. He began to ask the core questions: why are these buildings here, who did they serve, who designed and built them, why do they look as they do, how were they paid for, what did they mean to the community, what religious, social, economic and architectural history do they hold? What do they tell us about this Cynon Valley, and how does this fit into the incredibly complex story of Wales in the Industrial Age. And absolutely vitally, these were questions he answered by going out and doing the research in the field. Photographing, documenting, studying the buildings themselves – there is no substitute for this. As he did so, chapels were literally disappearing around him. His fieldwork records and preserves a rich history, but it's one that is fading fast. In the late nineteenth century Nonconformists were proud to state that they were opening a chapel a week in Wales – today they are being demolished at the same rate.

Until quite recently, there has been no 'official' attempt to record the disappearing chapel heritage of Wales, most of the work has been done by inquisitive amateur local historians, architecture fans, denominational historians, and we are grateful for their time and effort. Today, proper professionals from the best-equipped agencies like CADW and the National Building Record Offices, and the Royal Commission, are hard at work documenting everything they can about the Welsh chapel buildings. CAPEL, The Chapels' Heritage Society, has a lively and hardworking membership, busy recording chapel culture and history all over Wales. The National Library, Aberystwyth, the National Museum, Cardiff, the Glamorgan Records Office, and St. Fagan's Museum of Welsh Life, are becoming great repositories of masses of material relating to chapel history and culture. Nearer to home, the Aberdare Central Library and the Cynon Valley Museum also hold valuable and extensive records. But the work of these agencies and organisations is fairly new, and cannot replace the kind of dedicated and in-depth study we see in the fieldwork of Mr. Jones here in the Cynon Valley – work which was well-advanced when I first saw it in 1995, when I was invited to speak about chapel architecture at Ramoth Chapel, Hirwaun. As a fellow friend-of-chapels, and amateur historian of their culture, I am delighted to see Mr. Jones' excellent research into the Cynon chapels bear fruit in the form of this publication. It adds to the core knowledge we have of chapels and their meaning, and is especially timely as we continue to lose these symbols of an extraordinary and dynamic period of Wales' history. May I offer him thanks and congratulations on his work, and compliments to the Cynon Valley History Society for bringing it to publication.

Professor Anthony Jones CBE
President of The Art Institute of Chicago.
Autumn 2004.

INTRODUCTION.

At the turn of the twenty-first century, here after just over 250 years of Nonconformist religious witness is a written and illustrated guide to the history and art contained within the walls of our chapels, which over the years have been used for worship and praise, refuge and prayer, and was throughout the ages the hub of activity for countless social gatherings, recreation, education and community meeting for much of the population of the Cynon Valley. The purpose of studying the past is to seek a fuller understanding of the forces that have shaped what we are today. Research can play an important part in defining our cultural identity; it does this not only through studying our fine chapels and other worthy buildings, but also by preserving and interpreting the material evidence of their past and providing literature and art to reveal to us the history of our rich local heritage.

Over the past twenty years of research and documentation of 180 places of worship of all Non-conformist denominations throughout the Cynon Valley, most of them photographed externally and internally, I have herein attempted to present a complete and definitive treatise of the historical and artistic tradition of our fine religious edifices, and what may to us and future generations become a useful means from which to learn and appreciate how much in the course of time has been dedicated to the faith and diligence of so many. Furthermore it has been my aim and wish over many years to perhaps rekindle a dwindling interest for some, and to engender and broaden an awareness of our distinctive social history and splendid chapel heritage. For others it is hoped it will become one of the first convenient means that we people of Cynon Valley and others elsewhere have at our disposal to enter into the artistic and rich splendour of the chapels that dominate and form such an important part of our landscape.

Whatever their architectural design, various forms and styles, good and indifferent, grand or simple, dull or bold, love them or loathe them, our chapels more than anything else give our valley a unique and inimitable character and appearance, and in their absence no part of the Cynon Valley would be spiritually or culturally the same. They indeed form a striking and noticeable part of the local landscape and without them much of our valley and hillsides would comprise a uniform row of endless terraced houses.

As with all things that may be too familiar to us, the chapels above all are only too sadly missed when they fall into decay and are finally pulled down and cleared away. It is only then that we wished we had driven and turned away the bulldozer, and exploited all avenues to save them or at least to ensure that they were preserved and put to some good alternative use or similar useful function. How sad it has become to realise that only one third of the chapels recorded and built are today active and open for worship, whilst a third have disappeared from the scene altogether, and the remainder have been converted to other uses or remain vacant or derelict.

The decline in chapels is due to many governing factors that ultimately lead to closure and demolition; this is studied in a later chapter. Today many chapels are struggling to keep their doors open in some cases with less than a dozen faithful members, whilst a handful of chapels are thriving with activity with an abundance of members, young and old.

Bygone days witnessed our forefathers worshipping and meeting in humble and simple surroundings; barns, cottages, each other's houses, the open air, upper rooms of public houses and even tents. There was no pretence to grandeur or importance and these modest abodes were found at the time to be adequate to meet their spiritual needs; a modest beginning to their 'cause' but nevertheless a bold start. We shall read later of the early Dissenters and their meetings held in remote secret conventicles to avoid persecution, and how through the Toleration Act of 1689 the Nonconformists became at last free to build their own Meeting Houses, and later the chapels for the purpose of worship. After the 1689 Act the early Nonconformists continued their meetings and services without suffering their former fears and they started building small chapels, simple in design, around the late eighteenth century and early nineteenth centuries. Then came iron and coal; canals and railways; new industries were formed and rapidly expanded, and the population increased dramatically by the influx of English speaking immigrants and others throughout Wales, seeking work in the Cynon Valley. Together with the many famous religious revivals from the early eighteenth to early twentieth centuries this changed everything, and chapels were thereafter built at an incredible rate.

As numbers and memberships grew, chapel funds increased enabling the building and often rebuilding and enlargement of bigger and grander chapels. Furthermore, competition between the various denominations and religious sects often created rivalry in striving to build larger and more commodious edifices in order to accommodate and attract larger numbers of worshippers into their chapels. The ebb and flow continued as the years went by until sadly today the chapels continue to decline and fall into disrepair through a combination of lack of finance and neglect, and eventually to disappear from our local scene at an alarming rate. Half the total number of chapels recorded were built between 1751 when Hen-Dy-Cwrdd, Trecynon was founded, and 1869. Hen-Dy-Cwrdd (The Old Meeting House) is the oldest Nonconformist chapel in the Cynon Valley. After about 1910 when chapel building reached its peak in the Cynon Valley the rate of chapel building levelled off. The sharpest increase in the rate of demolition was between 1960 and 2000, when about 45 chapels out of a total of 180 were demolished.

In his 'History of Llanwonno' written in 1888, the notable Rev. William (Gwilym) Thomas, known in Literary circles as 'Glanffrwd' (b.1843 – d.1890) of Ynysybwl, reminds us of the chapels which in his time had long since gone. I quote below his unique poetic style of writing:

> "The old chapels long since gone, where once could be heard the strains of song and praise of a past century, where our faithful forefathers knelt at the Throne of God, and where a host of souls was saved; a place consecrated by the sermons, prayers, tears and sighs of pilgrims who have long since departed to a better world. Instead of Holy song and the refrains of melodious hymns, one now hears the patters of children's feet and the whistles and laughter of boys and girls many of whom know little or nothing of the sanctity and holiness of these former revered places of worship and Houses of Prayer."

Old chapels have an endearing and captivating charm, even if some of them have succumbed to the ravages of time and fallen into heaps of grey stones and rubble. But they have their story to tell, for many things have happened in and around them; If only we knew! They are a kind of centre around which are gathered fond memories and traditions of the old folk, old customs, and the old way of life which now have gone forever. Somehow we feel that the old chapels, the old grey walls of this and former generations are all we have to remind us of the simple and good life lived by our forefathers; God-fearing and peaceful wise men, and what wise men they were! Great characters and faithful stalwarts with foresight, and good proud giants among men of the chapels long since gone. Oh! – How full our valley still is of these fine old chapels. Let us then visit and enter them while we are able, and wonder and ponder upon events there in times gone by. We are indeed thankful to our admirable forefathers for all their devotion and sacrifice, and through whose untiring efforts we have entered into such a rich chapel inheritance. In these fast living modern days of the twenty-first century when many of us appear obsessed with the value of material things and secular interests, we would do well to pause for a little while and remember and take pride in our glorious heritage and outstanding chapel history.

Chapels disappear and time changes everything, but we know there is a time to break down and a time to build up; a time to cast away stones and a time to gather stones together; a time to reflect on past times and a time to forget; but the history and memories left behind we cherish, and they will surely remain in our hearts and minds forever.

I now invite you all to visit the wonderful chapels of our beloved valley. Join me and meander through the following pages of history and bygone days to discover something of their distant past, and in so doing rescue their wealth of memories and stories from neglect and oblivion. Let us then avail ourselves and enter these splendid and familiar holy places, a number still thankfully spared and open to us, which speak about God, and about you, about all of us, His people, about our past and future and the vision and courage of our forefathers, who at great personal sacrifice and human toil proudly built for us –

CHAPELS OF THE CYNON VALLEY.

Alan Vernon Jones, M.R.I.C.S.
Chairman of the Cynon Valley History Society.
Cwmdare.
Autumn 2004.

Chapter 1

CHAPEL HISTORIES, DRAWINGS AND PHOTOGRAPHS

		Page No.
(i)	**Introduction**	**1**
(ii)	**Chapel Name and Denomination**	**1**
(iii)	**Address and Locality**	**1**
(iv)	**Date Built**	**1**
(v)	**Current Use**	**2**
(vi)	**Brief History**	**2**
(vii)	**The Drawings and Photographs**	**2**
●	**Chapel References, numbers 1 to 180**	**3 to 164**

"I was glad when they said unto Me
Let us go into The House of The Lord".
Psalm 122, verse 1.
Inscription on stone plaque located in the forecourt of Elim P.C.,
Monk Street, Aberdare. (Built 1863; Demolished 2001).

(i) Introduction
This chapter deals with the history of each chapel and other places of Nonconformist worship of all denominations located throughout the Cynon Valley from Ynysybwl in the South to Penderyn in the North. For ease of reference a table is shown in Appendix C listing all 180 chapels in alphabetical order. Also, the chapels are shown in order of each of the twenty-four localities, South Central and North as shown in Appendix D.

(ii) Chapel Name and Denomination
Each chapel has a Reference Number, (Ref. No's 1 to 180). The name of each chapel is followed by the Denomination in abbreviated form e.g. W.B. = Welsh Baptist, and so on. The various denominations are explained in Appendix E.

(iii) Address and Locality
The street or road name is shown for each chapel, followed by the locality or town. For the purpose of convenience and clarity, I have divided the Cynon Valley into three separate areas, viz. South, Central and North. Each area comprises eight towns or villages, making a total of twenty-four localities. See Appendix B.

(iv) Date Built
This refers to the year of erection of a chapel and is usually the date of completion and opening followed, where applicable, by the date of rebuilding, extending, enlargement, refurbishing, restoration, alteration or repair. The date of the beginning or founding of the "Cause" of a particular chapel is shown

in the "Brief History" text, and is not necessarily the date the chapel was built, as many "Causes" began by holding meetings and services in another chapel, private house or hired rooms, including public houses, usually in the "long room" above or adjacent to the public bar area.

(v) Current Use

The current use of each chapel is indicated as at Autumn 2004. This will naturally henceforth continually change over the passage of time as a consequence of closure, vacancy, conversion to another use, demolition or redevelopment of a vacant site after demolition. "Still Active" denotes the chapel remains open for public worship.

Chapels active, vacant/converted or demolished

As at Autumn 2004 the current position of the 180 chapels erected in the Cynon Valley since 1751 is as follows:-

Active	=	63	35%
Vacant	=	11	6%
Converted	=	50	28%
Demolished	=	56	31%
No. Built	=	180	100%

(vi) Brief History

The history of each chapel has been researched and collated over a period of some past twenty years, and research material has been obtained from several primary and secondary sources, including the following:

* Chapel history booklets.
* Interviewing Ministers, Deacons, Secretaries and chapel members.
* Consultation and research at Aberdare Central Library and Mountain Ash Library; Glamorgan Record Office, Cardiff.
* Chapel Minute Books.
* Local newspapers including the old Aberdare Times (from 1862 to 1902), The Aberdare Leader (1902 onwards), Mountain Ash Leader and The Western Mail.
* Notes from research papers of W. W. Price and Rev. I. Parry, research room, Aberdare Central Library.
* Other references – see Bibliography and Further Recommended Reading list, Appendix G.

Chapel Photographs Galore!

In his private collection of photographs of Chapels of the Cynon Valley, over a period of 20 years (1984-2004), Alan Vernon Jones has compiled a total of 2300 photographs, plus 330 chapel drawings and maps. They cover the 180 places of Nonconformist worship and chapels throughout the entire Cynon Valley, and are contained in three large A3 volumes totalling 540 pages.

Have you any Chapel Photographs?

There must be hundreds if not thousands of old photographs relating to chapel buildings and the social aspects of chapel life in the ownership of many private individuals in the locality as well as chapel secretaries etc. Why not pass these on to the Central Library and Cynon Valley Museum for copying and placing on their Archives?

(vii) The Drawings and Photographs

The drawings produced in this book were prepared in 1978–80 by a team of young people. They were engaged under a Job Creation Project, promoted and organised by the Planning Department of the former Mid Glamorgan County Council, with the financial support of the Manpower Services Commission. Of the 600 or so Nonconformist chapels that were photographed, surveyed and recorded in Mid Glamorgan, 108 were in the Cynon Valley. Measured drawings were prepared of every chapel and included plans and main elevations. Historical information was collected wherever possible. Some thirty young people were employed during the two-year period of the scheme. Their backgrounds varied considerably, but many having learnt new skills found permanent work in similar fields. The project justified itself in this respect whilst producing a valuable record for posterity of one of the most important building types in architectural terms of the Glamorgan valleys.

Those employed on the Cynon Valley District area were: Ian Ball (sadly deceased), Bruce Carr, Chris

Evans, Mick Gittens, Ray Lewis, Dave Morgan, Kevin Pearson, Ieuan Rees, Brian Smith, Tim Walpole, Terry Wilkinson and Martin Howarth Williams. Thanks must be given to Warne John, whose brilliant idea initiated this project and who together with Elizabeth Evans organised the day to day running of the project. (Employees of the former Mid Glamorgan County Planning Department). The drawings and other records are now kept at the Glamorgan Record Office, County Hall, Cardiff, and through their kind permission the Society acknowledge reproduction of them in this book. All photographs throughout this book were taken by Alan Vernon Jones, except where otherwise indicated and credited.

CHAPEL REF. NO. 1.

NAME & DENOMINATION: **BETHEL C.M.**

ADDRESS / LOCALITY: **ROCK TERRACE, YNYSYBWL.**

DATE BUILT: **1786 – REBUILT 1876. CLOSED CIRCA 1960/70**

CURRENT USE: **CONVERTED TO A DWELLING HOUSE IN 1978.**
THE VESTRY WAS DEMOLISHED AT THE TIME OF CONVERSION.

BRIEF HISTORY: The oldest Non-conformist chapel in Ynysybwl, located adjacent to 'Pleasant View'. The First chapel, built in 1786, was originally slightly above New Bethel, and was known as Fanheulog Llanwynno Chapel, also Fanheulog Bethel. It was converted into two dwellings circa 1880, named "Bethel Cottages". In 1876 the second Bethel was built on a piece of ground belonging to the old chapel; It was closed in the 1970's and was converted into a dwelling house in 1978. It is believed that John Wesley preached at Bethel in 1786.

Rev. William Thomas ('Glanffrwd') tells us that in 1774 the first public worship in Ynysybwl was held in a cottage named Rhyd-y-Gwreiddyn (i.e. Source of the Stream), located west of Fanheulog, and about one mile south west of Ynysybwl, following the River Ffrwd. It was here that early meetings of the Nonconformists took place when they first came to the district of Ynysybwl. Glanffrwd also informs us that the great and notable Howell Harris (1714 – 1773) preached in Llanwonno and Ynysybwl in 1736, before Old Bethel (1786) was built. Services were held at various places around 1770, including 'Ty–tan–wal' located near Mynachdy, and there is no doubt that in this old farmhouse Howel Harris delivered powerful sermons. According to the old Welsh Methodists they met at Ty-tan-wal (the house under the wall) and "observed clear signs of God's presence among them; the congregations numbered 30 – 45 and would give rise to a 'hwyl' and hearty thanksgiving and praise."

The religious census of 1851 states – "Vanhayly (Fanheulog) chapel, Calvinistic Methodist, erected 1786. Space – free 4; other 6; standing 100. Present – morning 40 scholars, afternoon 65; evening 95. George Davies, Deacon, New House, Llanwunno.

Rhyd-y-Gwreiddyn, Ynysybwl. An early meeting-place of Nonconformists established 1774. Taken circa 1885.

New Bethel, built 1876

4

CHAPELS OF THE CYNON VALLEY

CHAPEL REF. NO. 2

NAME & DENOMINATION: **EBENEZER W.W.M.**

ADDRESS / LOCALITY: **ROBERT STREET, YNYSYBWL**

DATE BUILT: **1892**

CURRENT USE: **CONVERTED TO A WAREHOUSE FOR STORAGE OF MARKET STALL GOODS. OWNED IN 1996 BY MR. DAVID FOX OF PONTYPRIDD. THE STORE IS REFERRED TO LOCALLY AS 'HARRODS' OR 'THE EMPORIUM'.**

BRIEF HISTORY: Front elevation remains unaltered, but the interior has been taken out. Located between No's: 95 & 97. The chapel was a branch of the English Wesleyan Chapel, Thompson Street. (Ref: 9.) The Minister circa 1930 was Rev. Lewis Edwards.

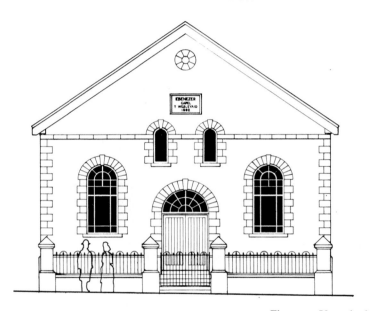 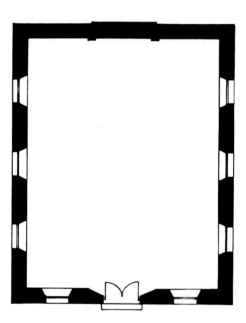

Ebenezer, Ynysybwl.

Minister – Rev. Lewis Edwards, Deacons & Sunday School Teachers and children circa 1930.

(Stephen Thomas collection.)

CHAPEL REF. NO.3

NAME & DENOMINATION: ENGLISH CONGREGATIONAL E.Cong.

ADDRESS / LOCALITY: ROBERT STREET, YNYSYBWL

DATE BUILT: 1906

CURRENT USE: CLOSED, CIRCA 1960. USED FOR MANY YEARS AS A STORE BY MESSRS. ELLIS & DENTON, BUILDING CONTRACTORS. CONVERTED TO A 5 BEDROOM DWELLING HOUSE 2002/3, NAMED "YR HEN CAPEL" – THE OLD CHAPEL. LOCATED ADJACENT TO NO. 175 ROBERT STREET.

BRIEF HISTORY A branch of Tabernacle W.I. (Ref: 8). The 'cause' commenced in 1896. Memorial stones laid on 8th. October 1906 by Miss Jennet Williams, Cribindy Farm, Ynysybwl, and Miss Jennie E. Morgan, Gurnos House, Ynysybwl. (Four stones in total). Seating for 350. Gwilym Gower was a prominent member and deacon when the chapel opened in 1906. Also commonly referred to as "New Road Congregational Chapel". One of the first chapels to close its doors in Ynysybwl. Nearby stands 'Aelwyd' formerly the Church Hall, now sadly in a derelict condition. First minister was Rev. William Ebenezer Davies, 1899 – 1900. Rev. Peter Lewis was minister here in the 1950's.

English Congregational Chapel, Ynysybwl.

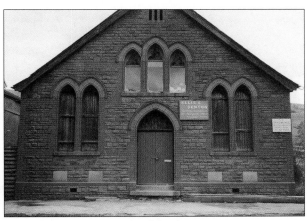

Taken in 1995.

CHAPEL REF. NO. 4

NAME & DENOMINATION: GOSPEL HALL G.H.

ADDRESS / LOCALITY: AUGUSTUS STREET, YNYSYBWL

DATE BUILT: 1926

CURRENT USE: STILL ACTIVE.

BRIEF HISTORY The 'Cause' commenced in 1906, by Mr. Archibald Mc.lay, then Managing Director of a firm of Printers & Stationers settling in Cardiff in 1902. In 1906 discussions took place with Mr. James, a Christian farmer and deacon, who owned Mynachdy Farm, Old Ynysybwl; he had recently withdrawn from his chapel owing to certain convictions derived from the scriptures over sectarian procedures. Mr. Mc.lay spoke to Mr. & Mrs. James, and a Mr. Salter, a farm labourer, and they gladly followed his teachings and agreed to be baptised in a mountain stream dammed up for the purpose, but ice needed breaking first! An assembly of Christian Brethren in Ynysybwl had thus been formed in 1906 with gospel meetings held at Windsor Cottage, Ynysybwl (now the home of David & Marjorie Harris), and later in Robert Street, in what has become 'Jeans' florist shop. As numbers grew, special gospel outreach meetings were held, and permission was given by the local miners to use the Lesser Hall of the Workmen's hall in Windsor Place. (Destroyed by fire in May 1992, replaced by flats.) Membership further increased and in 1926 a Gospel hall was built at the top of Augustus Street, opposite the site of the former Salvation Army Citadel. Many miners who were then on strike helped with the construction work. During the Second World War, evacuees helped to swell the Sunday School numbers to 200.

    Thanks to Mr. G. B. Rees for the preparation of this historical account.

Taken in 1926.

Taken in June 2002.

The Gospel Hall during construction work in 1926.   *(Stephen Thomas collection.)*

CHAPEL REF. NO. 5

NAME & DENOMINATION: **JERUSALEM W.P.**

ADDRESS / LOCALITY: **THOMPSON STREET, YNYSYBWL.**

DATE BUILT: **1888**

CURRENT USE: **CLOSED 1976 – CONVERTED TO A BUILDER'S STORE. LOCATED ADJACENT TO NO.1 THOMPSON STREET, ON A CORNER PLOT.**

BRIEF HISTORY: The 'cause' began in a room of a house in the village in 1885, by a number of local miners under the auspices of the Calvinistic Methodists. In 1888 the chapel was built by the Williams Brothers of Cribinddu Farm. William & Edward Williams became deacons, and they contributed generously to chapel finances. The first minister was Rev. D. Jones, or "Jones the bugail (shepherd)" as he was best known. The Rev. Isaac Morris was minister from 1913 –25, followed by Rev. T.M. Lloyd of Treorchy 1925 – 31, whose wife was in charge of the Sunday School and Band of Hope. Membership in the 1920's – 1930's was 350, and in 1938 was 270. The Rev. Randall Jones (former collier) ministered from 1938 – 46, followed by Rev. H. Glyn Davies 1946 – 55, and Rev. J. L. Mathias, 1955 – circa 1970. Miss Rosina Davies, a famous evangelist once preached in Jerusalem after a successful American visit. A united Christmas Gymanfa Ganu was broadcast on BBC radio in 1936 – Mansel Thomas was the conductor. In 1976 Jerusalem joined with Noddfa (Ref: 6.), where at present they worship in Welsh. Mrs. Nansi Valentine's father, John Davies, was a stonemason in Lady Windsor colliery, and a prominent deacon and organist for 35 years. In 1932 he was presented with an "Illuminated Address" done by hand, this is proudly displayed in Mrs. Valentine's home.

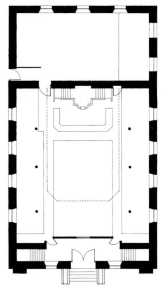

    This historical account was kindly prepared by Mrs. Valentine, who will celebrate her 90th. birthday in 2003.

Jerusalem, Ynysybwl.

Taken in 1986.

CHAPEL REF. NO. 6

NAME & DENOMINATION: **NODDFA. W.B.**

ADDRESS / LOCALITY: **HIGH STREET, YNYSYBWL.**

DATE BUILT: **1889.**

CURRENT USE: **STILL ACTIVE.**

BRIEF HISTORY: Located on a corner plot on the junction of High Street and Thompson Street. Architect/Designer – Rev. Dr. Roberts of Pontypool. Builder – Charles Jenkins & Sons, Porth. Building cost, £1,290, seating for 650. Early recollections from a descendant of Watkin Edwards, who stayed at Gelli Wrgan mentions a baptism of two people in 1786, in the River Cynon. The 'cause' began with meetings and services held in the kitchen of Gelli Wrgan farmhouse in 1885.

In August 1885, Rev. Edward Roberts and Mr. Dewi Cule met local residents to inspect land on which to build a chapel. Prior to this, many open-air meetings were held in the old Bethel Chapel (Ref: 1), the only Non-conformist chapel in Ynysybwl at that time. Later in 1885, meetings and services were held in a rented room in the Robertstown Hotel. During this period, many converts were baptised in the River Clydach, and at times ice had to be broken before baptisms could proceed.

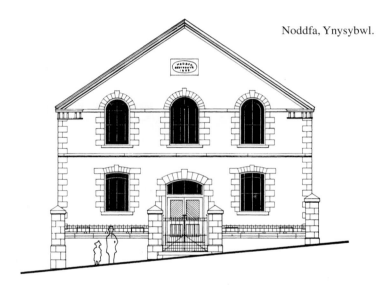

Noddfa, Ynysybwl.

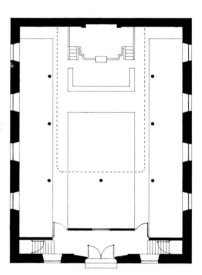

Taken in 1986.

In May 1886, land was chosen and building of the chapel discussed. By April 1888 the chapel had become Independent, and Noddfa was built in only ten months, completed by May 1890. Everyone, including the ladies, helped by carrying stones from the river for the building. There were 121 members in 1890. 176 members in 1938 with 150 in Sunday School – 136 members in 1947. Initially there was no pulpit; a table on which was placed a large bible was used instead.

The memorial stone was laid by Mr. George Evans of Sunnyside House, Pontypridd, on 10th. May 1890. The first minister was Rev. William Barker Jones (1891-95), followed by Rev. E.J. Williams; Rev. Owen Jones and Rev. Gwilym Davies. Secretary's were- Mr. John Isaac; Mr. W.D. Arnold; Mrs. Nansi Valentine and Miss Anne S. Arnold. The present Treasurer is Miss Elizabeth Valentine, and the organist is Mrs. A.S. Arnold. (From 1949 to 2003 –53 years service!). The religious revival of 1904/5 swelled numbers, but membership fell after the Second World War. In 1976 the chapel became Undebol Gymraeg (United Welsh Church); Members joined Noddfa from Jerusalem (Ref: 5), and some from Tabernacle (Ref: 8), to make up around 80 members for 1976. Present membership – 15.

Thanks to Mrs. Anne S. Arnold for preparing this history.

CHAPEL REF. NO. 7

NAME & DENOMINATION: **PRESBYTERIAN CHURCH. E.P.**

ADDRESS / LOCALITY: **GLYN STREET, YNYSYBWL.**

DATE BUILT: **1896.**

CURRENT USE: **STILL ACTIVE.**

BRIEF HISTORY: The 'cause' commenced as a result of the decision by the elders of Jerusalem W.P. (Ref:5) to establish an English speaking chapel for the English-speaking miners entering the valley to work in the newly opened Lady Windsor Colliery. The chapel was formed by William Thomas, a successful grocer known throughout the village as "Thomas Bach", who was to serve as chapel secretary for 55 years. The first meetings were held in the Long Room of the Robertstown Hotel, and as numbers increased, a small chapel was built on the present site.

A larger chapel was later built in 1896, as an extension to the older chapel, which then became the vestry.

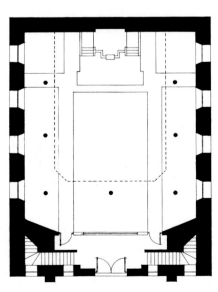

Presbyterian Church, Ynysybwl.

The chapel is of Gothic design with a slate spire on a square tower base. Attractive tracery windows adorn the front elevation. Seating capacity for 500, including the gallery. The foundation stone was laid by Rhys Davies Esq. Merthyr. 18th. May 1896. An annual donation from the bequest of Lord Davies – Ocean Coal Company, of Llandinam was welcomed, especially during the 1930 depression years.

Between 1927 and 2002 the chapel has been ministered by Rev. Dr. Richards; Rev. Wynne; Rev. Charles Owen; Rev. Norman Ellis; Rev. D.K. Smith and Rev. Alvan Richards-Clarke.

Presbyterian Church, Ynysybwl, taken in 1986.

No minister at present. The vestry is now used by Ysgol Feithriw – the movement to establish Welsh language nursery schools. The Three Valley's Choir Festivals were sometimes held here in the past.

Thanks to Mr. Malcolm Burnell for preparing this historical account.

CHAPEL REF. NO. 8

NAME & DENOMINATION: **TABERNACLE. W.I.**

ADDRESS / LOCALITY: **OTHER STREET, YNYSYBWL.**

DATE BUILT: **1886.**

CURRENT USE: **STILL ACTIVE.**

BRIEF HISTORY: The 'cause' commenced in 1885, when a group of young local people were asked why they had not attended Bethel Methodist Chapel (Ref: 1). They claimed that they were not Methodists, but Welsh Independents, and would attend a W.I. chapel if one became available. Consequently in August 1885, the first meetings and services were held in the bar of the newly built Windsor Hotel, and some weeks later in the upper room of the hotel. The chapel was formed on 9th. October 1885 with a communion service officiated by Rev. Robert Thomas, Minister of Carmel W.I. Penrhiwceiber (Ref: 29.).

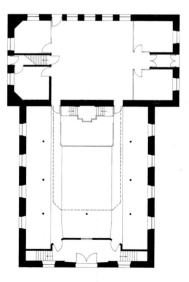

Tabernacle, Ynysybwl.

Tabernacle, Ynysybwl, taken in 1986.   Deacons of Tabernacle, circa 1900.

The following year the chapel was built in Other Street at a cost of £1,490, with seating for 600. The memorial stone was laid on 4th. October 1886 by T. Williams Esq. J.P., of Gwaelod-Y-Garth House, Merthyr Tydfil. The first preacher was Rev. John Williams, 'Yr Hafod' during the opening services on September 11th. & 12th. 1887. Past ministers include – Rev. R.O. Evans (1888-1889); Rev. R.C. Lloyd (1889-1909); Rev. Arthur Jones (1919-1927); Rev. P.H. Lewis (1929-1956). Current minister Rev. Hiefin Elias. Membership in 1892 was 321. Sunday School membership increase during the 1904/5 revival period necessitated the building of a new hall on top of the vestry. Present membership is just over 20.

Thanks to Mr. Idwal Davies for supplying this information.

CHAPEL REF. NO. 9

NAME & DENOMINATION: **WESLEYAN. E.W.M.**

ADDRESS / LOCALITY: **THOMPSON STREET, YNYSYBWL.**

DATE BUILT: **1903.**

CURRENT USE: **STILL ACTIVE.**

BRIEF HISTORY: In 1887 William Lawley came to Ynysybwl to live, and found there was no English 'cause' in the village. He had to walk each Sunday to the Wesleyan Chapel in Pontypridd. In the 1890's he commenced a 'cause' in the home of Mr. & Mrs. Jarman, Thompson Street; the mother chapel in Pontypridd helped to set up the 'cause'. From Thompson Street they moved to an empty shop

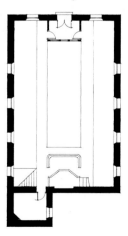

Wesleyan Chapel, Ynysybwl.

in Robert Street, and thereafter met in a small timber building in Thompson Street. The chapel received much support from many who had arrived in the village from Cornwall at the turn of the century.

Built in 1903 by Williams Brothers, Cribin Du, Ynysybwl, at a cost of £845, with seating for 200. The memorial stone was laid on Nov. 5th. 1903 by Miss Nancy Morgan of Gurnos House, Ynysybwl. Mr. Thomas Price was one of the founder members, and Mr. Trevor Main was the last organist. It closed as a Methodist Chapel in 1987, and later became the "Cross Roads Christian Community Centre", a branch of Ebenezer W.W.M. (Ref: 2.) Located adjacent to Nos. 40 & 41 Thompson Street.

CHAPEL REF. NO. 10

NAME & DENOMINATION: **ZION. E.B.**

ADDRESS / LOCALITY: **ROBERT STREET, YNYSYBWL.**

DATE BUILT: **1890. REBUILT IN 1895 & 1905.**

CURRENT USE: **STILL ACTIVE.**

BRIEF HISTORY: The 'cause' was founded in 1887, by Thomas Bound, Owen Lloyd and Thomas Pitchford. First meetings were held in a house in Robert Street and as numbers increased, they held services in the Long Room, Robertstown Hotel (let rent free). In 1890 Zion was built at a cost of £500, by William Bros., of Ynysybwl. Rebuilt in 1895, extended in 1905 as a result of the 1904/5 revival, cost (1905) – £2,000. Seating for 500. Services held in Workmen's Hall and Noddfa (Ref: 6) during the 1905 extension work; opened by Alderman T.J. Hughes on 6th. September 1906. Preacher – Rev. Joseph Ellison, minister at that time. Rev. David John Anthony was minister for 38 years, he died in 1985. The Jarman family has a long association with the chapel, reaching back over six generations. 1943 membership was 164, 1978 membership was 85.

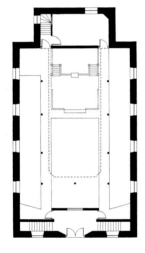

Zion, Ynysybwl.

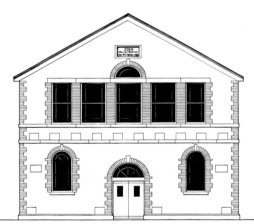

Taken in 1986.

CHAPEL REF. NO. 11.

NAME & DENOMINATION: **BETHANIA W.I.**

ADDRESS / LOCALITY: **MOUNTAIN ASH ROAD, ABERCYNON**

DATE BUILT: **1893. REBUILT 1898.**

CURRENT USE: **DEMOLISHED 1987. SITE NOW COVERED BY FLATS NAMED "BETHANIA" BUILT 1991**

BRIEF HISTORY: Founded by Rev. R.E. Williams of Bethania, Cilfynydd in 1891 by holding a Sunday School at the home of a Mrs. Yorath, 1 Woodland Cottages, Abercynon, and later in 'Bigfield House'; They then moved to a stable in the Basin. The first Bethania (Welsh Cong.) was built in 1893 but became too small for the growing membership; Consequently a new chapel was built in 1898 by W. Games of Abercynon at a cost of £3,500, with seating for 700. The original stone name plaque (1898) is now at the Dare Valley Country Park accommodation block, built into the main stone wall. Located adjacent to 46 Mountain Ash Road. The first minister was Rev. J.J. Williams, who later became Arch Druid. In the period 1894 – 1903, a number of members left Bethania to form Mount Zion English Baptist Chapel (Ref: 18.) i.e. Mynydd Seion. In 1938 Mount Zion joined Bethania, together with their minister Rev. J. Watcyn James. In the chapel there existed a remarkable and unusual keyboard instrument – an 'ORGAPIAN', made by E.W. Homes & Sons of Berkleyhead. It combined a wind organ and piano.

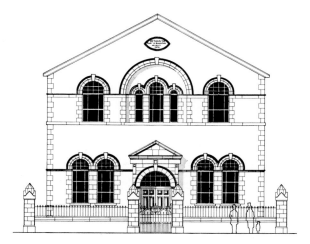 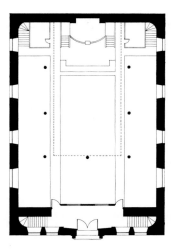

Bethania, Abercynon.

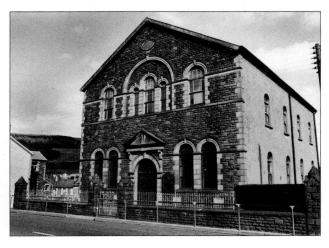

Taken in 1986.

CHAPEL REF. NO. 12

NAME & DENOMINATION: CALVARIA   W.B.

ADDRESS / LOCALITY: GLANCYNON STREET, ABERCYNON

DATE BUILT: 1888 – ENLARGED 1894

CURRENT USE: CLOSED 1981, DEMOLISHED 1983. SITE COVERED BY FLATS FOR THE ELDERLY NAMED 'CALFARIA', BUILT 1987/88.

BRIEF HISTORY: 1894 chapel Architect/ Designer Rev. Dr. Roberts of Pontypool. Builders – Howell Brothers of Navigation (i.e. Abercynon) Building cost £1,800. – Seating for 900. One of the largest chapels in the Cynon Valley. 32 members in 1888, 218 members in 1916, 100 members in 1939, first baptism reported in the River Cynon in 1835. The 'cause' commenced by holding the first services in the New Inn, The Basin, in 1850, and later in the Long Room above Thomas' shop in 1865. The first minister was Rev. J. F. Williams. The Sunday School/Vestry building was first built in 1888, at a cost of £285 and named 'Glancynon' followed by the chapel alongside in 1894 with a 'link' built to connect Chapel and Vestry. Chapel enlarged in 1904, cost £2,000. A "split" occurred in the membership in 1905 and some members left and built Nazareth in 1906 (Ref:19). The organist 1908 – 1920 was Bessie Thomas, followed by Edith Williams. The debt was cleared by 1939. The chapel closed with last service held on 8th. October 1981. History of Calvaria 1888 – 1938, is in Aberdare Central library.

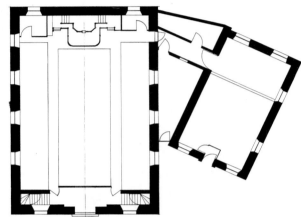

Calvaria, Abercynon.

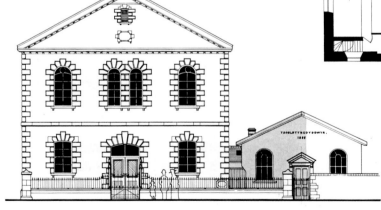

Taken in 1982.
(Brian Jordan)

CHAPEL REF. NO. 13

NAME & DENOMINATION: **CARMEL W.W.M.**

ADDRESS / LOCALITY: **MOUNTAIN ASH ROAD, ABERCYNON**

DATE BUILT: **1898**

CURRENT USE: **CLOSED IN 1985, DEMOLISHED 1999 FORMERLY USED AS AN ELECTRICAL CONTRACTOR'S STORE CIRCA. 1980-1990 SITE VACANT 2004.**

BRIEF HISTORY: Building cost £2,000. First meetings held in 1892 in the home of Mr.& Mrs. Matthew Morgan, 41 Ynysmeurig Road, later moving to the upper room in the Carne Park Hotel. In April 1894 they built a small timber chapel for £120, on land where the Wesley Cottages stand; 23 members in 1894, but numbers swelled to 103 by 1898 when the new chapel was built. Membership in 1913 was 175 with 200 in Sunday School, and 75 members in the Band of Hope. Memorial stone laid by Master D. 0. Harris Davies, Abercynon, and Dr. A.T. Jones, Mountain Ash.

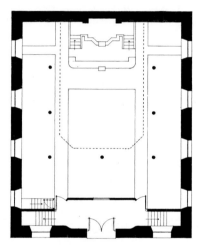

Carmel, Abercynon.

Taken in 1986.

CHAPEL REF. NO. 14

NAME & DENOMINATION: **CENTRAL FORWARD MOVEMENT F.M.**

ADDRESS / LOCALITY: **EDWARD STREET, ABERCYNON.**

DATE BUILT: **1906 – ENLARGED 1909.**

CURRENT USE: **CLOSED 1966. BECAME CHAPEL OF REST FOR F. SMITH & SON, FUNERAL DIRECTOR, CIRCA1980-90. VACANT AS AT 2004.**

BRIEF HISTORY: The Forward Movement was a home missionary movement establishing churches in the Cynon Valley in the early 1900's, formed by Rev. John Pugh, (b.1846-d.1907), Cardiff. He was a Calvinistic Methodist minister who in 1891 began an Evangelical campaign in a tent in Cardiff, before establishing churches in Abercynon, Mountain Ash and Penrhiwceiber in the early 1900's. The 'cause' commenced in a room of a coffee house in Gertrude Street – site of Lindsay Constitutional Club. The ground leased on 1st. November 1892 from Mrs. E. A. Bradley, Ynysmeurig Road Farm Estate. Leasehold of the building is dated 19th. December 1906, to Rev. Dr. John Pugh, the founder. The front of the chapel was altered in 1909; Formerly it had a small "sentry-box" type of porch. The Free Mission was for the English speaking whilst Tabernacle (Ref: 8.) was for Welsh speakers, both were part of the Presbyterian Church of Wales. Was also the Presbyterian Church in Wales at one time, and a branch of the Calvinistic Methodists. Also used as a Sunday School. Date of 1909 depicted on two separate terracotta scrolled plaques. Located adjacent to No.5 Edward Street.

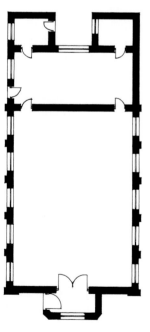

Central Forward Movement, Abercynon.

Taken in 1986.

CHAPEL REF. NO. 15

NAME & DENOMINATION: **ENGLISH CONGREGATIONAL. E.C.**

ADDRESS / LOCALITY: **YNYSMEURIG ROAD, ABERCYNON.**

DATE BUILT: **1886 – ENLARGED 1898.**

CURRENT USE: **CLOSED 1992 – COMPLETELY DESTROYED BY FIRE IN FEBRUARY 1995, DEMOLISHED SOON AFTER. SITE VACANT AS AT 2004.**

BRIEF HISTORY: There was no Welsh Congregational place of worship in the Basin (Abercynon) in 1886; the nearest chapel was Libanus Welsh Congregational at The Graig, Quakers Yard. Architect – T. Roderick of Aberdare. Builder (also a publican) F.W. Games, Abercynon. Some anxiety was felt at the time by members of the Temperance Society in allowing the publican, Mr. F.W. Games to build the chapel! Building cost £2,150, seating for 600. The chapel is of Gothic appearance. The vestry was built first in 1886 and the chapel erected over it in 1898; the height of the structure was a source of wonder to school children. The oldest chapel in Abercynon, the 'cause' began in "Spragues" in Station Terrace, and later in the Taff Vale Railway's station waiting room, officiated by the Station Master, Mr. Hiscox; for many years a large Bible was always to be seen on the table. The first minister was Rev. Morgan Jenkins 1896 – 1937 (died 1943). No minister from 1886 – 96. Bert Wilton was organist for 44 years (1916 – 60). The organ, built in 1908 for £500, was removed to Blaengwawr School, Aberaman, after the chapel closed in 1992. Memorial stone laid by Miss A. Roderick on behalf of the Sunday School children 1898. The stone name plaque comprised an attractive three-leaf clover design. 43 members in 1886; 301 in 1919; 350 in Sunday School. The chapel became a United Reformed Church in 1972.

English Congregational Chapel, Abercynon.

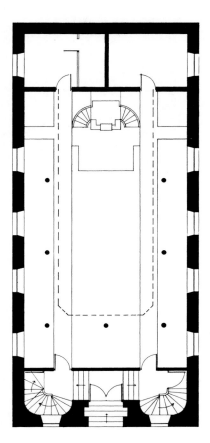

CHAPEL REF. NO. 16.

NAME & DENOMINATION: ENGLISH WESLEYAN. E.W.M.

ADDRESS / LOCALITY: MARTIN'S LANE, ABERCYNON.

DATE BUILT: 1897 – REBUILT 1928.

CURRENT USE: STILL ACTIVE.

BRIEF HISTORY: The 'cause' began in 1894 by holding meetings and services at the home of a Mr. Crump at No.10 Glancynon Terrace, and thereafter at the Carneparc Hotel, Carnetown. In 1897 an "Iron" chapel was built of corrugated zinc/iron sheets on the site of the present chapel, located opposite the old former Police Station, demolished in 1991. The old iron chapel was demolished in the 1920's, making way for the present building, opened in 1928 and built at a cost of £3,000. When Abercynon English Congregational Chapel (Ref:15) closed in 1992 (destroyed by fire, 1995), members joined the English Wesleyan Chapel.

The present chapel was extensively refurbished in 1995, and comprises a small sanctuary for worship and a large dual-purpose hall, which was originally the chapel area. Memorial stones were laid in 1928 by Mrs. G. Hodges, Aberdare; Lord Mayor of Cardiff; Sir W. Reardon Smith, Cardiff and others. The chapel later became "English Wesleyan and United Reformed Church". Rev. Marshall Edwards, a member of the chapel, kindly contributed towards these notes.

English Wesleyan chapel, Abercynon – Postcard 1922.

Taken in 1986.

CHAPEL REF. NO. 17.

NAME & DENOMINATION: **MORIAH. E.B.**

ADDRESS / LOCALITY: **MOUNTAIN ASH ROAD, ABERCYNON.**

DATE BUILT: **1897 – REBUILT 1905.**

CURRENT USE: **STILL ACTIVE.**

BRIEF HISTORY: The 'cause' commenced in 1893, in a room known as "The Old Surgery" in the Basin, owned by Mr. Thomas Thomas. Thereafter in 1895 the newly gathered fellowship moved to the Thorn Hotel Assembly Room, where they discussed and decided upon building a new chapel. The builder was Mr. Lewis of Pontypridd; the cost £296. The chapel was opened by November 1897. Membership soon increased necessitating a larger chapel, built in 1905 by Mr. Spratt of Tonypandy; the cost £1,595. It took only seven months to build and was opened on April 1st. 1906. The memorial stone was laid by (among others) Gwilym Jones Esq. Solicitor, Mountain Ash. Mr. W. H. Gabriel was organist 1947 – 1986; Miss M.S. Jones was Sunday School teacher for 62 years (1922 – 1984). A fine interior and a beautiful internal balcony balustrade are well worth seeing. The front railings are 'Art Noveau' style. Approximately 50 members as at 2003. Present lady minister is Rev. Joy Owen.

Moriah was a branch of Bethel English Baptist Chapel, Treharris, until 1895. In 1956, the chapel's first lady deacon was appointed. Centenary History Book 1893 – 1993, by Mr. W.H. Jones is at Aberdare Central Library.

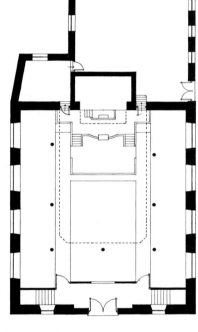

Moriah, Abercynon.

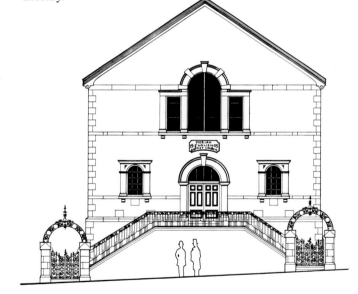

Taken in 1986.

CHAPEL REF. NO. 18.

NAME & DENOMINATION: **MOUNT ZION. E.B.**

ADDRESS / LOCALITY: **GLANCYNON TERRACE, ABERCYNON**

DATE BUILT: **1903.**

CURRENT USE: **CLOSED 1976   DEMOLISHED 1989 – SITE VACANT 2004 IN THE 1970's WAS USED AS A D.I.Y. STORE BY GRAHAM WILLIAMS.**

BRIEF HISTORY: Architect – Thomas Roderick, Aberdare. The 'cause' started in 1894, arising from members splitting from Bethania. W.I. (Ref:11). In 1905 the chapel debt was £605. In 1938 Mount Zion members joined Bethania W.I. (Ref: 11.) together with their minister Rev. J Watcyn James. Also known as "Elim Sunshine Corner", and in 1973 became Elim Pentecostal Church, of the Four Square Gospel Alliance, but closed in 1976, and lastly English Baptist, was also originally a branch of the Welsh Independents. A building with a plain façade. Adjacent to No.26 Glancynon Terrace.

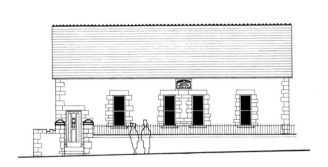
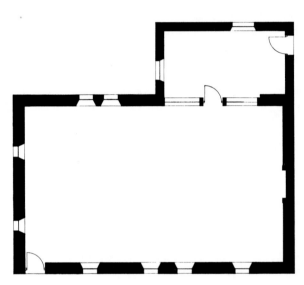

Mount Zion, (later Elim Pentecostal) Abercynon.

CHAPEL REF. NO. 19.

NAME & DENOMINATION: **NAZARETH.   W.B.**

ADDRESS / LOCALITY: **WELL STREET, ABERCYNON.**

DATE BUILT: **1906**

CURRENT USE: **CLOSED 1943. USED AS A STORE UNTIL 2002. FOR SALE 2004 – POSSIBILITY OF CONVERSION TO HOUSE OR FLATS IN THE FUTURE.**

BRIEF HISTORY: Seating for 400. The 'Cause' was founded in January 1906 with meetings held at Abercynon Girls School. Sister chapel to Calvaria W.B. (Ref: 12), but split away in 1905. Sold to the Church in Wales in 1943 upon closure, and then became known as the "Church Hall". Local enquiries suggest there are plans to build two houses on the site. During closure, throughout the Second

World War, the chapel was used for storing flour. Membership – 1916 was 80; 1932 was 30; 1938 was 24 – Sunday School membership was120 in 1916; 62 in 1928; and 10 in 1938. First minister was Rev. David Henry Davies, 1907 – 1909.

Nazareth, Abercynon – 1995.

CHAPEL REF. NO. 20

NAME & DENOMINATION: **SUNDAY SCHOOL W.C.M.**

ADDRESS / LOCALITY: **GLANCYNON TERRACE, ABERCYNON.**

DATE BUILT: **CIRCA. 1890**

CURRENT USE: **CLOSED 1970. CONVERTED. USED AS THE OSPREY FLY FISHING ASSOCIATION CLUBHOUSE.**

BRIEF HISTORY: Formerly a Sunday School and vestry belonging to and used by Tabernacle W.C.M. (Ref:21.) Used as a day infant's school circa 1930's, and in later years became a Meeting hall until its closure circa 1970. It was also referred to as 'Adam's Lounge' – the origin of this name is unclear. Located adjacent to No.1 Glancynon Terrace. Thanks to Mr. & Mrs. Harry Rogers for their contribution to these notes.

Taken in June, 2002.

CHAPEL REF. NO.21

NAME & DENOMINATION: **TABERNACLE. W.C.M.**

ADDRESS / LOCALITY: **EDWARD STREET, ABERCYNON**

DATE BUILT: **1898.**

CURRENT USE: **CLOSED 1991; DEMOLISHED 1993 SITE VACANT AS AT 2004.**

BRIEF HISTORY: The 'cause' commenced in 1892 by holding meetings in various houses, and at the Junction stables. The chapel structure sustained problems with land subsidence. Was formerly Welsh Presbyterian. Building cost was £2,000. Classical design style behind pulpit. Rev. Dr. D Ben Rees was minister at this chapel – He wrote "Chapels in the Valley" (1975).

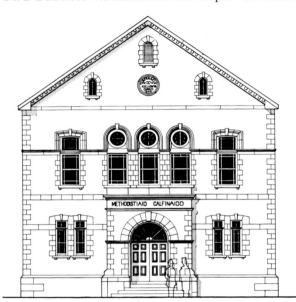

The Sunday school and vestry was built in 1893, and was detached from the main chapel nearer the road but on the same site; this was also demolished in 1993. As membership increased, a larger premises was built in 1898. The 1904/5 Religious Revival swelled numbers to 300.

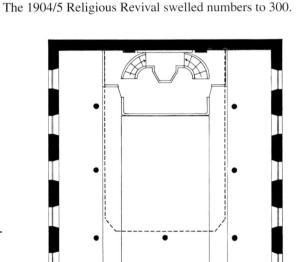

Tabernacle, Abercynon.

Taken in 1986.

Tabernacle Sunday School & Vestry, Abercynon. 1986.

CHAPEL REF. NO. 22.

NAME & DENOMINATION:	**CARMEL. E.M.**
ADDRESS / LOCALITY:	**MAIN ROAD, YNYSBOETH.**
DATE BUILT:	**CIRCA 1900.**
CURRENT USE:	**CONVERTED AND EXTENDED IN 1980 TO BECOME 'BRYNCYNON COMMUNITY CENTRE' AT A COST OF £47,000.**
BRIEF HISTORY:	Located oppositeNo.8, this former chapel named Carmel was a simple and plain building about 13m. by 10m. plan size with plain windows and a steep pitched slated roof. One of a total of four chapels to be built in the Ynysboeth area.

CHAPEL REF. NO. 23.

NAME & DENOMINATION:	**HEBRON. W. CONG.**
ADDRESS / LOCALITY:	**MAIN ROAD, YNYSYBOETH.**
DATE BUILT:	**1902.**
CURRENT USE:	**USED AS A SECURITY ALARM SUPPLIER STORE FROM CIRCA 1970 TO PRESENT DATE (2004).**
BRIEF HISTORY:	Seating capacity, 300. Now hardly recognisable as a former chapel building. Adjacent to No.6 Hebron Villas.

CHAPEL REF. NO. 24.

NAME & DENOMINATION:	**TABERNACLE. E.B.**
ADDRESS / LOCALITY:	**ABERCYNON ROAD, YNYSBOETH.**
DATE BUILT:	**1907.**
CURRENT USE:	**CLOSED CIRCA 1980/90 DEMOLISHED 1998. SITE VACANT 2004.**
BRIEF HISTORY:	The 'cause' commenced in 1900. Built in 1907 at a cost of £1,000. Seating for 350. Badly vandalised and derelict throughout the 1980's and 1990's. The

original commemorative silver trowel used for laying the memorial stone on 26 November 1906 was presented to John Williams Esq., and is now in the Glamorgan Record Office, Cardiff. 50 members in 1904; 22 in 1979 with 10 in Sunday School. In 1930 members from Bethany English Baptist chapel, Avondale Street (Ref: 25.), whose chapel was then in a poor structural condition, decided to amalgamate with Tabernacle. Services were conducted in both English and Welsh. The first minister was Rev. J.R. Davies (1907), followed by Rev. J. Frimston (1908). A bazaar held in 1908 swelled funds for the new chapel by £300.

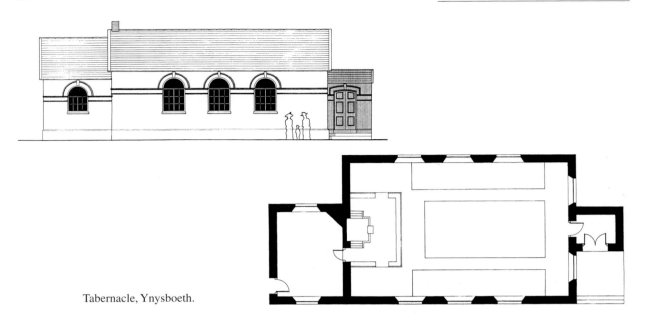

Tabernacle, Ynysboeth.

CHAPEL REF. NO. 25.

NAME & DENOMINATION: **YNYSBOETH CHAPEL. W.B. (BETHANY)**

ADDRESS / LOCALITY: **REAR OF AVONDALE STREET YNYSBOETH.**

DATE BUILT: **CIRCA 1890.**

CURRENT USE: **CLOSED CIRCA 1930. DEMOLISHED CIRCA 1940/50. SITE VACANT, 2004.**

BRIEF HISTORY: A small Welsh Baptist chapel located at the rear of 58 Avondale Street, and adjacent and south of the former Ynysboeth Isaf Farm. Shown on the 1870 Ordnance Survey plan as being a Welsh Baptist chapel named 'Bethany'. And on the 1900 O.S. plan as being Welsh Wesleyan Methodist chapel. It was also formerly an English Baptist chapel. The chapel fell into disrepair circa 1930; consequently members joined Tabernacle E.B. (Ref: 24.), where services were conducted in both English and Welsh.

CHAPEL REF. NO. 26.

NAME & DENOMINATION: **APOSTOLIC CHURCH. A.C.**

ADDRESS / LOCALITY: **RHEOLA STREET, PENRHIWCEIBER**

DATE BUILT: **CIRCA 1920.**

CURRENT USE: **CONVERTED MANY YEARS AGO INTO A DWELLING HOUSE.**

BRIEF HISTORY: Located adjacent to No.33 Rheola Street, Penrhiwceiber

CHAPEL REF. NO. 27.

NAME & DENOMINATION: **BETHEL. W.W.M.**

ADDRESS / LOCALITY: **OFF CHURCH STREET PENRHIWCEIBER.**

DATE BUILT: **1894.**

CURRENT USE: **CLOSED CIRCA 1970; CONVERTED TO A BUILDER'S STORE/WORK-SHOP IN THE EARLY 1990's**

BRIEF HISTORY: Modest front façade and simple seating plan layout. Remained derelict throughout the 1980's. Attractively renovated and decorated extensively during it's Centenary Year of 1994. The stone nameplate reads "Bethel Eglwys-y-Wesleyaid 1894."

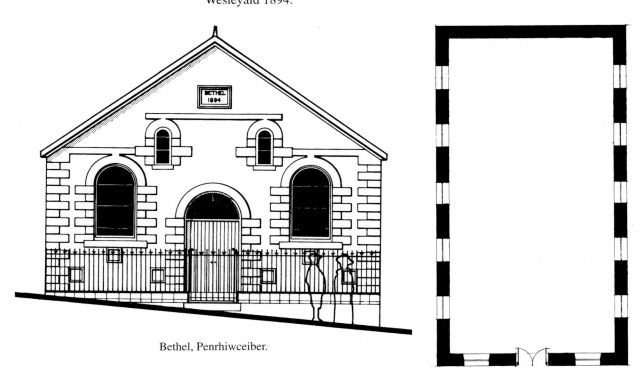

Bethel, Penrhiwceiber.

Stone name plaque.

CHAPEL REF. NO. 28.

NAME & DENOMINATION: **BETHESDA E.B.**

ADDRESS / LOCALITY: **PENRHIWCEIBER ROAD, PENRHIWCEIBER.**

DATE BUILT: **1885, REBUILT 1905.**

CURRENT USE: **CLOSED CIRCA 1980; DEMOLISHED 1996; SITE VACANT 2004.**

BRIEF HISTORY: The 'cause' commenced in 1884 when 14 members met and held services in a small zinc clad building. This chapel was soon found to be too small for the increasing membership, and so by 1885 a larger stone-built chapel was built by Mr. John Lewis of Gower Road, at a cost of £556, with seating for 300. The stone laying ceremony took place on 27th. April 1885. This building stood for only 20 years, and by 1905 membership had increased to 160 with 170 in the Sunday School, primarily as a result of the 1904 –5 Religious Revival. The old 1885 chapel therefore became too small for the swelling numbers, and in 1905 a larger chapel was built to seat 600, at a cost of £3,100. The architect was Mr. Henton, Aberdare, and the builder Mr. Price of Penarth. The original commemorative silver trowel presented to master John Williams and used for laying the memorial stone on 18th. September 1905 is in the Glamorgan Record Office, Cardiff. The stone was laid by R Cory Esq., and Alderman R. W. Jones, among others. The site on which the chapel was built was purchased from the executors of major V. H. Lee, after whom the nearby Lee Hotel (demolished 2004) was named. One of the founders of the 1905 chapel was Mr. Thomas Jones, D.C., of Penrhiwceiber House.

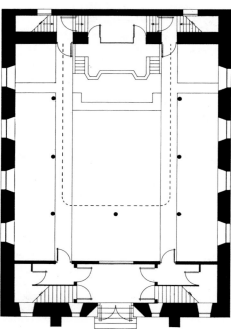

Bethesda, Penrhiwceiber.

    The front façade of the chapel was grand, although of a mixed Arts & Crafts design, complicated in detail; Full height battered buttresses framed a broad segment-headed window with flanking upper glazed loggia's under miniature hipped roofs. Inside was a two-manual harmonium by P. H. J. Trayser of Stuttgart. An interesting coloured postcard in the author's collection, dated 1905 shows the opening of the chapel by deacons and minister, and also a photograph dated 1910.

    Ministers include Rev. D. S. Davies 1888-1892 (first minister), followed by Rev. D. Hopkins B.A., Rev. Daniel Jones; Rev. W. Aerwyn Jones; and Rev. David Howells (1909). Mr. Joseph Rees was a prominent Choirmaster in the early 1900's. The original colourful illuminated address to commemorate his services to the chapel is kept at the Cynon Valley Museum; it was designed and painted by E. W. Holder, Bridge Street, Cardiff.

Taken in 1986.

Minister and Deacons at the opening of Bethesda in 1905.

CHAPEL REF. NO. 29

NAME & DENOMINATION: **CARMEL. W.I.**

ADDRESS / LOCALITY: **PENRHIWCEIBER RD. PENRHIWCEIBER.**

DATE BUILT: **1880, ENLARGED 1896.**

CURRENT USE: **STILL ACTIVE.**

BRIEF HISTORY: Between 1871 and 1880 prayer meetings and Sunday School meetings were held in various houses locally. In 1880 this continued in a house in Rheola Street, by both Methodists and Independents; The Methodists did not commence in Penrhiwceiber until around 1890. As the population of Penrhiwceiber increased and more workmen entered the colliery, sunk in 1873, they found a need to worship in a chapel of their own which would cater for their spiritual needs. In addition to the growing population seeking work in the local coal mine, a new chapel was required also to save the members travelling to Mountain Ash to attend Bethania W. I. (Ref: 48.). Plans were drawn for a new chapel on 12th. November 1880, the building was erected 1880-81, and opened on 9th. July1881. In 1881 78 members were transferred from Bethania W. I. Mountain Ash to Carmel. The memorial stone was laid by John Cory Esq., Cardiff, and Mr. E. Morris, Supply Store, Penrhiwceiber. It is the first of five Nonconformist chapels to be built in Penrhiwceiber Road alone. Carmel is a Grade 2 listed building and is the oldest chapel in Penrhiwceiber, providing seating for 700, built at a cost of £1183; It is the daughter chapel of Bethania W.I. (Ref: 48.) The vestry was built in 1886 (cost £230), and a manse provided (£250). The chapel was enlarged in 1896 at a cost of £2,500.

Notable ministers include Rev. Robert Thomas 1882 – 1905, student of Bala Collage, followed by his son, Rev. Job Thomas, and later Rev. Gomer Harris. This two storey chapel has a three-bay pedimental façade of coursed rock-faced pennant stone with rock-faced stone dressings. Moulded stone cornice under pediment with date plaque above, and upper rounded vent with keystones. The centre window has a 'Palladian' composition with corniced narrow side lights. Moulded stone band between floors. Large arched centre doorway with keystone. Gallery has canted angles on marble painted columns. A fine pulpit with two stairways with half landings and ornate turned balusters and ball-finial newels. Raked gallery pews. Coved cornice to plaster ceiling subdivided by painted wooden mouldings.

Handel Davies was organist of Carmel for 50 years (1930-1980); he died in 1982; he also conducted the chapel's choir for many years. Although modest and plain in external appearance, the chapel has a fine interior, and a large grand pipe organ of 1910, built by Norman & Beard of London and Norwich that cost £650, ornamentally decorated and well worth viewing. In 1934 the chapel and vestry were affected structurally by mining subsistence (repairs cost £350), later rectified by the National Coal Board, and again in 1996. The chapel debt was cleared by 1886.

300 members in 1896; 50 members in 1980.

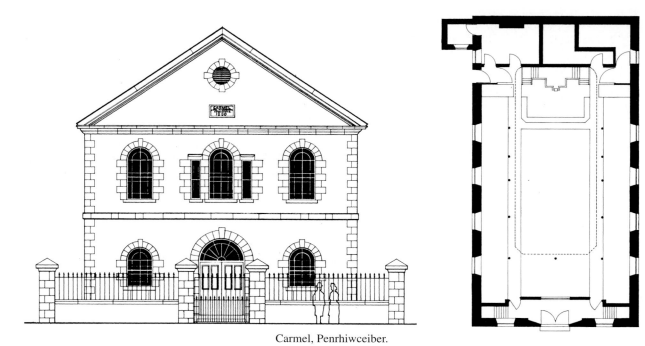

Carmel, Penrhiwceiber.

Taken in 1986.

CHAPEL REF. NO. 30

NAME & DENOMINATION: **HERMON W.C.M.**

ADDRESS / LOCALITY: **RAILWAY TERRACE, PENRHIWCEIBER.**

DATE BUILT: **1894**

CURRENT USE: **CLOSED 1980, DEMOLISHED 1995 SITE VACANT 2004.**

BRIEF HISTORY: Architect, T. Roderick, Aberdare. Building cost £4,000, seating for 800. Rev. Dr. D. Ben Rees was minister at this chapel; he wrote "Chapels in The Valley" (1975). A particularly mixed grand classical designed front façade built in sandstone; Impressive bar tracery work of circles in the tripartite main window. One of the largest chapels in the Cynon Valley. Dominated the scene from the valley basin. The main front doors folded and doubled up to open and close. A fine organ; ornate ceiling; curved pews on balcony. Memorial stone laid by Mr. David Roderick, Aberdare; Morgan Edwards, Aberaman; and Mrs. C. Jones, Tanybryn – Laid on 10th. December 1894. The fine 1,000 pipe, 23 stop, two manual, organ cost £400. 326 members by 1896. 186 members in 1931; huge decline in membership in the 1960's – 1970's.

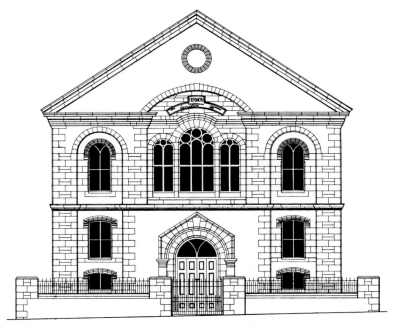

Hermon, Penrhiwceiber.

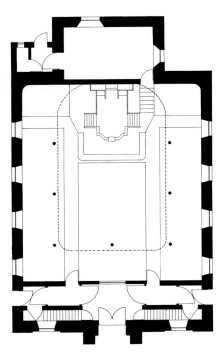

Taken in 1986.

CHAPEL REF. NO. 31

NAME & DENOMINATION: **HOPE P.M.**

ADDRESS / LOCALITY: **RHEOLA STREET, PENRHIWCEIBER**

DATE BUILT: **1907**

CURRENT USE: **STILL ACTIVE.**

BRIEF HISTORY: Built by T.W. Davies at a cost of £643. Six memorial stones laid on 8th. July 1907. Names include – D. A. Thomas Esq. M.P. – E. Morris Esq. D.C. – & Alderman R. W. Jones M.D. Up to 1883 a corrugated iron building existed on this site, belonging to Richard Cory, where the first services were held by the founder members of Jerusalem W.B. (Ref:32.) As at 2003, only six members attend this chapel. Deed of conveyance is dated 22nd. June 1888.

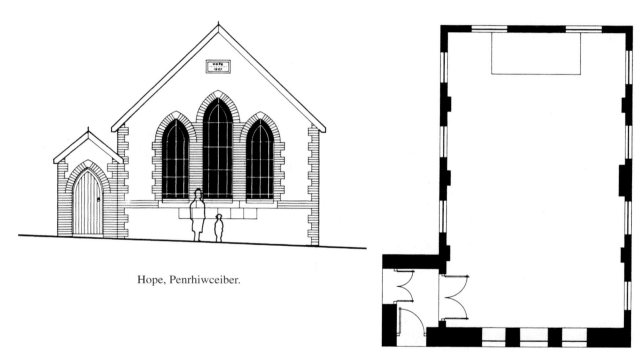

Hope, Penrhiwceiber.

Taken in 1986.

CHAPEL REF. NO.32

NAME & DENOMINATION: **JERUSALEM W.B.**

ADDRESS / LOCALITY: **PENRHIWCEIBER ROAD, PENRHIWCEIBER**

DATE BUILT: **1885**

CURRENT USE: **CLOSED CIRCA 1970; DEMOLISHED 1995; SITE VACANT 2004.**

BRIEF HISTORY: The 'cause' began in 1878 when several members from Rhos chapel, Mountain
Ash, (Ref: 61.) assisted a small number of Penrhiwceiber residents to start a
Sunday School. Meetings were held in 1882 in a house in Rheola Street, and a year later in a corrugated iron
building belonging to Richard Cory, on the site of the present Hope chapel (Ref: 31.). The first baptism took place
in the river Cynon near by in February 1883, performed by Rev. William Williams of Rhos W.B. By 1911
membership was 273, with 200 attending Sunday School; 1925-210; 1947-65. The chapel became free of debt by
1947. The first minister was Rev. J.B. Jones of Dowlais, Minister in 1904 was Rev. W.R. Jones. Built at a cost of
£1,900, seating for 700. Minister in 1895 was Rev. William R. Jones.

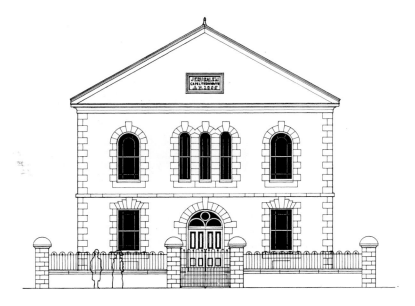
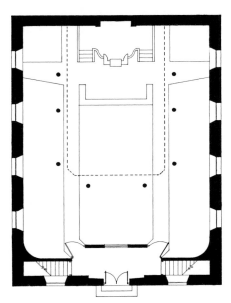

Jerusalem, Penrhiwceiber.

Taken in 1986.

CHAPEL REF. NO.33

NAME & DENOMINATION: **MORIAH C.M.**

ADDRESS / LOCALITY: **PENRHIWCEIBER ROAD, PENRHIWCEIBER.**

DATE BUILT: **CIRCA 1890**

CURRENT USE: **CLOSED JUNE 1949; DEMOLISHED 1964; BUNGALOW BUILT CIRCA 1967, NAMED 'CORRIDA'**

BRIEF HISTORY: Located between No's 206 & 210, and behind Canaan chapel (Ref: 38.) Front stone boundary wall and large pillars of the old chapel are still visible. Seating for 600. The first of five (from a total of 9) chapels to be demolished in Penrhiwceiber to date. (Four were demolished in 1995/6 alone) Closed in 1949 with 45 members, only 12 of whom were 'regulars'.

CHAPEL REF. NO.34

NAME & DENOMINATION: **PENUEL E.P.**

ADDRESS / LOCALITY: **PENRHIWCEIBER ROAD, PENRHIWCEIBER**

DATE BUILT: **1883**

CURRENT USE: **CLOSED LATE 1980'S; DEMOLISHED 1995; SITE VACANT 2004.**

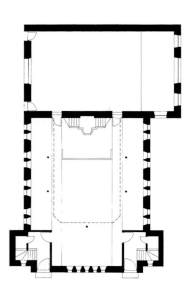

Taken in 1993.

BRIEF HISTORY: The first Methodist chapel in Penrhiwceiber. Originally Welsh Presbyterian, but later in 1950 became English Presbyterian. Built at a cost of £1,000. Mrs. Florrie Jones was organist for 50 years, up to the early 1950's. Was located between No's 102 & 104 Penrhiwceiber road. Seating for 400. A vestry was added in 1887. Continued as a Welsh Presbyterian chapel until 1894 when Welsh speaking members then transferred to Hermon W.C.M. (Ref: 30). No minister after 1965. Notable minister was Rev. Morfydd Llwyn Owen, a hymnist and poet of renown who died in her early 20's.

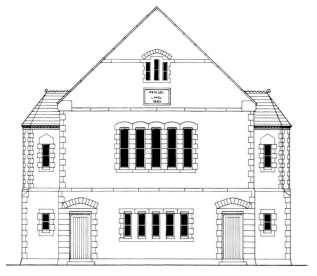

Penuel, Penrhiwceiber.

CHAPEL REF. NO.35

NAME & DENOMINATION: **BETHEL W.I.**

ADDRESS / LOCALITY: **GLYNGWYN STREET, MISKIN.**

DATE BUILT: **1903**

CURRENT USE: **DEMOLISHED 1995 SITE VACANT & FOR SALE 2004.**

BRIEF HISTORY: Architect – T. W. Millar, Mountain Ash. Built at a cost of £2,947, with seating for 600. Donations given by members of Carmen W.I. (Ref: 29), the sister chapel. Mother chapel to Bethania W.I., Mountain Ash (Ref: 48.). Located opposite No.12 Glyngwyn Street. Previously Welsh Congregational chapel located in Consort Street, near the corner of Bailey Street, being a zinc-clad structure built in 1896, and demolished in 1900 to make way for the new Bethel W.I. (1903), Glyngwyn Street. A Sunday School was formed in 1873, held in the Long Room of the Bailey Arms, under the supervision of Henry Eynon. In 1891 Rev. Jones of Bethania (Ref: 48.) discussed with John Davies of the Bailey Arms, the provision of a place of worship for the Welsh Independents in Miskin. With the support of Bethania they held a Sunday School and weekly meetings at No. 33 Victoria Street; this became too small so they erected the afore-mentioned zinc clad chapel in 1896. 42 members in 1896 with 150 in Sunday School. Debt cleared completely by 1923. The Welsh Development Agency at one point intended to acquire the vacant site under a Joint Venture Project. Demolition work in progress in 1995 was filmed for an H.T.V. documentary entitled 'On The Chapel Trail', directed by Hywel Davies, and presented by Professor Anthony Jones. Memorial stones laid by Mr. Gwilym Jones, Solicitor, Mountain Ash; Master Taliesin Millar, Forest Cottage and others, on 4th. January 1904.

Bethel, Miskin.

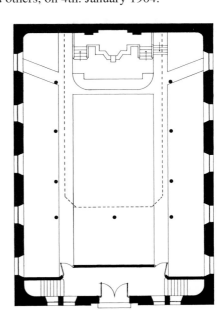

Taken in 1986.

CHAPEL REF. NO.36

NAME & DENOMINATION: **BETHESDA E.M.**

ADDRESS / LOCALITY: **GLYNGWYN STREET, MISKIN.**

DATE BUILT: **1891**

CURRENT USE: **STILL ACTIVE**

BRIEF HISTORY: Built at a cost of £350, with seating for 160. The oldest chapel in Miskin. Architect Thomas Roderick, Aberdare. The 'cause' began in a house in Victoria Street. It was originally Primitive Methodist and one-time a branch of Ebenezer P.M., Mountain Ash. (Ref: 52.). The vestry schoolroom was built in 1903. Original colour washed drawings on linen are in Cynon Valley Museum.

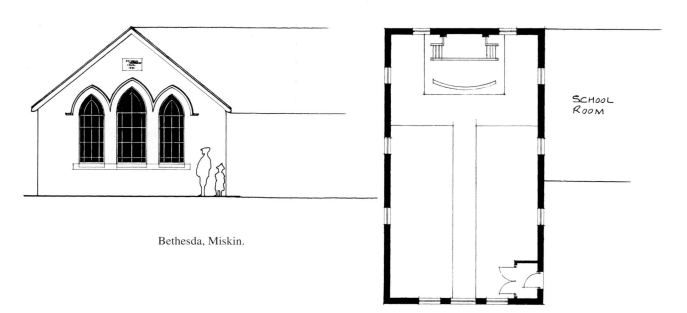

Bethesda, Miskin.

Taken in 1986.

CHAPEL REF. NO.37

NAME & DENOMINATION: **BRYNGOLWG E.F.C.**

ADDRESS / LOCALITY: **WINDSOR ROAD, MISKIN.**

DATE BUILT: **1907**

CURRENT USE: **STILL ACTIVE.**

BRIEF HISTORY: The 'cause' commenced circa 1900 as a Presbyterian chapel, and was built in 1907, Architect was T.W. Millar, Mountain Ash. Located opposite No.26 Windsor Road. A plain front façade with dressed stone walls and smooth red facing bricks to openings. The Mission Hall was established as a result of the influx of the English speaking working class from Somerset and neighbouring counties. In the 1920's-1930's the Mission Hall was used as a soup kitchen to help the needy during the 1926 strike and the depression years around this period. It became a sister chapel to Duffryn Street English Calvinistic Methodist Chapel, Mountain Ash (Ref: 53.). The chapel closed around 1946, was then sold, and became a button factory up to 1954. From 1946 to 1954 the lady members worshipped in the Gardener's Hut at the bottom of Windsor Road, now the site of the Cynon Taf Housing Development. It later became a garage. In 1954 the members bought back the Mission Hall and it became a Free Gospel Hall. The lady members went around collecting money to purchase the chapel, and Mr. Evans, Bank Manager, helped by giving a loan, but the members had to give their house deeds as financial security and collateral. In 1986 it became the Evangelical Free Mission Hall; it remains so to this day with about 24 members. It was also used as a temporary "overflow" for the nearby infants' school for a short period. The pews came from Bryn Seion, High Street, Mountain Ash (Ref: 51.) upon its closure in 1956. The first minister was Jack Davies, who lived in 20 Windsor Road; he later emigrated to Australia. He was minister from 1918 to late 1930's. William (Billy) P. Hodges was minister 1986 – 1988. The minister and elders from Duffryn Street E.C.M. chapel (Ref: 53.) conducted services at Bryngolwg Mission Hall from the late 1940's, up to the early 1960's, during which time membership was around 50 with a flourishing sisterhood and Sunday school. The annual sports day held at the field of Lan Farm after Sunday school anniversary was a memorable event when children and adults took with them baskets of sandwiches and would be met by an ice-cream van. Outings to the Cwm and Barry Island were also to be enjoyed. The present minister from 1995, is Rev. Peter Brake.

Thanks to Rev. Peter Brake, Mrs. Harding and Mrs. Winnie Beynon, for their kind help in compiling this account.

Bryngolwg, Miskin. 1986.

CHAPEL REF. NO.38

NAME & DENOMINATION: **CANAAN E.C.**

ADDRESS / LOCALITY: **PROSSER STREET, MISKIN.**

DATE BUILT: **1903**

CURRENT USE: **STILL ACTIVE. SINCE 1993 HAS BEEN THE KINGDOM HALL, JEHOVAH'S WITNESS (MOUNTAIN ASH BRANCH.)**

BRIEF HISTORY: Architect: G. A. Treharne M.I.M.E, Aberdare. Builder: T. W. Davies, building cost £1,200, seating for 350, vestry seating for 300. Gothic arch to front elevation (now altered) was typical of English Congregational chapel design. The 'cause' began in a simple temporary zinc clad structure in 1903. The original E. Cong. Chapel closed in 1977. Became the Kingdom Hall, Jehovah's Witness Mountain Ash branch in 1993. The original Mountain Ash Kingdom Hall was founded in the late 1940's, and in the 1950's was known to meet and worship in the Gwalia Hall, Penrhiwceiber. 27 members moved from the Aberdare branch in 1976 – (80 members at this time) – to join the Mountain Ash branch, and in 1993 they purchased Canaan chapel where they currently worship. The first minister was Rev. Thomas Gwilym Jones, 1904-1905. There was no permanent minister, at least after 1950. Rev. Idris Evans, minister of Providence E.C. (Ref: 60.) 1935-40, assisted in the services during the late 1930's. Rev. John Henry Latham, also of Providence, assisted 1941-45.

Original colour washed drawings on linen cloth, of the original English Congregational Chapel are in the Cynon Valley Museum.

Thanks to Mr. Norman Morris for contributing to these notes.

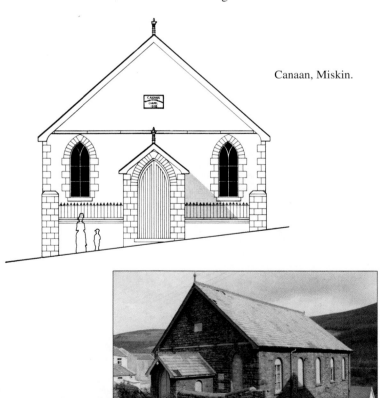

Canaan, Miskin.

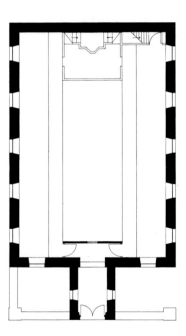

Taken in 1986.

CHAPEL REF. NO. 39

NAME & DENOMINATION: CHRISTADELPHIAN HALL C.H.

ADDRESS / LOCALITY: GLYNGWYN STREET, MISKIN. AND OTHERS.

DATE BUILT: 1912.

CURRENT USE: STILL ACTIVE.

BRIEF HISTORY: Mountain Ash Ecclesia, Glyngwyn Street, Miskin. John Marshall, founder of the Aberdare Ecclesia visited mountain Ash in 1912 and preached occasionally by invitation at Bryngolwg Mission Hall (Ref: 37.). He left due to disagreements over doctorial beliefs. James Moore who lived at Llanwonno Road, was secretary of Bryngolwg Mission Hall, and in the 1930's was instrumental in starting meetings of the Christadelphians at the home of Mr. Vaughan, Bailey Street, Miskin; Later they met at the Candle King grocers' shop at Commercial Street, Mountain Ash. In the late 1930's they moved yet again to a rented room belonging to the former Miners' Library reading room, which later became a Spiritualist Meeting Room at Glyngwyn Street, Miskin. In 1960 they refurbished this building and provided the Christadelphian Hall we see today. Membership in 2002 is 24 with a thriving Sunday School. A zinc clad structure located adjacent to the Post Office and No. 53A Glyngwyn Street.

REF. 39A.
ABERAMAN ECCLESIA, GWAWR STREET. ABERAMAN.

Founded in 1863 and later established at Gwawr Street at the rear of No's 144-145 Brook Street; the oldest Christadelphian Ecclesia in the Cynon Valley. They had close links with the Ecclesia at Swansea and Mumbles, founded by Richard Goldie in 1863. During this period the Aberaman Ecclesia met at various members homes. In 1884 they converted a building used originally as a stable for cows. The builder was Harry Llewellyn, a local colliery contractor. They worshipped here for 80 years, up until 1964 when the old building was demolished and rebuilt, and later refurbished, to provide the Ecclesia we see today. A prominent founder of the Aberaman Ecclesia was Earnest Harford, a local businessman who kept metal/tin workshops at Cardiff Road, near the Blaengwawr Inn, and near Penderyn Place, Aberdare

REF. 39B.
ABERDARE ECCLESIA, JENKIN STREET, ABERDARE.

In the early 1880's, Christadelphians living in Aberdare decided to leave the Aberaman Ecclesia and find a place of their own in which to meet and worship. They first met at the Assembly Room in Cardiff Street (later became (a) Crockers, and (b) Undeb). In July 1883 meetings and lectures were held at the Temperance Hall, Cynon Street, Aberdare (later became the Palladium), and also at the British School. The following year (1884), the brethren began meetings presided over by Brother William Pugh, stepfather to John Marshall, who became one of the founders of the Aberdare Ecclesia. In the 1930's members met in a room above Burton's Clothier's Shop, 9 Canon Street (formerly the Queen's Hotel-1861-1923.) They stayed here until 1957 when they then moved to No.35 Gadlys Road. On the 14th. September 1975 they moved to their present building, opposite19/20 Jenkin Street, Aberdare, which was formerly a Miners' Lamp factory, and in earlier times was a flour mill.

Another 'leading light' and founder of the Aberdare Ecclesia was Brother John Marshall who kept a School of Commerce at No.19 Whitcombe Street (later Clark's Dentists) Brother Marshall died circa 1980, aged 93. Membership in 2003 – 22.

GENERAL NOTES ON THE CHRISTADELPHIANS.
The movement was founded in America in 1848 by a London Physician, Dr. John Thomas (died 1871), son of a minister. The Christadelphians were originally known as the "Camberlites" then became the "Thomasites", named after Dr. J. Thomas. In 1864 they adopted the name Christadelphians, i.e. "Brothers of Christ". Leaders are called 'Arranging Brethren', i.e. lecturing, managing and presiding brethren, and are chosen by criteria as outlined in the scriptures. All are volunteers elected to their posts. The Ecclesia has no central organisation, each being

autonomous with no church hierarchy, no paid clergy or bishops. They appoint Servants and not Masters, and do not exercise authority but rather offer service. Regular Bible classes, and belief in the Bible as being the only authority – the 'Real Truth'. Members are encouraged to develop teaching, preaching and visitation duties, and to invite other Ecclesia to interchange and share preaching, fellowship, and worship.

The term' Ecclesia' is a formal church usage, and derives from the ancient Greek 'assembly' word – 'Called From' or to be 'Called Out'. The Cynon Valley has more Ecclesia (3) than any of the neighbouring valleys in the R.C.T. County Borough area.

Thanks to John Dunning; Clive Pavett; Ron Thomas and John Mayers for their help in compiling these notes.

CHAPEL REF. NO.40

NAME & DENOMINATION:	**GOSPEL HALL G.H.**
ADDRESS / LOCALITY:	**GLANCYNON TERRACE, MISKIN.**
DATE BUILT:	**CIRCA 1905.**
CURRENT USE:	**DEMOLISHED 1960, NOW A PRIVATE GARDEN AREA**
BRIEF HISTORY:	Located opposite No.11 Glancynon Terrace, near Springfield House.

CHAPEL REF. NO.41.

NAME & DENOMINATION:	**MISKIN BAPTIST E.B.**
ADDRESS / LOCALITY:	**PENRHIWCEIBER ROAD, MISKIN.**
DATE BUILT:	**CIRCA 1900, RENOVATED 1994.**
CURRENT USE:	**STILL ACTIVE.**
BRIEF HISTORY:	A thriving, active chapel extensively rebuilt and renovated in 1994, named Miskin Christian Centre. Originally known as 'The Old Mill', and later became

a Co-operative shop and factory. When Mount Pisgah E.B. (Ref: 43.) and Bethania E.B. (Ref: 28) were demolished in 1996 and 1995 respectively, members formed the new English Baptist Chapel.

CHAPEL REF. NO.42.

NAME & DENOMINATION:	**METHODIST CHAPEL E.W.M.**
ADDRESS / LOCALITY:	**HAWTHORN TERRACE, PERTHCELYN.**
DATE BUILT:	**1931**
CURRENT USE:	**DEMOLISHED 1952.**
BRIEF HISTORY:	Initially in 1931 the chapel was called 'The Primitive Methodist Mission Room', but some time later it was renamed 'Elim' English Wesleyan Methodist

Chapel. The original drawings dated 1931, by A.E. Alder, Architect, are at the Cynon Valley museum, and indicate that the chapel was built for the Rev. A. W. Baille and others. Formerly located near the lower end of Hawthorne Terrace (near no. 33), right hand side going down. Allotment gardens were located adjacent to the chapel. Built in 1931 to accommodate about 100 worshippers, this small chapel measured about 25 feet by 18 feet, a timber framed structure clad with flat asbestos sheets, with asbestos roof tiles and a small front entrance porch.

The chapel was demolished in 1952 (some sources suggest 1951) after only 20 years service, and the sections of the building were re-erected near the Hope chapel, Rheola Street (Ref: 31.), on the site of the present Penrhiwceiber Library. Upon closure of 'Elim' the members transferred to Darran Road English Wesleyan chapel (Ref: 54.) under the pastorate of Rev. Percy Large. Ministers include Rev. A.W. Baille (also a local councillor) Rev. Amlyn, and Rev. P. Large. Joe Sollis was caretaker and involved in many aspects of the chapel's activities, he lived in Pentwyn Avenue. Charlie Keepings (shop) was organist. Harold Albert Arbery was a lay preacher at this chapel. The chapel was renowned for its excellent Sunday School Anniversary services, and for the popular annual trips to Barry Island when up to five open charabanc busloads of excited children were conveyed to the seaside.

During the second World War, black American G.I. soldiers were based at Lletty Turner Field, where they had their training camp and canvas tents; they were there for about six months prior to "D-Day" in June 1944. The soldiers worshipped at Elim chapel during their army service at Lletty Turner field. Perthcelyn was without a place of worship from 1952; however services were recently held at Perthcelyn Community Centre, extensively refurbished in 2000, but it appears that they now no longer worship there. Lower Perthcelyn was also known as 'German-Town' so called after the German workmen who built the first houses there after the First World War, around 1918-1921. These included Dillington Terrace, Monmouth Street, and part of Glamorgan Street.

Thanks to Albert Bethel; Ernie Arbery; and Roy Davies for their help in collating these notes.

Opening day of the chapel in 1931. Left to right: Rear row, fourth from left – Mr. Harold A Arbery.

(Ernie Arbery)

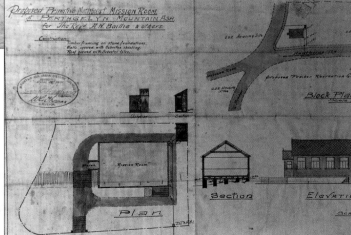

Methodist Mission Room. Later 'Elim' Perthcelyn.
Original colour-washed plans dated 1931.

CHAPEL REF. NO.43.

NAME & DENOMINATION: **MOUNT PISGAH E.B.**

ADDRESS / LOCALITY: **OAKLAND STREET, MISKIN.**

DATE BUILT: **1904.**

CURRENT USE: **CLOSED 1990; DEMOLISHED 1995; SITE VACANT 2004.**

BRIEF HISTORY: Architect – T. W. Millar, Mountain Ash. Built by T. W. Davies at a cost of
£2,400. Seating for 750, Vestry holds 350. Officially opened in February 1905.
Located opposite Nos. 6 & 7 Oakland Street. The 'cause' commenced in 1871 with a Sunday School held in Long
Room of the Bailey's Arms Public House, Miskin, whereby a number of members separated from Nazareth E.B.
(Ref: 58.) in 1900. Sister chapel to Rhos W.B. (Ref: 61.) and Nazareth E.B. (Ref: 58.) of Mountain Ash. Had 115
members by 1911, with 200 in Sunday School. The first minister was Rev. George Neighbour of Gloucester who
also ministered at the Brotherhood Chapel in Napier Street, Mountain Ash. (Ref: 50.); Rev John Protheroe was
minister in 1908. Fine harmonium organ made in Paris. Grand internal ornate balcony balustrade (pink and white).
Original colour washed drawings on linen cloth are in Cynon Valley Museum.

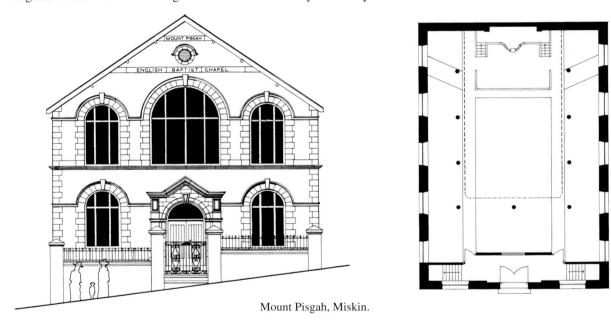

Mount Pisgah, Miskin.

Taken in 1993.

CHAPEL REF. NO.44.

NAME & DENOMINATION: SCHOOL ROOM W.I.

ADDRESS / LOCALITY: BAILEY STREET, MISKIN

DATE BUILT: 1891.

CURRENT USE: DEMOLISHED CIRCA 1950

BRIEF HISTORY: A zinc-clad structure built in 1891 as a School Room / Sunday School for Bethania W.I. Chapel (Ref: 48.) and Carmel W.I. Chapel (Ref: 29.). Original cost £340, seating for 80 children. Original colour washed paper plans drawn by J.W. Bevan of Woodland Street, Mountain Ash, are in Cynon valley Museum.

School Room (W.I.) Miskin 1891

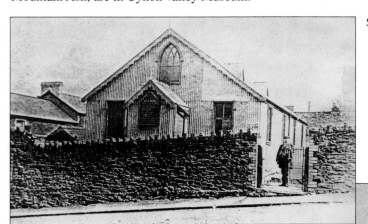

School Room (Welsh Independents) Miskin.
Original colour-washed plans dated 1891.

CHAPEL REF. NO. 45.

NAME & DENOMINATION: SUNDAY SCHOOL E.B.

ADDRESS / LOCALITY: OAKLAND STREET, MISKIN.

DATE BUILT: 1891.

CURRENT USE: DEMOLISHED 1955; SITE VACANT 2004.

BRIEF HISTORY: Indicated on the 1919 Ordnance Survey plan as being located just below Mount Pisgah E.B. (Ref: 43.) and opposite Nos. 1,2 & 3 Oakland Street, the building was of iron/zinc construction. Later became a dwelling house named 'The Cottage'. Local enquiries indicate the Sunday School was for Mount Pisgah E.B. Chapel, post 1904, but was originally a branch of Nazareth E.B. (Ref: 58.) in the 1870's.

CHAPEL REF. NO.46.

NAME & DENOMINATION: **WELSH BAPTIST W.B.**

ADDRESS / LOCALITY: **NEAR JOHN STREET, NEWTOWN.**

DATE BUILT: **1863.**

CURRENT USE: **THE CHAPEL CLOSED CIRCA 1925 AND LATER THE SITE BECAME A GARDENERS HUT AND MEETING HALL.**

BRIEF HISTORY: Founded and established in 1863, and named the 'Graig' School House, otherwise referred to as a 'Day School'. Built on the site of the present structure, and located between John Street and behind No. 1 Strand Street. (See also 1868 Ordnance Survey Plan.) It was originally Welsh Baptist, but later became English Baptist. Built at a cost of £600 in 1874, on land purchased from colliery owner Mr. John Nixon. Founded by Rev. William Williams (of Cardiff Road), David Jenkins, and Thomas Edwards. They conducted regular prayer meetings and supervised the thirty scholars of the Sunday School. First registered as a place of religious worship in 1879, it was originally a branch of Rhos W.B. (Ref: 61.). Sunday School teachers from Rhos included John Evans; William Williams (Junior); Mrs. William Williams and Thomas Wilmington. Nazareth E.B. (Ref: 58.) took over the Sunday School in 1904, and the deeds were transferred to them in October 1906. The existing simple timber clad structure on this site was more recently used as a Gardeners Association headquarters and is now a social meeting place where ladies meet twice weekly.

Thanks to Sian Rogers for translating part of this text.

Strand bridge on the Aberdare Canal. The ruins of the Welsh Baptist chapel is to the right of the picture.

(Glyn Davies Collection)

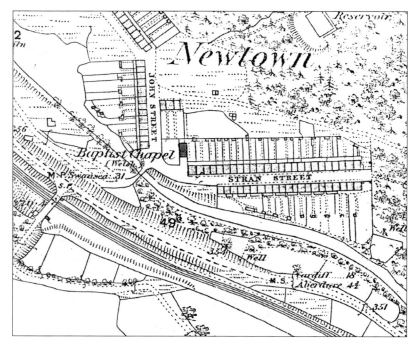

Welsh Baptist chapel (Graig school house), Newtown. Ordnance Survey plan – 1868.

CHAPEL REF. NO. 47.

NAME & DENOMINATION: **ZION P.M.**

ADDRESS / LOCALITY: **MARY STREET, NEWTOWN**

DATE BUILT: **1880.**

CURRENT USE: **STILL ACTIVE.**

BRIEF HISTORY: The 'cause' was founded by holding meetings at Nos. 3 & 4 Mary Street
                             Newtown in 1867. Meetings and services were held there until 1879 when it
was decided to build a new chapel for the Primitive Methodists, at a cost of £750.Stories of personal sacrifice
abound in the formation and building of the chapel, including the donation of a dram of coal from each miner
involved, to help to pay for the chapel. It is said that about thirty preachers have been 'raised' in Zion. Attractive
well maintained interior with yellow pine pews. Also to be seen is a Canadian harmonium, and a very attractive
fine china 'Love Mug' with two handles, dated 1882, inscribed with the name of the chapel. Renovated internally
in 1990; upper gallery remains intact; the vestry/Sunday School Room is annexed to the chapel. The original
colour washed drawings on linen cloth are in the Cynon Valley Museum. Mr. Andrew Wilson, chapel member and
organist, organised boat trips on the canal around the 1920's to the Basin at Abercynon, these were enjoyed as
Sunday School treats by the children.

Centenary booklet – 1880-1980, is at Glamorgan Record Office, Cardiff.

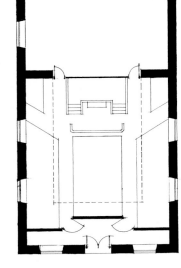

Zion, Newtown.

Taken in 1986.

Pulpit area, Zion, Newtown – circa 1950.

CHAPEL REF. NO. 48.

NAME & DENOMINATION: **BETHANIA W.I.**

ADDRESS / LOCALITY: **PHILLIP STREET, MOUNTAIN ASH.**

DATE BUILT: **1854, REBUILT 1859.**

CURRENT USE: **STILL ACTIVE.**

BRIEF HISTORY: The 'cause' began with a Sunday School built in 1850. Earlier meetings were held in the house of Daniel Rowlands, which later became the Glancynon Inn, opened in 1860. In 1852 Rev. Lewis of Cwmbach guided the cause and a decision was made to build a small chapel, built in 1854 at a cost of £320. Due to the Religious Revival of 1859, the first chapel became too small, and was therefore demolished. A new larger chapel (the present one) was built in 1859 at a cost of £950; it is a Grade 2 Listed Building, with seating for 750. The new chapel catered well for the spiritual needs of Allenstown (i.e. Caegarw) after the sinking of the nearby Deep Duffryn Colliery in 1855 (closed 1980). The front façade is rendered and is a fine classical design; overall pediment on a dentilled course; rusticated doorway; moulded surrounds to round headed windows. The interior is beautifully preserved and maintained. Ornate flat ceiling on a big cove with fine plaster ceiling roses picked out in red. The seating to the vestry is 'tip-up and raked' and is unique in its design as it can be converted to a table/bench. Enlarged with a vestry/school room built on at the side in 1887. Also in 1887, the roof of the chapel was raised to accommodate a new upper gallery. Original colour washed drawings of the large school room/vestry built in 1887, designed by Herbert Jenkins, Surveyor, are at the Cynon Valley Museum.

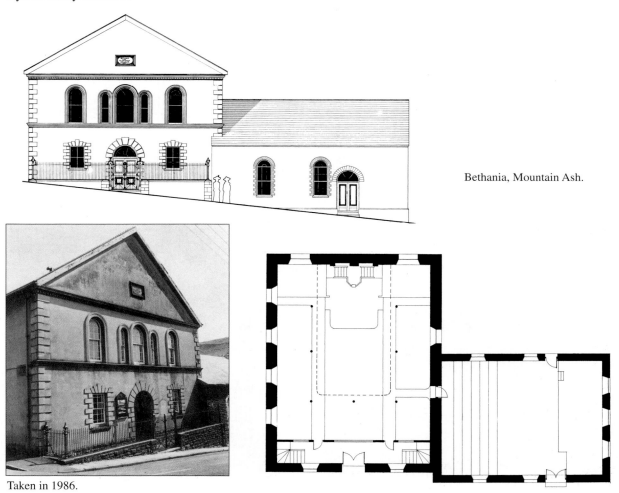

Bethania, Mountain Ash.

Taken in 1986.

Notable ministers include: Rev. Thomas Llewellyn 1854 –1888, died in 1892 aged 70; Rev. Owen Jones 1895; Rev. John Phillips 1911 –1945. Rev. Haydn Davies 1950 -1960. The chapel is mother chapel to Carmel W.I., Penrhiwceiber (Ref: 29.) A faithful member of Bethania was the notable conductor David Edward Coleman (Eos Hefin – 'Summer Nightingale' 1842 –1892), also known as 'Coleman Bach'. For many years he conducted the famous Bethania Welsh Congregational Chapel Choir, and he went on to become sectional conductor of the South Wales Choral Union, which won the Chief Choral prize at the Crystal Palace. London 1872-73. He kept a grocers and drapers shop at 54 Commercial St. Mountain Ash 1865-80. Membership in 2004 is 20, there is no Sunday School.

The Religious Census 1851 states – "Mountain of Zion – Welsh independent – part of a dwelling house 'erected' 1851. Space free 45; standing 35, present afternoon 10 + 35 scholars – Daniel Rowland, Deacon, Mountain Ash."

The words of 'Calon Lan' were written by Daniel James (b.1848 – d. 1920), a native of Mynyddbach, Swansea. He was otherwise famously known as the Welsh Bard and Poet 'GWYROSYDD', he came to live at Caegarw, Mountain ash, circa 1900, at the behest of the renowned local conductor Thomas Glyndwr Richards (b.1858 – d. 1935). The first public rendering of 'Calon Lan' was performed circa 1910 at Bethania W.I. Chapel, Mountain Ash. It was John Hughes of Llansamlet who put words to the music. The Mountain Ash and District Choral Society currently hold their practices and rehearsals in the vestry of this chapel.

CHAPEL REF. NO. 49.

NAME & DENOMINATION: **BETHLEHEM C.M.**

ADDRESS / LOCALITY: **PRYCE STREET, MOUNTAIN ASH.**

DATE BUILT: **1857, REBUILT 1900.**

CURRENT USE: **CLOSED 1980, DEMOLISHED 1990, FOR SALE AT £25,000. "HILLCREST MEDICAL CENTRE" BUILT ON SITE 1992/3**

BRIEF HISTORY: Rebuilt in 1900, designed by Mr. Thomas. Roderick, Clifton Street, Aberdare, cost £2,000 The 'cause' began in 1854 with meetings held in a private house in Commercial Street, and later in a house in Duffryn Street. Schoolroom added to the rear in 1857, cost £500, known as 'Capel Bach'. Memorial stones laid by William Lloyd, Draper, Commercial Street; Mr. Rees Evans,

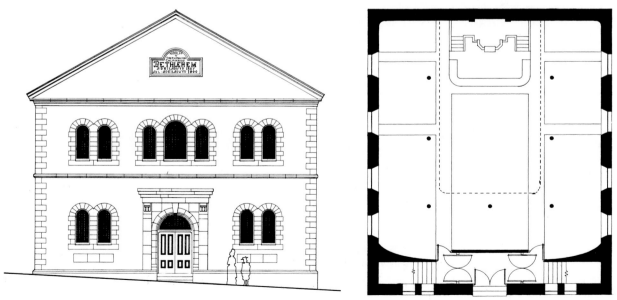

Bethlehem, Mountain Ash.

Grocer, and others. Rev. William Williams (b1812- d1897) ministered here 1870 – 1884; there was no permanent minister 1857-1870. Followed by Rev. M. Jones for 27 years, 1884 – 1911. Original colour washed design drawings are in Cynon Valley Museum. The vestry at the rear was used as an Infants' school 1942-1948 as a result of Duffryn Boys' school (built 1857) being destroyed by bombing/enemy action in June 1941. Bethlehem is the daughter chapel to Duffryn Street. E.C.M. (ref. 53). 280 members in 1923.

Evan Roberts, the 1904-05 Religious Revivalist worshipped here in 1899. There was a joint pastorate with Bethania (ref.48) in 1952. A new pipe organ was installed in 1953 at a cost of £950.

Drawings dated May 1872 of a proposed vestry room "to be built at Cynon Street" (now Pryce Street) are at Cynon Valley Museum.

Bethlehem, Mountain Ash. Taken in 1986

CHAPEL REF. NO. 50.

NAME & DENOMINATION:	**BROTHERHOOD L.C.**
ADDRESS / LOCALITY:	**NAPIER STREET, MOUNTAIN ASH.**
DATE BUILT:	**1912.**
CURRENT USE:	**CLOSED 1946. CONVERTED TO A CARPENTER/BUILDERS WORK-SHOP CIRCA 1960. NOW A PRIVATE HOUSE. (No.20-21)**
BRIEF HISTORY:	Founded as a "Labour Church" in 1912 by Rev. George Neighbour, 29 Gorsedd Street, Mountain Ash. He ministered there 1912 – 1929; He was also the first

Pastor of Mount Pisgah (Ref: 43.) in 1904. Rev. V.M.K. James took oversight of the church in 1937, he was also minister of Highland Place (Ref: 108.) 1932 – 1942. Alan Taylor was minister 1942-46. The chapel is also believed to have been Unitarian for a short time and named Mabers Chapel. The building is located in a row of stone terraced houses (built circa 1850), known as No's 20 – 21 Napier Street. The Minute Books (1930-1941) are held in the Glamorgan Record Office, Cardiff.

CHAPEL REF. NO. 51.

NAME & DENOMINATION:	**BRYN SEION. W.W.M.**
ADDRESS / LOCALITY:	**HIGH STREET, MOUNTAIN ASH.**
DATE BUILT:	**1864.**
CURRENT USE:	**CLOSED 1956, BECAME 'MOUNTAIN ASH JOINER'S' WORKSHOP. DEMOLISHED1989, NINE FLATS NAMED 'TY SEION' BUILT ON SITE, 1991/2.**
BRIEF HISTORY:	The 'cause' began in 1860, services held in Ebenezer P.M. Chapel (Ref: 52.). The first contractor failed to complete the building; David Harris, a faithful

member of Bryn Seion, finished it. A plain stone façade of simple design with little embellishment or architectural merit. Seating for 450. Located adjacent to No. 39 High Street. A School Room was located in the basement. Minister in 1895 was Rev. John James.

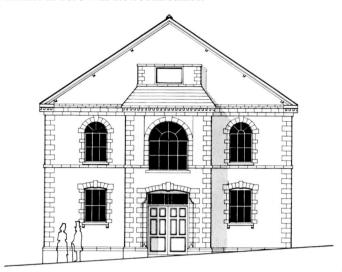

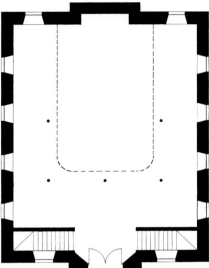

Bryn Seion, Mountain Ash.

Taken in 1986.

CHAPEL REF. NO. 52.

NAME & DENOMINATION:	**EBENEZER P.M.**
ADDRESS / LOCALITY:	**BRUCE STREET, MOUNTAIN ASH.**
DATE BUILT:	**1857, REBUILT 1860.**
CURRENT USE:	**CLOSED 1948; DEMOLISHED 1968. CURRENTLY (2004) AN UNATRACTIVE, VANDALISED 'AMENITY AREA'.**

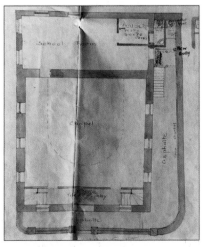

Ebenezer, Mountain Ash. Original colour-washed plan. Dated 1860.

BRIEF HISTORY: The 'cause' began in 1857 with services held in a house in Phillip Street; the first floor of the chapel was a Girls' School Room and a vestry was located at the rear ground floor. Seating for 450. After closure in 1948 the pews were transferred to Cefn Pennar E.B. (Ref: 66.). The 1857 chapel was built opposite the site of the second Ebenezer Chapel at the top of Bruce Street. Original colour-washed drawings are in the Cynon Valley Museum.

CHAPEL REF. NO. 53.

NAME & DENOMINATION: **ENGLISH CALVINISTIC METHODIST E.C.M.**

ADDRESS / LOCALITY: **DUFFRYN STREET, MOUNTAIN ASH.**

DATE BUILT: **1883.**

CURRENT USE: **CLOSED 1964; "DUFFRYN JOINERS" WORKSHOP, 1971 – 1995. PARTIALLY DEMOLISHED 1995-2003, DEMOLITION COMPLETED 2004.**

BRIEF HISTORY: Built in 1883 at a cost of £1,100, seating for 600. First meetings were held in 1882 at the 'Mountain Ash Coffee Tavern' in Commercial Street. School room and vestry were located in the basement. Three-quarter plan shaped balcony. 'Daughter' chapel to Bethlehem C.M. (Ref: 49.), and sister chapel to Bryngolwg Evangelical Free Church Mission Hall (Ref: 73.).

     The chapel vestry, located in the basement, was used as an infants school 1942-48 as a result of Duffryn Boys' School (built 1857) being destroyed by bombing/enemy action in June 1941, fortunately at night when unoccupied. Original drawings in Cynon Valley Museum.

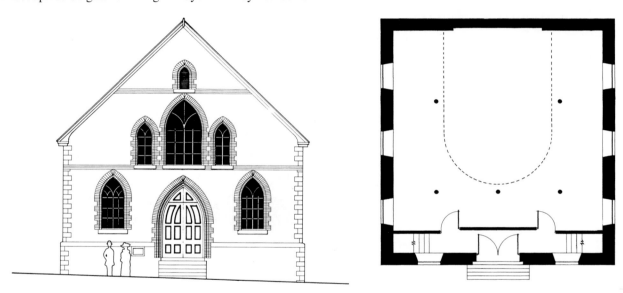

English Calvinistic Methodist (Duffryn St.) Mountain Ash.

Taken in 1986.

CHAPEL REF. NO. 54.

NAME & DENOMINATION: **ENGLISH WESLEYAN. E.W.M.**

ADDRESS / LOCALITY: **DARRAN ROAD, MOUNTAIN ASH.**

DATE BUILT: **1884.**

CURRENT USE: **CLOSED 1985; DEMOLISHED 1988. FOUR HOUSES BUILT ON SITE, 1989-90**

BRIEF HISTORY: The 'cause' began in 1862 in the town. Vestry built in 1863, followed by the main chapel in 1884, built at a cost of £1,000 with seating for 500. Rev. Idris Evans, minister of Providence E.C. (Ref: 60.) assisted in conducted services here during the late 1930's. Members from the Methodist (English Wesleyan) chapel 'Elim', Perthcelyn (Ref: 42.) transferred to this chapel upon the closure in 1951, under the care of Rev. Percy Large. Original plans in the Cynon Valley Museum.

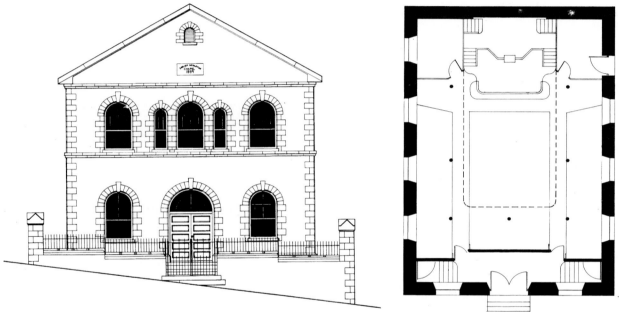

English Wesleyan Methodist (Darran Rd.) Mountain Ash.

Taken in 1986.

CHAPEL REF. NO. 55.

NAME & DENOMINATION: **FFRWD. W.B.**

ADDRESS / LOCALITY: **DUFFRYN ROAD, MOUNTAIN ASH.**

DATE BUILT: **1901.**

CURRENT USE: **CLOSED 1985. USED AS A DOCUMENT STORE ROOM FOR A LOCAL FIRM OF SOLICITORS.**

BRIEF HISTORY: A branch of the Welsh Baptists was established in 1876 as a Sunday School in the little mortuary chapel at Aberffrwd Cemetery (Ref: 57.), opened 1866. Ffrwd Welsh Baptist Chapel began its 'cause' in 1897, and in 1901 the chapel was built at a cost of £2,210. Architects – Morgan & Elford, Aberdare and Mountain Ash. Seating capacity – 600.

A severe façade of dark sandstone, used for the ashlar dressings as well as the rock faced walling. Mullion and transom windows without mouldings. Roof gable banded and punctuated with kneelers. Broad porch with entablature carried on stocky pseudo-Tuscan columns. 214 members in 1916 (150 in Sunday School); 106 in 1947; 25 in 1978. Pipe organ behind altar built by W. C. Vowles, Bristol. Baptistry under pulpit. Schoolroom and classrooms at the rear. Chapel debt of £3,500 cleared by 1943. Twelve memorial stones at the front laid on 26th. July 1900. Names include Mr. Howell Evans, draper; Emrys & Annie Jones, Emporium; Thomas Edmunds; Mr. & Mrs. Miles Morgan; Mr. & Mrs. T & A Evans of 14 Allen Street, Mountain Ash, etc.. Original colour washed drawings are in Cynon Valley Museum.

Ministers include – Rev. J. Glandwr Watkin (first minister); Rev. Fred Morgan; Rev. D. J. Thomas; Rev. Meredith Morgan & Rev. Elwyn Williams.

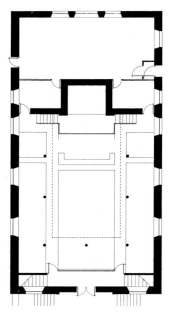

Ffrwd, Mountain Ash.

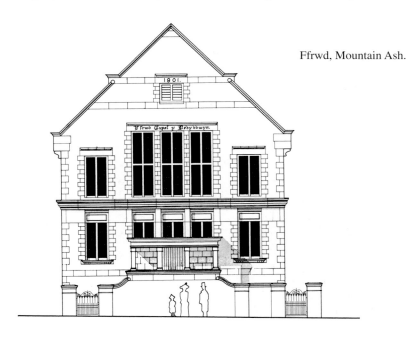

Taken in 1986.

CHAPEL REF. NO. 56.

NAME & DENOMINATION: **FFRWD YSGOLDY. W.B.M.R.**

ADDRESS / LOCALITY: **ALLEN STREET, MOUNTAIN ASH**

DATE BUILT: **1893**

CURRENT USE: **STILL ACTIVE.**

BRIEF HISTORY: Architect – Morgan & Elford, Aberdare & Mountain Ash. Building cost £344. Originally a Sunday School for Rhos W.B. (Ref: 61.); Also a School Room and meeting room. Trustees were from Rhos W.B. Now named "The Brethren". Original colour washed drawings in Cynon Valley Museum. The chapel is located adjacent to Nant-y-Ffrwd, ideally situated for baptism by submersion in that river at the turn of the century.

Ffrwd Ysgoldy, Mountain Ash. Taken in 1991.

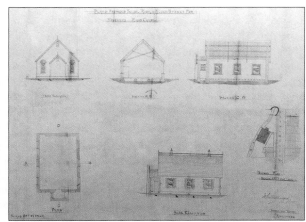

Ffrwd School-Room, Allen Street, Mountain Ash.
Original colour-washed plan, dated 1893.

CHAPEL REF. NO. 57.

NAME & DENOMINATION: **MORTUARY CHAPEL. M.C.**

ADDRESS / LOCALITY: **ABERFFRWD (OLD) CEMETERY, MOUNTAIN ASH.**

DATE BUILT: **1866.**

CURRENT USE: **DEMOLISHED CIRCA 1960.**

BRIEF HISTORY: Was located at the entrance to the cemetery, also used as a Sunday School for Rhos W.B. (Ref: 61.) The old cemetery was opened in 1866. The chapel was built out of native stone, in the Gothic style with a turret containing one bell. Formerly under the control of the Mountain Ash District Council, acting as the Burial Board.

The Mortuary Chapel at Aberffrwd (old) Cemetery overlooks the town centre of Mountain Ash. Taken circa 1955-60.

CHAPEL REF. NO. 58.

NAME & DENOMINATION: **NAZARETH. E.B.**

ADDRESS / LOCALITY: **CARDIFF ROAD, MOUNTAIN ASH**

DATE BUILT: **1841, REBUILT 1854 & 1901.**

CURRENT USE: **CLOSED DECEMBER 2002, MEMBERS TRANSFERRED TO PROVIDENCE CHAPEL (REF 60) CURRENTLY FOR SALE (2004) FOR £30,000 – 4,500 SQ. FT.**

BRIEF HISTORY: The oldest Non-Conformist chapel in Mountain Ash. Architect for 1901 rebuild was Tom W. Millar, Builder – Frank Mills, Mountain Ash. Seating for 650, cost £5,000. pedimented façade of sandstone, all openings round-headed in pairs with a central trio. There was a family of Baptists in Mountain Ash in 1786, who held services in various houses. In 1832 the Baptists began a cause in a house near the Bruce Arms, Commercial Street. Nazareth began their 'cause' in 1841 as a branch of Calvaria, Aberdare (Ref: 104.). Previous to 1841 members would have to walk four miles to Aberdare, or even further from Basin Isaf (Abercynon), to worship as there was no chapel then available at Mountain Ash or Abercynon. The first baptism took place in the River Cynon nearby in 1849. The entrance of the old 1854 chapel faced Cardiff Road. The Welsh Baptists moved from Nazareth to Rhos W.B. (Ref: 61) in 1860, and the English Baptists consequently took over Nazareth. Nazareth was a sister chapel of Mount Pisgah, Miskin (Ref: 43.) There were 294 members in 1899; membership increased dramatically to 498 in 1906 as a result of the 1904/5 Religious Revival; over 500 in the Sunday School. 1951 membership – 260.

Prominent ministers include: Rev. William Williams (the first minister) 1855-1892. (He received no college education): Rev. John Howells, 1877-1895 (D.1895 aged 46yrs.). Rev. J. Francis Jones, 1916- 1934. Tragically, he drowned in 1934 whilst camping with his army regiment in Porthcawl. In the 1940's, evacuees from London and Birmingham came to Nazareth; also black American G.I's worshipped here for a while in the early 1940's.

Major internal alterations were carried out in 1987, stripping out pews and flooring over the balcony level. Original drawings in Cynon Valley Museum.

Centenary booklet 1866 – 1966, written by Rev. Robin Davies is at Aberdare Central Library and the Glamorgan Record Office, Cardiff.

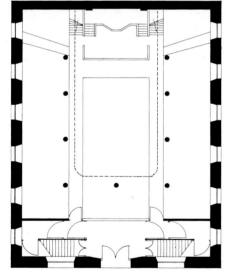

Nazareth, Mountain Ash.

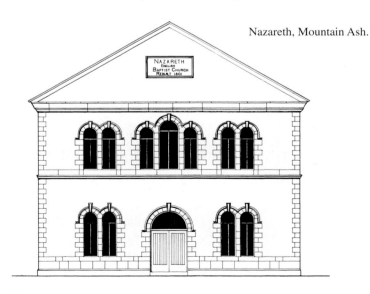

Taken in 1986.

CHAPEL REF. NO. 59.

NAME & DENOMINATION: **NODDFA (ELIM) P.C.**

ADDRESS / LOCALITY: **NIGHT STREET, MOUNTAIN ASH**

DATE BUILT: **1905.**

CURRENT USE: **STILL ACTIVE.**

BRIEF HISTORY: Grade Two Listed Building. Architects – Morgan & Elford, Mountain Ash. Builders – Jones Brothers, Barry. Cost (1905) £2,950. Seating for 700. Was originally Noddfa Welsh Calvinistic Methodist. Became Elim Pentecostal Chapel in 1947. Founded by the evangelist Mr. Percy Brewster of Cardiff. First services of the 1947 chapel were held in a tent erected in The Poplars Field, Caegarw, Mountain Ash, where there are now council houses. A few weeks later, the members purchased what was then Noddfa W.C.M. chapel, and later renamed it Elim Pentecostal Chapel (1947) known as Elim Christian Centre. There were 550 worshipping here at its peak in the 1940's – 1950's. Ministers include Pastors Quest; McAvoy; Maybin and Brown (11½ years). The present Pastor is Glesni Cunningham. First secretary – Sid Gilbert; First organist – Gloria Weeks.

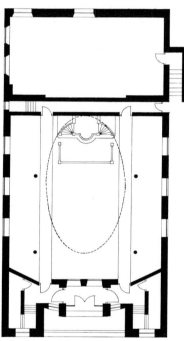

Elliptical plan to gallery; attractive ceiling in blue and white panels with two beautiful large ceiling roses. Unusual and rare bowed front between low side towers. Note the interesting and intricate wood carving of the words of the Lord's Prayer. The fine pulpit is exceptional with panelled grained wood, twin curving stairs and classical newels. Large baptism bath with coloured tiles. Steeply raked gallery pews curve to match the gallery shape. Stick banisters across gallery windows at front.

Original drawings in Cynon Valley Museum. Thanks to Roger Edwards for assistance with preparation of part of these notes.

Noddfa, (Elim), Mountain Ash.

Taken in 1986.

CHAPEL REF. NO. 60.

NAME & DENOMINATION: **PROVIDENCE E.C.**

ADDRESS / LOCALITY: **UNION STREET, MOUNTAIN ASH.**

DATE BUILT: **1869, REBUILT 1912.**

CURRENT USE: **CLOSED 1989, LAST SERVICE 26TH. FEBRUARY 1989. MAJOR CONVERSION & REFURBISHMENT 1993/4, INTO COMMUNITY CENTRE, COST £270,000 FRONT ELEVATION REMAINS UNALTERED. SOLD TO NAZARETH (REF: 58.), REVERTED TO A CHAPEL IN DECEMBER 2002. NOW CALLED PROVIDENCE BAPTIST CHAPEL.**

BRIEF HISTORY: The 'cause' commenced in March1869; meetings were held in the Long Room of the Baileys Arms, Miskin, and the Workmens' Hall, Mountain Ash. (Site of the present Town Hall). The memorial foundation stones were laid by Samuel Morley, M.P. and Henry Richard, M.P., followed by lengthy speeches at the Jeffries Arms (built 1852/5 – still open). The first 1869 chapel was designed by S.O. Harpour, Builder – William Hodges, Mountain Ash, at a cost of £850. Seating for 400.

The second (1912) chapel was designed by architect T.W. Millar M.S.A., Mountain Ash (£90 fee.), primarily of Gothic Perpendicular design. The builder was T.W. Davies, Mountain Ash. Building cost £2,250, seating for 600. Became the United Reformed Church in 1972. Prominent ministers; Rev. Daniel Jones, 1869-1871; Rev. Thomas Anthony, 1888-1909; Rev. Daniel Stanley Morgan, 1915-1923; Rev. John Keyworth Lloyd Williams, 1946-1955; Rev. Jean Sydney Wilkinson, first lady Congregational minister in the Cynon Valley. 1957-1964; Rev. James Ashford Hollyman, 1964-1970. Mr. N. Lukey-Davies (b.1903 – d.2003) was Sunday School Superintendent from 1928-1966. Mr. Austin Clift was treasurer 1954 – 1989. Organists include Gomer L. Davies, 1926-1963, and Alan Vernon Jones, 1960-1989.Original 1912 drawings in Cynon Valley Museum. Survey drawings by Alan Vernon Jones A.R.I.C.S., 1987 are in his private collection.

In the 1960's the chapel youth club enjoyed walks to Gelli Wrgan Farm, Llanwonno, and had milk and home-made bread kindly supplied by Mr. & Mrs. David Prosser, farmers. Mr. Prosser was a deacon of the chapel at one time. At times he would travel to chapel from his farm by tractor.

'History of Providence 1869-1987' written by Alan V Jones, is at Aberdare Central Library.

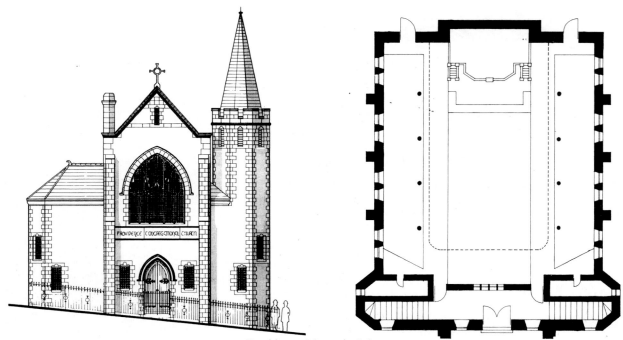

Providence, Mountain Ash.

Providence Chapel dominates the scene, taken from the bell tower,
Town Hall, Mountain Ash – 1974.   *(Brian Jordan)*

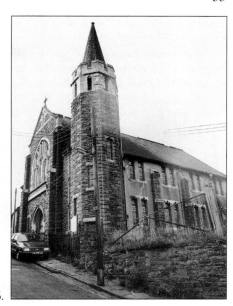

Taken in 1986.

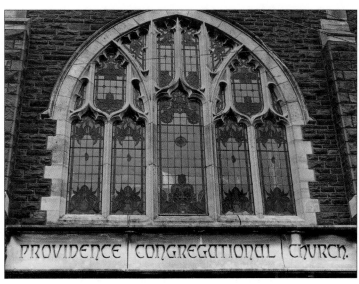

Gothic style tracery window with coloured leaded glass, 1912.

CHAPEL REF. NO. 61.

NAME & DENOMINATION: **RHOS. W.B.**

ADDRESS / LOCALITY: **OXFORD STREET, MOUNTAIN ASH.**

DATE BUILT: **1860.**

CURRENT USE: **CLOSED 1973; DEMOLISHED 1975; PUBLIC TOILETS AND AMENITY AREA BUILT ON SITE, 1988. BRONZE STATUE OF GUTO NYTH BRAN ERECTED ON THE SITE IN 1990.**

BRIEF HISTORY: The largest chapel in Mountain Ash, with seating capacity for 850. Original cost- £1,800. The Welsh Baptists moved from Nazareth (Ref: 58.) to Rhos in 1860 and the former Rhos (then English Baptists) transferred to Nazareth, just across the River Cynon. In 1883 Rhos built Ffrwd Ysgoldy (Ref: 56.). Rhos held a Sunday School in the small chapel located in the Aberffrwd public cemetery (Ref: 57.) before moving to Ffrwd Ysgoldy. There were 450 members in 1899, & 527 in 1905, falling to312 by 1911. In the 1890's the town's registrar's office was located in the vestry schoolroom basement.

After demolition in 1975 the fine organ built in 1900 (cost-£901), was given to Gwawr chapel, Godreaman (Ref: 85.). Rhos was sister chapel to Mount Pisgah (Ref: 43.), and a branch of Calvaria, Aberdare (Ref: 104.) Prior to demolition, fine survey drawings were prepared in 1974 by Chris King ARICS, MRTPI, of Cwmdare.

Prominent ministers include; Rev. William Williams – 1855-1891 (B.1812-D.1897.); Rev. T.T. Hughes – 1893 – 1906; Rev. R.S. Roger M.A. – 1908-1915; Rev. Daniel Jones – 1920-1948.

Centenary History of Rhos 1855 – 1955, 20 pages in Welsh, written by Rev. B.J. Jones B.A., is in Aberdare Central Library. Minute books 1886 – 1891/2/3 – 1906 to 1922 – 1942 to 1958, and Chapel History 1883 are at Glamorgan Record Office, Cardiff.

Taken in July 1975, a few months prior to demolition.   *(Brian Jordan)*

CHAPEL REF. NO. 62.

NAME & DENOMINATION: **SALVATION ARMY HALLS. S.A.**

ADDRESS / LOCALITY: **WOODLAND STREET, MOUNTAIN ASH & OTHERS.**

DATE BUILT: **1886, RENOVATED 1927**

CURRENT USE: **CLOSED CIRCA 1955. CONVERTED TO A LADIES CLOTHES FACTORY, LATELY USED AS A STORE, BELIEVED VACANT 2004.**

BRIEF HISTORY: Built in 1886, the Salvation Army preached in the streets of Mountain Ash since the 1870's. The organisation was founded by William Booth (b.1829-d.1912) in 1865, and is a Christian body which still performs valuable and worthy social work with the poor and needy. Known as "The Barracks", the foundation stone was laid in 1886 by Colonel Pepper of Salisbury. 56 members in 1896. 1947-50 Captain's Frost –Rigby – Clayton – & Hawkins. Early meetings were held in the old 'Workmens' Hall' (on the site of the present Town Hall). There also existed a Salvation Army in an old pawn shop in Mountain Ash. Original drawings in Cynon Valley Museum, drawn by Morgan & Elford, Architects, Mountain Ash. (Renovation work 1927.)

For convenience, the following brief histories of other S.A. Halls in the Cynon Valley are included here.

  (a). **Aberdare Salvation Army.**
      Located adjacent to No.14A Wind Street and opposite Nos. 63-65. Opened in January 2000, the
      building was formerly a domestic science centre for Town Church (Maerdy) School.

      In 1996 the S.A. held services at Ty Fry, (cottage meetings) and later at Soar W.M. (Ref: 114.) until
January 2000. In earlier days they were based near
the Rex Cinema, Aberdare until circa 1955. In
1878 they met at Maes-y-Dre, the old sawmills, before
transferring to Lamb Street, off High Street. 1954 –
Lieut's Kenneth Wilson. There were 600 converts in
Aberdare by 1925.

  (b). **Aberaman Salvation Army.**
      Formerly based at the Long Room, Regent Street,
      also based behind Mount Hill Street, Aberaman. They
      also held early meetings at the Temperance Hall and
      Long Room of the Lamb & Flag Inn, 165 Cardiff
      Road – (opened 1855, closed 1961). The Salvation
      Army Hall/ Citadel, otherwise known as 'The
      Barracks' then moved to the former Saron Ysgoldy
      W.I. (Ref: 76.) sold to the S.A. in 1928 for £688, now
      a Funeral Directors/ Chapel of Rest. (Proprietors Alan
      & Margaret Evans). 1954 – Lieutenant John
      Laurence.

  (c). **Rhigos Salvation Army.**
      An extension of Aberdare Salvation Army, set up in
      March 2002. Located off Heol Esgyn in the
      Community Centre.

  (d) **Cwmaman Salvation Army.**
      Located opposite the library (formerly a shop), near
      Cwmaman hall.

  (e) **Ynysybwl Salvation Army.**
      Was located at the top of Augustus Street – no longer
      exists.

Ladies of the Salvation Army, Aberdare branch,
circa 1900.

(Aberdare Library.)

    Thanks to Captain Michael Evan-Yates and his wife, Lieutenant Lindey Evan-Yates of Aberdare S.A. Wind
Street, for information.

    The Salvation Army were often to be seen in the streets performing outdoor band recitals on Sunday evenings,
they frequently visited public houses on Saturday evenings to sell their publication the "War Cry", where they
generally received a welcome and many purchasing customers. The "War Cry" first appeared on 22nd. December
1879.

CHAPEL REF. NO. 63.

NAME & DENOMINATION: **SOAR W.I.**

ADDRESS / LOCALITY: **HIGH STREET, MOUNTAIN ASH.**

DATE BUILT: **1904.**

CURRENT USE: **CLOSED 1964; USED AS A TEACHERS' CENTRE 1964-83. THEN AS
                             CAREERS CENTRE. FOR SALE, 2004.**

BRIEF HISTORY: The 'cause' commenced as a Sunday School in Duffryn Street chapel (Ref;
                             53.). Architect – T. W. Millar M.S.A., Mountain Ash, Builder – Jones Brothers,
Barry. Cost £3,000 – Seating for 700. Located opposite Police Station (built 1865), and adjacent to No.26. Massive
rusticated voussoirs to all windows. A branch of Bethania W.I. (Ref: 48.) 176 members were transferred from

Bethania in 1905. Hammond electric organ given to Nazareth E.B. (Ref: 58.) upon closure in 1964. Attractive coloured stained glass windows, an unusual design feature in Nonconformist Chapels. Original drawings in Cynon Valley Museum. Almost completely stripped out internally at 2002.

Memorial foundation stones laid 2nd. August 1904 by Gwilym Jones, Solicitor, Mountain Ash; Miss. G. Muriel Evans, Ffrwd Villa, Mountain Ash; Master Arthur T. Millar, Forest Cottage, Mountain Ash and Isaac George Esq., High Constable Aberdare and Miskin Higher. The notable founder and conductor of Mountain Ash Male Voice Choir, Thomas Glyndwr Richards (1885-1935) was born at Maesteg; he was an ardent member of Soar Chapel. He died in 1935 and is buried at Maesyrarian Cemetery, Mountain Ash.

The chapel was severely damaged by fire in 1936 and cost £800 to repair.

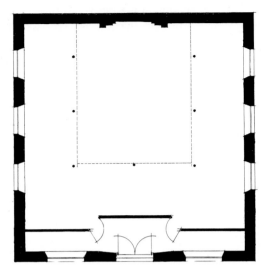

Soar, Mountain Ash.

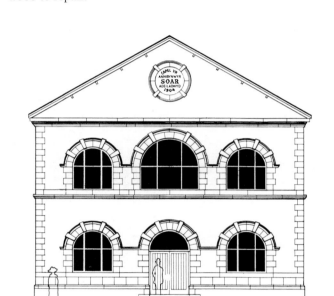

Taken 1986.

CHAPEL REF. NO. 64.

NAME & DENOMINATION: SAINT JOHN'S SC/G.H.

ADDRESS / LOCALITY: DOVER STREET, MOUNTAIN ASH.

DATE BUILT: CIRCA 1920.

CURRENT USE: DISCONTINUED CHAPEL ACTIVITIES CIRCA 1960, CONVERTED TO GARAGE/STORE

BRIEF HISTORY: A small chapel located adjacent to Aberpennar Cottage and opposite the Napier's public house. Formerly a Spiritual chapel/Gospel Hall in full use around 1940-1950.

CHAPEL REF. NO. 65.

NAME & DENOMINATION: **SUNDAY SCHOOL P.C.**

ADDRESS / LOCALITY: **IVOR STREET, MOUNTAIN ASH.**

DATE BUILT: **CIRCA 1905**

CURRENT USE: **STILL ACTIVE AS ELIM CHRISTIAN CENTRE.**

BRIEF HISTORY: Adjacent to No.1 Ivor Street. Shown on the 1960 Ordnance Survey map as being a Social Club, and on the 1919 survey as in use as a school.

CHAPEL REF. NO. 66.

NAME & DENOMINATION: **ENGLISH BAPTIST E.B.**

ADDRESS / LOCALITY: **TON COCH TERRACE, CEFNPENNAR.**

DATE BUILT: **1894.**

CURRENT USE: **STILL ACTIVE.**

BRIEF HISTORY: Located opposite No. 19, formerly known as 'The Baptist Mission Room'. A branch of Rhos W.B. (Ref: 61.), and daughter chapel of Nazareth E.B. (Ref: 58.). The first services were held in the front room of No.15 Ton Coch Terrace. Building cost in 1894 – £105. Seating for 300.

It comprises a corrugated zinc-clad structure. In 1954, the chapel became an Independent Chapel of the Baptist Faith and Order, served by keen lay preachers. Membership at present (2004) is about six worshippers.

English Baptist Chapel, Cefnpennar – Taken in 1995.

CHAPEL REF. NO. 67.

NAME & DENOMINATION: CAPEL BRYN MORIAH. W. CONG.

ADDRESS / LOCALITY: THE AVENUE (LOWER END, JOINING DUFFRYN ROAD) CEFNPENNAR.

DATE BUILT: CIRCA 1860.

CURRENT USE: DEMOLISHED CIRCA 1950.

BRIEF HISTORY: A small stone chapel located just below Cefn Pennar House, and near the former Lower Duffryn Colliery (Lower Pit) Cefnpennar. Remnants of the old stone ruins of the chapel are still visible at 2004. Some of the men and the Deacons were known locally as "The Bowler Hat Brigade"!

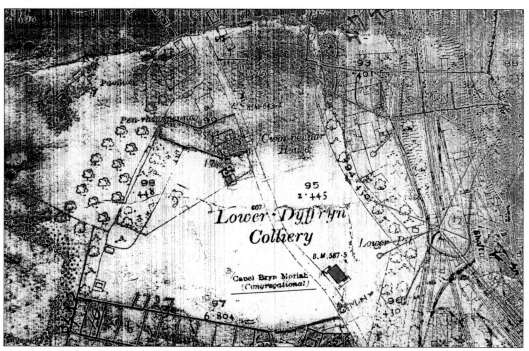

Capel Bryn Moriah (W. Cong.) Cefnpennar. Ordnance Survey Plan 1868.

CHAPEL REF. NO. 68.

NAME & DENOMINATION: BETHESDA W.B.

ADDRESS / LOCALITY: JOHN STREET, ABERCWMBOI.

DATE BUILT: 1864, RENOVATED 1904, 1938 & 1950

CURRENT USE: STILL ACTIVE.

BRIEF HISTORY: Cost £864 to build in 1864, seating for 600 containing boxed pews. Located between Nos. 70 & 71 John Street. A Grade 2 Listed Building; extensive renovations carried out in 1938 and 1950. A new vestry built in 1905 at a cost of £1,000. The 'cause' commenced in Cap Coch in 1854 (then a hamlet of only 40 houses) by a few members who came from Gwawr W.B. (Ref: 73.). In 1860 two homes were purchased in Jenkin Street and converted into a chapel, 39 members came there from

Gwawr W.B. 60 members in 1871 with 100 in Sunday School; 57 members in 1900 with 100 in Sunday School; 157 members in 1916. Two storey, three bay classical gable façade in painted stucco. Pedimental gable with plaque. Main front has four projecting piers to rusticated ground floor and has paired Corinthian pilasters above under main cornice. First floor arched windows, centre triplet with keystone to simple moulded surrounds. Interior raked gallery on plain cast iron columns. Pews in three blocks, all with hinged doors out to aisles. A very fine pulpit with joinery of excellent quality. Ceiling has plaster cornice and border, the rest is in two boarded rectangles. Large ornate multi-coloured roses on circular plaster panels set in stained herring-bone boarded wooden sections with diagonal ribs.

Memorial stone was laid by Mary Morgan, Abercwmboi, in 1864. First minister was Rev. James Jones – Rev. Matthias Jenkins 1900 – 1930, Rev. Arthur G. Llewellyn 1935 – 1962.

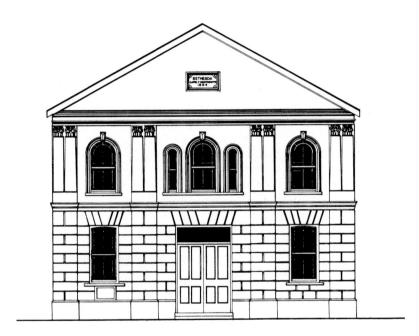

Bethesda, Abercwmboi.

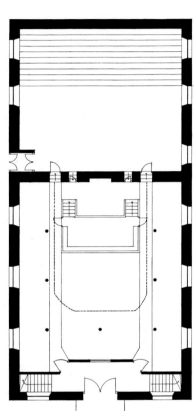

Taken 1986.

CHAPEL REF. NO. 69.

NAME & DENOMINATION: **BETHLEHEM W.I.**

ADDRESS / LOCALITY: **JOHN STREET, ABERCWMBOI**

DATE BUILT: **1860, ENLARGED 1875; RENOVATED 1899.**

CURRENT USE: **STILL ACTIVE.**

BRIEF HISTORY: As a result of the expansion of the iron and coal industries, the chapel was formed in October 1858. First services were held by Rev. John Bowen Davies of Aberaman, also known as 'Davis Bach', Caerdyddd. A number of followers rented a house nearby, the home of Thomas Lewis, to hold Sunday School and prayer meetings. In October 1858 23 members came from Saron W.I. (Ref: 77.). The chapel was built in 1860 at a cost of £700, with seating for 450. David Davis (Maesyffynon) laid the foundation stone in May, 1859. The chapel was renovated and the vestry built in 1899 at a cost of £1,000. Debt of £495 was cleared by 1913, first time free of debt since 1858. An organ was provided in 1920 at a cost of £1,000. The first minister was Rev. Robert Owen (1860-1862), followed by Rev. William Williams (1862-1875). Rev. Jonah Davies was minister from 1879 to 1897 and school master at Cwmdare; his son Gomer Lloyd Davies was organist here in 1900, and later at Providence E. Cong (Ref: 60.) from 1926 to 1963. He died on 5th. September 1971, aged 92. Rev. Morgan Price (1919 – 1944). Membership in 1890 was 160 with 247 in Sunday School; 1904 was 370 with 349 in Sunday School; 1914 was 308 with 216 in Sunday School; 1930 was 250 with 185 in Sunday School; 1954 was 143.

   Currently named 'Bethlehem Christian Fellowship' and 'Living Way Church'. All pews were taken out and replaced by removable chairs. False sheeted ceiling at balcony level to retain heat. The balcony balustrading, ceiling rose and cast iron gallery supports are of particular beauty and worth seeing.

   History Notes 1858 – 1914, by Rev. J Bowen Davies are in Aberdare Central Library.

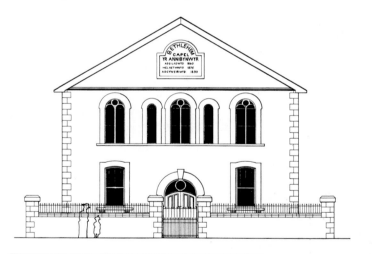

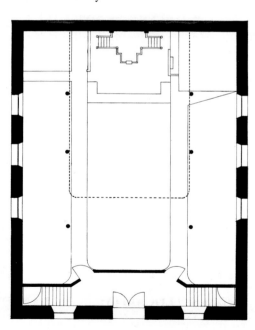

Bethlehem. Abercwmboi.

Taken in 1986.

CHAPEL REF. NO. 70.

NAME & DENOMINATION: **GRAIG STREET METHODIST E.M**

ADDRESS / LOCALITY: **SCHOOL STREET, ABERCWMBOI**

DATE BUILT: **1910.**

CURRENT USE: **CLOSED 1985, CONVERTED IN 1990 TO FLATS NAMED 'THE CHAPEL' NOS. 1 TO 4. VACANT & FOR SALE, 2004.**

BRIEF HISTORY: Located behind 87 Park View Terrace and Opposite/near Graig Crescent near School Street. A small chapel of plain and simple design with a small front porch entrance. Services were first held in a house owned by Mr. Finer, Park View Terrace. Deed of lease granted by Powell Duffryn Steam Coal Co. trustees for 99 years from 1st. November 1907. Freehold purchased in 1925. Foundation stone laid on 18th. August1910, chapel opened March 1913. Original members paid 2/6 (12½p.) annually. When Park View Terrace houses were built nearby, there developed a need for a new English Methodist chapel in the area, to meet the needs of new immigrants working at Aberaman Colliery. Members of Darran Road E.W. Methodist (Ref: 54.) contributed 50% of finance needed to build Graig Street Methodist Chapel, and also helped Mason Street chapel financially (Ref: 72.). In 1921-1923 the chapel was hired by the District Council for use as a Boys' Day School.

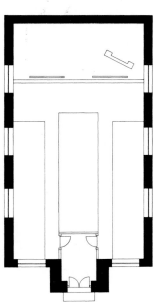

Graig Street Chapel, Abercwmboi.

CHAPEL REF. NO. 71.

NAME & DENOMINATION: **BEULAH E.B.**

ADDRESS / LOCALITY: **LLANDDEWI STREET, ABERAMAN.**

DATE BUILT: **1890.**

CURRENT USE: **CLOSED 1993. DEMOLISHED AUGUST 2002. OUTLINE PLANNING PERMISSION FOR TWO HOUSES.**

BRIEF HISTORY: At one time known as Carmel Bryn Sion. The 'cause' began in 1884; in circa 1860 served by the mother chapel, Carmel E.B. (Ref: 105.) First meetings held in the 'Long Room' of the Lamb and Flag Hotel, Lewis Street (opened 1855-closed 1961). The fine piped organ was one of the oldest in the Cynon Valley, purchased from St. David's E.P. Church, Aberdare (Ref: 111.) just before the First World War started. Seating for 320 (no gallery). The first minister from Penrhiwceiber, namely Rev. Luther Davies; he set up Trinity E.B., Cwmaman (Ref: 93.). 1911 – 69 members, 120 in Sunday School; 1938 – 76 members; 1947 – 56 members.

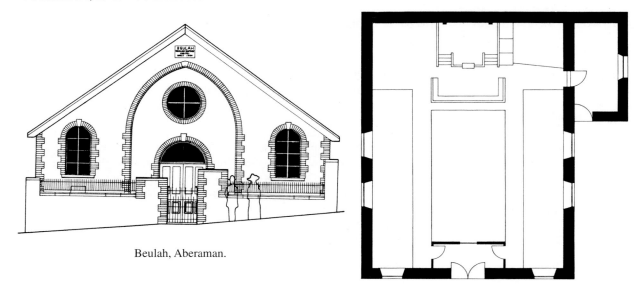

Beulah, Aberaman.

Taken 1986.

CHAPEL REF. NO. 72.

NAME & DENOMINATION: **ENGLISH WESLEYAN E.W.M.**

ADDRESS / LOCALITY: **MASON STREET, ABERAMAN.**

DATE BUILT: **1858, ENLARGED 1884 & 1938.**

CURRENT USE: **STILL ACTIVE.**

BRIEF HISTORY: First meetings held in houses at Mount Hill Street and Station Street. Built in 1858 by D. Grier with seating for 180. School Room built at a cost of £200 in 1884 (222 scholars in the Sunday School). Enlarged in 1884 to seat 300. Front extended in 1938 at a cost of £1,100; builder for this was Mr. Blackburn; architect was Edward Davies. Currently named 'Mason Street Methodist Church 1938' and located on a corner plot opposite No. 49 Commercial Street, and opposite the former Beaufort Arms public house (opened 1861-closed 1929), now No. 2 Commercial Street.

The Minister in 1958 was Rev. I. G. Pennant Lewis, the present Minister is Rev. Nicholas Lakin. In 1884 a thirteen-stop harmonium was purchased for £22. In 1924 the freehold was purchased for £25. Organist in 1958 was Miss E. Gulliver. Centenary booklet 1858 – 1958 is at Glamorgan Record Office and Aberdare Library.

Mason Street Methodist Chapel, Aberaman. Taken in 1986.

Opening ceremony, front extension of Mason Street Chapel, 1938.

Parade gathers outside Mason Street Chapel on 'Civic Sunday' 1961. Sarah Edwards is Chairlady, Aberdare Council.

CHAPEL REF. NO. 73.

NAME & DENOMINATION: **GWAWR. W.B.**

ADDRESS / LOCALITY: **REGENT STREET, ABERAMAN.**

DATE BUILT: **1849, REBUILT 1870.**

CURRENT USE: **DEMOLISHED CIRCA 1970. THREE TERRACED HOUSES BUILT ON SITE-1975, NAMED 'REGENTS CLOSE'**

BRIEF HISTORY: The 'cause' was formed in 1848 by members from Calvaria W.B. (Ref: 104.) First baptism in River Cynon in 1848. First meetings held in a large room near the King William Inn, Cardiff Road (opened 1848-closed 1871). Rebuilt in 1870 at a cost of £1,707-15-11. Vestry enlarged in 1890 at a cost of £900. The 1870 chapel had seating capacity for 850. The former Griffin Inn (opened 1856-closed 1936, now 290 Cardiff Road) was located almost opposite the chapel.

'Old' Gwawr was demolished circa1970, and members took over Hebron C.M. (Ref: 85.), Jubilee Road, Godreaman, which then became 'new' Gwawr W.B. (located between Nos.82 & 83 Regent Street. Formerly named 'Baptist Chapel (Particular)' – seating for 410. In 1871 Thomas Budd, a plasterer from Aberdare died following a fall from scaffold during renovation work.

270 members in 1859; 205 in 1916; 189 in 1925; 66 in 1955; 42 in 1963. Sunday School/Vestry attached at side, with graveyard at front. The 1851 Religious Census states – "Gwawr Chapel, Aberaman – Baptist, erected 1849. Present – morning 100 + 30 scholars, afternoon 60 scholars; evening 450 – Dewi Bevan Jones, Minister, Aberaman."

Minister in 1851 was Rev. Dewi Bevan Jones, Rev. Thomas Davies was minister for 33 years, 1875 – 1908. Rev. W. T. Francis was minister in 1911. The design of this chapel is classical and well-proportioned, with Doric pilasters, architrave and strong pediment in freestone. Well balanced openings with tall slim windows in outer bays, and a triple group of windows over a double entrance in the wider central bay.

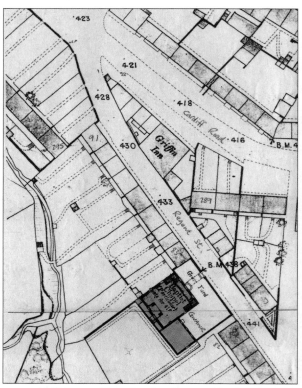

1868 Survey Plan, showing Gwawr, Aberaman.

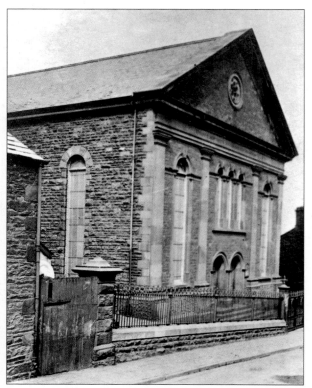

'Old' Gwawr, circa 1910. Demolished circa 1970.

CHAPEL REF. NO. 74.

NAME & DENOMINATION: **LIBANUS W.C.M.**

ADDRESS / LOCALITY: **LEWIS STREET, ABERAMAN.**

DATE BUILT: **1848 – REBUILT 1876.**

CURRENT USE: **CLOSED CIRCA 1985, CONVERTED TO FOUR FLATS, 2004.**

BRIEF HISTORY: Prior to building the chapel in 1848, a Sunday School was held in various houses nearby in Regent Street for several months. Libanus was erected in 1848 on a site in Regent street, Aberaman; from there it was re-built on its present site in Lewis Street in 1876. The chapel was built on land given by Crawshay Bailey. Cost of chapel in 1848 was £500. Seating for 550. In 1848 the preacher received 9 shillings (45p.) each Sunday Service and 2 shillings (10p.) per week for night services. Some members left Gwawr (Ref: 85.) and joined Libanus. A branch of Carmel C.M., Trecynon (Ref: 125.) 69 members in 1848; 16 in Sunday School. 85 members in 1853 with 140 in Sunday School. Electric lights installed in 1922. A gallery was installed in 1850. The 1851 Religious Census return states – "Libanus, Aberaman Welsh Calvinistic Methodist, erected 1847, space: free 180; other 330; standing 190. Present; morning 200; afternoon 229 scholars; evening 200, including teachers. William Morgan, Secretary, Aberaman Colliery.

Mr. R. Tom Davies was organist for 50 years, 1897 – 1947. Building improvements were carried out gradually over recent years (new windows etc.). Ornate ceiling centre rose; a fine pulpit; harmonium organ by H. Christophe, Paris. Fees for visiting ministers in 1848 varied from 3 shillings (15p.) to eight shillings (40p.).

Ministers include – Rev. E. Moses 1892-1900, Rev. J. Harris Jones 1903-1907.

Centenary history by D.J. Jones, 1848-1948 (in Welsh) is at Aberdare Library.

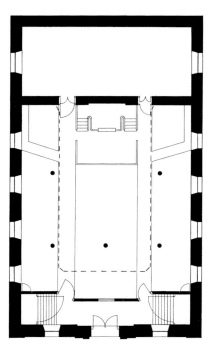

Libanus, Aberaman.

Taken 1986.

CHAPEL REF. NO. 75.

NAME & DENOMINATION: **PENTECOSTAL P.C.**

ADDRESS / LOCALITY: **CARDIFF ROAD, ABERAMAN**

DATE BUILT: **1910-ENLARGED 1923/26 & 1985.**

CURRENT USE: **STILL ACTIVE.**

BRIEF HISTORY: The 'cause' commenced in 1910 when a small group of people left Gwawr W.B. (Ref: 73.) and held services in various houses nearby. In 1919 the evangelist Stephen Jeffries came to the area and held a meeting in Libanus C.M. (Ref: 74.). Following this meeting people decided to form a church, and they purchased the Prince of Wales public house (opened 1865; closed 1917 – known locally as the 'Gin Palace'), 281 Cardiff Road, which is the site of the present church, and opposite the Castle Inn, opened 1853; still open. As numbers increased the building became too small. Between 1923 and 1926 the building was expanded with the work being carried out by the members, many of whom were miners and unemployed during the depression and 1926 strikes. In 1985 the church purchased the house next door (No. 280 Cardiff Road), and built a minor hall and kitchen, opened in October 1986.

Pastor's include:- Pastor D. Davies, the first minister, up to 1954; Pastor E. Lee 1957 – 1960; Pastor Phelps, 1960 – 1965; Pastor Cyril Chick, 1965 – 1971; Pastor Ian Jennings 1972 – 1975; Pastor Henry Drabble, 1975 – 1979; Pastor W. Morgan, 1980 – 1993 & Pastor C. Thomas, 1995 – 2000.

Over the years, over 40 members have taken up missionary work and pioneering new churches in Great Britain, Australia and America. The church is thriving and has a large number of young people.

Mrs. Maralyn Jones, a member of the church, kindly prepared part of this brief history.

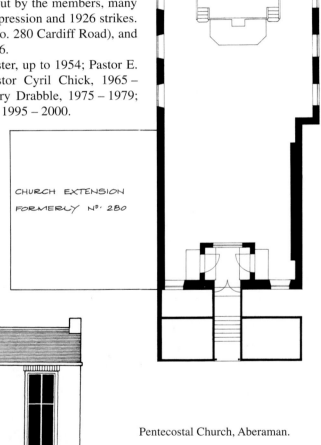

CHURCH EXTENSION FORMERLY Nᴼ. 280

Pentecostal Church, Aberaman.

CHAPEL REF. NO. 76.

NAME & DENOMINATION: **SARON YSGOLDY. W.I.**

ADDRESS / LOCALITY: **CARDIFF ROAD, ABERAMAN.**

DATE BUILT: **1896.**

CURRENT USE: **CONVERTED TO A FUNERAL HOME & CHAPEL OF REST IN 1985, OWNED BY ALAN & MARGARET EVANS.**

BRIEF HISTORY: Formerly a Sunday School belonging to Saron W.I. (Ref: 77.), from 1896 to 1928. From 1928 until the 1960's, it was a Salvation Army Hall/ Citadel, otherwise known as 'The Barracks'. Purchase price in 1928 was £688. Located adjacent to No.1 Wyndham Crescent. In the past the 'Nici-Naci' pit was located at the rear (now allotments). The colliery was also known as 'Williams pit' and 'Pwll Bara Menyn', located to the west of the old gasworks (opened 1846/50; closed 1912). Owned by David Williams of Ynyscynon.

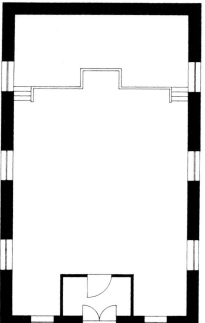

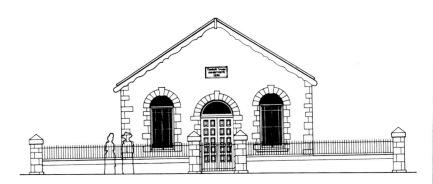

Saron Ysgoldy, Aberaman.

Taken in 1986.

CHAPEL REF. NO. 77.

NAME & DENOMINATION: **SARON W.I.**

ADDRESS / LOCALITY: **DAVIES STREET, ABERAMAN.**

DATE BUILT: **1849 – ENLARGED 1856; RENOVATED 1871 & 1890.**

CURRENT USE: **STILL ACTIVE.**

BRIEF HISTORY: Grade 2 Listed Building, located opposite No.34. The 'cause' started with the first meetings held in 1846, in the Lamb & Flag public house at 165 Cardiff Road (built 1845, closed 1961), and later at 242 Cardiff Road, under the care of Rev. David Price. Saron W.I. leased land on Abergwawr Farm from Jennet Roberts and Dr. James Lewis Roberts. The chapel was consecrated in August 1850. Building cost in 1849 was £719; enlarged in 1856 at a cost of £220, to provide increased seating capacity for 900. Renovated internally in 1890 at a cost of £1,600. One of the largest chapels in the Cynon valley, if not the largest, and is reputed to have a few more seats than others in this seating category, Viz: Calvaria (Ref: 12.); Ebenezer (Ref: 127.) and Siloa (Ref: 113.) The vestry at the rear was opened in 1863 and was formerly a 'British School for Boys and Girls', built at a cost of £300. Graveyard exists at the side. The recess formed behind for an organ was never used. A spacious wide interior of large proportions with gallery and a grand boarded ceiling; fine floral design stained glass in the vestibule doors. The entire chapel is beautifully maintained. Broad three-bay, two storey façade of fine classical design. Moulded string course between floors; upper floor with six pilasters flanking a broad centre bay with arched triplet windows.

Plain plinths. Caps below eaves. Ground floor is rusticated on a plinth with channelled pilasters at outer angles.

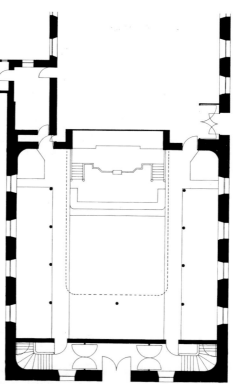

Ministers include – Rev. Glannant Jones for 42 years (1931 – 1973), the longest serving minister; Rev. John Davies (1854 – 1863); Rev. R. Rowlands (1864 – 1891); Rev. H. P. Jenkins (1893 – 1922). These three ministers served 99 years between them in the 109 year period 1864 – 1973. Mrs. Heulwen Evans A.L.C.M. was organist, 1960 – 2000. Membership in 1850 was 218. As at 2003 services are held in the large vestry behind the main chapel. A copy of "History of Saron 1846 – 1946", written in Welsh (24 pages), by Rev. Glannant Jones, is in Aberdare Library.

Saron, Aberaman.

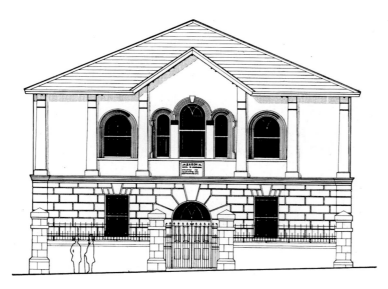

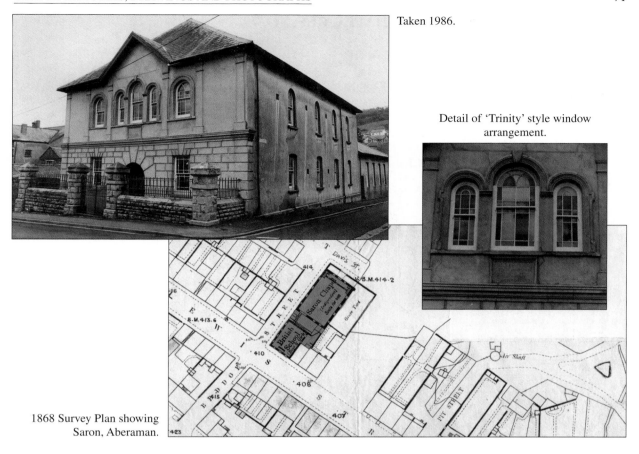

Taken 1986.

Detail of 'Trinity' style window arrangement.

1868 Survey Plan showing Saron, Aberaman.

CHAPEL REF. NO. 78.

NAME & DENOMINATION:	SEILOH C.M.
ADDRESS / LOCALITY:	REGENT STREET, ABERAMAN.
DATE BUILT:	CIRCA 1860.
CURRENT USE:	DEMOLISHED CIRCA 1970. 'REGENT COURT' FLATS NOW OCCUPY THE SITE.

BRIEF HISTORY: Located adjacent to Nos. 60 & 61. British School (Girls) attached. Bought from the Calvinistic Methodists in 1877, sold in 1962 (purchaser unknown). Seating for 404, including gallery. A Sunday School attached was a branch of Siloa W. Cong. (Ref: 113.).

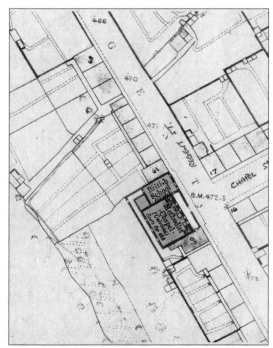

1868 Survey Plan showing Seiloh C.M., Aberaman.

CHAPEL REF. NO. 79.

NAME & DENOMINATION: SILOA. E.W.M.

ADDRESS / LOCALITY: YNYSLWYD ROAD, ABERAMAN

DATE BUILT: 1897.

CURRENT USE: CONVERTED TO A HOUSE IN 1982. WHITE UPVC CLADDING; TILED ROOF

BRIEF HISTORY:
Formerly A Sunday School, located opposite No. 8 Ynyslwyd Road. Also referred to as Siloa English Wesleyan, Ysgoldy Siloa, and used by the deacons of Siloa W. Cong. (Ref: 113.) Originally built as a 'halfway house' for people attending Siloa. Was never strictly used as a chapel – only as a Sunday School.

SILOA ENGLISH WESLEYAN CHAPEL.

PLANS ~ 1980

CONVERTED TO A DWELLING HOUSE IN 1982.

Siloa, Aberaman.
Plans drawn in 1980 (A.V. Jones).

Ysgoldy Siloa.
Taken circa 1910.

CHAPEL REF. NO. 80.

NAME & DENOMINATION: SILOH A.C.

ADDRESS / LOCALITY: CLUB STREET, ABERAMAN.

DATE BUILT: 1930.

CURRENT USE: STILL ACTIVE.

BRIEF HISTORY: Founded by George Forward & Nicolas Evans. The 'cause' commenced in 1921 in the Welsh School, Aberaman. As numbers increased, they bought a parcel of land in Club Street and built Siloh in 1930. Located opposite Nos. 1 & 2, a plain simple structure with a small front porch and rough stucco rendering to external walls. Daughter church of Apostolic Church, Trecynon (Ref: 123.)

Past Ministers – Rev. John Jones; Rev. T.N. Turnbull (1949); Rev. William James; Rev. Phillip Williams.

Siloh A.C., Aberaman. 2002.

CHAPEL REF. NO. 81.

NAME & DENOMINATION: ST. MARGARET'S, E.B.

ADDRESS / LOCALITY: BEDFORD STREET, ABERAMAN.

DATE BUILT: CIRCA 1870

CURRENT USE: DEMOLISHED CIRCA 1970; HOUSE BUILT ON THE SITE.

BRIEF HISTORY: Site now occupied by Nos. 6 & 7 Glamorgan Court.

CHAPEL REF. NO. 82.

NAME & DENOMINATION: TABERNACLE. E.M.

ADDRESS / LOCALITY: LLANDDEWI STREET, ABERAMAN.

DATE BUILT: 1855, REBUILT 1891

CURRENT USE: DEMOLISHED 1980. NOW SITE OF 'COMMERCIAL PLACE' FLATS, BUILT EARLY 1980'S.

BRIEF HISTORY: The 'cause' began in 1854 in Llanddewi Street, also known then as "Thomas Place". Foundation stone laid in February 1854 by David Williams, Engineer, Ynyscynon. Seating for 160; building cost £300. The chapel was built largely by the gratuitous labours of the members themselves. Rebuilt in 1891 with seating for 380, under the supervision of Rev. T Kench. Sunday School attached was built in 1912. Formerly Primitive Methodist; later became English Congregational. Home of "Duffryn Aman Ambulance Centre and Classes" up to demolition in 1980. In 1853 a Miss Mullen kept a schoolroom here with 45 pupils.

Located at the corner of Llanddewi Street and Commercial Street on a corner plot, and next to No. 10, just below Beulah E.B. (Ref: 71.). Membership in 1855 was 30.

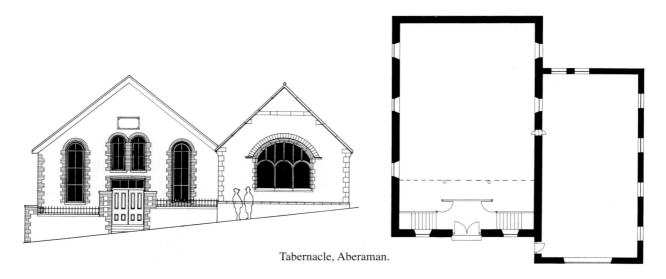

Tabernacle, Aberaman.

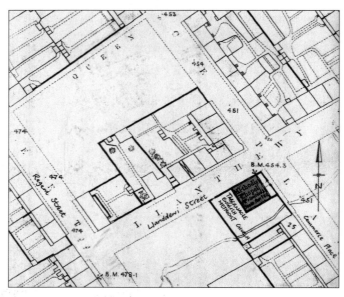

1868 Survey Plan showing Tabernacle, Aberaman.

CHAPEL REF. NO. 83.

NAME & DENOMINATION: **YNYSLWYD. W.B.**

ADDRESS / LOCALITY: **SUNNY BANK PLACE, ABERAMAN.**

DATE BUILT: **1862.**

CURRENT USE: **CLOSED 1996; DEMOLISHED 1998. SITE VACANT & FOR SALE 2003. THREE LINK HOUSES BUILT ON THE SITE, 2004.**

BRIEF HISTORY: The 'cause' commenced in 1858 as a Sunday School with a house attached, built at a cost of £254. Prior to this, meetings were held in the Long Room of the Albion Hotel, 60 Cardiff Road (opened 1864; closed 1934), later to become the Albion Lodging House. (Seating for 600 – cost £1,100.) A branch of Calvaria W.B. Chapel built in 1862 by David Morgan of Treorchy.

Named 'Ynyslwyd' after the estate on which it was built. Two vestries (upper & lower) plus caretakers' house. First minister was Rev. Thomas John ('Twrfab') (Ref: 104.) with 415 members in 1868, 550 in Sunday School. Membership dropped to below 300 at the end of 1876 as a result of mining subsidence. Membership in 1916 was 195 with 190 in Sunday School – 1928 was 231 with 217 in Sunday School – 1938 was 169 with 98 in Sunday School – 1847 was 122 with Sunday School down to 23. Fine new organ installed in 1912; attractive large central plaster ceiling rose. Memorial stone laid by Miss Davies, Ynyslwyd, 29th. May 1862. Local enquiries indicate the possibility of three link type houses being built on the site. Located adjacent to No. 1A Sunny Bank Street, and opposite 36-38 Sunny Bank Place. Ministers – Rev. R.E. Williams 1878-1911; Rev. T. Thomas 1935-1962. During the 1940's the organist was W. R. Thomas, otherwise known as the conductor of 'The Billy Thomas Accordion Band' which was popular in Aberaman during this period. Mr. Thomas resided at regent Street, Aberaman.

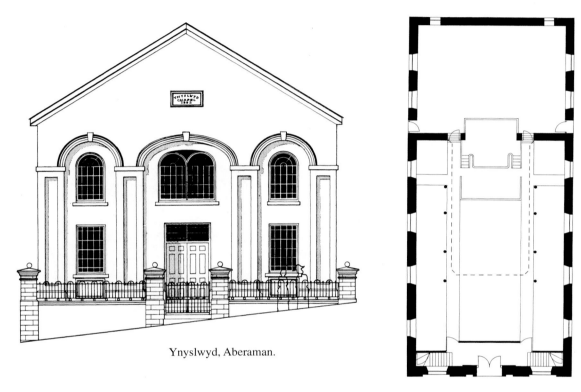

Ynyslwyd, Aberaman.

Ynyslwyd,
Aberaman.
1989.

CHAPEL REF. NO. 84.

NAME & DENOMINATION: **BETHANY E.C.**

ADDRESS / LOCALITY: **JUBILEE ROAD, GODREAMAN**

DATE BUILT: **1898**

CURRENT USE: **CLOSED 1995, SOLD FOR £20,000. CONVERTED INTO 4 FLATS, 2002/3.**

BRIEF HISTORY: Built by John Jones, Gwawr Cottage, with seating for 500. Located adjacent to No.55. Founded during the coal strike of 1898, under the direction of Rev. H.A. Davies, minister of Moriah Aman (Ref: 90.) from 1875 –1909 (Died 1922). Built on a plot of ground secured from the Powell Duffryn Company, Architect was Thomas Roderick, Aberdare. Building cost was £1,052. Schoolroom at the rear was designed and built by G.A. Treharne, Aberdare, at a cost of £175. Offspring of Tabernacle E.M. (Ref: 82.), and Saron W.I. (Ref: 77.). Memorial stones laid by D.P. Davies J.P., Ynyslwyd, and J.H. Powell Esq. London House, Aberaman, on 29th. August 1898. Commemorative silver trowel used by Mr. Powell is in a local private collection, as is a rare boxed travelling communion set. (Photographs in the author's

collection). First minister was Rev. John Solon Rees of Belmont Tce. Aberaman, (1900-1905), founder members include Alderman Thomas Williams of Gwaelodygarth, Merthyr, and William P Williams, postmaster, Aberdare. An attractive Bethany Sunday School banner of 1898 is in the Cynon Valley Museum. The front stone name plaque is of a three-leaf clover design with brick surround dressing. Fine central ceiling rose; attractive colourful capitals to cast-iron gallery support pillars. Membership numbers were drastically reduced in the 1930/40's due the trade depression period and conscription of young men for war service. 1938 membership was 114 with 120 in the Sunday School. The chapel had close social links with Providence E.C. chapel (Ref: 60.) Mountain Ash, particularly through the Youth Club activities in the 1950's – 1960's.

Taken in 1989.

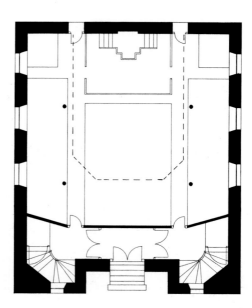

Bethany, Godreaman.

CHAPEL REF. NO. 85.

NAME & DENOMINATION: **GWAWR. W.B. FORMERLY HEBRON. C.M.**

ADDRESS / LOCALITY: **JUBILEE ROAD GODREAMAN.**

DATE BUILT: **1901.**

CURRENT USE: **STILL ACTIVE.**

BRIEF HISTORY: Architect – Thomas Roderick, Aberdare. Built by John Morgan & Sons, Aberdare at a cost of £1,740. Formerly Hebron C.M. Meetings and services were held in Aberaman Primary School while the chapel was being built in 1901. The 'cause' started in 1899 by holding meetings in the Board School, Aberaman. Old Gwawr W.B. (Ref: 73.) was demolished in the early 1970's and members took over Hebron in 1966, which was renamed (new) Gwawr W.B. Now named 'Gwawr Bilingual Baptist Church'. The chapel had an active Sunday School, Band of Hope and Young People's Society. Eighteen

members in 1966 (15 of whom were over 65 years of age). Magnificent organ given by Rhos W.B. (Ref: 61.) in 1975. The organ was operated by water driven pumps when at Rhos. A fine plaster ceiling rose and attractive capitals to gallery support pillars. There are also two harmonium organs – (a). A single manual with transportable/shifting keyboard, and (b). A 'University' two manual organ donated by Nazareth E.B., Mountain Ash (Ref: 58.). The first Minister was Rev. John Lewis (1901 – 1931). Membership, 1915 – 117; 1930 – 96; Sunday School averaged 40-60 pupils between 1915 & 1930. As at September 2003 the minister is Rev. Enid Jones (since 2002). Her husband, Rev. Arfon Jones ministered from 1960 to early 1980's (died 2001).

History of Hebron written in Welsh in 1917 by J. Lewis – copy in Aberdare Central Library.

Thanks to Rev. Enid Jones for details of her late husband.

Gwawr, Godreaman. 1989.

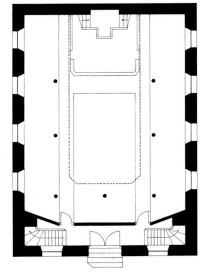

Gwawr, Godreaman.

CHAPEL REF. NO. 85A.

Having covered the Welsh Baptists, the English section of the Baptists in Godreaman. i.e. **CHURCH of CHRIST. E.B.** Foundry View, can be dealt with here for convenience.

CURRENT USE.   Closed/demolished circa 1960. Located between No.1 and Forge View Cottage, converted to dwelling accommodation circa 1960-62.

BRIEF HISTORY.   This chapel, named the Church of Christ English Baptist, was formerly a School Room, founded about 1870 to provide for the influx of English speaking immigrants from Ireland and various parts of the South West of England. i.e. Somerset, Devon, etc. They came to Godreaman seeking work in the ironworks (closed circa 1865), and Aberaman Colliery, (opened 1866 – closed 1962), located on the other side of the River Aman and opposite Foundry View. Many of the chapel members resided at Foundry View, Forge View, Incline Row and other nearby houses. The chapel was small, accommodating about 150 – 200 worshippers. It was a thriving chapel with a large membership and an active Sunday School, looked after by Maggie Davies the teacher and a prominent, active chapel member. It was a branch of the Church of Christ chapel in Commerce Place, Aberaman, long since demolished. The popular rallies and cantatas drew large congregations, and were at times joined by other chapels of the same denomination from Merthyr, Treharris, Aberfan and Griffithstown. New officers were appointed each year thereby allowing most members to participate in the various aspects of chapel work; a "post for life" was not the norm. The closure of the chapel arose principally out of the demise of the Aberaman Colliery located opposite. The whole of Incline Row located downhill and other nearby properties were demolished in the early 1960's, following the colliery closure in 1962 and this led to the decline in membership numbers. After closure the chapel became a button factory for a short period and at some time in the late 1960's it was converted into a bungalow. Prior to closure the members met (1959-60) in the vestry of Salem W.B. (ref: 88.).

Thanks to Mrs. Ivy Thomas, a former member of the chapel, for her kind help in compiling these details.

CHAPEL REF. NO. 86.

NAME & DENOMINATION: **NODDFA. W.I.**

ADDRESS / LOCALITY: **CWMAMAN ROAD, GODREAMAN**

DATE BUILT: **1900.**

CURRENT USE: **CLOSED 1980; CONVERTED INTO 'CWRT NODDFA' FLATS, 1995.**

BRIEF HISTORY: Built in 1900 as a result of the large increase in Population of Godreaman. Located opposite No.24. Daughter chapel of Moriahaman W.I. (Ref: 90.). Rev. H. Aeron Davies built Forge View School Room in 1877 for the Sunday School, he became minister of Moriah Aman (Ref: 90.) – 1875-1909. Band of Hope and prayer meetings were held there until the building of Noddfa Chapel in 1900, seating for 500. Several memorial stones were laid on 12th. November 1900, including E.M. Hann Esq. The Oaklands, Aberaman; D.E. Williams Esq. J.P., Hirwaun; Thomas Williams Esq. J.P., Gwaelodygarth House, Merthyr Tydfil, and Morgan John Esq., Preswylfa, Aberdare, officially opened in July 1901.

Noddfa, Godreaman. Taken in 1989.

A pleasing front façade; pediment broken by a stone arch to commemorate an unusual shaped stone name plaque. A fine pitch pine pulpit. This chapel was known in the 1930's for its notable orchestra. Soup kitchens were also held here in the depression years of the 1930's. During the second world war evacuees from Birmingham used the vestry as a schoolroom. Became free of debt in 1935. Mrs. Afonwy Jones (nee.Thomas) L.R.A.M., was precentor/ organist in the early 1900's. Ministers include Rev. Henry Aeron Davies – 1901-1903; Rev. Thomas Thomas – 1904-1916; Rev. Enoch Lewis – 1917-1920; Rev. Henry Thomas B.A. – 1921 –1925. Membership 1905 – 154 with 135 in Sunday School; 1914 – 176 with 162 in Sunday School; 1930 – 100 with 74 in Sunday School.

Taken in 1989.

Noddfa, Godreaman.

CHAPEL REF. NO. 87.

NAME & DENOMINATION: **PENTECOSTAL P.C.**

ADDRESS / LOCALITY: **BRYNMAIR ROAD, GODREAMAN**

DATE BUILT: **1920**

CURRENT USE: **KNOWN TO EXIST IN THE 1950'S BUT CLOSED MANY YEARS AGO. STILL VACANT, DILAPITATED & BOARDED UP, 2004.**

BRIEF HISTORY: Formerly a stable, converted into a place of worship by William Cook in 1920, and named 'Pentecostal Free Mission Hall – Assemblies of God'. Located opposite No's 99 & 100 Brynmair Road. Local enquiries confirm the chapel was for some time before closure used as a Salvation Army Hall. Damaged by fire in 1959. Referred to as "Cwmaman Pentecostal Church" and also as "Brynmair Road Mission Hall". Pastor in charge in 1961 was A.H. Phelps.

Pentecostal Chapel,
Godreaman. 2002.

CHAPEL REF. NO. 88.

NAME & DENOMINATION: **SALEM W.B.**

ADDRESS / LOCALITY: **BRYNMAIR ROAD, GODREAMAN**

DATE BUILT: **1905.**

CURRENT USE: **CLOSED 1970 AND DEMOLISHED. SITE REMAINS VACANT, 2004.**

BRIEF HISTORY: Seats for 320; Building cost £1,928. Founded in 1904 in a house belonging to W.T. Davies. In 1905 meetings were held at the newly opened Aberaman Hotel, Brynheulog Terrace. Six members came from Sion W.B. (Ref: 91.) and two from Bethesda W.B. (Ref: 68.). Also in 1904 other meetings were held in a room at the Fforchneol Arms public house, 196 Brynmair Road, opened 1872, still open. Used as a carpenter's shop (Emrys Jones) circa 1965 – 1970. Located between No's 6 & 8, and opposite No 200 Brynmair Road. Near/opposite Fforchneol Arms. First minister was Rev. G Llechidon Williams (1905-09). Minister (1931-1961), was Rev. W. Christmas Jones. Membership – 1916 – 80 with 92 in Sunday School; 1925 – 103 with 99 in Sunday School; 1937 – 54 with 74 in Sunday School; 1947 – 51 with 25 in Sunday School

CHAPEL REF. NO. 89.

NAME & DENOMINATION: **BETHEL P.M.**

ADDRESS / LOCALITY: **CWMNEOL STREET CWMAMAN.**

DATE BUILT: **1872 – REBUILT 1911 – RENOVATED 1951**

CURRENT USE: **CLOSED CIRCA 1985; CONVERTED TO 'BETHEL HOUSE' FLATS (7) IN 1997.**

BRIEF HISTORY: First services held at the old Co-operative Shop in 1872. The founders were called 'Ranters', due to their somewhat high-spirited manner of worship. The first Elementary School sponsored by the Nonconformist British Society was formed here in 1864, and set up by Charles Griffiths and William Thomas. The chapel was formally established in 1872. No date on the chapel façade. A gallery was built in 1875, thereby increasing the seating capacity from 100 to about 150. Memorial stones laid in 1911 by Mrs. A. Phillips, Aberdare, and Rev. W.D. Morris, Minister of Soar C.M. (Ref: 92.), on behalf of the Welsh Calvinistic Methodists and Congregational chapels, Cwmaman. The chapel was rebuilt in 1911 to the Gothic appearance we see today, and the front elevation remains unaltered, but has been decorated. Membership in 1912 was 80, with 200 in the Sunday School. The chapel was extensively renovated in 1951 at a cost of £1,295.

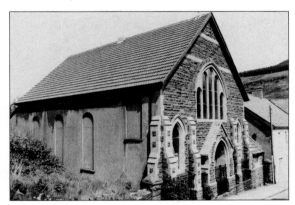

The first organist was Miss Isabella Burns, daughter of Thomas Burns M.E., who later married Rev. Thomas Humphreys, minister of Sion W.B. (Ref: 91.). Mr.W.H.John was precentor and conductor of the choir for 60 years until well over 80 years of age. Prominent member was George Rule M.E., chief mechanical engineer of Shepherd's Old Pit, and William Wilcox, Printer (1881). Bethel received many new members who came to Cwmaman to seek work from Cornwall, Somerset and the Forest of Dean. Other members included managers and agents of the Cwmaman Coal Co. Consequently the chapel became known as "the bosses chapel". The chapel is located near the old Great Western Railway (Aman branch) and stone bridge.

Taken in 1986.

Bethel, Cwmaman.

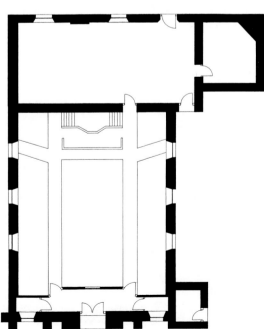

CHAPEL REF. NO. 90.

NAME & DENOMINATION: **MORIAHAMAN W.I.**

ADDRESS / LOCALITY: **FFORCHAMAN ROAD, CWMAMAN**

DATE BUILT: **1855 – REBUILT 1893.**

CURRENT USE: **STILL ACTIVE.**

BRIEF HISTORY: The oldest chapel in Cwmaman, located Adjacent to No.29 Fforchaman road. The 'cause', was started by J. Davies, Cardiff – Minister of Saron (Ref: 77.) as a Sunday School in 1853. Prayer Meetings were first held in a house in Mountain Road and later in a house in Pit Row (Cwmneol Colliery). In 1854 further services were held outside one of the houses in Gate Row. The first chapel opened on 2nd. October 1855; 27 members from Saron (Ref: 77.) began the 'cause' here. The 1893 chapel had seating for 650 (Gallery holds 250). 1905 membership was 435; 1912 membership 300. First minister was Rev. John Davies until 1858; Rev. Henry Aeron Davies – 1875 – 1909, (died 1922.) – he was founder and trustee of the Cwmaman Institute 1860; Rev. John Rees 1859 – 66; Rev. John Evans 1867-1874; Rev. E.J. Owen, 1911-1921; Rev. Alun Garner 1923-1928.

Moriahaman, Cwmaman.

Refurbished 1995 to become 'Christian Fellowship Church' (Pentecostal). The chapel was closed 1988 – 1990. Interesting external façade recently tastefully decorated and attractive external lights installed. In 1876 a manse was built near Goosebury Hill, and named 'Spring Hill Villa'. Job Lewis was a senior deacon and a poet of renown.

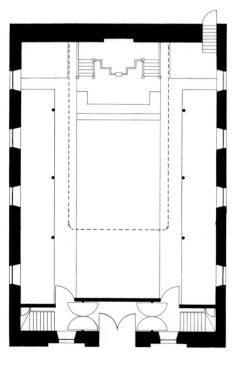

Taken in 1995.

FURTHER NOTES – (Ref: 90A).
Relating to the sister chapel to Moriahaman W.I., namely – BRYN MORIAH (Ysgoldy) Cwmaman – YR ANNIBYNWR (W.I.), built in 1906; closed circa 1930's.

Became a cookhouse for the nearby Glynhafod School during the 1939/45 war. The chapel has been used for various factory purposes, namely (a) For making copper storage tanks, (b) For making packing cases, (c) Used as a button factory.

The chapel became Apostolic circa 1960, but eventually closed circa 1985; it has remained closed since that date. A prominent member connected with this chapel was a Mr. Walter Love. The building was also in use as a Sunday School for Moriahaman W.I., located opposite Nos. 34 – 37, and adjacent to No.86 Brynhyfryd Street, Cwmaman. Sadly, it is now (2004) in a run-down derelict condition.

Thanks to Mrs. Alsie Evans (of No.35) for supplying details of Bryn Moriah (Ysgoldy).

CHAPEL REF. NO. 91.

NAME & DENOMINATION: SION W.B.

ADDRESS / LOCALITY: CWMNEOL PLACE, CWMAMAN

DATE BUILT: 1859, REBUILT 1870 & 1891.

CURRENT USE: STILL ACTIVE.

BRIEF HISTORY: Designed by Thomas Roderick, Aberdare (1891 chapel). First prayer meetings were held in the house of John Weeks, Fforchaman Road, in 1856. Eight members from Gwawr (Ref: 85.) held Prayer Meetings and Sunday School 1851-59. Building commenced in 1858 on a site known locally as "The Bloody Spot" after its previous use as a venue for cock-fighting. The chapel was erected voluntarily by the pioneers; women carried stones in their aprons from the River Aman for building the first chapel in 1859, and the men assisted in the building works after their normal days work was over. The design at the time was said to be "plain and old-fashioned". The original 1859 chapel named 'Baptist Chapel Particular' was much smaller than the chapel we see today; it was 30ft. by 30ft. – with no gallery, and cost £300, rebuilt in 1870 at a cost of £425. In 1883 the vestry was built at a cost of £254. It had only 200 seats whereas the 1891

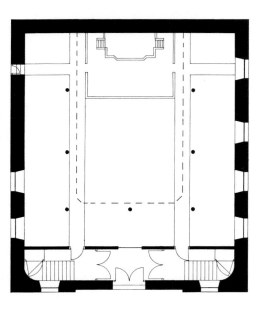

Sion, Cwmaman.

existing chapel holds 600 and cost £1,787. 1912 membership was 412; 420 by 1928; 140 in 1955; 100 in 1960. An additional room was added to the vestry in 1902. A Manse was built in 1897 at a cost of £448, named 'Rose Aman Cottage', located at the bottom of Fforchaman Road. A branch of Gwawr W.B. (Ref: 73.) and daughter chapel of Trinity E.B. (Ref: 93.) and Salem W.B. (Ref: 88.) First baptism in 1858 performed by Rev. T.E. Jones of Bethania (Ref: 96.). The first minister was Rev. Ebenezer Morgan, 1859-1864. Rev. T.T. Davies from 1864 to 1866. Longest serving minister was Rev. Thomas Humphreys, 1868 to 1910, he was also founder trustee of Cwmaman Hall and Institute; he baptised 1,700 members during his 42 years at Sion, and died in 1911. The chapel sustained extensive damage in January 1916 by a Tornado; in the meantime members held services in the Public Hall and Institute nearby.

Sion, Cwmaman. 1986.

Beautifully decorated ceiling roses in red, blue and yellow; fine boarded ceiling. Front elevation has been rendered in white spar dash granite chippings. The chapel has a two-manual harmonium by Alexandre Pere of Paris, and an exquisitely carved oak chair in front of the pulpit. A copy of the centenary booklet (1859-1959 is kept in the Glamorgan Record Office, Cardiff.

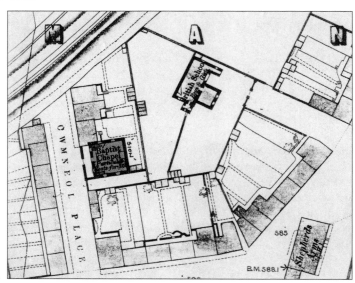

1868 Survey Plan, showing Sion, Cwmaman.

CHAPEL REF. NO. 92.

NAME & DENOMINATION: **SOAR. W.C.M.**

ADDRESS / LOCALITY: **FFORCHAMAN ROAD, CWMAMAN.**

DATE BUILT: **1859-REBUILT 1869 AND 1895.**

CURRENT USE: **CLOSED JANUARY 1992; DEMOLISHED 1998, SEMI-DETATCHED HOUSES (18 & 18A) BUILT IN 2000.**

BRIEF HISTORY: Located adjacent to No.19, and opposite No.161 Fforchaman Road. 1895 chapel had seating for 650; built at a cost of £3,070. The 'cause' was formed in 1859 during the Religious Revival period led by Dafydd Morgan. The first Methodist chapel to open in Cwmaman. Early meetings were held at the home of Thomas Anthony, Engineer at old 'Shepherd's Pit'. In 1868 David Bevan opened his coal level, driven towards Cwmneol Waun Fawr Field. Soar chapel stood above it! Vibrations from the

coal workings caused subsidence, and consequently the chapel collapsed in 1868, but was rebuilt the following year, 1869, with a school house located at the rear. The first minister was Rev. W. Telfilan Griffiths, followed by Rev. William Davies; Rev. W.D. Morris for 40 years -(1886-1926). Membership reached 350 in 1912. Originally a branch of Libanus W.C.M., Aberaman (Ref: 74.), and an 'offspring' of Saron, Aberaman (Ref: 77.). Memorial stone laid in 1895 by D.A. Thomas Esq. M.P.

In 1878 the first Cwmaman village Eisteddfod was held under the auspices of Soar chapel.

Soar, Cwmaman. 1986.

Soar, Cwmaman.

CHAPEL REF. NO. 93.

NAME & DENOMINATION: TRINITY E.B.

ADDRESS / LOCALITY: PROSPECT PLACE, CWMAMAN

DATE BUILT: 1908.

CURRENT USE: CLOSED 1992 – FOR SALE 1994 FOR £25,000; CONVERTED IN 2000 INTO AN ATTRACTIVE BUNGALOW NAMED 'TRINITY BUNGALOW' THE ORIGINAL 1908 NAME PLAQUE REMAINS.

BRIEF HISTORY: The 'cause' commenced in March 1899 in the vestry of Sion W.B. (Ref: 91.). Services conducted by David Hussey of the Baptist Forward Movement. Other meetings followed at the Public Hall, Cwmaman in January 1902; among those present were Rev. Thomas Jones, of Carmel, Aberdare and James Griffith of Calvaria, Aberdare. The 'cause' was originally set up by Rev. Luther

Davies of Penrhiwceiber, one time minister of Beulah, Aberaman (Ref: 71.). The first minister was Rev. George Hinchcliffe from 1903 to 1905, a mining engineer from Barnsley, Yorkshire. He was followed Rev. M.J. Thomas (1907-1912). Rev. Rees Owen was minister, 1928-1960. The chapel was plain, small and simple in design with a front porch entrance and seating for 150. In 1903 there were 200 children attending the Sunday School, 100 members by 1912, down to 12 members in 1978. Internally there was no pulpit but a raised platform for a preaching area, with timber balustrading and a plain lectern. Gas lamp fittings remained intact up to the date of conversion. Herringbone parquet block floor; pitch pine pews; harmonium by D.W. Karn Co. Ltd. of Woodstock, Canada. Mr. Anthony Kedward of, Aberaman was a prominent senior deacon of this chapel, and Arthur Dunning, of Forge View was one of the stalwarts of the chapel for 45 years (died 1946).

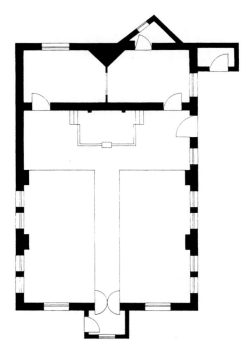

Trinity, Cwmaman.

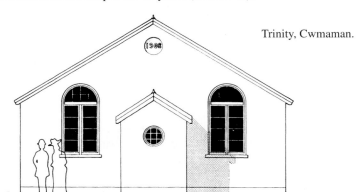

Taken in 1986.

CHAPEL REF. NO. 94.

NAME & DENOMINATION: **ABERNANT-Y-GROES UCHAF. UN.**

ADDRESS / LOCALITY: **CHAPEL ROW, BRIDGE ROAD, CWMBACH.**

DATE BUILT: **1840, REBUILT 1879.**

CURRENT USE: **CLOSED CIRCA 1970; DEMOLISHED 1992. SITE REMAINS VACANT 2004.**

BRIEF HISTORY: 1840 building cost was £650, providing seating for 150-200. The old Baptist Chapel ('Penuel') of Abernant-y-Groes was purchased by the Unitarians in 1856. The 1851 Religious Census states that it was then called 'Particular Baptist', 1840, with about 450 members (but only seating for 200!) and 120 scholars. Details given by John David Williams, Minister, Cwmbach. The ground on which the chapel was built was bequeathed to the chapel by William Thomas Davies in 1840. Ministers include Rev. John David Williams 1851; Rev. T.E. James 1855-1858; Rev. Evan Williams Lloyd, 1859. John Morgan was one of the principal founders, and treasurer of the chapel (b.1832-d.1917). Rhys Evans (b.1779-d.1867), born at Ton Coch, became a school master at Aberpennar (i.e. Mountain Ash) and was an active member of this chapel, his father was Edward Evans of Ton Coch. In 1935 the chapel became 'The Apostolic Church of Cwmbach'. The former Cynon Valley Borough Council carried out a survey in 1994 of the graveyard attached to the chapel, graves date from around 1845 – 1860. The 1879 chapel has a simple front façade with a name plaque set in a pediment. Long vertical round-headed windows; front porch entrance; grand central ceiling rose; ceiling level lowered to retain heat, thus covering the attractive original ceiling. A small front upper gallery on one side only.

Abernant-y-Groes Uchaf, Cwmbach

Circa 1900.   Taken in 1986

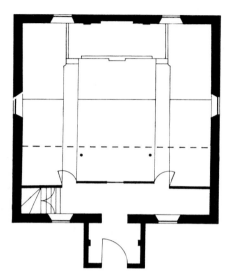

The Chapel and The Square, Cwmbach. Circa 1930

CHAPEL REF. NO. 95.

NAME & DENOMINATION: ABERDARE KINGDOM HALL. J.W.

ADDRESS / LOCALITY: CWMBACH ROAD, PLASDRAW.

DATE BUILT: 1972.

CURRENT USE: STILL ACTIVE.

BRIEF HISTORY: Located opposite Aberdare Girl's Comprehensive School, Cwmbach road. Named 'kingdom Hall of Jehovah's Witness'. The 'cause' commenced locally in 1943, when meetings were then held by small groups in 22 Victoria Square, Aberdare. In 1952 they moved to the British Legion premises in Regent Street, Aberaman; membership at this time numbered 9 adults and 6 children. After18 months, in 1954, they moved to Lewis Street, Aberaman where a room was used for worship and meetings. In 1955 they moved to 185 Cardiff Road, Aberaman, the old grocer's store (Kingdom Hall), where numbers increased to 16 adults and 10 children. In 1964 they moved yet again!, this time to the old Moose Hall in Seymour Street, Aberdare; now numbering 27 adults and 13 children. Membership now grew rapidly, and by 1972 there became a need for larger premises, consequently in 1972 they purchased a building and garage owned by Mr. Joshua Davies, who used it as a grocery and supply store serving local shops. The members demolished the building to window cill level and built and enlarged it to the present Kingdom Hall building. All work was carried out voluntarily by the membership. The hall was opened and dedicated on 22nd. December 1972. Membership at the time of writing is 80, including 8 young children. There is no paid minister as members share in preaching; the elders conduct services and meetings and share this with other neighbouring branches. The Ministerial Servants support the body of Elders, and all aspects of work, visitations of the sick, etc. Worship is carried out voluntarily with no rigid procedure of personal financial contributions or set form of Tithe-giving. There are just two Kingdom Hall's in Cynon Valley – This one and Prosser Street, Mountain Ash (Ref:38.).
Thanks to Mr. Norman Morris for providing details for these notes.

CHAPEL REF. NO. 96.

NAME & DENOMINATION: BETHANIA, W.B.

ADDRESS / LOCALITY: OFF BRIDGE ROAD, CWMBACH.

DATE BUILT: 1858 – REPAIRED/RENOVATED 1950

CURRENT USE: CLOSED CIRCA 1980; DEMOLISHED 1995. SITE VACANT 2004.

BRIEF HISTORY: First services held at 'The Square' at Abernant-y-Groes chapel in 'Upper Cwmbach'. Incorporated 15th. January 1845. Designed by Rev. William Lewis, who also designed other Baptist chapels near the locality. Built at a cost of £1,100 with seating for 580. 469 members in1906; 273 in 1932; 129 in 1947. Membership was at its highest during and shortly after the 1904/5 Religious Revival period. An 'offshoot' of Penpound, i.e. Calvaria W.B. (Ref: 104.), Aberdare. Severely damaged by enemy war action; bombed on the 30th. May 1941. The vestry built in 1865 was completely destroyed; services in the meantime were held in Penuel chapel school room (Ref: 102.) and Bryn Seion W.I. (Ref: 97.). After the 1941 bomb damage, Bethania W.B. was restored 1950/51, and reopened on the 14th. April 1951.

Bethania, Cwmbach taken in 1951.

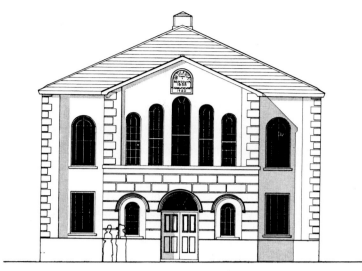

Bethania, Cwmbach

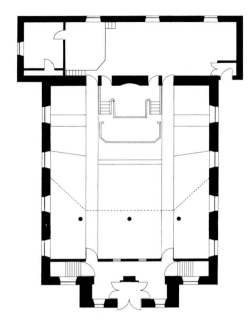

Ministers – Rev. Morgan Lewis was first minister in 1845, he died of Cholera in 1849.

Rev. William Harris – left in 1862. Rev. T.E. James in the 1850's. Rev. James, 1903 – 1927.

Only 15 members in 1978; a few years later the chapel was forced to close through lack of members.

Taken in 1986

CHAPEL REF. NO. 97.

NAME & DENOMINATION:	**BRYN SEION. W.I. (WELSH SECTION).**
ADDRESS / LOCALITY:	**TIRFOUNDER ROAD, CWMBACH**
DATE BUILT:	**1858 – ENLARGED 1889**
CURRENT USE:	**CLOSED DECEMBER 1999; PARTIALLY DEMOLISHED 2002/3 FOR CONVERSION TO RESIDENTIAL USE**

BRIEF HISTORY: The Welsh Independents started their 'cause' in 1799 at the home of Timothy Davies, Cwmbach, then in 1809 they moved to a converted dwelling in a house named 'Penpound'. In 1858 they built their chapel and named it 'Bryn Seion'; the designer was J Owen, and the cost was £1,000. They had 70 members and 70 in Sunday School at that time. In 1899 the chapel was enlarged and extensively renovated at a cost of £1.050, a Sunday School/Vestry was built and attached at the rear; the seats were arranged on a sloping floor. Membership in 1809 was 26; by 1850 it was 70; and by 1860 had increased to 300 as a result of the 1859 Religious Revival. In 1905 membership was at it's highest at 574, but by 2000 had fallen to only 12 members. Rev. Jonah Morgan (b.1814 – d.1888) was minister for 32 years, 1856 – 1888.His oldest daughter Anne, who died at the early age of 22 in 1862, married Thomas Morgan Thomas (b.1828 – d. 1884) who in 1858 left Cwmbach to become a missionary with the London Missionary Society, serving in central Africa (1858 – 1870). He died in 1884 aged 56, at Matabeleland and is buried at nearby Inyathi in the depths of Africa. He studied at Brecon College prior to becoming a missionary. A gathering took place on 10th. May 1858 for a farewell presentation to Mr. & Mrs. Thomas; this coincided with the opening of the new chapel. It was reported that (quote) – *"1200 drank tea in the new chapel and choirs from several chapels were present including Bethania W.I. Mountain Ash; Siloa W.I. Aberdare; Ebenezer W.I. Trecynon and Heol-y-Felin W.B. Trecynon."* – The main chapel closed in 1970 and services thereafter were held in the vestry until final closure when the last service was held on 13th. December 1999, with just five lady members present.

Ministers include Rev. D.M. Davies-1888-1907; Rev. R.H. Davies- 1909-1921; Rev. Dr. W.B. Thomas-1923-1927; Rev. H.P. Hughes- 1932- Fred Rees and W.J. Davies were organists here for many years.

A magnificent 'Monkey Puzzle' tree stands prominently at the front of the chapel site. This chapel was used as a setting in a television drama in the early 1990's and caused controversy among local residents because the script involved drug use etc. The chapel had a fine pipe organ, Built by Norman & Beard of London & Norwich, 1909, and a grand, beautifully carved pulpit. Also a harmonium made in Paris by H. Christophe & Etienne, supplied by Harmston & Co, Piano and Organ Merchants, Aberdare.

The entire debt of the chapel was cleared by 1944. Thanks to Miss Sheila Cameron of Caernarfon for supplying details from her research regarding Thomas Morgan Thomas, and to Margaret Harris of Cwmbach for her assistance.

Bryn Seion (Welsh Section), Cwmbach.

Taken in 1986.

CHAPEL REF. NO. 98.

NAME & DENOMINATION: BRYN SEION. E.C. (ORIGINALLY W.I.) (ENGLISH SECTION).

ADDRESS / LOCALITY: TIRFOUNDER ROAD, CWMBACH

DATE BUILT: 1846 – REBUILT 1852.

CURRENT USE: DEMOLISHED CIRCA 1965. COUNCIL HOUSES BUILT ON SITE CIRCA 1970. (85 – 96 TRE-TELYNOG).

BRIEF HISTORY: The 'cause' commenced in 1843. The first chapel built in 1846 was a small structure with seating for 150 and referred to as 'Capel Bricks'. Its cost was £66, cared for by Rev. David Price. The second chapel built in 1852 was larger with seating for 320, and built at a cost of £329. The Minister in 1850 was Rev. John Lloyd, followed by Rev. Henry Lewis in 1852.

The chapel was originally Welsh Independent, but when Bryn Seion W.I. (Ref: 97) was built in 1858, this chapel was thereafter used by and transferred to the English speaking Independents and later became Primitive Methodists. The chapel was demolished around 1965, having been located between Old Oak Row and Victoria Row (also demolished about the same time as the chapel). The former Co-Operative Store, founded in 1860, was located adjacent to the chapel and a commemorative plaque marking the site can be seen on one of the houses in Tre-Telinog.

This chapel was located almost opposite Bryn Seion W.I. (Ref: 97.). The Religious Census of 1851 records – *"That in morning services there were 59 plus 20 scholars, and evening service 75; There is space for almost 100 to sit and for 50 to stand. Details supplied by Rev. John Lloyd, Minister."*

A copy of the history booklet 1845 – 1945, by David Edward Williams is in Aberdare Central Library. The Ordnance Survey of 1868 clearly indicates the Welsh And English sections of Bryn Seion.

1868 Survey Plan showing both Welsh and English Sections of Bryn Seion, Cwmbach.

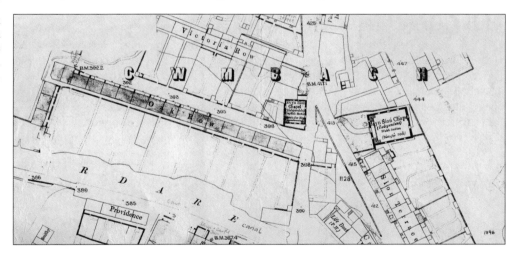

CHAPEL REF. NO. 99.

NAME & DENOMINATION: BRYN SEION (YSGOLDY). W.B.

ADDRESS / LOCALITY: CWMBACH ROAD, CWMBACH.

DATE BUILT: 1858.

CURRENT USE: CLOSED CIRCA 1960; CONVERTED TO A HOUSE NAMED "LONG WAIT" CIRCA 1970.

BRIEF HISTORY: Listed as a Sunday School on the 1900 Ordnance Survey map. Located behind Ynyscynon Street, and opposite No. 35 Cwmbach Road. Formerly a branch connected with Bethania Welsh Baptist Chapel (Ref: 96.).

CHAPEL REF. NO. 100.

NAME & DENOMINATION: **CARMEL W.I. (YSGOL SABBOTHOL)**

ADDRESS / LOCALITY: **WATERLOO STREET, CWMBACH**

DATE BUILT: **1895.**

CURRENT USE: **CONVERTED TO A HOUSE – 1970 NAMED 'CARMEL HOUSE'.**

BRIEF HISTORY: Built in 1895 at a cost of £350. Formerly a Sunday School branch of Bryn Seion W.I. (Ref: 97.). Listed as a Sunday School on the 1900 Ordnance Survey map.

CHAPEL REF. NO. 101.

NAME & DENOMINATION: **EBENEZER, C.M.**

ADDRESS / LOCALITY: **TIRFOUNDER ROAD, (SION TERRACE) CWMBACH.**

DATE BUILT: **1851-REBUILT 1864 REPAIRED/RENOVATED 1908**

CURRENT USE: **STILL ACTIVE AS 'PENTECOSTAL COMMUNITY CENTRE'**

BRIEF HISTORY: The 'cause' began in 1848 as a Sunday School where meetings were held in the house of Dafydd Sims, Old Lletty Siencyn House; known later as 'Canal House', Canal Road. In 1851 a small chapel was built on farm land known as 'Tir Bach' i.e. 'Little Ground' located between No.11 Richards Terrace and No.6 Tir Founder Road, directly opposite No.1 Greenfield Terrace. The chapel had seating for about 150-200 worshippers, and was named 'Capel Lletty Shiencyn'. It is believed this chapel closed circa 1930's and was converted into four small cottages, namely No's. 5-6-7& 8 Tir Bach. Numbers 5-6-7 were from the main chapel and No.8 was from the rear vestry; during renovations recently a chapel bell was discovered hanging in the roof space of the present cottages. The congregation remained in Tir bach (Capel Lletty

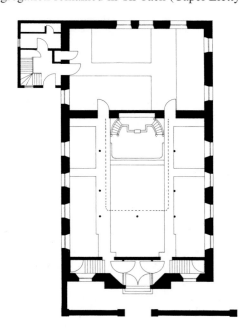

Ebenezer, Cwmbach.

Shiencyn) from 1851 to 1864. In 1852 some members joined the little chapel from Libanus C.M., Aberaman (Ref. 74.) – built in 1848. A larger new 'daughter' chapel was built in 1864 in Sion Terrace, and they named it 'Ebenezer'. The builder was David Edwards, Trecynon, and the cost was £1,300, with seating for 500. The vestry was built in 1870. In 1908 Ebenezer was repaired and renovated, architect for this work was Thomas Roderick, Aberdare, building work by Jones Bros., Penydarren, Merthyr. The cost was £2,170. The former houses at Canal Terrace and

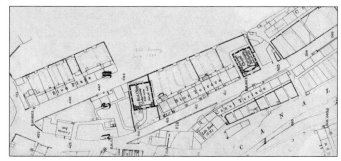

1868 Survey Plan showing Ebenezer Chapel.

the 'Life Boat' public house were located directly opposite Ebenezer chapel, (now an open grassed area). The pub was located at No.2 Canal terrace, Cwmbach, opened in 1864 – closed 1907. Ebenezer C.M. is a branch of Carmel C.M., Trecynon (Ref: 125.). The chapel closed temporarily in 1982 and later reopened as a Pentecostal chapel; in 2003 named 'Pentecostal Community Centre'. Notable ministers include Rev. E.J. Poolman, 1952 – 53, and Rev. Robert James 1963 – 1972.

Copies of the Welsh language centenary history booklet (1851 – 1951), by Gomer Jones, are in Aberdare Library and the Glamorgan Record Office, Cardiff. Thanks to Mr. Ken Collins (C.V.H.S. Treasurer 1979 –to date.) for his assistance in researching these notes.

Ebenezer, Cwmbach, taken circa 1930.

Taken in 1986.

CHAPEL REF. NO. 102.

NAME & DENOMINATION: **PENUEL. W.B. (YSGOLDY BEDDYDDWR – BAPTIST SCHOOL).**

ADDRESS / LOCALITY: **CWMBACH ROAD, CWMBACH**

DATE BUILT: **1906**

CURRENT USE: **CLOSED CIRCA 1960-70, CONVERTED TO A HOUSE IN 1975 NAMED "PENNY WELL SPENT", A PLAY ON WORDS – PENUEL = PENNY WELL!!**

BRIEF HISTORY: The 'cause' commenced in 1898. The chapel was built in 1906 at a cost of £700. It was formerly a Welsh Baptist Sunday School. Located between No's. 20 & 21 Cwmbach Road, and near Well Place. Was a branch Sunday School for Bethania W.B. (Ref: 96.).

Penuel, Cwmbach, circa 1910

CHAPEL REF. NO. 103.

NAME & DENOMINATION: **BETHANIA. C.M.**

ADDRESS / LOCALITY: **WIND STREET, ABERDARE**

DATE BUILT: **1853- REBUILT/ENLARGED 1884**

CURRENT USE: **CLOSED CIRCA 1990. VACANT & DERELICT 2004.**

BRIEF HISTORY: The front façade is an imitation based on the design of the church of San Andrea at Mantua, Italy; designed by Leon Battista Alberti (1404-72) in 1470 with the introduction of an arch across the face of the façade sometimes producing a discordant effect in some chapel designs; standard gable façade; The giant arch contains the date plaque over triartite window with oculi over each square-headed small pane light.

Pennant sandstone; windows of mixed design at different levels; dentils to a gable verge and central arch is only slightly recessed so it appears as a line without depth across the surface; a somewhat concealed entrance approach up a long flight of steps, almost hidden from public view!

Architect – Evan Griffiths, 'The Poplars' High Street, Aberdare (1853 chapel), built by David Evans, Aberdare, at a cost of £1,600. Seating for 550. Grade Two Listed Building including the Sunday School. The chapel is almost hidden from view and located behind and to the side of the Black Lion Hotel. Thomas Roderick (b.1854-d.1922.) Architect, was a prominent member; he designed the school-room.

Chapel erected in 1853 on a field, part belonging to Ynyslwyd Farm otherwise known as 'Cae Tirion', formerly a branch of Carmel E.B. (Ref: 105.) The 1852 deeds of the property contained permission (quote) – "to build one chapel or meeting house, and one stable to be used only by persons or travellers frequenting the said chapel." – In 1852 the 'cause' began with holding a Sunday School in the long room of the Black Lion Hotel, under the auspices of the Mother chapel at Carmel E.B. (Ref: 105.). A new vestry was added in 1866; the chapel was extensively remodelled in 1884 by Rev. William Jones, Ystrad, at a cost of £1,300.

Prominent minister's include – First minister, Rev. David Saunders D.D.1857 – 1862; Rev. William James for 38 years, 1870 – 1908; died 1908. He attended Trefecca College 1865 – 1869. Bethania is said to be

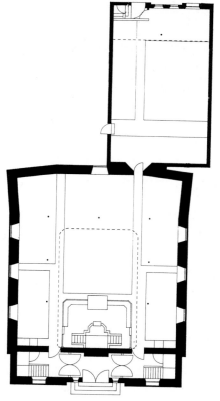

Bethania, Aberdare.

the first chapel in Wales to start the Gymanfa Ganu. Sunday School and caretaker's cottage attached to the main chapel in 1889 – Thomas Roderick, Aberdare was architect, John Morgan, Clifton Street was the builder. Renovated during the Religious Revival of 1904/5 at a cost of £594; new organ installed in 1904 at a cost of £585, positioned over the 'Set Fawr' with arched panelling. Note the blazing bible carved on the stone wall plaque over the front entrance door. The chapel had 284 members in 1925; 141 in 1953, followed by a sharp decline in numbers 1960 – 1990. A magnificent pulpit and gallery balustrading; the raked gallery corner is on fluted cast iron columns with palm-like capitals and a collar band of similar leafy pattern, ornate ceiling rose; grand pipe organ by Messrs. Norman & Beard of Norwich. Mr. W. Beddoe Stephens was organist at one period. Chris King, A.R.I.C.S., M.R.T.P.I., of Cwmdare, made meticulous survey drawings in 1993. 1854 – 1954 centenary history (in Welsh) and "Hanes Bethania" by John Mills, 1917, are in Aberdare Library.

Front façade of Bethania, 1993.

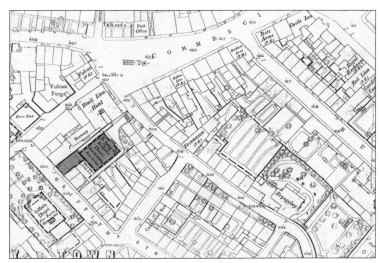

1868 Survey Plan showing Bethania, Aberdare.

CHAPEL REF. NO. 104.

NAME & DENOMINATION: CALVARIA. W.B.

ADDRESS / LOCALITY: MONK STREET, ABERDARE

DATE BUILT: 1811; REBUILT 1852; RENOVATED 1859.

CURRENT USE: STILL ACTIVE.

BRIEF HISTORY: Grade 2 Listed Building. 1852 chapel designed by Thomas Joseph, a colliery engineer from Hirwaun. With seating for 840, it cost £1,400 to build. The renovation work carried out in 1859 was designed by Thomas Davies, architect – the builder was Abraham Richards. 'Calvaria Hall', built in 1871 is attached. Graveyard in grounds. Sunday School established in 1807 by a number of young men from Sion Welsh Baptist Chapel, Merthyr. In 1809, Rev. Christmas Evans among others, officiated here when owing to the crowded condition of the place the floor gave way but no-one was seriously hurt. In 1811 the members leased a small piece of land from Griffith Davies Esq., Ynysybwl, and built a chapel where later Carmel E.B. (Ref: 105.) once stood. In 1852 Calvaria was built. 4747 members were received between 1845 and 1901. Membership in 1862 was 1,000 – 1871 was 470 – 1899 was 537 – 1906 was 493 – 1916 was 420 – 1925 was 395 – 1955 was 200 – 1961 was 183 – and by 2003 it was 19, with average evening attendance of 6. A copy of the 1812 – 1912 Centenary History by James Griffiths, and 1852 – 1952 history (in Welsh) by Rev. Huw D. Thomas and Maldwyn E. Jones are in Aberdare Library. The 'cause' commenced in 1804 in the home of Lewis Richards – known as "Little Chapel", at Penpound where Carmel E.B. (Ref: 105.) once stood; the chapel was in fact also referred to as 'Penpound' Welsh Baptist. In 1807 they started a Sunday School in a room at the Farmers' Arms, and also later in a room above the old 'Market House' (rent – £1 per year) which later became the Town Hall. When Penpound became too small for the Welsh Baptist congregation, they built Calvaria in 1852 on the opposite side of Carmel (Ref: 105.), and left the old chapel to the English Baptists. The first minister was Rev. William Lewis (1813 – 1815). Rev. Dr. Thomas Price (b.1820 – d.1888) was minister for 42 years from 1846 to his death in 1888, and was formerly minister of Carmel E.B, Aberdare (Ref: 105.), he is buried in the chapel graveyard. Dr. Price performed 1596 baptisms by his 40th. anniversary as minister. Rev. James Griffiths was minister from 1890 to 1930, and Rev. D. Herbert Davies from 1932 – 1947. The chapel is adorned with an extremely ornate interior with craftsmanship of a high order, including a beautiful boarded ceiling with a single deeply undercut rose. The balcony balustrading is particularly attractive, comprising bonded cast iron front with intricate foliage design. There are box-type pews. The platform and steps up to the 'Set Fawr' have cast iron newels with gilding and ball finials and 'barley twist' balusters. The fine organ with simple Gothic type casing was built in 1903 and cost £850. Detailed survey plans drawn in 1994 by Chris King A.R.I.C.S., M.R.T.P.I., of Cwmdare. The large vestry behind (Calvaria Hall) is dated 1871. The main chapel has a fine classical three-bay front with moulded cornice quoins and plinth and squared rock-faced Pennant sandstone; overall pediment; round-headed entrance doorway and wheel window, in slightly projecting centre bay. Sunday School banner dated 1807, by Keesey of Birmingham is in Cynon Valley Museum.

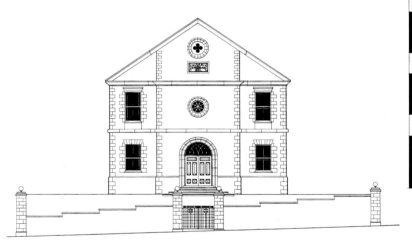

Calvaria, Aberdare.

Interior of Calvaria, circa 1910.

Pulpit and organ, Calvaria, Aberdare. Circa 1952.

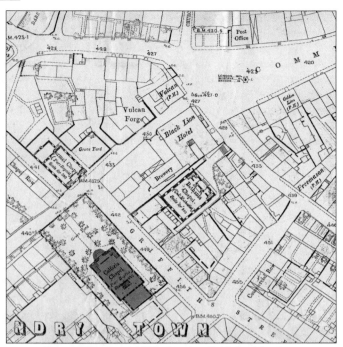

Survey Plan dated 1868, showing Calfaria, Aberdare.

CHAPEL REF. NO. 105.

NAME & DENOMINATION:	**CARMEL. E.B.**
ADDRESS / LOCALITY:	**MONK STREET, ABERDARE**
DATE BUILT:	**1863.**
CURRENT USE:	**CLOSED CIRCA 1960. DESTROYED BY FIRE IN 1970. A SCHOOLROOM (ABERDARE PARISH HALL) BUILT ON PART OF THE SITE IN THE 1970'S; REMAINDER OF SITE OCCUPIED BY POST OFFICE DEPOT UNTIL 2002, NOW CONVERTED TO WEATHERSPOON'S RESTAURANT**

BRIEF HISTORY: In 1799 both the Welsh Independents (Ebenezer (Ref: 127.) and Carmel started their 'cause' together in the same place in a small cottage. Formerly a branch and sister chapel of Calvaria W.B. (Ref: 104.), seating for 380. Other meetings were held from house to house in 1850, with Rev. Dr. Thomas Price assisting. The following year meetings were held in a large room belonging to the Horse & Groom Inn, (then located at 11 High Street, Aberdare – built in 1835, closed in 1871). The later meetings were held at the Black Lion Hotel (opened 1811). Also referred to as 'Particular Baptist' and previously called 'Penpound' of the Welsh Baptists (opened 1812), and later removed into Calvaria W.B. (Ref: 104.); Carmel was consequently left for the English Baptists. The Religious Census of 1851 states that Carmel was founded in 1812, enlarged in 1832 and rebuilt in 1851 at a cost of £1,200. These details were supplied to the census returns by Rev. Dr. Thomas Price of Rose Cottage, Aberdare. Formerly a graveyard was attached to the side of the chapel. Foundation Memorial Stone was laid in 1863 by Mrs. Wilkinson of Cwmpennar. The first minister was Rev. James Cooper, 1852 – 1854, followed by Rev. James Owen; Rev. T.A. Price; Rev. D. Rees Jenkins; Rev. Thomas Jones, 1873 – 1905, who baptised 1200 people during his 32 years ministry at this chapel. Professor Tom Jones was organist and conductor for 50 years, 1891 – 1941. The chapel had 101 members in 1873; 436 in 1906; 298 in

1925; 217 in 1932 and 205 in 1947. Sunday School membership between 1925 and 1947 varied from 109 to 284. In 1917 controversies and differences arose over a matter related to the Trust Deeds; followers left Carmel and formed Christchurch E.B. (Ref: 118.) in July 1918. The chapel was located almost exactly opposite Calvaria (Ref: 104.), and opposite and facing Griffith Street. A copy of the Centenary History 1852 – 1952, is in Aberdare Central Library. 1840 Sunday School banner is in Cynon Valley Museum, Aberdare.

Carmel, Aberdare. Circa 1930.

Carmel, Aberdare. 1976

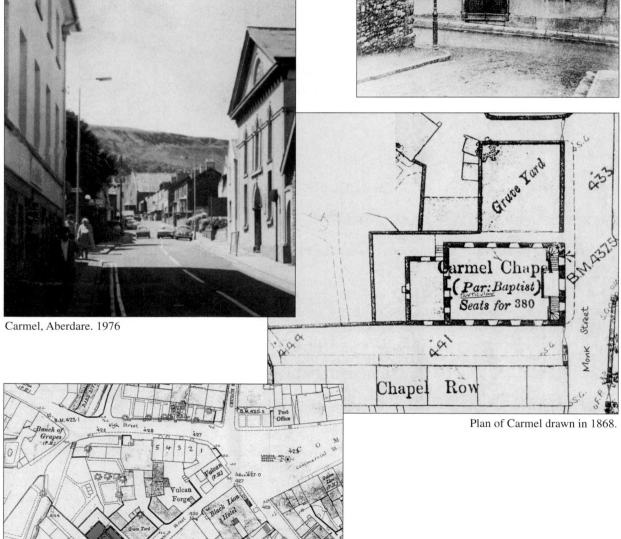

Plan of Carmel drawn in 1868.

1869 Survey Plan showing Carmel, Aberdare.

CHAPEL REF. NO. 106.

NAME & DENOMINATION: **ELIM. P.C.**

ADDRESS / LOCALITY: **MONK STREET, ABERDARE**

DATE BUILT: **1863.**

CURRENT USE: **MAIN CHAPEL CLOSED 1995, DEMOLISHED 2001 – VESTRY AT REAR REMAINS INTACT & STILL USED FOR WORSHIP (2004)**

BRIEF HISTORY: Formerly named Bethesda Primitive Methodist, (see 1868 Town Survey Plan). Seating for 250, plain design; simple internal layout. Became a Pentecostal chapel in 1942. Located at Clifton Place, between No's 64 and 66 Monk Street. Foundation stone was laid in 1863 by Mrs. Wilkinson of Cwmpennar. The Primitive Methodists first appeared in Aberdare during the first half of the 19th. Century, and during the 1840's about 30 members met in a cottage in Mill Street, Trecynon; their pastor was a Rev. Mr. Mullin. Later a room at the Temperance Hall (built in 1858) was used. Later they built Bethesda Primitive Methodist School Room at the rear. Elim Pentecostal Church commenced meeting at 28 Canon Street, and at Whitcombe Street, Aberdare. In 1938 they moved to 'Cole's Bazaar' at 56A Dean Street, Aberdare. They were also called 'The Four Square Gospel Church', renamed 'Elim' in 1942.

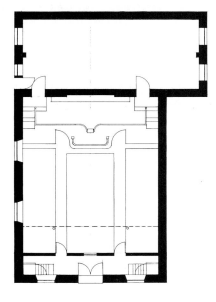

Elim, Aberdare.

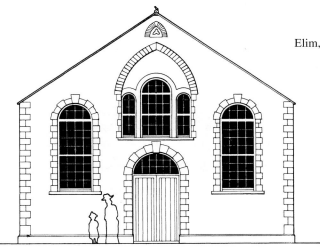

Taken in 1995

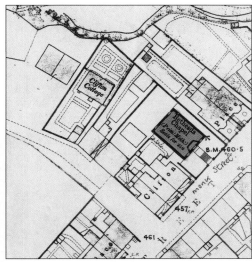

1868 Survey Plan showing Elim (formerly "Bethesda"), Aberdare.

CHAPEL REF. NO. 107.

NAME & DENOMINATION: **ENGLISH WESLEYAN. E.W.M.**

ADDRESS / LOCALITY: **GREEN STREET, ABERDARE.**

DATE BUILT: **1841, REBUILT 1859, ENLARGED 1864.**

CURRENT USE: **STILL ACTIVE.**

BRIEF HISTORY: The second 1859 chapel is a Grade 2 Listed Building. In 1864 it was enlarged to provide the chapel we see today, known more commonly as Green Street English Wesleyan Methodist Chapel. A classical design; simple with pilasters dividing the façade into panels and finished in colour wash rendering. Plain entablature and tapered pilasters with high bases flanking each bay. In the late 1830's the English Wesleyan's first met at Moss House, Abernant, and there they held services and decided to build a new chapel for themselves, built in 1841 at a cost of £200, with seating for 200. It was built on a site once occupied by Messrs. Hodge & Sons, clothiers, at the bottom of Victoria Square, now No.23 Commercial Street, next door but one to the Boot Hotel. The foundation stone giving the detail 1841 was for a long time kept in the passage off William Hodge's house at what was then No.23 Victoria Square. It was later kept at the back of Gadlys Cottage, the home of Mrs. Gilbert Hodge, and when the latter was demolished to make room for the Western Welsh garage (built in 1939) it was cemented into the floor outside the garage, but no longer visible. The English Wesleyan Methodists then built their present chapel in 1859 to accommodate swelling numbers as a result of the great 1859 Religious Revival; seating for 400, and located in Green Street opposite Aberdare Central Library. It was built on the site of the former Swan Inn (built 1844) and adjacent shop and cottage; these were destroyed by fire in September 1858, and the chapel was built on the site the following year, the freehold costing £266. In 1850 there were 22 members, and 22 in the Sunday School, but numbers increased dramatically in the 1860's. The 1851 Religious Census states that the chapel was erected in 1841, 12 month average attendances were – Afternoon's 40 – Evenings 76. Only 14 chapels were listed in this census, George Walls was the chapel steward. A Sunday School was built at the rear in 1864; galleries were provided in 1867 at a cost of £225, allowing increased seating capacity to around 550 – 600.

Numerous memorial plaques exist internally. Attractive pipe organ and exquisite pulpit as is the rail enclosing the pulpit area. Coloured acanthus ceiling rose. Bracket cornice and keystone ornamented by figureheads and

Green Street E.W.M. Chapel, Aberdare.

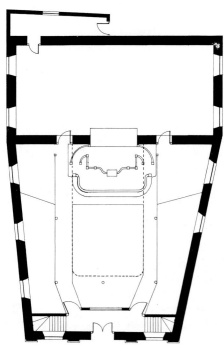

panelled pilasters with bosses. Raked gallery following the splayed angles of the side walls. Tall cambered arch behind the organ at the back of the 'set fawr'. Mr. A.E. Harmston was organist 1896 – 1916, Mr. Lionel Langley organist and piano teacher 1916 – 1945;

Mr. Byron Davies from 1951 – 1966, and Mr. Sheridan George organist from 1966 to date.

The three manual pipe organ from Trinity Methodist chapel, Risca, was rebuilt in 1993 at a cost of £20,000, and contains over 1500 pipes and is one of the largest in the Cynon Valley, rebuilt by Roger Taylor of Burrington, near Bristol. The original organ was built in 1877 by Peter Conacher of Huddersfield. In the 1860's the chapel was immediately surrounded by no less than six public houses! In 1857, the first Superintendent Minister was Rev. Edward Russell, assisted by Rev. George Cartwright, Rev. Fred Peacock minister 1958. Centenary booklet, 1859 – 1959, is in Aberdare Central Library.

Green Street Chapel. Aberdare, 1986.

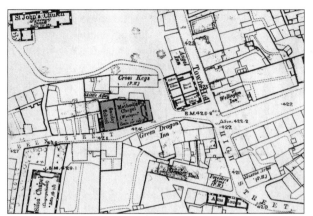

1868 Survey Plan.

CHAPEL REF. NO. 108.

NAME & DENOMINATION:	**HIGHLAND PLACE, UN.**
ADDRESS / LOCALITY:	**MONK STREET, ABERDARE.**
DATE BUILT:	**1860 – RENOVATED 1996**
CURRENT USE:	**STILL ACTIVE.**

BRIEF HISTORY: Architect – H. J. Paull, Cardiff, built by Thomas Charles, Llandilo, with seating for 300; and at a cost of £1.000. The chapel was erected primarily to cater for the English speaking Unitarians in the locality; chief founders included Messrs. J. Jones, chemist; Evan Thomas; Arthur Jones and Richard Lewis, 'Fairfield'. Gothic design, stone façade with sandstone ashlar dressings; Transeptal plan layout; Bold Dec tracery, shafted entrance doorway. Daughter chapel of Hen-Dy-Cwrdd, Un. (Ref: 129.), Built in 1860 largely under the influence of Lewis Noah Williams (b.1845 – d.1919) – Son of William Williams 'Y Carw Coch' (Bardic name) – He lived at the Stag Inn, Trecynon (opened 1860 – closed 1910) In 1860 L. N. Williams established the Lamp Works in Graig Street; later became famous as 'The Cambrian Lampworks' (still trading today as 'Thomas & Williams', Robertstown.). Founder

Highland Place Chapel, Aberdare, circa 1900.

(Berry Collection)

member – Rhys Hopkin Rhys, a well-known public figure. School-Room built in 1877 at a cost of £550. Manse built in 1874 at a cost of £800. Owing to various complicated and untoward difficult circumstances related to the mortgage and building costs of the schoolroom, services were discontinued and the chapel was closed and boarded up for 8 years (1882 – 1890) L.N. Williams was instrumental in reopening the chapel in 1890. Prominent ministers include – the first minister Rev. Charles Frederick Biss 1861 – 1863; Rev. John Joseph George 1864 – 1882, (died 1905 aged 83); Rev. Mary Constance Harris was Aberdare's first lady minister 1928 – 1931; Rev. David Jacob Davies, 1945 – 1957; Rev. J. Eric Jones from 1962 up to his retirement in 2003, longest serving minister. He held many important roles within the denomination including President of the General Assembly of Unitarians and Free Christian Churches; he was also a School Governor and Chairman of the Ebenezer Choral Society, Trecynon. The minister as at November 2003 is Rev. John Clifford. Prominent organists include Miss Sophia George, over 50 years (died 1952), She was former headmistress of the Higher Standard School, and daughter of the above mentioned Rev. J.J. George. Mr. Carlyle Whitcombe was organist for over 40 years. The organ was built in 1915 at a cost of £400, and is similar to the one at Saint Winifred's, Penrhiwceiber. The highly successful Women's League was formed in 1911. Interesting design worth viewing is the rear balcony balustrade, moulded iron tablets set into the panelling. The building was extensively renovated in 1996/7 at a cost of £86,000. History of the chapel – 1860 to 1985 by Rev. J. Eric Jones (24 pages in English) "A City Set on a Hill", and a copy of the centenary booklet (1860 – 1960) are available at Aberdare Central library.

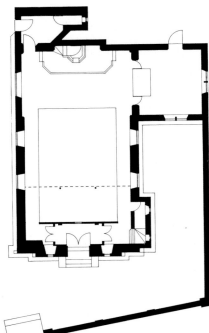

Highland Place Un. Chapel, Aberdare.

Taken in 1986.

Taken, circa 1900.

Berry Collection.

CHAPEL REF. NO. 109.

NAME & DENOMINATION: **MORTUARY CHAPEL. EC/DC.**

ADDRESS / LOCALITY: **ABERDARE CEMETERY.**

DATE BUILT: **1858.**

CURRENT USE: **DEMOLISHED FEBRUARY 1982.**

BRIEF HISTORY: Designed by W. S.
Rampling previously an Aberdare surveyor, who also
designed Tabernacle E.C. in 1859 (Ref: 115.).
Indicated on the 1868 Town Survey plan as being
named The 'Episcopal Chapel' and the 'Dissenter's
Chapel'. The two chapels were separated by a linked
Port – Cochere structure surmounted by a spire, thus
allowing separate access. A fine drawing dated 14th.
February 1865 is in Aberdare Central Library, and is
shown opposite.

The Mortuary Chapel, Aberdare. 1865.
(Aberdare Library)

The Mortuary Chapel, Aberdare. Circa 1970.

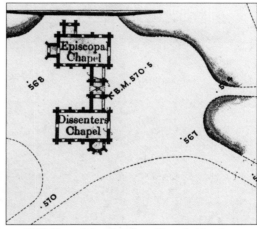

1868 Plan of the Mortuary Chapel, Aberdare.

CHAPEL REF. NO. 110.

NAME & DENOMINATION: **NAZARETH. W.C.M.**

ADDRESS / LOCALITY: **ABERNANT ROAD, ABERDARE.**

DATE BUILT: **1860 – REPAIRED/RENOVATED 1905**

CURRENT USE: **CLOSED 1965; 1966 CONVERTED TO A BUILDER'S MERCHANT/
STORE KNOWN AS GREGORS LTD, LATER BECAME HARCROSS,
NOW (2004) JEWSON.**

BRIEF HISTORY: Built at a cost of £1,770 to seat 500, gallery for 200. Foundation Memorial
stone laid 30th. August 1860, officially opened on 7th. July 1861.
Schoolroom/Vestry added at the rear in 1905 at a cost of £1,850. A branch of Bethania C.M. (Ref: 103.); several
members left Bethania to commence the cause at Nazareth in 1860. Located opposite Aberdare Railway Station,

and adjacent to the old iron bridge crossing the Taff Vale railway line. Centenary history in Welsh (1860 – 1960) is in Aberdare Central Library. The freehold of the site was purchased in 1920. There were dangerous signs of subsidence in October 1927 and services were held in the vestry until strengthening work was completed. Nazareth was supervised by the pastor of Bethania W.I. (Ref: 48.) up to closure in 1965.

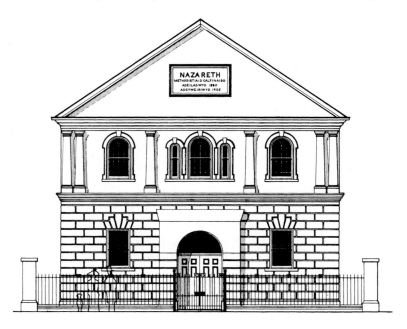

Nazareth, Aberdare.

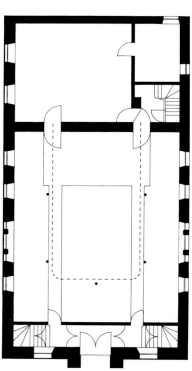

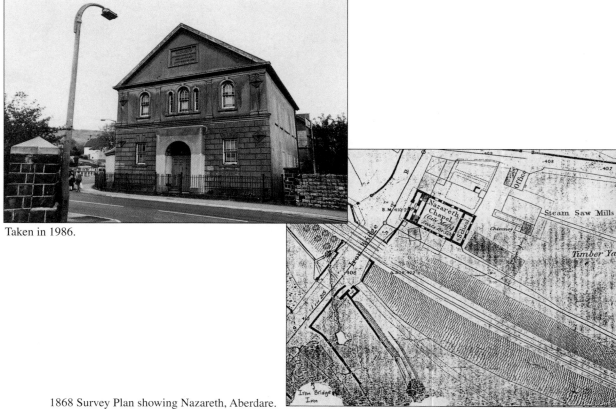

Taken in 1986.

1868 Survey Plan showing Nazareth, Aberdare.

CHAPEL REF. NO. 111.

NAME & DENOMINATION: **SAINT DAVID'S. E.P.**

ADDRESS / LOCALITY: **HIGH STREET, ABERDARE**

DATE BUILT: **1877.**

CURRENT USE: **CLOSED 1952. CONVERTED TO A TELEPHONE EXCHANGE CIRCA 1960; VACANT FOR MOST OF THE 1970'S; BUILDERS MERCHANTS (MENDHAM'S) IN 1979. CONVERTED TO OFFICES AND EXTENSIVELY REFURBISHED 1993 VIA W.D.A. GRANT AID. MANAGED BY SOCIAL SERVICES AS 'COMMUNITY MENTAL HEALTH TEAM' TO THIS DATE (2004).**

Taken circa 1900, before the removal of the 85ft. high spire, taken down circa 1960.

BRIEF HISTORY: Designed by W. Douglas Blessley, who also designed the 1876 Great Western Hotel, and Prince of Wales Theatre, Cardiff. Built at a cost of £4,600, St. David's was built arising from a dispute at Trinity W.P., (Ref: 116.) whereby the English Calvinistic Methodists returned to Trinity in 1875 and the English Presbyterians consequently built St. David's as a result of this change. A hall was built adjoining the chapel. Seating in main chapel is for 400. Formerly used by the Scottish Presbyterians, later became English Wesleyan Methodist. A fine banquet was held in the Black Lion Hotel after the laying of the foundation memorial stone by Miss Davis of Maesyffynon. Several changes of use over the past 50 years, however the front elevation remains unaltered, and has recently been cleaned and repaired. The former 85 ft. high spire was taken down circa 1960 (St. Elvan's spire is 189 ft. high). The beautiful pipe organ was sold circa 1910 to Beulah E.B., Aberaman (Ref: 71.), and was one of the oldest pipe organs in the Cynon Valley. The building is of geometrical Gothic design, with blue pennant sandstone and Bath stone dressings. First minister was Rev. John Evans M.A. (1876 – 1882); in 1886 the minister was Rev. J. Foulks; in 1901 Rev. John Robertson M.A. The chapel closed in 1952 with 50 members. Membership decline was attributed to the fact that the town was "overchurched".

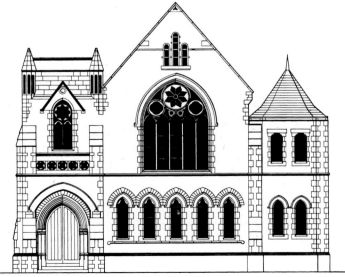

Saint David's, Aberdare.

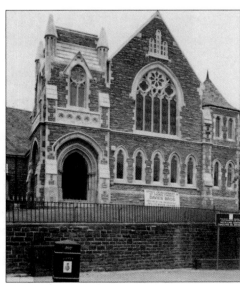

Taken in 1994

CHAPEL REF. NO. 112.

NAME & DENOMINATION: **SION. E.W.M.**

ADDRESS / LOCALITY: **CROSS STREET, ABERDARE**

DATE BUILT: **1850**

CURRENT USE: **CLOSED 1961; DEMOLISHED 1962 SITE REDEVELOPED 1980'S TO PROVIDE A 'PAY & DISPLAY' CAR PARK.**

BRIEF HISTORY: Located at the junction of Cross Street and Wind Street; opposite the former police station (demolished July 2002 – rebuilt 2004); The Dare Foundry (iron and brass) with moulding shed and workshop was formerly located at the rear of the chapel in the 1870's. The chapel had seating for 500, including gallery. Smooth rendered lime mortar external walls; pediment with name plaque; moulded string course separated floors. The Wesleyan Training School (later a vestry/Sunday school room) was at one time attached behind, built 1859. This was also called 'The Wesleyan Day School'.

Sion, Aberdare, circa 1960.

1868 Survey Plan showing Sion Chapel.

CHAPEL REF. NO. 113.

NAME & DENOMINATION: **SILOA. W.CONG.**

ADDRESS / LOCALITY: **GREEN STREET, ABERDARE.**

DATE BUILT: **1844-REBUILT 1855. RENOVATED 1890 AND 1957.**

CURRENT USE: **STILL ACTIVE.**

BRIEF HISTORY: Grade Two Listed Building. The 'cause' commenced in 1841 by Rev. T. Rees. Membership increased considerably as a result of the powerful Religious Revivals of 1849 and 1859. Early meetings were held (1841-1843) in the Long Room of the Boot Hotel, Aberdare. The first chapel was built in 1844 at a cost of £600, and was rebuilt and enlarged in 1855 at a cost of £719. The debt was cleared by 1860. Extensive renovations were carried out in 1890 at a cost of £1,100. The architect for this work was Thomas Roderick, Clifton Street, Aberdare; the builder was Michael Thomas of Graig Street. Present seating is for 900, and is one of the largest chapels in the Cynon Valley, more or less comparable with Calvaria

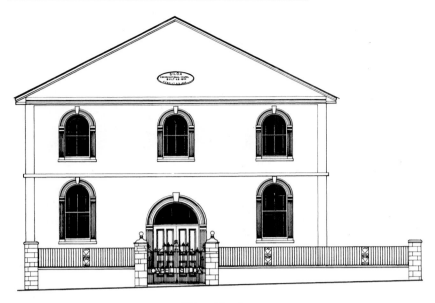

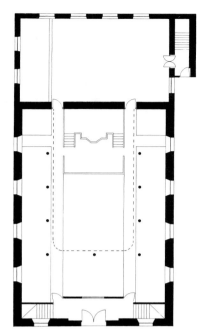

Siloa, Aberdare.

(Ref: 12.); Saron (Ref: 77.); and Ebenezer (Ref: 127.). Renovated again in 1957. Membership details – 300 with 280 in Sunday School, 1853: 661 by 1899; numbers reached a peak during the 1904/5 Religious Revival of 761. 645 members in 1923; 363 in 1954 and 191 by 1964. Notable ministers include – Rev. Dr. David Price, founder, 1843 – 1878; Rev. David Silyn Evans, for an incredible 50 years, 1880 – 1930 (b.1850-d.1930); Rev. R. Ivor Parry, 1933 – 1965 (b.1908 – d.1975). The first three ministers served an astonishing 117 years between them, and the chapel was only without a permanent minister for five years during the 122 year period. William John Evans was organist and choirmaster for 50 years (1886 – 1937); his son was Ivor Evans, former Principal of University College, Aberystwyth. Services have been held in the vestry since1980 due to a sharp decline in membership. As at 2003 there are 38 members with 15 in the Sunday School – about 15 attend evening service, on average. A magnificent organ, and fine joinery throughout. Attractive colourful stencil decorative work to the gallery support columns. Four plaster roses in the herringbone boarded ceiling. Galleries on three sides. Simple classical 'set fawr' with quatrefoil punched newels capped by ball finials, pitch pine furnishings. The simple yet classic designed façade is divided into storey heights by raised string courses and the round headed windows are accentuated by moulded surrounds, keystones and fluted architraves. The whole formal design is emphasised by colour-washed rendering. A graveyard exists within the chapel grounds. Iron boundary railings have 'barley twist' uprights. The Religious Census of 1851 states – "Erected 1844; space free 235; other 265; Present morning 331 + 162 scholars; Afternoon 224 scholars; Evening 430." Details supplied by David Price, Minister.

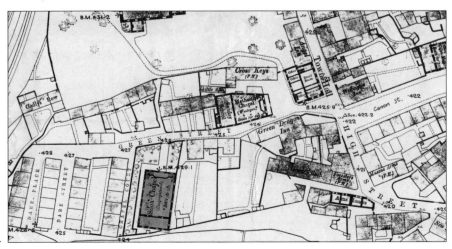

1868 Survey Plan, Siloa, Aberdare.

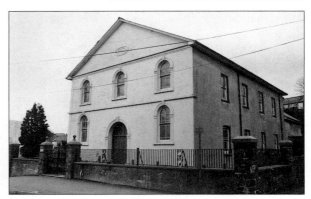

Siloa W. Cong., Aberdare. 1903.   Taken in 1986.
(Berry Collection)

Centenary Book 1843 – 1943 is in Aberdare Central Library. Attractive Sunday School banner and band of Hope banner are in Cynon Valley Museum, Aberdare. Thanks to Mr. Stephen Morris for his contribution to part of these notes.

CHAPEL REF. NO. 114.

NAME & DENOMINATION: **SOAR. W.M.**

ADDRESS / LOCALITY: **WIND STREET, ABERDARE.**

DATE BUILT: **1858.**

CURRENT USE: **CLOSED CIRCA 1970, CURRENTLY (2004) USED AS A YOUTH CLUB 'CANOLFAN ABERDARE URDD GOBAITH CYMRU'.**

BRIEF HISTORY: Seating for 550. The 'cause' commenced in a dwelling house in 1854 by the Welsh Wesleyan Methodists, under the leadership of David Davis of Maesyffynon, later became Welsh Independents. Front façade remains unaltered but internally has been extensively altered and adapted to suit youth club activities and the like. First minister in 1854 was Rev. William

Soar, Aberdare.

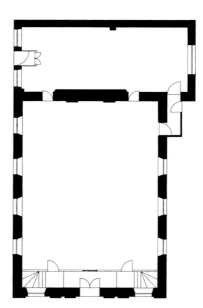

Jones, when the services were held in a dwelling house – later Rev. John Davies 1867 – 1904. Became Independent under Rev. Aeron Davies. 1924 – 1959. History booklet 1859 – 1950 is in Aberdare Central Library. In 1956 the Mormon Church held meetings here for a period, but this was short-lived and never fully materialised. Membership in 1905 was 71 with 50 in Sunday School – 1914 was 120 with 125 in Sunday School , and 1930 was 52 with 40 in Sunday School.

Soar, Aberdare, 1986.

CHAPEL REF. NO. 115.

NAME & DENOMINATION: **TABERNACLE. E.C.**

ADDRESS / LOCALITY: **STATION STREET, ABERDARE.**

DATE BUILT: **1856, REBUILT 1859, RENOVATED 1875.**

CURRENT USE: **CLOSED 1970; DEMOLISHED 1973 REDEVELOPED AS 'TESCO' STORE; 'WILKINSONS' FROM 1999.**

BRIEF HISTORY: First meetings held in 1841 in the Long Room of the New Inn, 13/14 High Street, Aberdare. (Built circa 1840-closed 1910.). The 1856 chapel had seating for 450, designed by Rev. B. Owen, Merthyr Tydfil; Built by Messrs. Jones & Morris at a cost of £823. Foundation stone laid on 7th. March 1856 by Hon. Mrs. Thompson, Chepstow. 156 members in 1857; 136 in Sunday School. 'Mother' chapels were Ebenezer W.I. (Ref: 127.); Siloa W. Cong. (Ref: 113.); and Saron W.I. (Ref: 77.). The 1859 chapel was designed by W. S. Rampling (previously a surveyor); he also designed the Mortuary Chapel, Aberdare (Ref: 109.). Built by W. Rees at a cost of £800, with seating for 543. W. Rees also built the Temperance Hall, Aberdare. The former Police Court and Roberts Arms public house, 2 Station Street, Aberdare (opened 1861 – closed 1923) were located near the chapel. The chapel was primarily of Gothic design, a typical style of

Tabernacle, Aberdare, circa 1950.

many English Congregational chapels in Cynon Valley. The design was laid down and decided by the land owner, the Marquess of Bute; built out of a need for an English Congregational cause due to increase in the English speaking population and influx of English workers into the area. Ministers include – Rev. John Cunnick, 1857 – 1860; Rev. D. M. Jenkins, 1865 – 1871; Rev. J. Farr, 1872 – 1881; Rev. J. Morgan Jones, 1902 – 1913; Rev. T. M. Jeffreys, 1914 – 1920; Rev. E. R. Davies, 1922 – 1930; and Rev. Percy Thomas, 1936 – 1940. A new pipe organ was built in 1891 by Messrs. Thompson & Shackell of Cardiff. Mr. Edward Moses was organist for an incredible 65 years! from 1888 until his death in 1953. In 1879 a 'Band of Hope' was formed. Membership in 1905 was 140;

1923 – 200; 1945 – 104; 1957 – 76. A sharp decline in membership followed from 1960 until closure in 1970. By the late 1960's the chapel was in serious financial difficulty, and membership was very low. Copies of the Centenary booklet, 1857 – 1957 (20 pages, in English) are in Aberdare Central Library and the Glamorgan Record Office, Cardiff. 57 page history by D. M. Richards is also in Aberdare Library. Minute Books, 1913 – 1922 and 1953 – 1968 are in Glamorgan Record Office. Upon closure in 1970 the furnishings and vessels were distributed among other chapels in the locality, and to Aberdare General Hospital.

Interior of Tabernacle taken from rear gallery circa 1950.

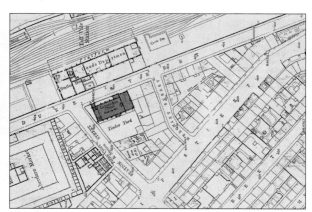

1868 Survey Plan showing Tabernacle, Aberdare.

CHAPEL REF. NO. 116.

NAME & DENOMINATION:	**TRINITY. W.P.**
ADDRESS / LOCALITY:	**WEATHERALL STREET, ABERDARE.**
DATE BUILT:	**1867-RENOVATED 1894, EXTENDED 1909.**
CURRENT USE:	**STILL ACTIVE.**

BRIEF HISTORY: A Grade 2 Listed Building, a classical design; rendered and colour-washed. Entrance is crowned by an open pediment into which a bold semicircular recess is inserted and supported by pairs of Corinthian pilasters flanking the central ionic-arcaded windows. The 'cause' commenced in 1856 by establishing a Sunday School in a building on the site of the present Town Hall. Further meetings and services were held in1867 in the vestry of Bethania C.M. (Ref: 103.). In the same year Trinity was built by Simon Richards, Cardiff Street, Aberdare, at a cost of £1,300. (This firm of builders was established at Aberdare by his father, Daniel Richards, in 1834.) Architect/ designer – Evan Griffiths, Aberdare. Seating for 700 – built to a classical design theme. Foundation stone laid on the 7th. October 1867 by Mrs. Williams, widow of 'Alaw Goch' of Ynyscynon, and Mordecai Jones, Brecon – proprietor of Nant Melyn Colliery. Underneath the foundation stone a casket of white marble was deposited containing coins of the realm dated 1867, plus copies of newspapers and a few periodicals. Remodelled/renovated in 1894; Pediment is broken by a giant arch over recessed central two bays with lettering. Outer advanced bays are flanked by composite pilasters with a plain frieze. Semi-circular headed central windows

Trinity, Aberdare, circa 1900.

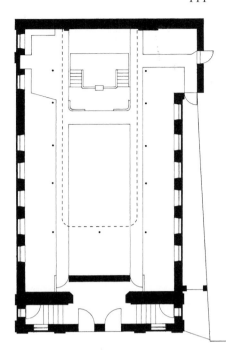

Trinity, Aberdare.

with moulded heads. Ionic pilasters and balustrade aprons. Inscribed and foliated date stone. The façade continues around the corner to left with composite pilasters flanking narrow end bay. Hall added by J. Llewellyn Smith in 1909, including new organ (total cost £3,500). Membership in 1893 was 118 – and by 1910 was 274, and by 1967 was 142. The chapel was formerly English Calvinistic Methodist, later becoming Presbyterian Church of Wales. Prominent founder of Trinity was Walter Lloyd (d.1883). In 1917 the chapel debt was a staggering £2,145, but unemployed members paid off the debt by 1934. The chapel features a grand pipe organ and fine polished boarded ceiling, galleries on three sides, pillar supports with clustered shafts and moulded caps and annulettes. Prominent Ministers; First Minister was Rev. John Evans, 1868 – 1875. Rev. Edwin Williams, 1877 – 1883; Rev. G. Humphrey Evans, 1919 – 1925; Rev. D.O. Calvin Thomas 1927 – 1938; Rev. S. Ifor Enoch, 1941 – 1953; Rev. Gwillym Evans, 1955 – 1965. Rev. Glaslyn Bowen 1966 – 1992.

Centenary booklet 1867 – 1967, written by Rev. Glaslyn Bowen, is in Glamorgan Record Office and Aberdare Central Library. History booklet 1867 – 1917 is also in Aberdare Central Library.

Opening Day of Trinity New School alterations, 1909.

CHAPEL REF. NO. 117.

NAME & DENOMINATION: **BETHEL. W. Cong.**

ADDRESS / LOCALITY: **RAILWAY STREET (top end of Tudor Terrace), GADLYS**

DATE BUILT: **1860 – REBUILT 1913.**

CURRENT USE: **CLOSED LATE 1980'S, VACANT & DERELICT THROUGHOUT 1990'S. DEMOLISHED NOV/DEC. 2003, DETACHED HOUSE BUILT ON THE SITE IN 2004**

BRIEF HISTORY: Grade 2 Listed Building, two-storey classic design, somewhat insipid with big crude windows and deformed pilasters – central round-headed doorway in a channelled concave surround; pedimented gable – full height channelled quoins with full width dentilled corniced moulding. Round arched cavetto moulded central entrance with broad channelled architrave and dropped keystone. String course between floors. The gable had semicircular arches recess inscribed 'Bethel 1860' cavetto moulded voissoirs. Designed by Mr. Evan Jones, Aberdare; built in 1860 at a cost of £747 by David Jones, Mason and John Edwards, Carpenter (costing £207 and £540 respectively). Seating for 600.

The 'cause' commenced in 1858 by 30 followers from Salem W. Cong. (Ref: 122.); Minister then was Rev. William Harrison, followed in 1859 by Rev. Hugh Hughes ("Huw Tegai"), previously minister of a Manchester Independent Chapel – He tragically collapsed whilst preaching from the pulpit in 1864, and died 3 days later. Minister was Rev. Robert Evans (1866 – 1877); and Rev. D. Onllwyn Brace (1885 – 1888). They held their services in 'Bethel Bach' St. John's Place, Heol-y-Felin. Originally composed of Wesleyan reformer's who worshipped at Pentwyn Bach, Trecynon. Membership in 1890 was 245 with 257 in Sunday School; 1905 was 344 with 270 in Sunday School; 1914 was 280 with 210 in Sunday School. Rebuilt in 1913 at a cost of £2,975; pipe organ cost £420. Later became Welsh Baptist. The two cottages opposite served as accommodation for the caretaker. The chapel is adjacent to No.2 Railway Street, and near Tudor Terrace. Formerly an elaborate interior, richly adorned with herringbone boarded and coved ceiling with roses, four smaller roses repeated in the corners,

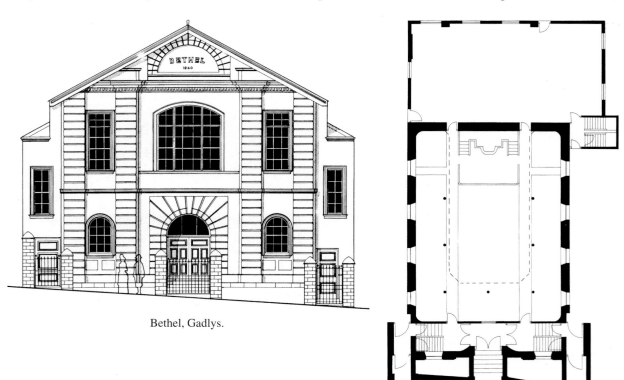

Bethel, Gadlys.

raked gallery. Rectangular galleried interior with organ chamber to far end. Raked gallery with panelled front carried on cylindrical columns, continued around behind the 'set fawr' with inset memorial tablets. Semi circular front to set fawr with Doric columns, set canu in front. The staircases opened on to the gallery through round arches. Coloured glass to lobby. Vestry/Schoolroom at rear. Memorial stones laid by Mr. Lewis Jones, deacon and local preacher. During demolition work in November 2003 bricks were found bearing the inscription 'D.R. Llewellyn, Aberdare.' (from Llwydcoed brickworks)

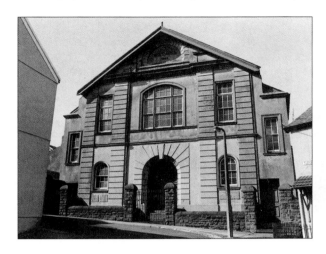

Bethel, Gadlys, 1986.

Bethel Chapel, Gadlys, circa 1900. Rebuilt in 1913. Demolished 2003.

The organ at Bethel, Gadlys, circa 1962. Organ built 1913 at a cost of £420.

CHAPEL REF. NO. 118.

NAME & DENOMINATION: **CHRISTCHURCH. E.B.**

ADDRESS / LOCALITY: **EAST AVENUE, GADLYS**

DATE BUILT: **1920, REBUILT 1979**

CURRENT USE: **STILL ACTIVE.**

BRIEF HISTORY: Built in 1920 at a cost of £1,400 with seating for 280. The 'cause' was founded in July 1918 when members first met at Gadlys Central School. A split from Carmel E.B. (Ref: 105.) occurred arising from a disagreement in connection with the taking of communion and on conflicting pacifist views held by some members during the 1914 – 1918 Great War. Many members who strongly sympathised with Rev. Thomas Edmunds, B.A., over a matter related to the Trust Deeds and holding of Communion services left Carmel E.B. and founded Christchurch in 1918. The chapel was built in 1920 and opened in 1921. It was refurbished/rebuilt and re-opened in 1979 on the same site at a cost of £1,200, much of the work being done by volunteer members. There was only £5 in the chapel funds before they started work in 1979. During the 1939 – 1945 war the chapel was used as a "British Restaurant" & kitchen for the poor and needy of the district. First minister – Rev. Wm. Bound; then Rev. Wm. Walters; Pastor Mansel Jones; Rev. Gwilym Jones. Rev. William Bryant was Pastor 1935 – 1944. Membership in 1936 was 65 – in 1960 was 49 – and in 1979 it was 30. Members in Sunday School varied from 90 to 34 between 1925 and 1947. History booklet at National Library of Wales – Manuscript No. 10350c. Thanks to Mr. Keith Evans for help with compiling these notes.

View of pulpit and Sunday School Banner, circa 1930.

CHAPEL REF. NO. 119.

NAME & DENOMINATION: **GADLYS. W.B.**

ADDRESS / LOCALITY: **RAILWAY STREET (top end of Tudor Terrace), GADLYS**

DATE BUILT: **1864**

CURRENT USE: **CLOSED 1980 – CONVERTED TO FLATS 1995**

BRIEF HISTORY: Grade 2 Listed Building with rendered front crowned by a pediment carried on four elegant Ionic pilasters, cement rendered with plinth. Round arched gallery windows with sills broader and segmental arched to centre over main entrance. The 'cause' commenced in 1858 as a Sunday School held from house to house until a school room was built in 1859 (opened on 6th. February), with three houses at a total cost of £372-3-4, under the care of Rev. Dr. Thomas Price. 49 members came from Calvaria W.B. (Ref: 104.), to form the new chapel at Gadlys, built on land leased from Dr. J L. Roberts of Gadlys Uchaf Estate. It became a separate chapel in June 1865. First baptism 5th. April 1863. Architect – Thomas Joseph (colliery engineer); 1864 building cost was £675. 1911 membership was 195; seating for 600. This chapel was located opposite Bethel W. Cong. (Ref: 117.), demolished Nov./Dec. 2003, and adjacent to No's. 1 & 2 Railway Street. The façade is tastefully decorated and remained unaltered during conversion work. New organ dedicated in 1940. Minister (1876-

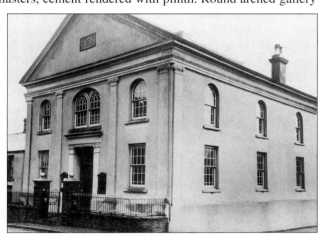
Gadlys Chapel, taken in 1981.

1900) Rev. Ben Evans (Telynfab). Available at Glamorgan Record Office, Cardiff – Minute books 1907 – 1957, also papers of Rev. Ben Evans (drafts of sermons) 1844 – 1900. Prominent member was the well-known historian John Davies (Pen Dar – b.1864 d.1940). During the 1870-1880's the daughter of the landlord of the Glandover Inn, 98 Gadlys Road (opened 1870, still in business), was organist at this chapel for several years.

Thanks to Mr. Doug Williams (C.V.H.S. committee member) for his help in researching these notes.

Gadlys W.B. Chapel, Gadlys.

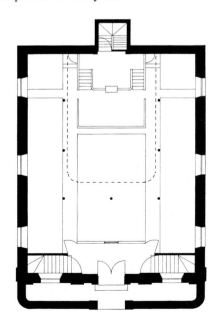

CHAPEL REF. NO. 120.

NAME & DENOMINATION: **BETHEL. W.B.**

ADDRESS / LOCALITY: **ABERNANT ROAD, ABERNANT.**

DATE BUILT: **1856 – ENLARGED 1862 & 1895.**

CURRENT USE: **STILL ACTIVE.**

BRIEF HISTORY: Located adjacent to Bethesda W.I. (Ref: 121.) The 'cause' commenced as a Sunday School in 1846, under the care of Rev. John Thomas. Minister in 1857 was Rev. Dr. Thomas Price of Calvaria W.B. (Ref: 104.) where he was also minister from 1846 until his death in 1888. Dr. Price baptised many candidates in the River Cynon near The Trap, and also in the stream a little above the school-room, which along with a house was built in 1856 at a cost of £344-18-3. this proved too small and was therefore taken down in 1861, and the chapel was enlarged and reopened in December 1862. A Baptism well was provided and first used in October 1867. The debt of £800 was cleared by 1873. Rebuilt in 1895 at a cost of £2,000. The chapel was a branch of Calvaria W.B. (Ref: 104.)

Bethel, Abernant, circa 1900.

and had 240members in 1880 with 241 in the Sunday School; 398 members in 1925; 395 members in 1916 with 200 in the Sunday School; 165 members in 1955; 137 members in 1963. 47 young men from Bethel left to serve in the War in 1914. Rev. John Fuller was minister 1869-1872; he died in 1872 from Smallpox and is buried in Aberdare Cemetery- about 10,000 people attended his funeral. Rev. John Mills was minister 1876 – 1909. Enlarged in 1895 and renamed – cost £2,000 – seating for 750. Grand ceiling rose; fine pipe organ to the side of the pulpit; this chapel is well maintained and cared for. Religious Census of 1851 states – "space free 48; other 72; present morning 40; afternoon 26; standing 40;scholars, evening 54; – David Davies, Abernant (1851)." Only 8 members attending in February 2004. Centenary booklet (1856 – 1956) is in Glamorgan Record Office, Cardiff.

Bethel, Abernant.

CHAPEL REF. NO. 121.

NAME & DENOMINATION: **BETHESDA. W.I.**

ADDRESS / LOCALITY: **ABERNANT ROAD, ABERNANT.**

DATE BUILT: **1860 – REBUILT 1906.**

CURRENT USE: **CLOSED 1995, CONVERTED 1999 INTO A HOUSE NAMED 'MONSERRAT'**

BRIEF HISTORY: Located adjacent to Bethel W.B. (Ref: 120.). 1860 chapel built by Thomas Roberts and Samuel Parker at a cost of £260; Seating for 300; opened 5th.May 1861 by Rev. Dr. David Price, who ministered here 1861 – 1872, and was also minister of Siloa W.Cong. (Ref: 113.) 1843 – 1878. The first minister was Rev. Thomas Pugh, originally a minister in America for 15 years. Rev. Dr. Price of Siloa took charge of the Communion services once a month until Rev. Isaac J. Evans became minister 1873 – 1909. Other ministers were Rev. T. Emrys James 1914 – 1918; Rev. W. Walters 1921 – 1947. Organist in 1901 was Lettitia Jones; singing conductor was John Thomas. Bethesda is daughter chapel to Siloa W.Cong. First services were held in a cottage belonging to Peggy Jones of Fireman's Row – 1858 – 1861. Up to 1874 the chapel was used as a 'British School', the first school in Abernant where lessons took place in the chapel basement. In 1860 26 members came to Bethesda from Siloa to form the new 'cause'. Richard Fothergill, coal owner, helped to meet the cost of building the chapel in 1860; he helped financially on condition that the chapel be used as a school during the week. In 1881 paraffin lamps were updated to gas. The 1904-5 Religious Revival swelled numbers considerably, necessitating the rebuilding of the chapel in 1906, at a cost of £1,252; opened on 22nd. December 1906 by Mr. William Moses. By 1911 the entire chapel debt was cleared. Membership in 1860 was 36, by 1890 it was 89; 96 in 1905 with 90 in Sunday School – 124 in 1930 with 130 in Sunday School. By 1993 numbers were drastically reduced to 10 members, and in 1995 the chapel closed. In its day the chapel had a fine polished boarded

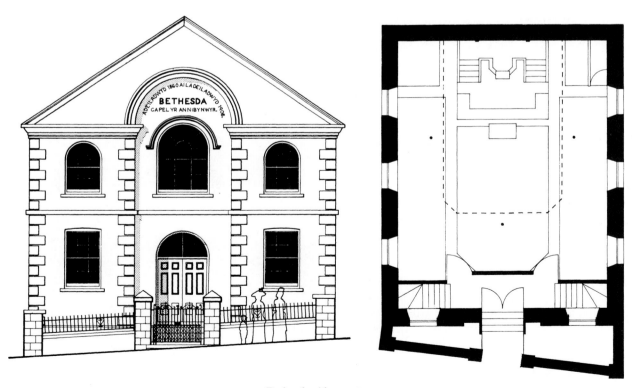

Bethesda, Abernant.

ceiling with a large central rose and a harmonium made in Paris; there was no pipe organ. 1858 – 1958 centenary booklet is in Aberdare Central Library. Thanks to Mr. Tom Griffiths for his help in compiling some of these notes.

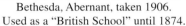

Bethesda, Abernant, taken 1906.
Used as a "British School" until 1874.

Bethesda, Abernant. 1993.

CHAPEL REF. NO. 122.

NAME & DENOMINATION: SALEM. W. CONG.

ADDRESS / LOCALITY: BRIDGE STREET, ROBERTSTOWN

DATE BUILT: 1841, RENOVATED 1899

CURRENT USE: STILL ACTIVE.

BRIEF HISTORY: A Grade 2 Listed Building, with two storey long-wall facade with highly symmetrical elevational treatment. In 1835 there occurred a 'split' at Ebenezer W.I. (Ref: 127.) when Rev. Joseph Harrison went out and left with 15 members and formed Salem. He was forced to leave because he admitted his willingness to administer baptism by total immersion to believers who desired it. Members met in various houses in turn, and later held meetings in the Long Room of the White Lion Inn, located near the bottom park gates at 56 Gadlys Road, opened 1841, still open, and near the old toll gates at the lower end of the Common. Worshippers had to walk through the bar to reach the Long Room of the pub, and this was

frowned upon by the chapel founders who objected to strong drink, being teetotal and good Templars. In 1836 they built a wooden hut known locally as 'Ty Planca' (House of Planks). This became too small so they thereafter decided to build Salem across the river from 'Ty Planca'. The founders carried huge stones from the River Cynon to build the chapel after their normal days work, in their spare time. They built Salem in 1841 at a cost of £550 – on land leased from Dr. James Lewis Roberts, on a site known as Gadlys Uchaf Farm. The chapel is well maintained and seats 600, and is almost exactly square on plan, with a tall hipped slated roof, wide eaves, tiled cresting with hooked finials. Classical details to 'set fawr' with paired columns; round arched classical 'reredos' behind with painted pilasters and keystone. It is located adjacent to the Gadlys Arms; and was at one time known as 'Tresalem' A Sunday School/

Salem, taken circa 1900. Note Gadlys Arms adjacent,
owned by Philip Harrison.

Vestry is attached at the side, built in 1899 and the adjacent 'Salem cottage' is occupied by the caretaker and his wife.

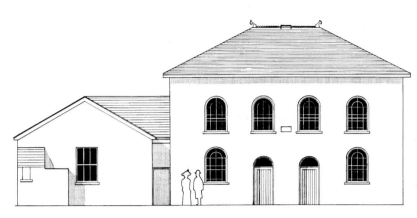

Membership was 15 in 1837; 6 in 1840; 65 in 1841; 25 in 1842 and 100 in 1851 with 70 in the Sunday School. Prominent ministers include – Rev. Joseph Harrison, from 1836 to his death in 1851; Rev. J.D. Rees (40 Years 1882-1922). This chapel is well worth seeing, particularly the fine interior and magnificently decorated ceiling rose and canted ceiling. Cast iron columns with foliage capitals. The chapel was remodelled in 1899. A railed graveyard is located at the front; last burial was in 1883, of Mrs Elizabeth Morgan.

Note – The Islamic Centre is located in St. Johns in the vestry alongside, behind Salem. History of Salem (Tresalem), Robertstown 1836-1936, 56 pages in Welsh, by Daniel Thomas & David Thomas is in Aberdare Central Library. Religious Census 1851 states – "Salem, Independents. Erected 1841. Space free 12; Other 276; Present morning 94 + 41 scholars, evening 91 + 80 scholars. – John Harrison, Elder, Gadlys.

Ref. 122 (A). Islamic Centre, Robertstown.

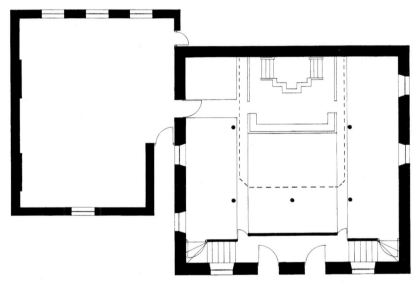

Salem, Robertstown.

Taken in 1974.

Taken in 1995.

CHAPEL REF. NO. 123.

NAME & DENOMINATION: APOSTOLIC (BABELL). A.C.

ADDRESS / LOCALITY: DAVID STREET, TRECYNON.

DATE BUILT: 1910

CURRENT USE: STILL ACTIVE

BRIEF HISTORY: 'Babell' Translation – Tabernacle/Tent. The 'cause' commenced in 1910 after the effects and influence of the 1904-5 Religious Revival, and the emerging progress of the Pentecostal movement. James Forward was a prominent founder of the church in 1910 and was then a member of Heol y Felin W.B. (Ref: 130.). In 1911 the assembly progressed further at the Pentwyn Bach Mission, Trecynon, in the charge of Mrs. Shepherd, familiarly known as 'Mother Shepherd. Meetings were also held in the homes of Brothers Tom Leach and James Forward. In 1916 25 members met in the cellar beneath Brother Ben Edwards house near the Golden Lion public house, 1 Cynon Place, Trecynon, (built 1848; closed 1939), but they came under considerable opposition there by the landlord as a result of the enthusiastic and noisy worshipping; much verbal abuse was expressed by the landlord and others in the pub, and eventually they threw buckets of water on the worshippers in an attempt to quell the noise! In 1920 they moved to the Park School (now Comin) for twelve months. In June 1921 they moved into a new building at Robertstown – their new 'Babell' but during the War in 1942 the building and land was requisitioned for a factory. In 1942 they moved to their present building in Trecynon, where in 1950 and 1986 refurbishment was carried out; the building was a former billiards hall, and also a former public house (1867-1909) named the "Park View Inn", No.17 Hirwaun Road. Seven other assemblies were formed in the area at Aberdare, Aberaman, Cwmbach, Abernant, Penrhiwceiber, Mountain Ash and Hirwaun around the early 1920's. 2003 approximate membership 70. The Aberdare Apostolic chapel first met at Whitcombe Street, Aberdare; also called "Aberdare Four Square Gospel Chapel" where they met at Canon Street. They later moved to 'Cole's Bazaar Stores' in Dean Street.

Ref. 123 (A). Apostolic Church, Aberaman.
Ref. 123 (B). Apostolic Church, Cwmbach.
Ref. 123 (C). Apostolic Church' Abernant.
Ref' 123 (D). Apostolic Church, Mountain Ash.
Ref' 123 (E). Apostolic Church, Hirwaun.

Apostolic Church (Babell), Trecynon. Taken in 1986.

CHAPEL REF. NO. 124.

NAME & DENOMINATION: **BRYN SION. C.M. (CARMEL. E.B.)**

ADDRESS / LOCALITY: **MILL STREET, TRECYNON.**

DATE BUILT: **1862, REBUILT 1899**

CURRENT USE: **STILL ACTIVE.**

BRIEF HISTORY: Grade 2 Listed Building. Architect (1899 chapel) Thomas Roderick, Aberdare.
                               Built with seating for 600, at a cost of £550 by David Davies, Trecynon.
Membership in 1897 – 400. The 'cause' commenced in Pentwyn Bach as a result of the 1859 Religious Revival, in
which Dafydd Morgan was actively involved. Formerly welsh Calvinistic Methodist; now named Carmel English
Baptist. Interesting and grand Roll of Honour is displayed. Extremely ornate panelled coffered ceiling and cornice
work fluted and bracketed; The ceiling was installed in 1930. The whole interior has a strong classical appearance.
Central rose with small rosettes to the ribs. Baptism bath; the 'Set Fawr' (big seat) came from a chapel in the
Rhondda. Panelled reredos behind the 'set fawr', framed by twinned Ionic cabled pilasters with deep dentil
cornice. Raked gallery with wood panelled front carried on cast iron columns. Inpost band links gallery windows,
Vestry/ Schoolroom attached at the rear. Beautiful pulpit with an exquisite curved staircase, galleries on three
sides. The façade has a double width window with a single central opening. A plain façade in rock-faced Pennant
Sandstone sneck rubble. The chapel was incorporated in 1838; opened for worship in 1862, rebuilt 1899 at a cost
of £580.

Rev. Dr. Thomas Price (1820 – 1888) was minister at Carmel (Ref: 105.) and later became minister at Calvaria
W.B. (Ref: 104.) Jessie Millicent Griffiths (1905 –2003) was organist here for many years and also at Emmanuel
E.F.C. (Ref: 126.). Sunday School banner dated 1860 is in Cynon Valley Museum.

Bryn Sion chapel, Trecynon was the first chapel in Cynon Valley to be visited on 13th. November 1904 by the
great Revivalist and Evangelist **Evan Roberts** (1878 – 1951) during the Religious Revival in Wales, 1904/5.

Bryn Sion, Trecynon.

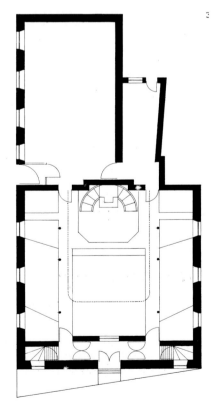

Trecynon was the first town outside his home town of Loughor, near Swansea, for Roberts to commence holding his great Revival Meetings and services. The Revival broke out in Loughor during the first weeks of November 1904, and quickly spread throughout the Cynon Valley and the whole of Wales. The second chapel visited by Roberts, also in Trecynon was Ebenezer W.I. (Ref: 127.) on 14th. & 15th. November 1904. (See chapter 7 for full details). The chapel became a Baptist chapel in the 1970's when the immersion baptismal font was installed.

Bryn Sion (now Carmel), Trecynon, 1986.

Bryn Sion, Trecynon taken circa 1900. To the right is the building "J.Thomas, Draper, Milliner and Outfitter". Note Ice Cream cart to the left of the photograph

CHAPEL REF. NO. 125.

NAME & DENOMINATION: CARMEL. C.M.

ADDRESS / LOCALITY: HIRWAUN ROAD, TRECYNON.

DATE BUILT: 1829, REBUILT 1896.

CURRENT USE: CLOSED/SOLD 1988; DEMOLISHED 1989; REPLACED BY A NEW PLAIN BRICK BUILDING IN 1993 – SEE REF.125A.

BRIEF HISTORY: The first Calvinistic Methodist chapel in Aberdare; In 1799 members used to walk from Cefnpennar; Aberaman; Cwmaman and other distant places to the first Meeting House until the 1829 chapel was built. The 1896 chapel was built by Messrs J. Morgan & Son at a cost of £2,500 including the organ, with seating for 750. First meetings of the Calvinistic Methodists were held in 1799, in the house William Jenkin, shopkeeper, at the rear of the present Mackworth Arms Hotel (25 Gadlys Road, built 1867 – still open), five members were present. Later in 1801 services were held in the loft of the old shop of Evan David in Dare Court, behind 53 High Street. For some time after they also worshipped in the house of Thomas Pugh, a Mason, near the Aberdare Cemetery, and thereafter they moved to the home of William Pugh, Llwydcoed. In 1806 the first Calvinistic Methodist chapel in Trecynon was built, namely 'Pentwyn Bach' at St. John's Place, above the old Tram Road. The chapel was later called 'Gospel Hall', with 30 members in 1806. The

 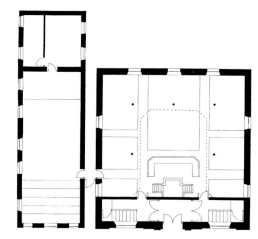

Carmel, Trecynon.

building seated 300, with no gallery. By 1829 Pentwyn Bach became too small for the growing congregation, so a new chapel was built in Hirwaun road at a cost of £1,000, seating about 700. Membership in 1829 was 152 with 260 in the Sunday School, 1901 membership was 400-500. Whilst the chapel was being built services and the Sunday School were held in the upstairs of "The Mill" and the long room of the Boot Hotel, Aberdare. The old 1829 chapel was of long wall façade design; the pulpit was flanked by the two entrance porches. An original water colour painting of the 1829 chapel by E Harris, dated 1888, once hung in Siloh Vestry, Trecynon. (Ref: 133.); a photograph is in the author's collection. The adjacent vestry of Carmel was built in 1873, and behind was a small stable where horses could be kept for visiting preachers who travelled to the chapel on horseback. £1.50 was spent on providing hay for the horses, and 7/6d. (approx. 37p.) was given to the ostler for taking care of the animals, together with 1/- (5p.) for tobacco and pipes and 2/- (10p.) for beer, and the same for gin! When the Calvinistic Methodists under the instigation of Evan Griffiths, Ty Mawr, moved from Pentwyn Bach chapel, they built their second chapel in 1896 at a cost of £2,394; a Grade Two Listed building. Services in the meantime were held at Ysgol Comin. A hand-pumped pipe organ was installed in 1896. The vestry was enlarged in 1933 at a cost of £1,000. In the 1940's evacuees from Ilford used the vestry as a schoolroom. The original stone name plaque of the 1829 chapel is built into the main stone wall of the accommodation block at the Dare Valley Country Park. The chapel debt of £800 was cleared in 1944. The Sunday School closed at the end of the 1970's. Carmel Dramatic Society was a notable success from the early 1900's to well into the 1950's. Past ministers include Rev. J.H. Lloyd, 1879; Rev. David Morgan Jones, 1883-1892; Rev. Henry Thomas Stephens, 1893-1922 – his son Mr. W. Beddoe Stephens was organist at Bethania C.M. (Ref: 103.) in the 1920's; Rev. Ivor Glyndwr Richards, 1937-1945; Rev. John David Eurful Jones B.A-B.D., 1960-1966; Rev. Evan Emrys Evans B.A., 1968-1971 and Rev. Glaslyn Desmond Bowen, 1984-1992.

Carmel C.M., Trecynon, circa 1900. Built in 1829 of "Long Wall Façade" design.

Taken in 1986.

Membership numbers – 160 – 179 (1830-1918), steady decline after 1918, then 108 in 1955; 60 in 1970; 36 in 1985; and 4 in 1996. Religious Census of 1851 states – "Erected 1829; space free 150; other 250; standing 100; present morning 296; afternoon 240 scholars; evening 347. – Evan Griffith, Deacon, Grocer – Hirwaun." Carmel chapel sadly closed in 1988. The remaining members transferred to Siloh (Ref: 133.) and stayed there up to the closure of Siloh in 1996 with only 4 members. A copy of "History of Carmel, Trecynon, 1799-1996" by Elfed Davies (published 2002), is in Aberdare Central Library.

Thanks to Mr. Elfed Davies for his contribution to these notes.

CHAPEL REF. 125A.

THE BRETHREN MEETING ROOM, TRECYNON.

It is opportune here to deal with this 'cause' whose chapel is built on the site of the former Carmel C.M. chapel, Hirwaun road, Trecynon.

The origin and history of Christians known as 'Brethren' in the Cynon Valley commenced about one hundred years ago, in the early 1900's, when a few believers gathered together in fellowship on a scriptural basis; They found confirmation in the Scriptures that "One is your Master, All ye are Brethren" – (Matthew 23. verse 10).

Initially Bible readings and communion Services were held in various houses including the home of Mr. Ioan Evans in Church Row, Trecynon. Later a Meeting Hall was acquired in Bell View, Trecynon where the 'Lord's Supper', Gospel preachings, prayer meetings and Bible reading classes were held. The Brethren have no permanent clergy and there is no laity divide, no church hierarchy and no ordained priesthood. Autonomy is exercised in each local church. About 1925 a larger building known as "Broniestyn Lane Meeting Room" was built at the rear of Carmel C.M. chapel, Hirwaun Road, Trecynon, and accessed by a lane off Broniestyn Terrace. Carmel Chapel and the adjoining house were purchased and demolished in 1989. The Brethren built a new plain brick Meeting Room on the site, completed in 1993; it has been used regularly since that date.

The Brethren, also known in some areas as 'The Plymouth Brethren' is a religious Christian Protestant sect characterised by simplicity of belief and founded in Dublin about 1827, by Rev. John Nelson Darby (b.1800 – d.1882).

Thanks to Mr. Peter Jones of the Brethren, Trecynon, for the preparation of part of these notes.

CHAPEL REF. NO. 126.

NAME & DENOMINATION:	**EMMANUEL. E.F.C.**
ADDRESS / LOCALITY:	**BELL STREET, TRECYNON.**
DATE BUILT:	**1941, REBUILT 1953**
CURRENT USE:	**CLOSED IN THE 1980'S – 1989; CONVERTED TO DAY NURSERY "NOAH'S ARK NURSERY" IN 1989**

BRIEF HISTORY: Formerly named 'The Evangelical Free Church' Located between 36 & 37 Bell Street, also known as the 'Mission Hall' and 'Free Gospel Mission'. Officially opened on 15th. March 1941. The original hall was burnt down in March 1953; during renovation and rebuilding work the services and meetings were held in the vestry of Hen-Dy-Cwrdd chapel located nearby. The present chapel (rebuilt 1953) is the second chapel to have existed on the site. Prominent member was Jessie Millicent Griffiths (1905 – 2003), she was organist at Emmanuel for many years and also at Bryn Sion (Carmel Ref: 124.) She died in 2003 aged 98 years. This chapel closed circa 1980 after about 40 years of Christian witness.

Emmanuel, Trecynon, 1995.

CHAPEL REF. NO. 127.

NAME & DENOMINATION: **EBENEZER. W.I.**

ADDRESS / LOCALITY: **EBENEZER STREET, TRECYNON.**

DATE BUILT: **1811; REBUILT 1829; RENOVATED 1852; REFURBISHED 1902.**

CURRENT USE: **STILL ACTIVE.**

BRIEF HISTORY: In 1799 both the Welsh Independents (Ebenezer) and what was then the Calvinistic Methodists (Carmel – Ref: 105.) started their 'cause' together in the same place in a small cottage. The 'cause' continued in 'Tyr Capel', licenced in 1804 – the house of Timothy Davies near Carmel, (Ref: 105.), Monk Street. In 1811 Ebenezer was built. Land was offered by Griffith Davies of Blaengwawr but it was decided to build at Trecynon (Heol -Y-Felin). Stones were gathered here and there on the open Common above Trecynon and carried to the chosen site. Dafydd William Dafydd donated better quality stone from a quarry on his Cwmdare farm – Dyffryn Dar, and lime came from an old kiln in Trecynon, sited at the bottom of the present Harriet Street. Transportation of materials was difficult as there were no roads, only primitive tracks, and stone bridges were not built before 1789. Evan Giles of the Dare Inn, a contractor owning horses and carts provided free transport to the site. Building took place in 1811; the builders were Morgan Shon Morgan, John Richards of Penywaun, and Thomas Philip Richards. Despite much free labour and materials, the expenses came to £250, and £6 for the lease. Money was borrowed from members and appeals were made and funds were raised through concerts and Gymanfa Ganu. William Shencyn loaned £40 and other sums came from Morgan Davies, Cefnpennar and Dafydd Shencyn. There were no seats and no gallery; seats were made by the members and were varied in appearance and quality, due to expense and the skill factor. However, a gallery was built in 1823 at a cost of £60. The chapel was rebuilt in 1829 (£800), during the Religious Revival period – designed by Joseph Harrison. The stone name plaque reads – "Ebenezer, October 9th. 1829 (translated) – 'Until now The Lord has helped us' – Protestant Dissenters." The chapel was renovated in 1852; the three upper windows of the façade with Corinthian pilasters belonging to the 1852 building and was heightened in 1874-5. The porch opening in the centre projects under three equilateral gables faced with red terracotta rosettes (1902). The façade is most striking for its lean-to lobby with three gables; pediment treatment is given by an overall cornice. Central bay has fluted marble effect cast iron columns. The chapel was refurbished in 1902 when a lavish and extensive refit took place. Architects were Owen Morris Roberts and Son, of Portmadoc, Gwynedd – seating for 900 and a cost of

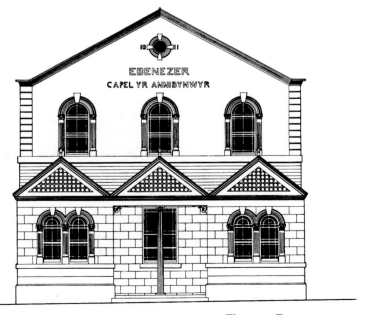

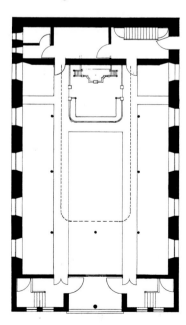

Ebenezer, Trecynon.

£1,700. The 1902 refurbishment provided a very fine interior with high-class joinery work throughout. The pulpit and 'big seat' all elaborately fretted and decorated with ebony pilasters, and two magnificent ceiling roses encircled with rosettes. The coved ceiling and beautiful roses have radiating ribs to boarded edge and central band; and dentil cornice. The raked gallery is carried on marble effect cast iron columns; panelled front with foliage ornament inset in a darker wood. Quatrefoil panels to organ in recess above 'set fawr'. The pipe organ has 794 pipes, two manuals and was installed in 1938, restored in 1983. There are numerous interesting internal memorial plaques of past ministers, including Rev. Dafydd Jones 1813 – 1815; Rev. Joseph Harrison (1817 – 1835), he was of Scottish descent born 1789; he played a prominent part in the building of Ebenezer in 1829; such was his enormous drive and effort that the chapel was known for many years as 'Harrison's Chapel'. Also recorded are – Rev. Dafydd Jones 1813 – 15 Rev. John Daniels 1836 – 1840; Rev. Dr. Thomas Rees 1840 –1844; Rev. William Edwards 1844 – 84; Rev. Grawys Jones 1885 – 1925; Rev. William Morse B.A. 1929 – 1959; Rev. R.O. Thomas 1961 – 1986. Membership in 1828 – 17; 1829 – 71; (increase due to the Religious Revival that year); in 1853 – 340 with 225 in Sunday School. 1907 membership – 564; 1918 – 365; 1954 – 330. A graveyard exists in the chapel grounds. 'History of Ebenezer, 1811-1898 (in Welsh, 119 pages) written by J. Treharne is in Aberdare Library. Mr. Edward (Ted) Evans was organist for 50 years, 1930 – 1980. Fine detail plans were drawn in 1984 by Chris King A.R.I.C.S., M.R.T.P.I., of Cwmdare. Ebenezer was renowned for its fine orchestra, formed in 1904, but has a century of musical tradition prior to this. The present chapel is a Grade 2 Listed Building. The school room built in 1860 at a cost of £588, is located opposite. Joseph Harrison, as a member, was among those who carried stones from the Common (before 1811) to enable building of the original chapel. He later became minister of Salem (Ref: 122.). In 1828, Rev. J Harrison baptised 86 infants and between 1817 & 1828 more than 1600 were baptised by him. Ebenezer was mother chapel to Cana, Penywaun (Ref:143.). A devout Member and Deacon of Ebenezer, David Emlyn Thomas (1892 – 1954) was Labour M.P. for Aberdare 1946 – 54, and the last former miner to represent the constituency in Parliament. His daughter Mrs. Margaret Morris formerly of Broniestyn Terrace, Trecynon, (now living at Rhiwbina), served as Chapel Secretary for many years. Thanks to Mr. Elfed Bowen (C.V.H.S. committee member) for providing some of the history notes.

Ebenezer, Trecynon, 1986.

"Old" Ebenezer, Trecynon. Pre 1902.

Capel Ebenezer – "Tyr Capel". Services held here commencing in 1804, near Carmel Chapel, Monk St., Aberdare.

CHAPEL REF. NO. 128.

NAME & DENOMINATION: ENGLISH WESLEYAN. E.W.M.

ADDRESS / LOCALITY: LLEWELLYN STREET, TRECYNON.

DATE BUILT: 1887; REBUILT 1905

CURRENT USE: MAIN CHAPEL CONVERTED INTO A PRIVATE HOUSE IN 2000/ 2001 NAMED 'WESLEYAN HOUSE'. SUNDAY SCHOOL/HALL CONVERTED INTO ADJOINING GARAGE.

BRIEF HISTORY: Foundation stone laid by D.A. Thomas J.P. of Ysguborwen. A local newspaper dated August 1887 reported that several current coins of the Realm were inserted into a cavity in the stonework during the laying of the foundation stone. Photograph of a water-colour painting dated 1888 by E. Morris is in the collection of A.V. Jones. The chapel later became Llewellyn Street Methodist Chapel, Trecynon. A Hall/Sunday School attached, built in1905. Harmonium organ made in Woodstock, Canada – no pipe organ, no upper gallery, seating for 300. John Beale Arnold (d.1927) was a prominent founder member, and for over 50 years was superintendent of the Sunday School. James Rogers (b.1833 – d.1892), was superintendent of the Sunday School for 16 years. Member James Field, also a local preacher (b.1831 – d. 1905). Silver tray presented to the chapel by Mrs. James Harrison in May 1898. Previously Pentwyn Bach, sold to the Welsh Wesleyans 1890.

The re-building of the chapel in 1905.
The members and children gather together in Edward Street.

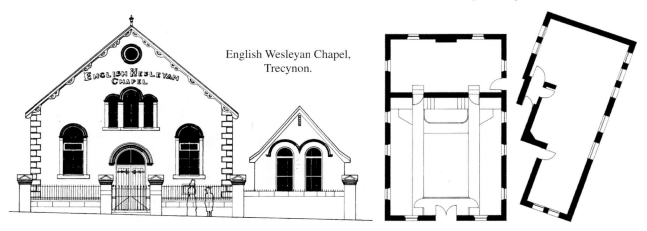

English Wesleyan Chapel, Trecynon.

Taken in 1986.

CHAPEL REF. NO. 129.

NAME & DENOMINATION: **HEN-DY-CWRDD. Un.**

ADDRESS / LOCALITY: **ALMA STREET, TRECYNON**

DATE BUILT: **1751 – REBUILT 1862.**

CURRENT USE: **CLOSED 1994 – VACANT, BOARDED UP 2004, FUTURE USE UNCERTAIN**

BRIEF HISTORY: Founded in 1751 – the 1862 chapel is a Grade 2 Listed Building. The oldest Nonconformist chapel in the Cynon Valley; The ancient St. John's Parish Church (founded 1189) and Hen-Dy-Cwrdd chapel were the only two places of worship to be built in the parish up to 1811.Famously known as 'The Old Meeting House', the origin and establishment of Hen-Dy-Cwrdd can be traced back to 1751, and it was established on this site by Dissenting members of the Cwm-Y-Glo Chapel on the Merthyr mountain. The original lease was granted on 5th. March 1751 by Theophilus Richards (b.1704 – d.1794) and revised by his son Richard Richards on 12th. December 1796. Rev. Ivor Parry confirms that it was originally known as 'Ty Cwrdd Godre Hirwaun'. The appearance of the first 1751 old chapel was that of a simple and modest cottage, or a humble Inn with a front porch entrance, and outside stone stairs. This small structure was demolished in 1861 and the present, much larger chapel was built in 1862 at a cost of £753 – 15 – 4 d. precisely. The Architect was Evan Griffiths (Junior), Aberdare, son of Evan Griffiths 'Ty Mawr' owner of the largest trading establishments in Aberdare during the first half of the 19th. Century, and a staunch Methodist. He was also owner of barges that carried freight on the Aberdare Canal. The 1862 chapel was designed to "be simple and strong, reflecting Unitarian beliefs in liberty, tolerance and forbearance" The chapel has a square shaped interior, galleried on three sides, the deep gallery fronts moulded; the cast-iron columns supporting the gallery have acanthus capitals. Symmetrical cement rendered gable front, channelled below gallery windows. Round attic window. Round arched doorway with broad voussoirs and keystone below inscribed plaque. String course over gallery windows, arched up over semi-circular headed paired windows with dividing pilaster.

   Notable ministers include:- Owen Rees 1756 – 68, (b.1717 – d.1768) – buried in St. John's Churchyard, facing the main road. David Evans, 1769. Edward Evans of Ton Coch (poet & author b.1716-d.1798), Minister 1772 – 96, also buried at St. John's Churchyard. John Davies 1796 – 1803. David Oliver (b.1765-d.1815) Minister 1803 – 06. John Jones 1806 –11. Thomas Evans (Tomos Glyn Cothi), politician, 1813 –33. (b.1764 – d.1833) , a prolific hymn writer. John Jones 1833 – 63, and his son Rees Jenkin Jones M.A. 1864 –72 and 1879 – 1909, lived in Broniestyn House. (b.1835 – d.1924). J. Glynne Davies 1910 –13. E.R. Dennis 1916 until his death in 1949, he

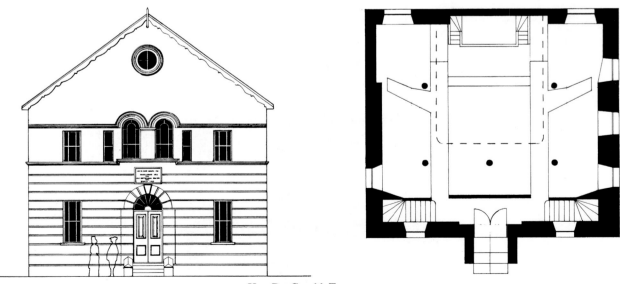

Hen-Dy-Cwrdd, Trecynon.

Hen-Dy-Cwrdd, Trecynon, circa 1910.
To the right is the old Mount Pleasant Inn.

Hen-Dy-Cwrdd, Trecynon, circa 1900.

was a well-known dramatist and founder of The Little Theatre, Aberdare. D. Jacob Davies B.A. 1952 – 57. J. Eric Jones B.A. 1962 until closure. Prominent members include Griffiths Rhys Jones 'Caradog' (b.1834-d.1897); Rhys Hopkins Rhys (1819 – 99) of Llwydcoed; W.W. Price, notable local historian; Thomas Dafydd Llewellyn; Evan Thomas developer of miners' safety lamp. Although the chapel closed in 1994, the 'cause' was being maintained by the members transferring to Highland Place (Ref: 108.), under the ministry of Rev. J. Eric Jones, until his retirement in 2003. The graveyard surrounding the chapel is sadly overgrown and unkempt, the earliest burial is that of a young child in 1797. In 1782 there were 43 members; the preacher received £9 per annum; by 1800 the salary had risen to £21.p.a. Register of baptisms kept by Rev. Edward Evans (1772 – 79) is in Glamorgan Record Office. The parents of baptised children are recorded as coming from Aberdare, Llanwonno and Merthyr Tydfil. Copies of the bi-centenary history book, 1751 – 1951, 86 pages in Welsh, by Rev. D. Jacob Davies B.A. (minister 1952 – 57) are kept by G.R.O. and Aberdare Central Library.

The 1751 Chapel drawn from ancient written descriptions.
Rebuilt 1862

Artist's impression of the original chapel built in 1751. The oldest Nonconformist Chapel in the Cynon Valley.
(Doug Williams)

CHAPEL REF. NO. 130.

NAME & DENOMINATION: **HEOL-Y-FELIN. W.B.**

ADDRESS / LOCALITY: **BELL STREET, TRECYNON**

DATE BUILT: **1852 – RESTORED/ENLARGED. 1893 – RENOVATED 1905.**

CURRENT USE: **STILL ACTIVE.**

BRIEF HISTORY: At the commencement of Ysguborwen Colliery, Llwydcoed in 1849, a great many Baptists came to Trecynon and met together for prayer meetings and Sunday School classes at the old Wesleyan Chapel, St. John's Place. Grade 2 Listed Building. Two storey classic design; low angled pediment and abbreviated Doric pilasters to upper floor; ground floor plain; disproportionally large round-headed window forms a podium to the upper part of the building. Architect: Thomas Joseph, a local engineer from Hirwaun, and a colliery entrepreneur who came to Aberdare to open a colliery. Seating for 800, building cost £900. It

Heol-Y-Felin, Trecynon, 1986.

became a self-governing chapel in 1855. 470 members in 1916; 237 members in 1947; 495 in Sunday School in 1911. A consistently high membership between 1860 & 1916 (350 –500). Highest recorded number being 500 in 1906. During the Religious Revival, 95 were baptised in December 1904. New classrooms were added in 1905. A branch of Ramoth W.B. (Ref: 151.), the chapel has been blessed with many notable ministers including – Rev. William Harries 1862 – 1902 (d. 1911), president of the Welsh Baptist Union 1891/92. Rev. W. Cynoc Williams, 1903 – 1941. (two ministers covering 79 years!). Minister in the 1950's was Rev. Daniel Meredith Morgan. The 'cause' commenced in 1846 by holding a Sunday School and Prayer Meetings in various houses nearby. Several members of Calvaria, Aberdare (Ref: 104.) joined the new chapel. Rev. Thomas Price was in charge of the Sunday School and also at Carmel (i.e. Penpound) in 1847. Rev. Thomas Price used to baptise converts in the River Cynon nearby. When Thomas Joseph moved from Hirwaun to Heol-y-Felin, many Hirwaun Baptists moved with him.

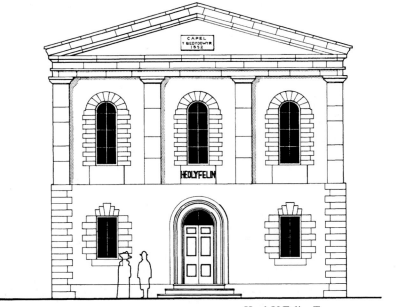

Heol-Y-Felin, Trecynon.

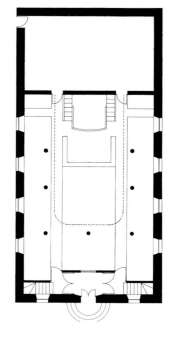

They and Carmel – Penpound members who lived in Heol-y-Felin (Trecynon) took over Pentwyn Bach but retained their membership at Carmel (Ref: 125.), and Ramoth, Hirwaun (Ref: 151.). A white marble monument is displayed of Owen Harris dated 1905 – a member and Deacon for 30 years. Other beautiful marble plaques to various ministers are also displayed. A fine organ built by Gray & Davison, London; boarded ceiling on a deep coving with handsome single plaster ceiling rose; excellent quality joinery in pulpit and balcony, iron balustrading with tulip pattern of Art-Nouveau influence. Raked upper gallery on all four sides on tapered cylindrical iron columns painted in imitation of 'scagliola' work, manufactured by Dare Fychan Foundry – D.R. Lewis 1852. The pulpit has Art-Nouveau influence in the metalwork, circa 1900. There is a graveyard within the chapel grounds. First minister was Rev. Benjamin Evans of Hirwaun, 1852 – 1861. The chapel was a branch of the W.B. at Cwmdare and Llwydcoed, as well as Ramoth, Hirwaun. 1901 membership was 400. History books from 1915 (99 pages) and 1952 are held at Glamorgan Record Office.

CHAPEL REF. NO. 131.

NAME & DENOMINATION: **NODDFA. W.B.**

ADDRESS / LOCALITY: **MOUNT PLEASANT STREET, TRECYNON.**

DATE BUILT: **1905.**

CURRENT USE: **CONVERTED INTO A HOUSE, 2002.**

BRIEF HISTORY: The 'cause' commenced in 1904 as a result of a 'split' from Heol-Y-Felin W.B. (Ref: 130.); first meetings held at the Public Hall, Trecynon; first baptism in River Cynon in 1905. Architect – T W. Millar, Mountain Ash. Builder – D. Rees, Trecynon. Seating for 600 – building cost £2,500. Vestry at rear, added in 1906. Thirty eight memorial stones laid including Rev. William Harris; Miss E. Harrison of Maesgwyn Tce. Cwmdare; R. Llewellyn, Bwllfa; T W. Millar, Architect; Mrs. Daniel, Llwydcoed House. The first minister in 1907 was Rev. D. Hopkins B.A. Prominent minister for 25 years, Rev. William David Lewis (b.1886 – d. 1942.). The debt of £3,000 was cleared in 1947.

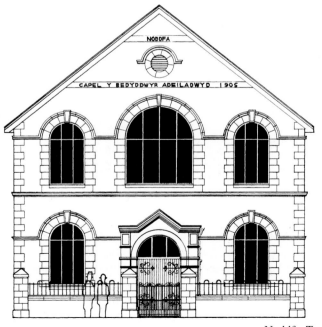
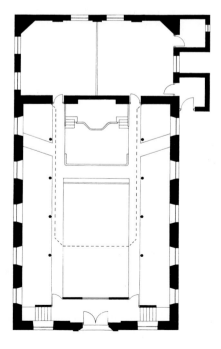

Noddfa, Trecynon.

At Aberdare Central Library – A silk cloth print of the chapel, deacons and Sunday School children, presented to Mary Evans, 1906 (Ref: RB.15 – W. W. Price collection). Interesting framed photographs of ministers and groups; watercolour of chapel building by Tom Thomas, Abernant, circa 1950. Note the clock by Runge, Aberdare – the twelve numerals depicted by 'Dilynwch-yr-o'en' (i.e. 'Follow the lamb), presented by the children. Attractive coloured stained glass windows, and fine cast iron balcony balustrading. Elegant pulpit with beautiful cast iron decorative front. Note the cast iron front door brackets. Fine organ behind pulpit framed by a grand stone arch and fluted pillars.

Noddfa, Trecynon, 1986.

Members and children gather outside Noddfa, circa 1905.

(Joseph Thomas)

CHAPEL REF. NO. 132.

NAME & DENOMINATION: PENTWYN GOPEL HALL. G.H.

ADDRESS / LOCALITY: ALMA STREET, TRECYNON.

DATE BUILT: CIRCA 1860.

CURRENT USE: STILL ACTIVE.

BRIEF HISTORY: Prior to 1870 'Pentwyn Mission', later named 'Pentwyn Gospel Hall', situated at the bottom of Belle Vue Lane, Trecynon, was the engine-house for a small coal mine across the valley. The building was hired temporarily by Mother Shepherd (b. 1836 – d. 1930.) for her Evangelical Meetings. The early Brethren joined Mother Shepherd for a short period. Captain Mother Shepherd (nee Pamela Morgan), born at Talywain, Monmouth, was sent from Salvation Army headquarters in 1878 and opened the Mission Hall at Pentwyn Bach, Trecynon, and became actively associated with Women's Guilds in various chapels, Sewing Guilds and Temperance groups etc. There were, however, some doctrinal problems connected with the early brethren so they later moved and held 'House Meetings' at the home of a Mrs. Price of Harriet Street, Trecynon. These meetings became appropriately called 'Mrs. Price's Meetings. They became so large that the worshippers resorted to hiring a room at the Miner's Institute, located at 'The Square', Trecynon. Later the Brethren purchased the old engine house building and named it Pentwyn Gospel Hall. The building became structurally unsafe, so the local brethren purchased the vestry/Sunday School belonging to 'Hen-Dy- Cwrdd (Ref: 129.), they renovated it, and named it Mount Pleasant Gospel Hall, located at Alma Street, Trecynon. There was a charge of one penny per week to use the old vestry for schoolroom purposes. An extension and entrance lobby was built at the front circa 1960, attached to the old vestry, built circa 1860. About 8 members continue to worship here.

Thanks to Mr. Byron Lloyd for his contribution towards the preparation of these notes.

Members of Pentwyn Bach Chapel; later Gospel Hall, circa 1930. Located at the bottom of Belle Vue Lane.
(Doug Williams)

Pentwyn Gospel Hall, Trecynon, 1995.

CHAPEL REF. NO. 133.

NAME & DENOMINATION: **SILOH. W.I.**

ADDRESS / LOCALITY: **MOUNT PLEASANT, TRECYNON.**

DATE BUILT: **1889 – REBUILT 1902.**

CURRENT USE: **CONVERTED 2002/3 INTO A FUNERAL SERVICES BUILDING FOR GARAGING HEARSES, STORING COFFINS ETC. FOR RICHARDS FUNERAL SERVICES.**

BRIEF HISTORY: 1902 Architect – Thomas Roderick, Aberdare. Located adjacent to the Coliseum Theatre. The 'cause' was founded in 1887 by Rev. David Onllwyn Brace who left Bethel W. Cong (Ref: 117.) with 50 members to join Siloh W.I. Members first met in the Swan Coffee Tavern of Evan Hopkins (built 1860-closed 1910), Bell Street, and also at the house of Richard Wigley,

Bell Street. Later, as membership increased they met at Park School (Ysgol-Y-Comin). A gallery was added in 1904, which increased seating capacity to 550. The Sunday school/vestry attached at the side was built in 1916 at a cost of £700. In 1901 the debt was £1,000. Memorial stones laid in 1916 by Master Thomas H. Roderick, Leaholme, Aberdare; W. M. Llewellyn Esq. M.E., D.C., of Bwllfa House, Aberdare and Miss R. Morfydd Davies, Ardwyn, Trecynon. Membership in 1905 was 154 with 165 in Sunday School; 1914 – 144 with 160 in Sunday School; 1930 – 138 with 147 in Sunday School.

Notable minister – Rev. J. Sulgwyn Davies for 43 years, 1891 – 1934 (d.1939.) Grand ceiling rose; fluted cast iron gallery supports with colourful capitals; Harmonium made in Battleboro, Vermont, U.S.A. by Estey Organ Co. 20 members transferred from Carmel (Ref: 125.) and worshipped in Siloh from 1988 until its closure in 1996.

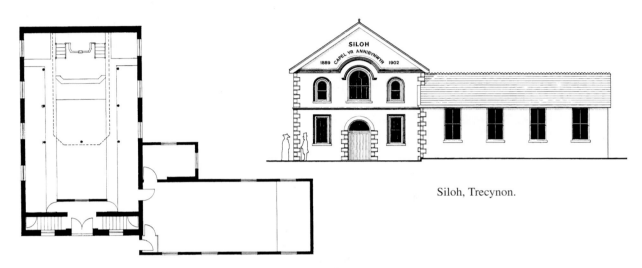

Siloh, Trecynon.

Siloah W.I. Chapel in the foreground, circa 1925.

(J.F. Mear)

Siloh, Trecynon, 1995.

CHAPEL REF. NO. 134.

NAME & DENOMINATION:	**CWMDARE MISSION HALL. M.H.**
ADDRESS / LOCALITY:	**CWMDARE ROAD, CWMDARE.**
DATE BUILT:	**1920 – REBUILT 1950. RENOVATED 1960 & 1971. EXTENDED 1976.**
CURRENT USE:	**STILL ACTIVE.**

BRIEF HISTORY: The Evangelical Free Mission Hall of Cwmdare is located adjacent to 'Harrisonville' and opposite No's 37 & 38 Bryn Terrace. The Mission 'cause' commenced in 1911 primarily as a result of a need to cater for the English-speaking chapel population of Cwmdare, as the only three Nonconformist chapels in the village at that time catered for Welsh speaking members, namely Elim W. Cong. (Ref:135.); Old Nebo W.B. (Ref:137.), and Gobaith C.M. (Ref: 138.) – now Nebo Newydd W.B. The founders of the Mission included Mr. & Mrs. Albert Collier, (Welsh Methodists) and Lewis Evans (a member of Gobaith). First meetings were held in Cwmdare Primary School, The Square, in 1911 and continued there until 1921; however, a small temporary chapel was opened on May 5th. 1914 on the site opposite No's 30 to 34 Bryn Terrace (now occupied by houses) located a little lower down from the present site; this chapel stood only for a few years. Mrs. Mabel Lewis recollects sitting at the children's desk in front of a coal fire; Mother Shepherd visited the Mission occasionally; Campaigns, Cantatas and Concerts were held as well as the giving generously of voluntary contributions and door to door collections – these efforts helping to swell funds. In 1920 the well-known Harrison family leased land to the church elders on which to erect a church; later the church purchased the ground (August 1946 at a cost of £100.). The land formed part of the Maesgwyn Estate. By 1920 finance increased enabling a church to be built opposite No's 37 & 38 Bryn Terrace. Tyssul Davies supplied some of the bricks for the foundation, and many members gave their free time to help. An old army hut was acquired from Brecon, left over from the 1914-18 War, a little later, as membership increased, a larger hall was purchased for £200, formerly used as a workmen's canteen on the Rhigos Road, and was of galvanised steel construction and affectionately called the "Tin Mission". Situated in the middle was a coal stove which used to smoke the meeting out if the wind blew in a particular direction, making it almost impossible to see the preacher in the pulpit! Mr. D. R. Llewellyn of 'Fairfield', Aberdare, allowed members to use thousands of bricks from the old Gadlys brick kilns, the site of the former National Welsh Bus Depot, Gadlys. After the bricks were cleaned they were packed on to a station trolley and transported to the main road to Cwmdare. Tyssul Davies assisted with his horse and cart in bringing the bricks and other materials to the site. Cwmdare Mission Hall was officially opened on March 8th. 1920 by Mrs. D. R.

Cwmdare Mission Hall. "The Mission", as it was once called, was the result of a Movement began in 1911 to provide a place of worship for Nonconformists in Cwmdare to worship in English. In this photograph, the overhead wires can be seen which powered the trolley buses which once ran up and down the hill, at the bottom of which one had to change to a tramcar.

Llewellyn and Mother Shepherd was also present to represent the Salvation Army. The gates were given in memory of Mrs. Ann Jane Harrison by her daughter Lady Marian Williams and Dame Phyllis Harrison. During building works services were held at the Harrison's home at Harrisonville. In 1950, Rev. Jack Sands, a converted boxer, was a frequent visitor at the Mission when young people saw the need of a personal saviour.

Mr. Islwyn Jones, contractor, Hirwaun, built a new hall in 1950 followed by extensive renovations in 1960. In the early 1970's Keith Gardner supervised the young people's work under the title of "The Pioneers". The Mission Hall was further refurbished in 1971 and in 1976 a new extension was built under the supervision of Mr. Nicholas Hullett. In the 1940's & 50's the notable evangelists David Matthews, Jack Sands and Jack Bell preached at the Mission and Elim chapel was borrowed for the entire week. In 1973, 1975, & 1977 the prominent Welsh evangelist Rev. David Shepherd preached here. Band of Hope and Singing Schools were regularly held along with occasional Prayer Meetings at the lodging house in Abernant Road. Pastors include – Pastor Joe Griffiths, 1961 – 1974; Pastor Haydn Rule 1974 – ??; he was formerly Butchery Manager at Aberdare Co-operative Society. Treasurers include – David Edwards, 1920; Laurence Seldon – 1940 – 1969. The first organist was Benji Jones; the present (2004) Pastor is Rev. Jeffrey Gilbert B.A. History booklet (19 pages) entitled "70 years of Witness" – 1911 to 1981, is in Aberdare Central Library.

CHAPEL REF. NO. 135.

NAME & DENOMINATION: **ELIM. W. CONG.**

ADDRESS / LOCALITY: **BWLLFA ROAD, CWMDARE.**

DATE BUILT: **1859. ENLARGED 1868. REBUILT 1902.**

CURRENT USE: **CLOSED 1998 – VACANT 2004.**

BRIEF HISTORY: Architect of 1902 chapel – Charles Thomas, Abertawe. Builders – Messrs. Jones Brothers, Barry. Built at a cost of £500, with seating for 550. The 'cause' commenced chiefly as a result of the great Religious Revival that swept through the Cynon Valley and the whole of Wales in 1859. Fifty members were 'released' in 1859 from Ebenezer, Trecynon (Ref: 127.) to establish a Welsh Congregational chapel in Cwmdare. Elim is a branch of Ebenezer. The Welsh Congregationalists formed the branch at Cwmdare in 1859 and built a vestry; in August 1867 a new chapel was opened, this being above the vestry and named 'Elim'. The chapel was rebuilt and re-opened in May 1903; it was set back a little further from the road than the old chapel. Formerly named 'Particular Baptist'. Memorial stone laid on 11th. August 1902 by Rees Llewellyn,

Elim, Cwmdare.

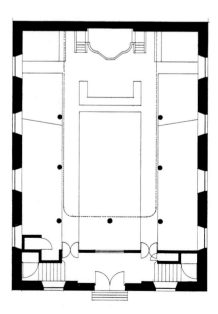

Bwllfa House, Cwmdare and J. W. Evans of Gyereithiwr, Hirwaun. First minister – Abraham Matthews (1859-60. b.1832 – d.1899.); he became one of the pioneers of the Welsh Settlement in Patagonia and emigrated to there in 1865, he also ministered at Horeb W.I. (Ref: 139.). Rev. Hugh Hughes ("Huw Tegai") – 1860 –1862, also ministered at Bethel, Gadlys 1962 – 1868. Rev. David Griffiths, 1869 – 98. Rev. William Aneurin Jenkins 1920 – 30. Rev. David Owen Davies ministered here from 1961 until his retirement in 1981; he died 20th. October 1989. The chapel has a plain façade built in local pennant dressed and coursed stonework, with round-headed door and window openings. The two manual pipe organ is located at the side of the pulpit within the upper gallery area.

This charming picture shows the assembly of The Annual Sunday School Demonstration, circa 1910, taken outside Elim. On the extreme right the members of Nebo are also forming up in Bwllfa Road.

Elim, Cwmdare, 1986.

CHAPEL REF. NO. 136.

NAME & DENOMINATION: HOPE SUNDAY SCHOOL. W.B.

ADDRESS / LOCALITY: BWLLFA ROAD, CWMDARE.

DATE BUILT: 1858.

CURRENT USE: CONVERTED TO A DWELLING HOUSE

BRIEF HISTORY: A branch of Nebo W.B. (Ref: 137.) and opened September 12th. 1858. Shown on the 1868 Town Survey Plan as now being No's 78 – 79 Bwllfa Road, and opposite No. 32. The Welsh word for 'Hope' – Gobaith, became the name of the new Welsh Baptist chapel built in 1875 (Ref: 138.).

CHAPEL REF. NO. 137.

NAME & DENOMINATION: NEBO. W.B.

ADDRESS / LOCALITY: BWLLFA ROAD, CWMDARE

DATE BUILT: 1858 – REBUILT 1867 & 1900, FAÇADE REBUILT 1950

CURRENT USE: DEMOLISHED MARCH 1977, DETACHED HOUSE ON SITE. ADJACENT TO 'Y MANS' HOUSE.

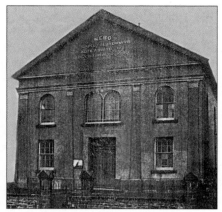

Nebo Cwmdare, circa 1900.

BRIEF HISTORY: This chapel was located adjacent to No. 29 Bwllfa Place and opposite No's 8 & 9 Dare Road. The 'cause' commenced in 1856 by holding prayer meetings and a Sunday school, later in September 1858 a small chapel was opened and formed into a church in 1860. Originally baptisms were carried out in the Nantmelyn stream, and later in the River Dare below the Dare Inn, before making use of a pool built outside the new chapel. A larger chapel was built on the same site in 1867. Built by D. Bevan of Hirwaun at a cost of £1,800, 'old' Nebo had seats for 500 and was originally named 'Particular Baptist'; an infant's school and 'British School' for boys and girls was attached at the rear of the chapel. The façade of the chapel was rebuilt in 1950 at a cost of £1,200, A new organ was installed in 1954 – supplied by Victor Freed, Aberdare. This Selma Lincoln electric organ replaced the old reed instrument that had served for thirty years. Membership in 1911 was 155, with 180 in Sunday School. Ministers include – Rev. William Harris, 1867 – 1871; Rev. Joseph Evans, 1872 – 1877; Rev. William Thomas, 1882 – 1907; Rev. William Aerwyn Jones ("Jones Nebo"), 1909 until his death in 1951. The chapel was demolished in 1977 and members took over Gobaith W.B., which was renamed Nebo Newydd (New Nebo) – (Ref: 138.).

Nebo, Cwmdare. In the process of demolition in 1977.

CHAPEL REF. NO. 138.

NAME & DENOMINATION: NEBO NEWYDD. W.B. FORMERLY GOBAITH. C.M.

ADDRESS / LOCALITY: CWMDARE ROAD, CWMDARE.

DATE BUILT: 1861 – REBUILT 1875 AND 1907 – REFURBISHED 1977.

CURRENT USE: STILL ACTIVE.

BRIEF HISTORY: The original building at the beginning of this 'cause' was Hope (Gobaith) Sunday School (Ref: 136.). This chapel was built in 1861 as a result of the effects of the Religious Revival of Dafydd Morgan in 1859. Mordacai Jones, proprietor of Nant Melyn Colliery allowed stones to be taken from Nant Melyn to rebuild the chapel in 1875; it was built by John Morgan, Aberdare, for £800, and later rebuilt in 1907. The 1907 chapel was designed by Thomas Roderick, Aberdare, and cost £2,500. It is located at 'Gobaith Terrace' opposite the Primary School. 'Old Nebo' W.B. (Ref: 137.) was demolished in 1977 and members there took over Gobaith C.M. and renamed it Nebo Newydd (New Nebo). It was refurbished in 1977 to become the new 'home' of the Welsh Baptists, opened by Rev. J. Clement Davies of Newcastle Emlyn. The stone name plaque on the side of the chapel reads – "GOBAITH CALVINISTIC METHODIST 1875".

A superb pipe organ made by Blackett and Howden; reconstructed in 1977 by Morgan & Lloyd, Organ Builders, Aberdare. It occupies almost the width of the chapel. Sunken baptismal bath with railed surround. Fine pulpit, magnificent ceiling rose. Rev. Thomas Powell was minister from 1906 – 1936. 1931 membership was 305 – 1966 membership 71.

History in Welsh (14 pages) is in Aberdare Central Library.

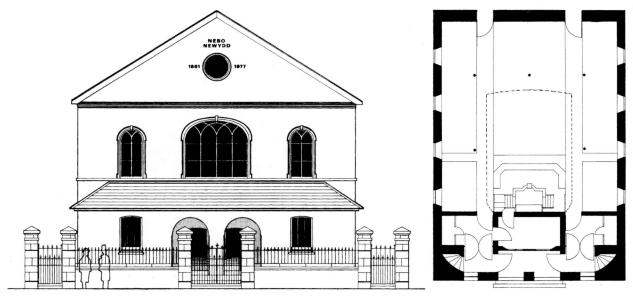

Nebo Newydd, Cwmdare.

Nebo Newydd, formerly Gobaith C.M. was provided with a porch in 1907 after this photograph was taken (1973). Following the demolition of Old Nebo in 1977 the chapel was re-named "Nebo Newydd", the new home of the Welsh Baptists in Cwmdare

Nebo Newydd, Cwmdare, taken in 1986. A plaque reads – "A Gorwyd (opened) gan y Parch J. Clement Davies of Castell Newydd Emlyn Mai 12th 1977".

CHAPEL REF. NO. 139.

NAME & DENOMINATION: HOREB. W.I.

ADDRESS / LOCALITY: HOREB TERRACE, LLWYDCOED.

DATE BUILT: 1859 – RENOVATED 1933.

CURRENT USE: STILL ACTIVE.

BRIEF HISTORY: The 'cause' was founded in 1846. In 1859 members transferred from Ebenezer W.I. (Ref: 127.) and built Horeb at a cost of £800, to seat 350. The vestry at the rear was formerly a 'British School' maintained by voluntary contributions, it was the original school for Llwydcoed from 1871 until 1890, renovated in 1933 at a cost of £200. At this time (2004) services for a small gathering of members are held in the vestry at the rear. The well-known and accomplished Llwydcoed Brass Band hold practice sessions in the vestry. On display is a white marble memorial plaque in memory of Rev. William Samlet Davies, of 23 Windsor Villas, Trecynon, minister here for 52 years from 1871 to 1923; he died in 1923 aged 82. The first minister was Rev. Abraham Matthews of Bala Collage 1859 – 65; he left for Patagonia in 1865 and was succeeded by Rev. Thomas of Abercanaid, 1865 – 1871. He was also minister at Elim W. Cong. (Ref: 135.). Rev. D.J. Warlow was minister 1936 –1951, and also a County Councillor. Membership in 1890 was 195 with 180 in Sunday School; 1905 – 222 with 272 in Sunday School; 1914 – 193 with 167 in Sunday School, and 1930 – 214 members.

Horeb, Llwydoed, 1986.

Horeb, Llwydcoed.

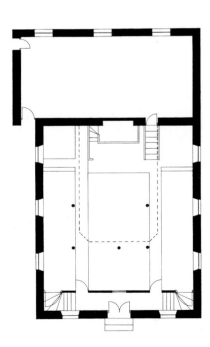

CHAPEL REF. NO. 140.

NAME & DENOMINATION:	**MORIAH, W.C.M.**
ADDRESS / LOCALITY:	**BRYN MORIAH (MORIAH PLACE) LLWYDCOED.**
DATE BUILT:	**1843 – REBUILT 1852 – RENOVATED 1891.**
CURRENT USE:	**CLOSED CIRCA 1980; FOR SALE 1986; DEMOLISHED 1988; DWELLING NAMED 'MORIAH BUNGALOW' BUILT ON SITE 1992.**

BRIEF HISTORY: The original chapel built in 1843 at a cost of £400, was demolished circa 1851 to make way for the Merthyr to Hirwaun railway line. The new 1852 chapel was re-located and built lower down the road in Moriah Place. It was again rebuilt on the same site in 1891. Located next to No. 14; a plain smooth rendered façade with little embellishment. Seating for 450 with gallery on three sides, almost square on plan. Front vestibule entrance with staircase both sides to gallery. Rev. Margam Jones was minister of Moriah for twenty years, he was also a renowned poet and philosopher.

The Religious Census of 1851 states – *"Moriah, Llwydcoed, Calvinistic Methodist. Erected 1839 space free 16; other 72; standing 150; present morning 135; afternoon 111; scholars evening 148; average (2 months) morning 140; afternoon 115; evening 140. – Edward Pugh (his mark) Deacon and Farmer, Llwydcoed.* [Authors note – other sources suggest building date to be 1843.]

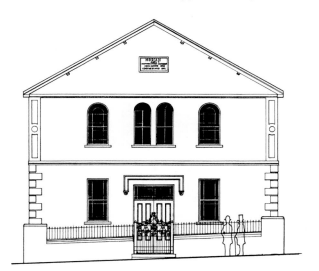
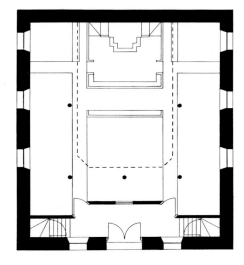

Moriah, Llwydcoed.

The original Moriah Chapel built 1843. The first chapel in Llwydcoed.

(Jean John and Russell John)

Moriah Chapel circa 1930. Rebuilt 1891. Demolished circa 1980.

(Jean John and Russell John)

CHAPEL REF. NO. 141.

NAME & DENOMINATION: SOAR. W.B.

ADDRESS / LOCALITY: KINGSBURY PLACE, LLWYDCOED

DATE BUILT: 1859 – REBUILT 1873.

CURRENT USE: **CLOSED EARLY 1980'S – FOR SALE 1986. DEMOLISHED 1996; DETACHED HOUSE BUILT ON THE SITE 2004.**

BRIEF HISTORY: The 'cause' commenced in 1847 in the house of Thomas Dyke of Llwydcoed; first Sunday School held in Miners Row in 1855; members also held services in the house of William and Mayonel Davies, Pentrebach, and at the house of Evan Thomas, Blacksmith, until the chapel was eventually built in 1859, with seating for 380. The first minister was Rev. Daniel Jones 1876 – 98, a deacon sent from Heol-Y-Felin, W.B. (Ref: 130.) other ministers include – Rev. D.G. Price, 1900 – 1907; Rev. Vaughan Pugh, 1907 – 1920; Rev. Christmas Jones, 1838 – 1954; and Rev. D. Meredith Morgan. First precentor was Simon Thomas, 1857 – 59, also from Heol-Y-Felin W.B. The vestry attached at the side was built in 1892 at a cost of £300. 80 members in 1911

with 60 in Sunday School. Between 1911 & 1947, membership was 82 – 52; with 90 in Sunday School in the 1930's. The chapel design was simple with a long sloping roof to one side; lime mortar rendered with a wide front porch. Located adjacent to No. 8 Kingsbury Place.

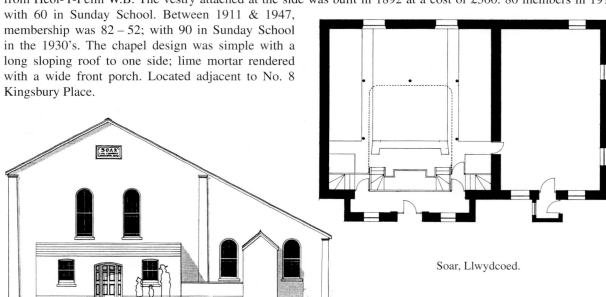

Soar, Llwydcoed.

Taken circa 1920. Demolished in 1996.

CHAPEL REF. NO. 142.

NAME & DENOMINATION: BETHEL. P.C. (NOW 'REHOBOTH')

ADDRESS / LOCALITY: HEOL BRYN GWYN, PENYWAUN.

DATE BUILT: 1954.

CURRENT USE: STILL ACTIVE.

BRIEF HISTORY: Located adjacent to St. Winifred's Church in Wales, and next to No. 45 Heol Bryn Gwyn. The 'cause' began with a small group from the Hirwaun Mission Hall holding open-air meetings in Penywaun in the late 1940's. They also held meetings at Cana W.I. chapel (Ref: 143.). In 1949 they held services in the old former Welfare Hall adjacent to Cana chapel and opposite No. 12 Gwladys Street. As the village and population of Penywaun developed and expanded, membership increased, swelled by new converts to the Gospel, along with a thriving Sunday School, which in the 1960's reached a peak of 200. In the early 1950's they purchased a plot of land from the Aberdare Urban District Council, and built the present church; the foundation stone was laid on 1st. July 1954. The church was built at a cost of £3,000; the contractor was Mr. R. Davies. Bethel Pentecostal Church was re-named Rehoboth, which translates to "the Lord has made room for us". It was re-named in 1996 with the arrival of the present minister, Pastor W. Stewart. The church was also at some time called "Four Square Gospel Church". Present membership (2004) is 20.

Bethel (now Rehoboth),
Penywaun, 1995.

CHAPEL REF. NO. 143.

NAME & DENOMINATION: CANA. W.I.

ADDRESS / LOCALITY: GWLADYS STREET, PENYWAUN.

DATE BUILT: 1856 – ENLARGED 1892.

CURRENT USE: CLOSED 1994. MAJOR CONVERSION INTO A COMMUNITY CENTRE, 1995-7, AT A COST OF £300,000 THROUGH THE PENYWAUN ENTERPRISE PARTNERSHIP. RENAMED 'CANA CENTRE'.

BRIEF HISTORY: A small schoolroom/vestry was built first in 1856 at a cost of about £40, followed by the chapel built on in 1892. Seating for 100, building cost -£353. Memorial stone laid by Margaret Haig Thomas, Llanwern, on 11th. April 1892. Formerly a branch of Ebenezer W.I. (Ref: 127.). New vestry added, built in 1907 at a cost of £600. First minister was Rev. J. Grawys Jones (1885-

1925) also minister of Ebenezer, Trecynon; he travelled to Cana chapel on horseback from stables at the rear of the Ebenezer chapel house, 'Bryngafael', in Cemetery Road, Trecynon. The horses were owned by his next-door neighbour and were hired out mainly to Bwllfa Colliery. In 1887 Ebenezer donated a harmonium to Cana (cost-£16.), it remained there until the chapel closed in 1994. Members now worship at the vestry of St. Winifred's Church in Wales, Penywaun.

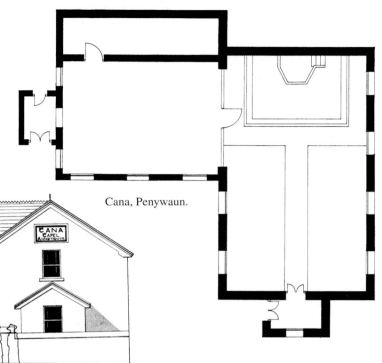

Cana, Penywaun.

Taken in 1986.

CHAPEL REF. NO. 144.

NAME & DENOMINATION: **BETHEL (OLD). W.C.M.**

ADDRESS / LOCALITY: **BETHEL PLACE, HIRWAUN.**

DATE BUILT: **1823 – REBUILT 1836 & 1856. ENLARGED 1893.**

CURRENT USE: **DEMOLISHED LATE 1960'S – 'NEW' BETHEL BUILT ON SITE 1974 (SEE REF: 145.)**

BRIEF HISTORY: Located next to the old former No. 8 Bethel Place. The 'cause' commenced in 1806 when services were held in a house provided by Mr. George Overton. In 1822 a house in Merthyr Road, Hirwaun, was licenced for preaching by the W.C. Methodists and also the Baptists. Prior to 1823 meetings were also held in 'Capel Harris', but during the year they felt the need to build a chapel of their own. A spot was chosen above the river at Heol-y-Felin. Women carried stones from the riverbed in their aprons or in baskets on their heads, whilst the men built the walls. There were 30 members in 1823. The chapel then accommodated 120 worshippers; it had an earthen floor, and was not paved. Enlarged in 1836, enlarged again in 1856, redesigned by Rev. Evan Harris of Merthyr, benches provided in 1866. The expansion of the Welsh Calvinistic Methodists was originally led in Hirwaun by a shop-keeper named Evan Griffiths, who later moved to Aberdare (Ty Mawr).

A Deed dated 1823 and endorsed 'Bethel, Hirwaun' states:- *"That the Marquis of Bute leased a plot of land to the* Methodists *on 2nd. February 1823."* It contains a covering clause as follows:- *"In the event of the ironworks at Hirwaun ceasing to be carried on, an allowance of a moiety of the rent shall be made during the period of the stoppage or discontinuance of the works"*. The chapel obtained a licence to worship on 26th. November 1824; with 36 founder members and accommodation for 120. In 1823 Bethel was built at a cost of £678, with seating for 600. The Religious Revival of 1829 boosted numbers with 140 new members. The prime instigator of the move of Aberdare Calvinistic Welsh Methodists from Pentwyn Bach was Evan Griffiths.

The vestry was built in 1893 and the chapel was renovated at a cost of £1,700. Formerly, a graveyard existed at the rear. This burial ground became very full with victims of the Cholera Epidemic of 1849. First minister was Rev. Edward Matthews, Cardiff, in 1829. Rev. W. Josiah Williams – 1866 – 1912. Rev. David Teify Davies – 1916 – 1943. Architect Mr. Thomas of Glandwr designed the 1836 chapel, building cost was £500. Prominent members include – The Bevan family; Mathews of Ewenny, and David Watkins Jones, better known as Dafydd Morgannwg. The 1851 Religious Census states – *"Bethel, erected 1823. Space free 160; other 183; standing 57. Members present – morning 213 scholars; general congregation 271; scholars 230. – Signed, Morgan Davies, Elder, Grocer."*

Centenary booklet 1823 – 1923, written by Rev. David Teify Davies (31 pages) is at Glamorgan Record Office. 1823 – 1973 history booklet by Dilwyn Roderick, B.A., is at Aberdare Central Library.

Old Bethel, Hirwaun, circa 1910.

Bethel Place and Old Bethel Chapel, circa 1972.

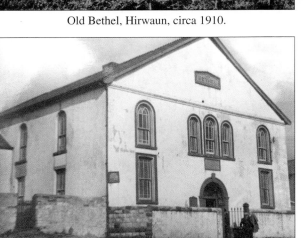

Bethel, Hirwaun. Circa 1960.   *(John F. Mear)*

Hirwaun undertaker, Rees Overton Jones, looks proudly at his new hearse as it passes Bethel Chapel, circa 1900.

(C.V.H.S.)

CHAPEL REF. NO. 145.

NAME & DENOMINATION: BETHEL (NEW). W.C.M.

ADDRESS / LOCALITY: BETHEL PLACE, HIRWAUN.

DATE BUILT: 1974.

CURRENT USE: CLOSED IN THE LATE 1990'S, CONVERTED TO PROVIDE A SPACIOUS DETACHED DWELLING 2000.

BRIEF HISTORY: Built in 1974 to replace 'old' Bethel (Ref: 144.) which was demolished in the late 1960's. Opened on 14th. January 1975, a brick built structure comprising chapel, vestry, kitchen and toilets. Fell into disrepair and was forced to close late 1990's. As a result of closure members worshipped temporarily in Mount Pleasant E.C. (Ref: 149.), but eventually joined Nebo W.I. (Ref: 150). The original stone name plaque of the 'old' Bethel, dated 1823-1836-1856 (Ref:144.) has been incorporated into the boundary wall of the newly converted house. The new chapel served its purpose for less than 25 years. Its membership (old chapel) was 500 in 1931, and (new chapel), 143 in 1965.

CHAPEL REF. NO. 146.

NAME & DENOMINATION: BETHESDA, A.C.

ADDRESS / LOCALITY: HIRWAUN ROAD, HIRWAUN.

DATE BUILT: CIRCA 1950.

CURRENT USE: DEMOLISHED LATE 1960'S. SITE OCCUPIED BY PRIVATE HOUSE NAMED 'RAVENDELL'.

BRIEF HISTORY: Located adjacent to Gamlyn Terrace, a branch of Trecynon Apostolic Church. (Ref: 123.). Members from Trenant, Trewaun, Penywaun attended this chapel as well as those from Hirwaun. Prior to the chapel opening circa 1950, meetings were held at the Old Meeting Hall near the Police Station, Hirwaun.

Thanks to Mr. & Mrs. Gareth Davies for their help with this script.

CHAPEL REF. NO. 147.

NAME & DENOMINATION: ENGLISH WESLEYAN, E.W.M.

ADDRESS / LOCALITY: PENYARD ROAD, HIRWAUN.

DATE BUILT: 1876.

CURRENT USE: STILL ACTIVE.

BRIEF HISTORY: An offshoot of Soar W.W.M (Ref: 152.) The only English Wesleyan Methodist chapel in Hirwaun. Founded by a group of Trustees from the English Wesleyan Methodist chapel in Green Street, Aberdare (Ref: 107.). The chapel was officially opened on 17th. October 1876. Meetings of the Welsh Wesleyan Methodists (Ref: 152.) had already been taking place as early as 1824 in Hirwaun prior to the building of this English section of the Wesleyan Methodists. In 1876 the chapel was served by ministers of the Aberdare Wesleyan Methodist Circuit. The freehold of the ground was generously left to the Trustees by the owner of the Bodwigiad Estate in his will dated 1925; however there were difficulties regarding the mines and mineral rights, but this was resolved in 1932 and the freehold handed over to Rev. H.G. Humphreys.

The chapel had a thriving Band of Hope; Youth Club; Wesley Guild; Boys Brigade; an excellent Sunday School and 'Sunshine Corner'. The organist in 1976 was Charles Donnelly; chapel conductor was G. Collier, founder of the well-known 'George Collier Choir'. The chapel at one time had an orchestra which accompanied the singing. The main chapel closed in 1986 and became a builder's store in 1990; consequently the members now hold their services in the vestry. Harmonium organ by Estey Organ Co., of Battleboro, Vermont, U.S.A. Ministers include – Rev. J. James; Rev. William Harris; Rev. T. Lloyd Rees; Rev. D.H. Brenton and Rev. D.C. Williamson.

Taken in 1986.

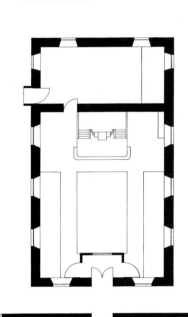

English Wesleyan Chapel, Hirwaun.

CHAPEL REF. NO. 148.

NAME & DENOMINATION: **MISSION ROOM. M.R.**

ADDRESS / LOCALITY: **HIGH STREET, (AND OTHERS) HIRWAUN.**

DATE BUILT: **CIRCA 1890**

CURRENT USE: **DEMOLISHED CIRCA 1950**

BRIEF HISTORY: Was located behind Hirwaun Community Centre, and at the rear of No.5 High Street, off/near 'Penhow'. Shown on the 1900 Ordnance Survey map. A zinc-clad Pentecostal Chapel was built near the Pandy Pond, Hirwaun, circa 1950-60, supervised by Pastor Cole – (no connection with the aforementioned Mission Room). The 'Peniel Pentecostal Mission' was founded in 1902 and located off Merthyr Road, Hirwaun. The 'Free Pentecostal Mission' of Hirwaun opened in 1938 and local enquiries suggest it was named 'Jerusalem Pentecostal Church'.

CHAPEL REF. NO. 149.

NAME & DENOMINATION: **MOUNT PLEASANT. E.C.**

ADDRESS / LOCALITY: **HARRIS STREET, HIRWUN.**

DATE BUILT: **1866.**

CURRENT USE: **STILL ACTIVE.**

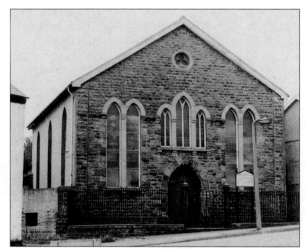

Taken in 1986.

BRIEF HISTORY: Founded in 1864; founder members were D.E. Williams J.P.; William Williams of the London Warehouse; and Daniel Joseph Davies, Carpenter. Located adjacent to No.17 Harris Street. Parent chapel of Nebo W.I. (Ref: 150.). Built in 1866 to cater for the influx of English speaking workers/ immigrants who came to the place to work in the extensive and long-established ironworks, the chapel opened on 26th. December 1866. The drive to set up the new chapel was supported by affluent businessmen and colliery officials of Hirwaun who subscribed generously; D.E. Williams, J.P., gave £300; William Williams of Bryncynon gave £200.... Etc. First meetings were held in 1864 in the Long Room of the Belle Vue Inn, Cross Street, and later in the larger Long Room of the Beehive Inn, 44 High Street; opened 1844, closed 1922, as numbers expanded meetings were transferred in June 1866 to the British School Room. Several members left Nebo W.I. (Ref: 150.) to help the new 'cause', and soon the chapel was built at a cost of £1,150, of Gothic appearance with seating for 300 and a small rear gallery where also the pipe organ was located, installed in 1870. The first minister was Rev. Daniel Jones of Brecon College (1866 – 1869); he left for Providence E. Cong. (Ref: 60.), where he ministered from 1869 to 1871. The second minister was Rev. D.M. Lewis M.A., 1876 – 1900. The last minister was Rev. George Arfyn Thomas. Original cast-iron railings to forecourt, date of chapel (1866) in a simple wooden plaque fixed to the front door. Baptismal font is from St. David's E.P. (Ref: 111.). Attractive ceiling rose in pink, brown, cream and yellow. Centenary booklet 1866 – 1966 is held at Aberdare Central Library and Glamorgan Record Office, Cardiff.

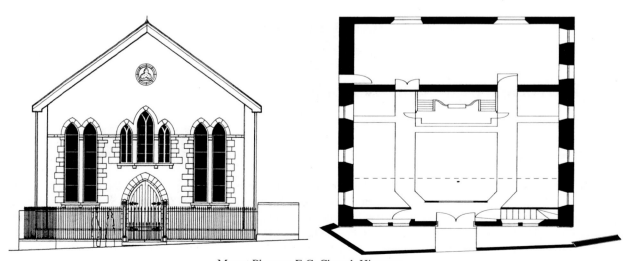

Mount Pleasant E.C. Chapel, Hirwaun.

CHAPEL REF. NO. 150.

NAME & DENOMINATION: NEBO. W.I.

ADDRESS / LOCALITY: MERTHYR ROAD, HIRWAUN.

DATE BUILT: 1823; ENLARGED 1836; REBUILT 1851; RENOVATED 1890.

CURRENT USE: STILL ACTIVE.

BRIEF HISTORY: The oldest Non-conformist chapel in Hirwaun. They met first in the early 1800's in a house provided by George Overton, in the early 1820's they held services in 'Capel Harris' and in 1823 built Nebo. Parent chapel of Tabernacle W.I. (Ref: 153.), and Mount Pleasant E. Cong. (Ref: 149.). Workers from home and away came to the Hirwaun Ironworks to seek employment, and also from other ironworks at Aberdare, Gadlys, and Llwydcoed. They strove to meet and worship together in a new chapel they could call their own. The Congregational Union of England and Wales was formed in 1832, and by 1851 a larger chapel was built at a cost of £1,100, with seating for 800. 250 members in 1853 with 200 in Sunday School. The formation and building of a Welsh Independent chapel in Hirwaun was encouraged by Thomas and Joseph Harrison of Ebenezer W.I. (Ref: 127). A 'split' occurred in 1879 when members broke away from Nebo and in 1881 they erected Tabernacle W.I. (Ref: 153.). The chapel is located adjacent to the club and No.1, formerly the Crawshay Arms public house, 53 High Street, (opened 1835, closed 1919.) First minister was Rev. Joseph Harrison (1823 – 1835); followed by Rev. William Williams (1841 – 1877 died 1877 aged 70); Rev. J. Rhydybont Williams (1878 – 1888); Rev. E. Wern Williams (1890 – 1924); Rev. Efonwy Hughes was minister in the 1930's; Rev. G. Stanley Davies (1950 – 1965). Minister from 1969 Harri Williams. The chapel was known as 'Pen-Nebo' at one time. A graveyard exists within the chapel grounds, and contains many victims of the 1849 Cholera

Taken in 1986.

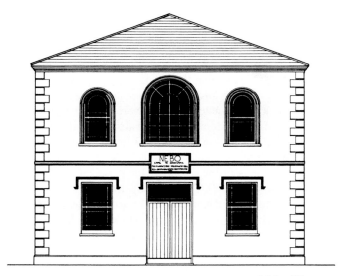
Nebo, Hirwaun.

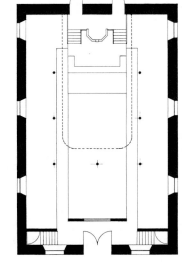

epidemic. History of Nebo 1823 – 1973 in Welsh, 12 pages, by Rev. Harri Williams is held at Aberdare Central Library. Religious Census of 1851 states – *"Erected 1821* (Author's note – other sources say 1823) *Space free 105; other 540; standing 420; present – morning 433 +260 scholars, afternoon 280 scholars, evening 500. – David Evan Williams, Deacon, 'Bristol House', Hirwaun."*

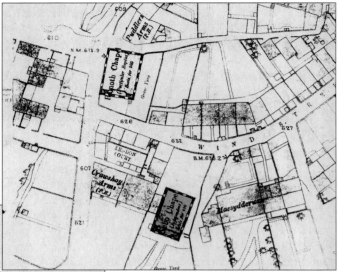

1868 Survey Plan showing Nebo, Hirwaun.

Nebo, Hirwaun, taken circa 1900.

CHAPEL REF. NO. 151.

NAME & DENOMINATION: **RAMOTH. W.B.**

ADDRESS / LOCALITY: **TREVENOCK PLACE, HIRWAUN.**

DATE BUILT: **1825; REBUILT 1840 & 1867; REFURBISHED 1994.**

CURRENT USE: **STILL ACTIVE.**

BRIEF HISTORY: The Religious Census of 1851 states that the chapel was – *"Ramoth, Hirwaun, erected in 1825 space free 213. Standing 210. Present; morning 275; afternoon 220 scholars; evening 340. Benjamin Evans, Minister, Hirwaun."* Four denominations were in Hirwaun as at 1806. The 'cause' commenced in 1811 in a house owned by Mr. George Overton of the Hirwaun Ironworks. In 1825 the chapel opened with 50 members, and was licenced for worship in August 1830. Ramoth was originally the 'daughter' chapel of Calvaria W.B. (Ref: 104.) until 1834, and 'mother' chapel of Heol-Y-Felin (Ref: 130.). At one time it was named 'Particular Baptist'. The costs of building are as follows – 1825 chapel – £250; 1840 chapel – £700. Designed by Rev. William Lewis, Aberdare. 1867 chapel £1,200. Designed by Rev. H. Thomas, Briton Ferry, with seating for 500. The chapel was built primarily to meet the needs of the ironworkers at Hirwaun. Ministers include – Rev. William Lewis – 1826 to 1834 (of Calvaria, Aberdare). Rev. Thomas G. Jones – 1835 to 1837; Rev. Benjamin Evans – 1842 to 1857; Rev. Evan John Hughes – 1923 to 1955 (died 1961 aged 70). There were eleven ministers between 1826 and 1955. Membership numbers – 50 in 1826; 97 in 1840; 165 in 1846; by 1849 membership increased to 178 as a result of the Religious Revival of that period; 194 in 1857; 524 in 1904 with 900 in the Sunday School! The high adult and children numbers are due to the 1904/5 Religious Revival, which had a marked effect in Hirwaun and elsewhere in the Cynon Valley. 40 were baptised during 1904. The beautiful pipe organ was installed in 1913 at a cost of £350, paid for by a grant from Andrew Carnegie. The chapel has a fine interior; grand boarded ceiling with a large centre rose beautifully decorated; high class plaster ceiling coving; pews have been removed and replaced with movable chairs. The gallery is intact. The old former 'Puddler's Arms' public house (built 1841 – closed 1907) stood directly behind the chapel and later became No.28 Trevenock Place. A graveyard exists at the side of the chapel and contains many victims of the Cholera Epidemic of 1849. A document at the Glamorgan Record Office indicates – *"Registration of a Meeting House for use as a place of worship by Particular Baptists, Hirwaun, 15th. June 1826."* History of Ramoth dated 1913, by Rev. A. S. Evans (112 pages in Welsh) is held at Aberdare Central Library. The chapel closed as a Welsh Baptist chapel in 1982, refurbished in 1994 with the aid of a council grant, and reopened named 'Assemblies of God'.

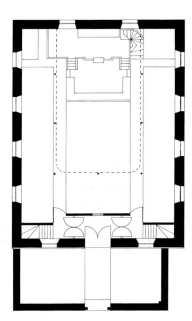

Ramoth, Hirwaun.

Taken in 1986.

In this photograph taken circa 1900, Ramoth is to the left and Nebo to the right. In between is the old Crawshay Arms Public House, 53 High Street, Hirwaun. The pub opened circa 1835 and closed in 1919.

CHAPEL REF. NO. 152.

NAME & DENOMINATION: **SOAR. W.W.M.**

ADDRESS / LOCALITY: **STATION ROAD, HIRWAUN.**

DATE BUILT: **1824 –REBUILT 1837 & 1886.**

CURRENT USE: **CLOSED 1977; DEMOLISHED DECEMBER 1981. SITE VACANT 2003. PART OF ST.THERESE OF LISIEUX R.C. CHURCH IS BUILT ON THE SITE.**

BRIEF HISTORY: The 'society/cause' was formed in 1805 by Rev. Edward Jones. Early meetings were held in an old barn located in Station Road where Renowden's Boot Repairers shop once stood. The first (1824) chapel was built by voluntary labourers, many belonging to the Bryant family. In 1837 the first chapel was converted into cottages and a new chapel built adjacent on the present site at a cost of £550, with seating for 260. The original chapel was of long wall façade design. David Davis of Blaengwawr (b.1797 – d.1866), grocer and owner of the 'London Warehouse' at 41/42 High Street, Hirwaun, was a leading member and was instrumental in the building of the 1837 chapel. He later moved to Blaengwawr where he there opened the colliery in 1843, and also a colliery at Ferndale. Minor improvements carried out in 1860; chapel rebuilt 1886 and opened by Master Frederick Lewis

Soar, Station Road, Hirwaun, circa 1905.

Davies, grandson of David Davies. Rent income from the 1824 chapel cottages was used to support the 'cause'. Until the building of the Sunday School in 1894, the school was held at the old barn of Renowden's Boot Shop. A graveyard once existed at the side of the chapel and contains many victims of the Cholera Epidemic of 1849.

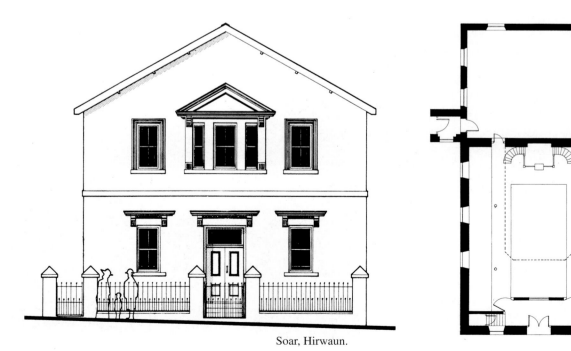

Soar, Hirwaun.

When the chapel closed in 1977 members transferred to the English Wesleyan chapel in Penyard Road. (Ref: 147.) and soon after a new Catholic Church was built on part of the site. In 1853 there were 450 members and 120 in the Sunday School. The chapel was located opposite St. Lleurwg's Church in Wales. The former Aberdare and Hirwaun Tramway was located behind Soar chapel. Religious Census of 1851 states – *"Erected before 1825 (author's note – actually erected 1824) space free – 240; other –180; standing-80; present morning 7 scholars; afternoon 111; evening 120. – Lewis Davies, Chapel Steward, Hirwaun."* On a stone tablet set high in the centre of the long wall façade of the 1824 chapel were the words – (translated from Welsh) – *"Wesleyan Chapel – Soar built Nov. 1824. Keep thy foot when thou goest to the House of God; for to draw nigh to hear is better than to give the sacrifice of fools. Ecclesiastes – 5"*.

The original Soar chapel on the right was built in 1824. Rebuilt 1837. The chapel on the left was built in 1886.

Soar Chapel. Rebuilt 1886.

CHAPEL REF. NO. 153.

NAME & DENOMINATION: **TABERNACLE. W.I.**

ADDRESS / LOCALITY: **BRECON ROAD, HIRWAUN.**

DATE BUILT: **1839 – REBUILT 1881.**

CURRENT USE: **CLOSED, OCTOBER 1970 – DEMOLISHED CIRCA 1972; HOUSE NO. 65 BUILT ON THE SITE.**

BRIEF HISTORY: Located adjacent to 'Hafod' bungalow. The 'cause' initiated in May 1839 by Rev. Joseph Harrison. A small chapel was built and named 'Capel-y-Drindod' (i.e. Trinity Chapel). W.I. This stood for only six years 1839 – 1845; it became too small and was converted into two houses named "Tai'r Capel". Much later, in 1879, a split occurred in Nebo W.I. (Ref: 150.), a section of over 100 members broke away and formed a new chapel near the old Victoria Hall, which later became the Billiard Hall, located behind the Palace Cinema. In 1881 Tabernacle was rebuilt to seat 400 worshippers; the foundation memorial stone was laid in June 1881 by Mr. Dafydd Evan Williams J.P. (died 1903 – buried in Penderyn), and Mrs. Williams. The first minister of the second chapel was Rev. Thomas Edmunds of Brecon

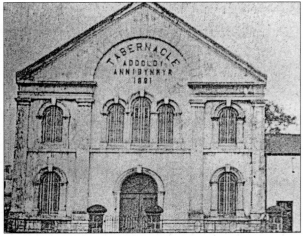

Tabernacle, Hirwaun, circa 1910.

College, 1885 – 1907, followed by Rev. Dervel Roberts, 1907 – 1917; Rev. E. Cefni Jones, and Rev. Benjamin Evans D.D. 157 members in 1882; in 1963 there were only 16 members. Tabernacle closed in 1970 with only 12 members and no minister; last service held on 22nd. October 1970. When the chapel was demolished in 1972 the foundation memorial stones were taken to Soar Chapel, Penderyn (Ref: 162.). Most of the furnishings were given to other chapels in Hirwaun; the organ went to a chapel in Ytradfellte. Tabernacle had a fine classical façade; broken pediment; semi-circular arch on three windows, with nameplate depicting 'TABERNACLE ADDOLY ANNIBYNWR 1888', this was inscribed below and within the arch. Thanks to Mr. Stephen Morris for his help towards part of these notes; he was the last treasurer of this chapel. Mrs. Gwyneth Jones was the last secretary.

Tabernacle and the street scene, Brecon Road, Hirwaun 1905.

Members gather outside Tabernacle, circa 1910.

CHAPEL REF. NO. 154.

NAME & DENOMINATION: **ZION (OLD). E.B.**

ADDRESS / LOCALITY: **FOUNDRY ROAD, HIRWAUN.**

DATE BUILT: **1900.**

CURRENT USE: **DEMOLISHED 1985.**

BRIEF HISTORY: The 'cause' commenced 1899 when a small gathering met in the house next door to Zion, occupied by the Bound family. Later services were held in the back of the Beehive public house – "*A nice little room – and we put a pulpit in it*" (quote by founders). The site of the 'Beehive' is now occupied by the Hirwaun library. Zion was built/opened February 1900, builder James Lee, Manchester. Seating for 110. A wooden frame with corrugated zinc sheets and affectionately known as "Zion Zinc". First minister was the evangelist Rev. G Harries, 1900 – 1903; Rev. Cefni Jones (Pastor of Ramoth, died 2000, aged 90); Rev. J. Edwards, 1931 – 1960; Rev. David Amos Thomas, 1960 to present (2002). Treasurers – Mr. S. Meadon, 50 years; Mr. W.L.L. Davies, 46 years. Secretaries – Arthur Weston, 20 years; Mrs. M.

"Old" Zion, Hirwaun, ("Zion Zinc") circa 1910.

Smith 33 years to date. Organists – Mr. S.H. Bennett, 20 years; Mr. Martin Thomas, 1990 to date. Membership – 1916 – 30; 1930 – 20; 1947 – 22. Sunday School averaged 40 – 70, 1916 to 1947.

CHAPEL REF. NO. 155.

NAME & DENOMINATION: **ZION (NEW). E.B.**

ADDRESS / LOCALITY: **FOUNDRY ROAD, HIRWAUN.**

DATE BUILT: **1986.**

CURRENT USE: **STILL ACTIVE.**

BRIEF HISTORY: One night in 1984 a devastating storm shook old 'Zion Zinc' and caused structural damage; it was soon decided the building was so unsafe it needed urgent attention. Old Zion was therefore demolished, and 'New Zion' was built in 1986 on the same site. It was built by Mr. Rossiter (S.R.G.) contractor of Hirwaun, at a cost of £1,500; Most of the cost was borne by only 12 members, who donated generously. This is a brick-built structure with seating for 120, located between 5 & 6 Foundry Road and near the Towers and Beacons multi-storey flats (demolished May 2004). Membership in 2002 is 36, with no Sunday School. Mrs M. Jones, a deacon of this chapel, will be 100 years old in December 2002.

"New" Zion, Hirwaun, 1995.

CHAPEL REF. NO. 156.

NAME & DENOMINATION: **BETHEL. W.M.**

ADDRESS / LOCALITY: **MOUNT ROAD, RHIGOS.**

DATE BUILT: **1839; REBUILT 1860; ENLARGED 1905**

CURRENT USE: **STILL ACTIVE.**

BRIEF HISTORY: The 'cause' began by holding services in the stable loft of Hendre Fawr, then in a house on The Bryn, circa 1800, and later at Penrhiw in 1805. In 1839 the members built a small chapel (18ft. by 12ft.) and named it 'Bethel'. It was rebuilt in 1860 on its present site, cost £214, carpentry £101, masonry £25. The chapel is simple and plain in design and located in a quiet pleasant rural setting, adjacent to Brick Yard farm, Cefn Rhigos. The chapel was described in the 'Aberdare Times' 1861 as being – *"A small but neat and substantial building"*. There is seating for 120, no gallery; the boarded ceiling is quaint in appearance with a small star-shaped centre rose set in a circular wood frame. The chapel was enlarged in 1905 (lobby

Taken in 1990.

added) building work done by Dan Jones of Hirwaun. A small devoted gathering of 10 members continue to worship here. Treasurer – for 50 years Glyn Rees (aged 88); organist for 50 years was Mrs. Mary Gwen Rees (died circa 1970), and the harmonium organ she played was built by Bridgeport Organ Co., Connecticut, U.S.A. Thanks to Mr. Evan John Jones, secretary since 1990, for preparing part of this historical account. In 1995 the circuit minister was Rev. Pamela Cram, English born, learnt Welsh especially for conducting services in Welsh. 52 members in 1878 – 14 in 1890 – 79 in 1945 – 23 in 1995.

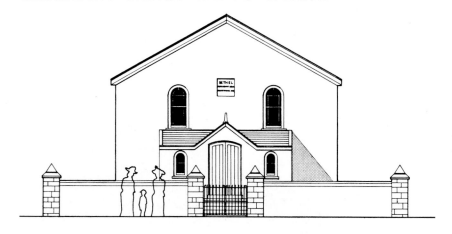

Bethel, Rhigos.

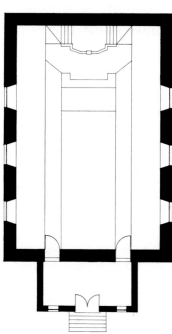

CHAPEL REF. NO. 157.

NAME & DENOMINATION: CALFARIA. W.I.

ADDRESS / LOCALITY: CWM ISSAC, RHIGOS.

DATE BUILT: 1844. REBUILT 1860. ENLARGED 1906.

CURRENT USE: CLOSED NOV. 2002 FOR SALE FEB. 2004. POSSIBILITY OF HOUSING DEVELOPMENT IN THE FUTURE

BRIEF HISTORY: The founding of the chapel in 1841 was assisted by members from Nebo W.I. (Ref: 150.); meetings were held in the house of Morgan Morgan. Land was given by the Marquess of Bute. A small vestry/hall (School Room) was built in 1844 for Prayer Meetings and occasional preaching, and up to 1872 it was used as a schoolroom. Located near Heol-Y-Graig. Ministers include – Rev. Williams (1841 – 1866); Rev. J. Jenkins (1919 – 1930). The last minister, Harry Williams ministered here from 1950 until 1983. Rev. J. Griffiths was a past minister. The chapel has fine pitch pine pews; gallery on three sides terminating on a curve to the wall. Handsome coloured capitals to gallery pillar supports, attractive ceiling rose. Seating for 550 (1906 chapel). The chapel was enlarged in 1906 by builder Dan Jones of Foundry Road, Hirwaun; he was also an undertaker and died in 1940. 1890 membership was 81; 1914 was 125; 1930 was 119. The old chapel (1841) was known as 'Capel-Y-Comin'. Last service held in November 2002, the members continue to worship in a nearby private house.

Old Post Card showing Calfaria, circa 1905.

Calfaria, Rhigos.

CHAPEL REF. NO. 158.

NAME & DENOMINATION: BETHEL (OLD). W.B.

ADDRESS / LOCALITY: YNYSFELIN, PENDERYN.

DATE BUILT: 1799 – REBUILT 1866.

CURRENT USE: DEMOLISHED 1914.

BRIEF HISTORY: The 'cause' commenced in 1793 with members from Seion Baptist Chapel, Merthyr Tydfil meeting regularly at Penpont Farmhouse, Cwm Taf, and later in a house at Ynysfelin. They built Bethel in 1799. This chapel is worthy of attention here even though no longer falling within the boundaries of Cynon Valley. However the chapel was formerly in the Parish of Penderyn but was demolished as a result of the construction of Llwyn Onn Reservoir which took place during the period 1914 – 1927. Now in the Parish of Vaynor. Ministered to for over sixty years by Rev. David Owen Davies, up to his death in 1853 aged 88.

"Old" Bethel, Ynysfelin, Penderyn, circa 1910.

CHAPEL REF. NO. 159.

NAME & DENOMINATION: BETHEL (NEW). W.B.

ADDRESS / LOCALITY: YNYSFELIN, PENDERYN.

DATE BUILT: 1927.

CURRENT USE: STILL ACTIVE.

BRIEF HISTORY: The 'new' Bethel was built in 1927 to replace the old Chapel lost under the aforementioned reservoir.

"New" Bethel, Ynysfelin, Penderyn, circa 1930.

CHAPEL REF. NO. 160.

NAME & DENOMINATION: **JERUSALEM. W.C.M.**

ADDRESS / LOCALITY: **CHAPEL ROAD, PENDERYN**

DATE BUILT: **1857 – RENOVATED 1908.**

CURRENT USE: **CLOSED 1986 – CONVERTED INTO 'JERUSALEM HOUSE', A PRIVATE RESIDENCE, 1989**

BRIEF HISTORY: Located adjacent to No.8 Chapel Road. Longwall façade design; plain but interesting layout. Pulpit close to the surrounding pews on all three sides, seating for 200 including gallery on one side at the rear. Chapel entered from side foyer. There were very few local founders of the chapel; most were farmers and quarrymen who came from outside the area. People came to work in the Foel Quarry, Penderyn, thus creating a need for a Methodist chapel in the area.

Jerusalem, Penderyn.

Jerusalem, Penderyn, 1986.

Name Plaque, Jerusalem.

CHAPEL REF. NO. 161.

NAME & DENOMINATION: **SILOAM. W.B.**

ADDRESS / LOCALITY: **PONTBREN LLWYD, PENDERYN**

DATE BUILT: **1823 – REBUILT 1857.**

CURRENT USE: **STILL ACTIVE.**

BRIEF HISTORY: The 'cause' commenced in 1823. The founders were from Ynysfelin, Cwm Taf, and local Penderyn farmers. One of the early ministers was Rev. Richard Howells, a Penderyn farmer, and also Rev. Gwilym Owen, son of 'Penderyn' who worked in Llwyn Onn Quarry and was helped and encouraged through Theological College; he later became president of the United School Movement. Siloam Chapel was rebuilt in 1857 at a cost of £450; architect was David Bevan of Hirwaun. 150 members in 1851 and 50 in the Sunday School. The Religious Census of 1851 states – *"Siloam Particular Baptist, erected about 1823, space for 150, average attendance – morning 60 + 51 scholars; evening 105. Details supplied by Rev. Daniel Evans, Minister, Penderyn."*

Ministers include Rev. Daniel Evans -1851; Rev. E. J. Hughes, B.A. – 1927 to 1961. Religious Revivals in 1828/29 boosted membership. Mrs. Valerie Owen, organist from 1960 to present day (2004), and is also secretary. Mrs. Elizabeth Mary Evans was secretary for over 30 years, died 1998 aged 94 years. 11 members at 2002. Note the Canadian manufactured harmonium with "mouse-proof pedals"! – Patented 24th. February 1887. The chapel is located near the Community Centre and Infants' School. A grave yard exists to the front and side of the chapel.

Siloam, Penderyn.

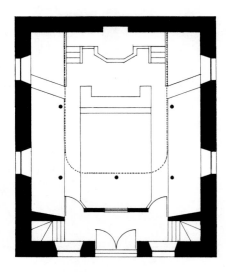

Siloam, Penderyn, 1986.

Old Post Card showing Siloam, circa 1900.

CHAPEL REF. NO. 162.

NAME & DENOMINATION: **SOAR. W.I.**

ADDRESS / LOCALITY: **CHAPEL ROW, PENDERYN.**

DATE BUILT: **1860 – REBUILT 1912.**

CURRENT USE: **CLOSED 1983 – USED AS A STORE BY 'TECLA' MUSIC PUBLISHERS.**

Soar, Penderyn, 1995.

BRIEF HISTORY: The founding of this chapel was assisted by Nebo W.I. (Ref: 150.), with the help of Rev. William Williams. First minister was Rev. Evan M. Evans, 1866 – 1873 (b.1817 – d.1882). Located near the Lamb Hotel. The pews, gallery and pulpit remain intact despite the chapel being used for storage purposes. The chapel interior has an attractive ceiling; original cast iron railings to the front forecourt; note – the gallery, built in 1873, unusually has no pillar supports and is cantilevered and believed to be the only one of its type in the Cynon Valley. Seating for 500. Many worshippers from Penderyn originally had to travel to Hermon W.I. chapel in nearby Ystradfellte, but soon they felt the need to build a Welsh Independent chapel of their own; they therefore built Soar W.I. chapel in 1860 at a cost of £270. An influx of quarrymen, ironworkers and rail workers from Carmarthenshire and nearby in the 1850's boosted the need for a Welsh Independent chapel in Penderyn. Soar was the main venue for concerts and Eisteddfodau etc., as it is the largest chapel in Penderyn. The 1912 chapel was designed by Mr. Thomas Roderick, Aberdare, whose fee was £45, and the builder was Mr. Dan Jones of Foundry Road, Hirwaun – he was also an undertaker and died in 1940; building cost was £883. History booklet 1860 – 1960, 34 pages in Welsh by Rev. Elwyn P. Howells, Cwmgwrach, is in Aberdare Central Library and Glamorgan Record Office, Cardiff. Thanks to Mrs. Nansi Selwood for contribution to part of these notes. Please refer to 'Hanes Plwf Penderyn' by Dewi Cynon for further history of Penderyn.

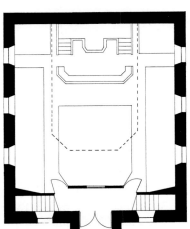

Soar, Penderyn.

Deacons of Soar, Penderyn. Circa 1900.

CHAPEL REF. NO. 163.   Christadelphian Ecclesia, Aberaman.   See Ref: 39a.

CHAPEL REF. NO. 164.   Christadelphian Ecclesia, Aberdare.   See Ref: 39b.

CHAPEL REF. NO. 165.   Salvation Army Hall, Aberdare.   See Ref: 62a.

CHAPEL REF. NO. 166.   Salvation Army Hall, Aberaman.   See Ref: 62b.

CHAPEL REF. NO. 167   Salvation Army Hall, Rhigos.   See Ref: 62c.

CHAPEL REF. NO. 168.   Salvation Army Hall, Cwmaman.   See Ref: 62d.

CHAPEL REF. NO. 169.   Salvation Army Hall, Ynysybwl.   See Ref: 62e.

CHAPEL REF. NO. 170.   Bryn Moriah (Ysgoldy), Yr Annibyniwr
                                  Bryn Moriah Sunday School,
                                  Welsh Independent, Cwmaman.   See Ref: 90a.

CHAPEL REF. NO. 171.   Islamic centre, Robertstown.   See Ref: 122a.

CHAPEL REF. NO. 172.   Apostolic Church, Aberaman.   See Ref: 123a.

CHAPEL REF. NO. 173.   Apostolic Church, Cwmbach.   See Ref: 123b.

CHAPEL REF. NO. 174.   Apostolic Church, Abernant.   See Ref: 123c.

CHAPEL REF. NO. 175.   Apostolic Church, Mountain Ash.   See Ref: 123d.

CHAPEL REF. NO. 176.   Apostolic Church, Hirwaun.   See Ref: 123e.

CHAPEL REF. NO. 177

NAME & DENOMINATION: **THE MORMON CHURCH. M.**

ADDRESS/LOCALITY: **HIRWAUN, ABERDARE & CWMBACH**

DATE BUILT: **1838–1845**

CURRENT USE: **NO LONGER IN EXISTENCE IN THE CYNON VALLEY.**

BRIEF HISTORY: **HIRWAUN BRANCH.** The Mormon Church, known as the 'Church of Jesus Christ Of Latter Day Saints' commenced their missionary activities in the Cynon Valley in 1838, making Merthyr Tydfil their headquarters, under the leadership of William Henchman and Captain Dan Jones. The first and earliest branch of the Mormon Church in the Cynon valley was established in Hirwaun; The 'cause' commenced in 1838 with 74 members (62 Welsh, 12 English speaking) at the Pandy, Tabernacle Row, located behind the present Glancynon Inn; They named their new church 'Tabernacle' – not to be confused with Tabernacle W.I., Hirwaun. (Ref: 153.) Morgan Evans, who lived in Hirwaun, was in charge of the church which catered for both Welsh and English speaking members. The Religious Census of 1851 states the following:-

> *"Tabernacle, Penderin (i.e. Hirwaun) latter Day saints. Morgan Evans and George Roger, English speaking, and John Davies for the Welsh section, Hirwaun. Erected (founded) 1838. Space free 500. Standing 50"*

In 1849 the president of the Hirwaun branch was Daniel Evans and there were 59 members. In 1850 the Hirwaun branch moved to the 'Patriot Arms' public house (closed 1928) located at 66 High Street, at the lower end of the street near the school where now there are flats. The Hirwaun church was licenced as a place of worship for the Mormons on 15th January 1850. By the early 1850's there appears no mention of this church at Hirwaun as Welsh Mormons joined their fellow worshippers in America in the 1850's.

ABERDARE BRANCH. The Mormon Church at Aberdare was established as part of the Merthyr district church. The 'cause' commenced in 1844 and started by holding meetings and services in the 'Welsh Harp Inn' located at 5 Commercial Street, Aberdare, and was the residence of Mr. Phillip Rees; This public house was opened in 1835 and closed in 1916, the site is now occupied by Woolworths Store. The Aberdare branch did not become licenced as a place of worship for the Mormons until 4th October 1848. One of the most prominent Aberdare Mormons around 1844–47 was William Howells, who later became a missionary in France in 1847. The Religious Census of 1851 states:-

"Latter Day Saints (Mormon Church) Aberdare. Space free 200. A spacious room adjoining another building, but not used exclusively as a place of worship. They meet on Sunday and other evenings of the week and will not contain more than 200 seated"

In 1849 the President of the Aberdare Branch was Joseph Davies, and there were 150 members. In 1847 there was a combined total of 85 Mormons in the branches of Hirwaun, Aberdare and Cwmbach. (The Religious Census, 1851 states there were 250 Mormons at Hirwaun, Aberdare and Cwmbach.) By 1854 the number rose to 277 members. However, the numbers continued to decline from around 1860 and by circa 1880 there was no trace of them anywhere in the Cynon Valley. Throughout this period and before, many members had already emigrated to America and joined the thriving Mormon Church at Salt Lake City, Utah, founded in 1847 by their president Brigham Young. Mormons were noted for their claim to spiritual gifts, particularly the gift of prophecy. The late Rev. Ivor Parry M.A. (1908–1975) informs us of an event in 1845 which appears to substantiate this claim; He tells us that a number of Mormons were employed at Powell's No. 1 Pit, Cwmbach (also known as Old Duffryn Colliery – opened 1840, closed 1901). It appears that one of them was warned in a vision not to attend work on a certain day in 1845; on this same particular day 28 lives were tragically lost in the colliery and it was claimed not one of the number was a Mormon; It was reported that they kept away from the colliery as advised through the vision of one of their members. (Reference source – "Theirs is The Kingdom" by W. J. Ashton – Salt Lake City – 1945). Another account written by the late Rev. Ivor Parry tells us that in 1849 a party of Mormons from Aberdare, under the leadership of Captain Dan Jones, emigrated to America in the "Buona Vista" liner. Stories abound concerning the rough Atlantic sea passage and the number of people who became ill during the voyage. Later, in 1852, a party of Mormons sailed to America including some from Aberdare. It was confirmed that some of them had dubiously become Mormons before embarking on their journey in order to obtain cheap passage fares with the help of "The Saint's Permanent Emergency Fund for New Orleans and St. Louis". Upon discovering their illegitimate and crafty motive they were promptly ex-communicated aboard ship! The prominent local historian W. W. Price (Watkin William Price M.A. 1873–1967) tells us that the Mormon Church held meetings at Soar W.M. Aberdare (Ref: 114) in 1956. In the 1950's & 1960's attempts were made to revive the Mormon Church in Aberdare, but this proved unsuccessful and short-lived, and never fully materialised. In 1960 two young American Elders of the Church of Latter Day saints came to Aberdare with the intention of voluntarily setting up a branch of their Movement. For a while they held weekly meetings on Sundays at the Aberaman Lesser Hall, and also a Youth Club called The Mutual Association. They were Dennis Encanbrack (aged 20) of Utah, and Clyd Merritt (aged 19) of Wyoming. They lodged at Pembroke Street, Aberdare where they stayed until 1962, returning to America afterwards to continue their studies. They spoke of the strong branch of the Mormon Church in Aberdare around 1844–1880, but as a result of mass emigration of the local branch to America around that time, there had been no established branch in the town at least since 1880. Despite their efforts a branch never materialised in the town, nor in any other part of the Cynon Valley during the twentieth century.

CWMBACH BRANCH. Little is known about this branch other than that in 1849 the President was a Mr. John Price, and there were 68 members.

A BRIEF HISTORY OF THE MORMON CHURCH – WORLDWIDE. The Mormons are members of a Christian sect known as "The Church of the Latter Day Saints" founded in Fayette, New York in 1830 by Joseph Smith (1805–1844). He received his first religious call in 1820, and in 1827 claimed to have had a 'vision' and had been granted the divine revelation of "The Book of Mormons" from an ancient North American prophet, and inscribed on gold plates concealed a thousand years before in a hill near Palmyra, New York State. Joseph Smith translated and published the 'Book of Mormon' on 6th April 1830. The church structure is hierarchical and authoritarian; Offices are staffed by lay members presided over by the Bishop and his two Councillors. The hierarchy is headed by the President, known as the Prophet. In 1844 Joseph Smith and his brother Hyrum were assassinated by an angry mob, due to Smith's assumption of monarchical powers and that Mormons practiced polygamy (abolished in 1890). Mormonism continues to thrive as a world-wide, rapidly growing religion. The church has its headquarters in Utah, western U.S.A., known as the "Mormon State" – the capital is Salt Lake City. The church has a worldwide membership of over eight million followers. Nearer to home, the Merthyr Mormon Church was formed in the late 1830's and by 1845 had gained at least 5,000 members.

The Religious Census of 1851 records 28 congregations of Mormons in Wales. In 1848, 249 Welsh Mormons emigrated to Salt Lake City, Utah, where the famous Tabernacle Choir had its origin among their number; Other groups followed and Mormonism in Wales declined as a consequence of this emigration. In 1949 there were about 25,000 Mormons of Welsh descent in America and there is an excellent collection of genealogical material relating to Wales. The Merthyr Church continues in being to this day, a thriving movement.

CHAPEL REF. NO. 178.   Jewish Synagogue, Aberdare. In the past the Jewish community in Aberdare met at their Synagogue in Seymour Street.

CHAPEL REF. NO. 179.   Brethren Meeting Room, Trecynon.   See Ref: 125a.

CHAPEL REF. NO. 180.   Church of Christ, English Baptist, Godreaman.   See Ref: 85a.

Name Plaque, English Congregational Chapel, Abercynon.

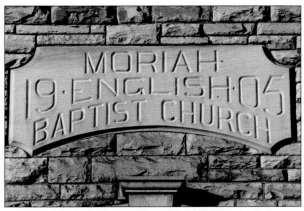

Name Plaque, Moriah E.B., Abercynon.

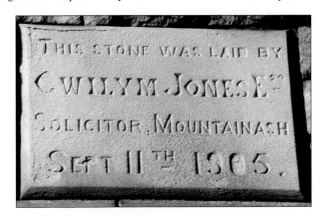

Memorial Stone, 1905,
Moriah E.B., Abercynon.

Interior, Moriah E.B., Abercynon.

Name Plaque, Bethel W.I., Miskin.

Name Plaque, Bryngolwg E.F.C., Miskin.

Memorial Stones, Bethel W.I., Miskin.

Bethel, W.W.M., Penrhiwceiber, 1904.
(Centenary photograph).

Coloured Post Card, Bethesda E.B.,
Penrhiwceiber, circa 1910.

Hermon W.C.M., Penrhiwceiber, dominating the valley scene, 1995.

168

Carmel W.I., Penrhiwceiber, 1993.

Bethel W.I., Miskin, 1994.

Bryngolwg E.F.C. (formerly The Mission Hall), Miskin,
1995

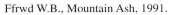

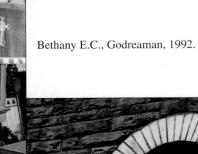

Ffrwd W.B., Mountain Ash, 1991.

Ffrwd Ysgoldy, W.B.M.R., Mountain Ash, 1991.

Bethany E.C., Godreaman, 1992.

Name Plaque, Bethany E.C., Godreaman.

Gwawr W.B. (formerly Hebron C.M.), Godreaman, 1995.

Bethel P.M., Cwmaman, 2002.

Bethania W.B., Cwmbach, 1965.

Bryn Seion W.I., Cwmbach, 1986.

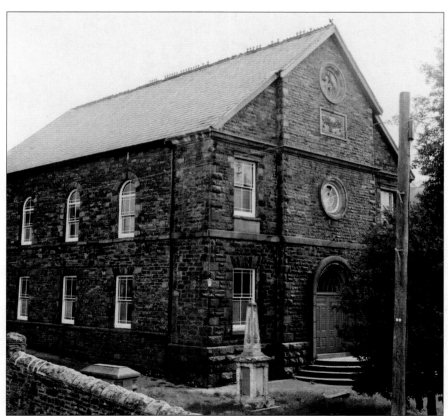

Calvaria W.B., Aberdare.

Green Street E.W.M., Aberdare 1995.

Elim P.C., Aberdare, 1986.

Highland Place Unitarian Church, Aberdare, 1995.

Carmel E.B., Aberdare, circa 1960.

Gadlys W.B., Gadlys, 1995.

Water colour painting, Gadlys W.B. Chapel, Gadlys. Painted by E. Morris 1894.

Bethel W.B., Abernant, 1995.

Salem W. Cong., Robertstown, 1990.

Bethesda W.I., Abernant, 1986.

Water colour painting, Carmel C.M., Chapel, Trecynon. Painted by E. Harris 1888.

Pentwyn Gospel Hall, Trecynon, 1995.

Window detail, Ebenezer W.I., Trecynon, 1995.

Water colour painting, English Wesleyan
Chapel, Trecynon. Painted by E. Morris,
1888.

Ebenezer W.I., Trecynon, 1995.

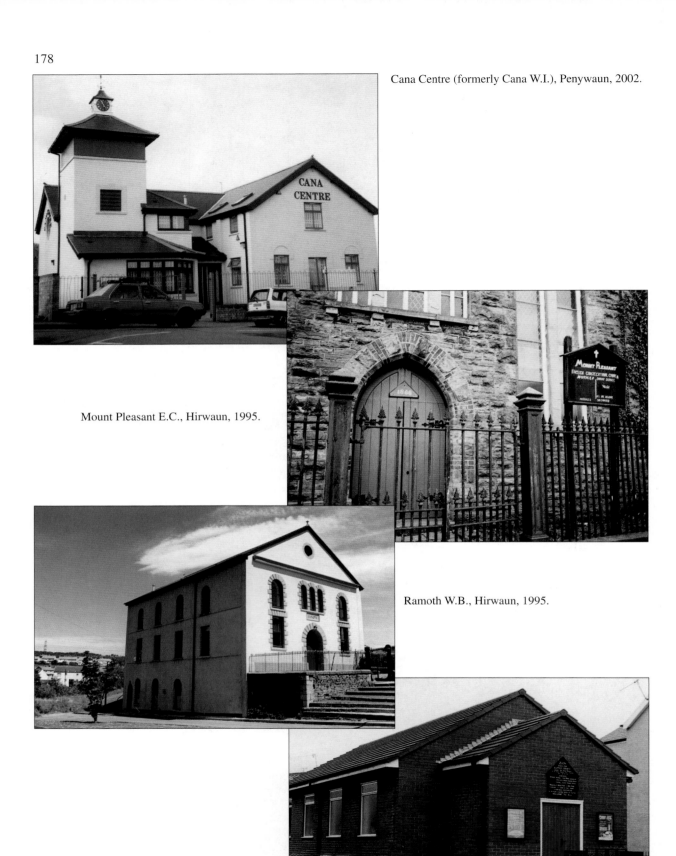

Cana Centre (formerly Cana W.I.), Penywaun, 2002.

Mount Pleasant E.C., Hirwaun, 1995.

Ramoth W.B., Hirwaun, 1995.

Zion E.B., Hirwaun, 1995.

Bethel W.M., Rhigos, 1990.

Soar W.I., Penderyn, 1995.

Siloam W.B., Penderyn, 1995.

Soar W.W.M., Hirwaun, circa 1960.

Doug Williams.

Rear of Soar W.W.M., Hirwaun, circa 1960.

Doug Williams

Chapter 2.

THE HISTORY OF NONCONFORMITY AND DISSENT
IN THE CYNON VALLEY 1642 TO 1920

Page No.

(i)   The Blaencanaid Conventicle 1642 –1689   181

(ii   Cwm-y-Glo Chapel 1689-1749   183

(iii) Separation From Cwm-y-Glo Chapel 1747-1751   185

(iv) Hen Dy Cwrdd Unitarian Chapel, Trecynon. Founded 1751. Rebuilt 1862   186

(v)   A Brief Outline of the Early Nonconformist Chapels of the Cynon Valley. 1751-1841 186

(vi) The Period of Persecution and Suppression of Dissent. The Various Acts 1661-1689 187

(vii) Relations Between the Established Church and Nonconformity 1850-1920   189

"Until now, The Lord has helped us."
– Protestant Dissenters, October 9th 1829.

Welsh to English translation of the chapel stone plaque
of Ebenezer W.I., Trecynon.

(i) The Blaencanaid Conventicle 1642-1689

Why and how did Nonconformity reach the Cynon Valley – resulting in a massive building programme
of chapels, which started in 1751 when the first Nonconformist chapel Hen Dy Cwrdd (The old Meeting
House) was founded in Trecynon? This chapter examines the local dissenters or nonconformists of the
seventeenth century up to 1920 when, in part (vii), we shall deal with the relationship of the
nonconformists and the established church in the Cynon Valley. The early Puritans and Dissenters
refused to conform to the principles, doctrine and practice of the Established Anglican Church. It was out
of this defiance to conform that they became commonly known as 'Nonconformists'.

Nonconformist chapel history in the Cynon Valley is complex and goes back over 360 years from 1642.
This was the period of the reign of King Charles I, 1625-1649, and the early part of the rule of the Lord
Protector, Oliver Cromwell. Reliable sources confirm that Nonconformity in and around our locality
began in humble and remote surroundings in the beautiful hillsides of the Merthyr Mountain between
Abernant and Heolgerrig over the Mynydd Aberdare (Aberdare Mountain) boundary. The earliest known
meetings were held in secret in an old barn of a farmhouse in the small village of Blaencanaid located half
a mile south of Heolgerrig and two miles north east of Abernant. The farm house was situated on the
Merthyr side of the ridge which separates the two valleys of Aberdare and Merthyr. The earliest known
evidence of this first conventicle in the locality is well documented as being in 1642 and certainly existed
circa 1655-60 when records confirm the Merthyr District and the neighbouring parishes of Vaynor and
Aberdare as being a focus of Puritan and Nonconformist religious activity. This was during a period just
three years after the first known Independent, Welsh nonconformist chapel was established in 1639 in
Llanfaches, near Newport, Monmouthshire by William Wroth, (died 1641), a native of Abergavenny, who
in 1617 became rector of Llanfaches, (source – "cofiadw 1923"). In 1649 the first Baptist Chapel in Wales
was established at Ilston on the Gower Peninsula.

In a converted barn attached to the lonely and secluded farmhouse at Blaencanaid about half a mile
from Cwm-y-Glo, a group of dissenters from Aberdare and Merthyr gathered together in 1642 to meet
and worship discreetly and in secret. This was their first meeting place. The history of the Blaencanaid

Conventicle from 1642 onwards is furnished only with the barest outline of information. Some sources state that the members were here for a period after 1642, whilst some tell us that they worshipped here until circa 1660. However the chance of it being in existence from as early as 1620 as some historians have written appears to be extremely doubtful, as the first Nonconformist chapel in Wales is widely claimed to be that of the Independent chapel at Llanfaches, Monmouthshire, founded in 1639.The old Blaencanaid farmhouse owned by a Nonconformist farmer was a little frequented spot where the founder leader and minister was Howell Lewis a Baptist minister, with, according to the late Rev. Ivor Parry, "a party of highland tribesman about him". He later left for Hengoed. His members had made an early home in this secluded retreat and many stories were told over the years of the courage of these early pioneers and the persecution they had to suffer from the early 1600's to around 1690 and, to a lesser degree, for some time after. By around 1670 it was estimated that there were already 300 to 600 people attending secret conventicles in Merthyr Tydfil.

Sometime between 1642 and the late 1660's, or as some sources state, "soon after 1642", the Dissenters left the Blaencanaid Conventicle and moved to another remote old barn at Cwm-y-Glo farm. This secret meeting place was part of a fairly large gabled farmhouse occupied by a Presbyterian farmer who allowed dissenting worshippers to use one of his empty barns as a conventicle. The hay in the barn was especially set aside on Sundays to accommodate the worshippers who stood throughout the services without fire to warm themselves on cold winter days, and they needed to wrap their feet in straw to keep warm. During the service others kept watch outside in all weathers to warn their fellow members of the approaching danger of any unwanted visitors. They continued their meetings in secret, forever mindful of the risk and danger of persecution and arrest. Such fears restricted their freedom of worship and they were forced to remain watchful and alert, knowing that they were always at risk of being betrayed by informers. Guards kept watch around and near this secret meeting place to avoid discovery by the authorities, both secular and ecclesiastical. They met only to hear the Word of God, often without official ministers or clergymen; they merely wanted to hold prayer meetings and simple services without harassment and to be free to worship in accordance with the teachings of the New Testament. They would meet at night to avoid being caught and were at all times vigilant and alert for the sound of the dreaded footsteps of informers. They would therefore have to worship quietly, without partaking in song for fear of hostile ears listening nearby.

This was a difficult period in the early religious life of the district and arduous years for Dissenters and Nonconformists. It was a time of trouble and persecution for those who exercised dissent and dared to be at variance with the Established Anglican Church and who did not conform to the requirements of the various Acts in force during the period 1660-1690. The Acts are described in detail in part (vi) of this chapter.

In his 167 page manuscript entitled "The History of Aberdare", written circa 1965 but never published – (copy at Aberdare Central Library) – the late Rev. R. Ivor Parry (1908-75) records in Chapter 13 the events surrounding the Blaencanaid Conventicle. He tells us that the earliest evidence of the beginning of Nonconformity and its rise in the vicinity of the Cynon Valley was established in the upper reaches of the Neath Valley and in Breconshire. The culture of the Cynon Valley was directly influenced by the social and religious activities of the area from Craig-y-Llyn to the Brecon Beacons. Rev. Ivor Parry further writes that Nonconformity came to the Aberdare Valley from such nearby places as Blaengwrach, Cwm-y-Glo and the afore-mentioned village of Blaencanaid where dissenting worshippers from Aberdare travelled over the mountain to meet in secret.

In the year 1665, the Nonconformists of the Parish of Aberdare became affiliated to a widely scattered puritan church in Breconshire, where meetings and services were held surreptitiously in remote places or in very small groups of not more than five persons in accordance with the terms of The Conventicle Act of 1664 This forbade the holding of any large gathering for worship except in the Anglican and Established form. The earlier Act of Uniformity 1662 was also aimed at the suppression of Dissent and limited the freedom and scope of Nonconformist worshippers thus forcing the early Dissenters to leave the Established Church. It was from this refusal to conform that Nonconformity came into being during the seventeenth century. Wherever larger gatherings took place the results were usually disastrous resulting in severe harassment and persecution. This is borne out by the "Episcopal Returns of 1669 – Diocese of Llandaff, Merthyr Tydfil Parish". In 1669 Vavasour Powell (b.1617-d.1670), a native of Knucklas in Radnoshire and one of the leading pioneers of Welsh Nonconformity, came to Merthyr where word got around and a congregation of some one thousand people gathered in the church yard. The rector, Rev. George Jones immediately reported this occurrence to the Deputy Lieutenant of the county, Edmund Thomas of Wenvoe, and confirmed that Powell was accompanied by a band of armed men. Powell was apprehended at his lodgings in Merthyr and was arrested by Major John Carr and taken to Cardiff and later Cowbridge, then to the Court of Pleas in London. He was committed to the Fleet prison where he died in 1670 aged 53. As early as April 1660, Powell was imprisoned by Sir Matthew Price, High Sheriff of Montgomeryshire for preaching in Welshpool. Powell spent a total of eleven years in thirteen different prisons. His crime was that he preached the Gospel in public without a licence to do so. He was a forceful and dynamic character and a powerful preacher and would travel a hundred miles a week drawing in large congregations in spite of the repressive measures laid down by the Clarendon Code of 1662, which imposed severe sentences and penalties on those who refused to conform to the Established Church.

Returning to the chapels of yesteryear, Rev. Ivor Parry states that at the other end of the valley on the side of the old road from Rhigos to the Neath valley was the Unitarian chapel of Blaengwrach. Services in this early Nonconformist Conventicle had been conducted there since the 1690's, (some sources indicate earlier, circa 1670) but the chapel was not built until 1704 and erected by Protestant Dissenters. The date of 1704 could be seen carved on a timber beam over the fireplace as late as 1857. Around this same period there is increasing evidence of the rise of Nonconformity in the areas immediately adjacent and surrounding the Cynon Valley. Further afield is the only Nonconformist chapel that still exists intact in anything like original form, converted from a cow house in 1696 and registered as a chapel in 1697, at Maesyronnen, Glasbury, Hay on Wye. This chapel was used as a conventicle before 1696 and known as a "barn chapel". Llanwenarth Baptist Chapel was established at Govilon in Monmouthshire in 1695 and enlarged circa 1750, and with Maesyronnen, these two are the oldest surviving Nonconformist chapels in Wales. Capel Groes Wen, near Caerphilly, built in 1742, was the first Calvinist Methodist chapel in Wales. Another example is Capel Pen-Rhiw (Unitarian); this chapel was converted from a barn in 1777 with the addition of a gallery and a high pulpit for the preacher. Originally located at Drefach, Felindre, Dyfed, it was removed and reconstructed in 1956 at the Museum of Welsh Life, St. Fagan's. Both Maesyronnen and Pen-Rhiw chapels are excellent examples of "barn chapels" of the 17th and 18th centuries, before the advent of purpose built Nonconformist chapels which first began to appear in the Cynon Valley about 1800.

(ii) Cwm-Glo-Chapel 1689-1749

Prior to the passing of the Toleration Act of 1689, Declarations of Indulgence were issued by Charles II in 1672 and later by James II in 1687 and 1688. These Statutes of Declarations suspended all laws against Catholics and Nonconformists but with the coming of the "Glorious Revolution of 1688" which swept King James II from his throne the Nonconformists were thereafter rewarded by the passing of the Act of Toleration in May 1689. After only three years of the reign of James II (1685-88), the Protestants King William III and Mary II were accepted as joint sovereigns on 13th February 1689. In this year also, the Bill of Rights came into force which defined what the Monarch could and could not do. The arrival of William III and Mary II was greeted by Dissenters with great relief. The burden of persecution was at last eased and conditions became easier for the Nonconformists enabling them to move forward and openly build chapels in which to worship freely. Also, it may be said here that through the 1689 Act, Presbyterianism was recognised as the official religion in Scotland. However, as will be studied later in the text, the law did not tolerate the Unitarians until much later in 1813.

Following the Act of Toleration 1689, which allowed the Nonconformists the freedom to build licensed Meeting Houses for the purpose of worshipping, the Aberdare and Merthyr Independents decided to move from their barn conventicle at Cwm-y-Glo to an even more remote place nearby and search for a piece of ground on which to build a chapel. Over the years membership had increased and the old conventicle had become too small. They were able to lease land near to the Cwm-y-Glo farm from the owner Captain D. Jenkins of Hensol and accordingly they took out a sixty-year lease commencing from 1689 and expiring in the year 1749. The members erected a new purpose built chapel they could now at last call their own; a simple stone building built around 1689-90 of austere and plain design about 30 feet by 18 feet plan size. The chapel was located in a quiet and secluded hollow, surrounded and screened by a dense copse and tall overhanging trees. The place was very remote and well hidden.

Ruins of the old chapel at Cwm-Y-Glo. Built circa 1689-90. Photograph taken circa 1950.

Under the 1689 Toleration Act the Dissenters were legally and theoretically free from persecution and harassment by opposing groups of the Established Church. However, despite the passing of the Act there remained inadequacies. These early Nonconformists were tolerated but alas not entirely free from persecution and they continued to be under close surveillance. Many of the new Meeting Houses formed after 1689 were destroyed by unruly mobs and the worshippers continued to be severely harassed and their chapels vandalised.

Throughout the 1680's there arose theological divisions and differences between the Calvinists and Armenians, the latter led to Arianism which had a strong following at this time and later Unitarianism came into being. The Meeting House at Cwm-y-Glo however, was Independent but was called Presbyterian because of its ruling body of ministers and elders. The term Presbyterian was used to designate Unitarian chapels but the term "Unitarian" did not actually come into use until 1813.

In 1874 Dafydd Morgannwg confirms that part of the old Meeting Place at Cwm-y-Glo was just barely standing, being 37 feet long by 19 feet wide with adjacent stables 20 feet by 15 feet. Even today (2004) the area has been cleared and remnants of the ruins and original walls are still visible sufficiently to distinguish the size and outline of the building.

Between 1689 and circa 1715 seven new Nonconformist chapels were built in Glamorganshire. At last after years of hiding and persecution the Nonconformists had openly established themselves without fear and were now licensed to build meeting houses. They had little money and little knowledge of building or architecture and therefore the few chapels that they managed to build were small and modest, almost akin to simple cottages. The first Dissenting chapel built in the Cynon Valley viz. Hen Dy Cwrdd, Trecynon, built in 1751 meets such a cottage-like description. Many early existing barns and cowsheds from around 1680 to the late 1700's were converted and modified to provide a simple room in which to worship, with crude seating or benching and a simple make-shift pulpit; often there was no seating and members had to stand. Professor Anthony Jones explains that these early Meeting Places were referred to as the "Barn-chapels". Surviving examples from around 1700-1800 are indeed rare throughout Wales and non-existent in the Cynon Valley.

(iii) Separation from Cwm-y-Glo Chapel 1747-1751

Following the passing of The Toleration Act 1689, the Aberdare and Merthyr Dissenters remained at Cwm-y-Glo from 1689 to 1747. However, a "split" occurred in the congregation in 1747. The Armenians (later to be Unitarians) who lived on the Merthyr side of the Aberdare Mountain broke away and left Cwm-y-Glo in 1747 and built their new chapel Hen Dy Cwrdd Cefn (Presbyterian) at Cefn Coed-y-Cymmer. This chapel followed Armenianism and eventually became Unitarian; it was rebuilt in 1853 and again in 1894. The founder member was Sion Llewellyn (1690-1776), a blacksmith from Cefn Coed who did much work in spreading Arminianism in Aberdare. In 1947 a memorial was unveiled in his memory at the Unitarian Chapel at Cefn Coed. This first separation had far-reaching consequences for the congregation at Cwm-y-Glo as other sections were also soon after to break away. Two years later in 1749 the Independent Dissenting worshippers from the Aberdare/Merthyr Mountain also left the old sanctuary and later established Hen Dy Cwrdd Meeting House in Trecynon in 1751. (See account written in "Ar Gomin Hirwaun- yn Heol Felin 1751"). A third "split" occurred in 1749; the Merthyr Independents moved from Cwm-y-Glo chapel and built their own meeting place at Ynysgau – i.e. Capel Ynysgau, Merthyr Tydfil.

In time, each of the three separate congregations became either Trinitarian as in the case of Ynysgau Chapel or Unitarian as with the Cefn Coed-y-Cymmer and Trecynon chapels. Three separate chapels therefore emerged from the old Conventicle thus revealing theological divisions which had always been a feature of the former Cwm-y-Glo assembly. It was as a consequence of this three-way split that Cwm-y-Glo eventually closed in 1752 when the remainder of the congregation thought to have comprised mainly Presbyterians also left the old chapel.

When separation finally came for the three congregations between 1747 and 1751, it was not only because of theological disputes but also due to the important fact that they had to consider finding a new meeting place, as the sixty year lease, granted in 1689 was about to expire in 1749. This was a significant and prominent historical turning point in the beginning of Nonconformity in the Cynon Valley, for it was as a consequence of the expiration of the sixty-year lease in 1749 that Cwm-y-Glo led to separation of the congregation on the Aberdare and Merthyr sides of the mountain. Cynon Valley was soon thereafter to have its first Nonconformist chapel, built in 1751 and named Hen Dy Cwrdd, The Old Meeting House, Trecynon, and along with the Parish Church of St. John the Baptist (founded 1189), these were the only two places of worship in the Cynon Valley during the 1750's.

I shall conclude this part of the chapter with a quote by Tom Lewis (Mab y Mynydd) from his book "The History of Hen Dy Cwrdd, Cefn Coed y Cymmer written in 1947. He reminds us of the stalwarts and pioneers of the old chapel at Cwm-y-Glo and of their determination and courage in the face of persecution. He writes, *The senseless wranglings which culminated so disastrously at Cwmglo are to be regretted, but nothing that occurred there can ever dim the lustre and the glory of the Dissenters' initial achievement. That must always be remembered. When we remember that to attend the services they journeyed from Aberdare, Gelligaer, Vaynor, Cwmtaf, and even from distant places in Monmouthshire, we cannot but admire their devotion, their courage and honesty of purpose. One of them, "old Saphin", found his way there, presumably astride his pony, from Bridgend. We are so accustomed, in our time, to accept the right to public worship as a part of our long heritage that it seldom occurs to us that that right was won for us after much suffering and travail of spirit. The memory of man is short and fleeting, and it is doubtful whether Nonconformists of today give Fathers of Cwmglo even a passing thought. The Dissenters lie in forgotten and unvisited graves, and should they return and make a pilgrimage to their old shrine today they would find there, (probably to their disgust), only a few feet of crumbled walls – a jumbled heap of sacred rubble. But if by men the ancient pile is remembered not, nature is less ungrateful, for throwing their protective arms and their tangled shadows athwart the ruins are a few sturdy oaks that might well have been silent witnesses of the persecution of long ago".*

(iv) Hen-Dy-Cwrdd Unitarian Chapel, Trecynon, founded 1751; rebuilt 1862.

When Hen-Dy-Cwrdd was founded in 1751, the small meeting house accommodated not more than 50 to 100 people, and was situated in what was then a field belonging to the old farm house of Gadlys Uchaf and known as Tir yr Neathe. The appearance of the chapel was that of a simple and modest cottage, or a humble Inn with a front porch entrance and tiled roof. In 1782 there were 43 members and the preacher received £9 per annum; by 1800 the salary had risen to £21 per annum. The first minister was Rev. Owen Rees inducted in 1756; he was born in 1717 and died in 1768 and is buried in St John's churchyard. The original lease was granted on 25th March 1751 by Theophilus Richards (1704-1794) and was revised by his son Richard Richards on the 12th December 1796. It was at the time described as, "a Meeting House for the Dissenting Protestants". In 1853 membership was 60; unfortunately the chapel is presently closed (2004) and boarded up and its future remains uncertain. A more detailed history can be found in Chapter 1, reference 129. The chapel was rebuilt in 1862 at a cost of £753-15s-4d precisely and the architect was Evan Griffiths (junior) of Aberdare and son of Evan Griffiths, Ty Mawr, a staunch Methodist and the owner of the largest trading establishments at Aberdare during the first half of the nineteenth century. The 1862 chapel was designed to be "simple and strong, reflecting Unitarian Beliefs in liberty, tolerance and forbearance".

According to Rev. Ivor Parry, it is believed that Hen Dy Cwrdd became Unitarian in 1813 under the ministry of Rev. Thomas Evans (1764-1833) – also known as Tomos Glyn Cothi – who ministered here 1811-1833, and was a prolific hymn writer. There is some debate as to whether Hen Dy Cwrdd was formed as a result of theological dispute or because of geographical convenience, i.e. the split from Cwm-y-Glo to Trecynon in 1749. Rev. Ivor Parry concludes however that it seems likely that doctrinal and theological differences between Calvinism and Unitarianism (Arminianism) proved responsible for the founding of Hen Dy Cwrdd. Even today this question is still open to debate and further research. Rev. I Parry further states that until further evidence is forthcoming there is no proof that Hen Dy Cwrdd was either Calvinistic or Armenian in the 1750's. However, his theory leans towards it being Calvinistic during this period. It should be noted here that the Armenians (Unitarians) did not become "free" from the Established Church until as late as 1813 because the Toleration Act 1689 only applied to those Dissenters who subscribed to the Triniterian creed (The Trinity).

(v) A Brief Outline of the Early Nonconformist Chapels of the Cynon Valley 1751-1841.

During this period, religious services and prayer meetings were held in a variety of different places including hired rooms above Public Houses (Long Rooms); in private houses and lofts of old shops; in barns and in Coffee Taverns. However, through the development of the Industrial Revolution of iron, coal industries and the expansion of the railways and canal, the population accordingly grew and by the early to middle 1800's there was a considerable demand for Nonconformist Chapels and these appeared on the scene in abundance throughout the early to middle 19th century. The first sign of Nonconformist Chapels appearing in increasing numbers was in the early 1790's and the various causes developed rapidly in the century to follow. Between 1751 when Hen Dy Cwrdd, Trecynon, was founded and 1790, there is no record of licensed places of worship appearing in the Cynon Valley. However, according to Glanffrwd's "History of Llanwonno", there is evidence that religious services and prayer meetings were being held in secret conventicles and meeting places in the Cynon Valley as early as 1774, namely, Bethel Calvinistic Methodist Chapel, Ynysybwl. (See chapter 1, Ref. 1).

The Calvinistic Methodists, Welsh Baptists, Wesleyan Methodists and Primitive Methodists entered the Cynon Valley encouraged by visiting preachers and religious revivalists of the early 19th century. Such denominations were soon to develop into permanent sects of worshippers to settle in their own respective chapels. By 1840 fifteen meeting places had been formed in the Cynon Valley and 23 alone in the Aberdare Parish by 1853, but it was not until the 1880's and 1890's that Nonconformity came to power in the lower half of the Valley (Penrhiwceiber, Abercynon etc.). By 1897 there were no less than 118 Nonconformist Chapels, accelerated by the growth of the coal industry and resulting population growth. The earlier chapels were predominately Welsh speaking but as English speaking immigrants flocked to the valleys to seek work in the expanding coal industry there was a demand for more and more chapels to be built to fulfil the needs of the increasing population.

Early Dissent in the Aberdare Valley around 1790 is associated with David Oliver, a native of Aberdare and a cobbler by trade. He preached occasionally at Aberdare and in 1791 baptised four adults in the River Cynon. He became minister of Hen Dy Cwrdd 1803-06. Prior to this period, a family of Baptists living in Mountain Ash held services in 1786 at various houses in the town. By the early 1800's the Unitarians held their meetings once a month in Troedyrhiw House, Mountain Ash, and also held "Sermon Meetings" on Sunday afternoons much later in the Mountain Ash Coffee bar or "Coffee Tavern", Commercial Street. In 1793 the "Cause" of Bethel Welsh Baptist, Penderyn, commenced at Penpont Farmhouse, Cwm Taf and later in a dwelling house at Ynysfelin. In 1799 they built Bethel. (See chapel ref. 158). Ebenezer Welsh Independents, Trecynon, commenced their cause jointly in 1799 with Carmel Calvinistic Methodists in a building at the rear of the present Mackworth Arms and in 1801 in the loft of an old shop in Dare Lane. They later held meetings in Tyr Capel (Chapel House), licensed in 1804 at the house of Timothy Davies near Carmel, Monk Street. In 1811 Ebenezer was built. In 1806 the first Calvinistic Methodist Chapel in Trecynon was built, namely "Pentwyn Bach" at St John's Place above the old tram road, – rebuilt in 1829 in Hirwaun Road (see chapel ref. 125). In 1804 Calvaria Welsh Baptist Aberdare started their "cause" in the home of Lewis Richard, known as Capel Bach and also called Penpound. In 1806 Soar Welsh Wesleyan Methodist, Hirwaun held early meetings in an old barn until they built their chapel in 1824. Also in 1806 Bethel Welsh Calvinistic Methodist, Hirwaun commenced their "cause" in a house provided by George Overton, until they built their chapel in 1873. Bethel Welsh Methodist, Rhigos commenced their "cause" in 1805 in a house in the Bryn, and in 1839 built their chapel. Nearby in Penderyn, Siloam started their "cause" in 1823 by local farmers. In 1811 Ramoth Welsh Baptist started their "cause" in a house, and their chapel was built in 1825. A little earlier in 1823 Nebo Welsh Independent, Hirwaun built their chapel. Salem Welsh Congregational Chapel was established in 1835 as a result of a split at Ebenezer, Trecynon. In 1832 Nazareth Welsh Baptist, Mountain Ash began their "cause" in the Bruce Arms Public House; their chapel was built in 1841.

The afore-mentioned chapels established between 1790 and the 1840's are a small selection of the total in the Cynon Valley. The period 1840 to 1900 saw a huge increase in chapel building, the histories of which are covered in detail in Chapter One, and includes 180 Nonconformist places of worship in the Cynon Valley.

(vi) The Period of Persecution and Suppression of Dissent. The Various Acts 1661-1689.

The Acts of 1661-1689 were primarily aimed at the suppression of Dissent and to limit the freedom and scope of the Nonconformist worshippers during this period of persecution. The Acts made it illegal for the Dissenters to worship according to their conscience. They had to conform or else go into hiding and worship in secret remote places. They would gather together in plain and modest conventicles to hold prayer meetings and simple services and hence they became known as "Conventiclers" or "Dissenters". They were also referred to as Puritans and later and more commonly as "Nonconformists".

We shall now examine the salient Acts of 1661-1689 relating to the Suppression of Dissent.

(a) THE CORPORATION ACT 1661

This Act restricted public office to Anglican communicants and prevented the Nonconformists taking part in local government and excluded them from holding municipal office. The 1661 Act was passed under the reign of King Charles II who reigned 1660-1685 and was brought back from exile and restored to the throne in May 1660.

(b) THE ACT OF UNIFORMITY 1662

Passed in April 1662 this Act required all ministers to give their assent to the rites and liturgy of the Church of England, and compelled all clergy to use the revised Prayer Book. Many clergy refused to obey and were ejected from their office. It required all clergymen to be re-ordained and to declare allegiance to the Book of Common Prayer. This and other measures forced the Dissenters to leave the Established Church and it is from this refusal to conform that Nonconformity arose. This fundamental change and dissent from the State-Established church eventually led to the birth of Nonconformity leading to the many religious denominations as we know them today. Following the Act, Nonconformists suffered considerably and were severely persecuted for their beliefs. The Act required clergy to give their total consent to all and everything prescribed by the Book of Common Prayer and to acknowledge that it was unlawful upon any pretence whatsoever to take arms against the King. The Dissenters separated from the Established Church because they wished to be free to worship in accordance with the teachings of the New Testament rather than the dictates of the Monarch or the Magistrate. They sought spiritual freedom and equality of all in the sight of God. As with the early Puritans the sermon was the chief feature of worship among the Nonconformists. However, a period of persecution was to prevail from 1660-1688 until the passing of the Toleration Act 1689, which was to change everything for the better for the long-suffering Dissenters.

(c) THE CLARENDON CODE 1661-1665

Named after Edward Hyde, First Earl of Clarendon (1609-74), these were repressive measures that imposed severe penalties on those who refused to conform to the Established Church. They were a series of Acts between 1661 and 1665 which secured and re-asserted the supremacy of the Church of England after the collapse of the Puritan Revolution in 1660. See details of these acts later in the text.

(d) THE CONVENTICLE ACT 1664

This Act forbade groups of more than five persons to assemble at any one time for the purposes of worship except to the requirements of the Anglican Church. This measure forced the Dissenters to meet in secret remote places in very small groups and whenever larger gatherings took place the results were usually disastrous. Severe penalties were enacted including transportation for seven years for a third offence.

(e) THE FIVE MILE ACT 1665

No Nonconformist or Puritan minister was allowed to teach, preach or settle within five miles of any town, borough or parish in which he had previously ministered and had a church living. It aimed at the destruction of Nonconformity in the towns. Nonconformity was recognised as lawful, but many restrictions were placed on their movements and activities. Nearly two thousand ministers resigned rather than submit to the measures laid down by the various Acts.

(f) DECLARATIONS OF INDULGENCE 1672

In 1672 Charles II issued Indulgences to Dissenters that enabled them to meet legally for worship under licence from the State, but this was withdrawn one year later in 1673. The Quakers who were in existence from around 1650 were however, heavily persecuted from as early as 1661 as were the Roman Catholics around this period. Their meetings were attacked and they were often imprisoned. The Baptists, Independents and Presbyterians were much less remorselessly pursued than the Quakers.

(g) THE TEST ACT 1673
Prevented Catholics taking any political office in England, restricted public office to Anglican Communicants and disqualified Dissenters from holding public office under the Crown unless they complied with a sacramental test. However, Nonconformists especially Baptists and Independents continued to meet in secret places and would eventually become the pioneers of many "causes" in later years.

(h) DECLARATIONS OF INDULGENCE 1687-88
Implemented under King James II (1685-88) and suspended all laws against Catholics and Nonconformists. Note – The Bill of Rights confirmed constitutional Monarch in England in 1689.

(i) THE GLORIOUS REVOLUTION 1688
Rescued the nation and the religion from the Catholic rule of James II, whose downfall and flight into exile to France led to the reign of Protestants William III and Mary II (1689-1702). In 1688 James II was expelled for trying to restore Catholicism as the official religion.

(j) THE TOLERATION ACT 1689
After almost thirty years of persecution the Nonconformists were rewarded by the passing of this Act in May 1689. The Act allowed Dissenters the freedom to build and worship in Meeting Places that had been licensed for the purpose by Justices of the Peace, whereas prior to 1689 they were forced to meet in secret. They were however required to take an oath of loyalty to the Crown and to accept the 39 Articles of the Church of England which had been adopted in 1563 when the C. of E. was established. The Dissenters were required to keep the doors of their Meeting Places unlocked during worship; to continue paying tithes and to serve as church wardens and parish overseers when chosen for such offices. They were tolerated but not truly free and were kept under close surveillance. From 1689 onwards chapels were built and openly acknowledged. By the end of the eighteenth century more than a hundred Nonconformist Chapels had been built throughout Wales. After many years of persecution the Nonconformists could now at last worship in peace, in their own purpose-built chapels. The 1689 Act allowed the Nonconformists to lay the foundations for what would become an extraordinary future of Nonconformist expansion. The Act enabled them to look forward to a better future. By 1700 about 12% of the population of South Wales were Dissenting Worshippers. Notwithstanding the passing of the Act many of the newly established Meeting Houses were destroyed by unruly mobs and the Dissenters continued to a certain extent to be persecuted by some of the opposing sections of the Established Church.

Such was the hostility that some preachers were even assaulted and at times the chapels were vandalised by opposing groups. Despite the inadequacies of the Act its passage meant that Nonconformists who had previously been persecuted by the Courts could henceforth look to the Courts to defend them and immediate steps were taken to profit from the measure. The chief need of the Nonconformists was suitable buildings in which to worship and this need was to be fulfilled in the coming years. Trinitarian protestant ministers were now permitted to conduct services without hindrance provided they swore the relevant oaths and registered their Meeting Places as licensed places for worship. The coming of the protestant William III and Mary II to the throne was greeted by Dissenters with great relief; the burden of persecution was at last lifted.

(vii) Relations between the Established Church and Nonconformity 1850-1920.
The late Rev. Ivor Parry, minister of Siloa, Aberdare tells us that even though there were obvious differences between the Nonconformist chapels and the Established Anglican Church the basic teaching and preaching were more or less similar. However, ill-will and opposition between "Chapel" and "Church" continued throughout the middle of the nineteenth Century and up to the early 1900's. Much acrimony and bitterness arose over the publishing of the Blue Book in 1847, (Report of the Royal

Commission on the State of Education in Wales) when Rev. John Griffiths the vicar of the Aberdare parish was ostracised and disgraced by the Nonconformists led by the Rev. Dr. Thomas Price, minister of Calvaria Welsh Baptist, Aberdare, for his accusations of immorality amongst the Welsh, particularly women. Rev. Dr. Price was a constant thorn in the flesh of successive vicars of Aberdare. The controversy and clash continued over the matter of Disestablishment, but the disagreement was eventually resolved with the disestablishment of the Welsh Church in 1920, as we shall read later.

Chapel and Church were not always at loggerheads. On a number of occasions Tabernacle English Congregational Church, Aberdare and St. Elvan's Church demonstrated their good will towards each other. On Christmas Day, 1858 Rev. John Cunnick (minister 1857-60) and his Tabernacle congregation joined the St. Elvan's service. In January 1870 during the wedding of Mr. M.G. Johnson, manager of Werfa colliery and his bride Miss Pardoe, which took place in Tabernacle E.C. chapel, St Elvan's gladly arranged for the ringing of their church bells in celebration.

"The Rivals – Church & Chapel" Contemporary Post Card.

(Courtesy of Kevin Adams 1904 Ltd.)

In 1840, Rev. John Davies, minister of Ebenezer Chapel, Trecynon wrote a book "The Nature of the Church from the Evangelical Standpoint", and many meetings continued during the 1840's over the issue of Church versus State. At Aberdare the relationship between the Nonconformist Chapels and Anglican Church deteriorated as a result of the publication of the "Report of the Royal Commission on the State of Education in Wales", in 1847. The report was predominantly prepared by Anglican witnesses (80%) and as such could hardly be expected to present a fair picture of a nation thoroughly Welsh and Nonconformist. According to the Report, the state of education in Wales was deplorable; the reaction of the Nonconformists was naturally that of indignation. Aberdare was in the mainstream of protest because of the great exception taken to the new vicar, 26 year old Rev. John Griffiths who had been in the parish for only six weeks. He had charged the people of Aberdare with immorality, improvidence and drunkenness!! Consequently, on 23rd February 1848 a mass protest meeting was held at Siloa Chapel, Aberdare and a report published on 7th March 1848. Over 2000 protesters attempted admission to Siloa, which seated only about 900. Prominent speakers included David Williams, Ynyscynon, David Davis, Blaengwawr and Rev. Dr. Thomas Price; the vicar declined to attend. All the speakers and protesters vehemently refuted the vicar's charges and articles were published in the press indicating this. Rev. John Griffiths was found to be instrumental in the charges and attacks and public reaction was extremely intense in 1848-1851. Relations between the Nonconformists and Anglican Church were at a low ebb during this period, unhappier than they had ever been before.

However, records proved alcohol was certainly a problem at the time. Even in 1837 there were 49 public houses in the Aberdare Parish alone, for a population of only 5000, besides numerous establishments selling beer. The Vestry reports and Baptismal reports also verified that there was much unchastity and illegitimacy. Rev. Dr. Thomas Price's counter-charge was that miners and colliers were doing good work. There were around 45 Friendly Societies in the locality providing sickness and bereavement benefits. It should be noted that the Nonconformist Chapels ruled that no member should frequent a public house after communion on pain of excommunication. The Report did great harm to the relations between the Anglican Church and Nonconformists. The fundamental debate on the relations between Church and State continued from the 1850's to the 70's. In 1853 a local Minister; Rev. Josiah Thomas Jones published a book on "Popular Objections to our Established Church".

In 1860 Rev. John Cunnick, minister of Tabernacle, Aberdare asked the vicar to sign a local petition in favour of the abolition of the Church Rate which remained a constant source of friction; the vicar refused. A further cause of dispute was the question of burial rights in the parish churchyard, when Anglican clergy sometimes refused to bury Nonconformists, especially unbaptised children. In 1860, Rev. Dr. Thomas Price was particularly disturbed over this issue when the vicar Rev. Evan Lewis refused the burial of a child, however the child was buried and Dr. Price preached outside the churchyard instead! By 1864 burials in the parish churchyard were prohibited and other smaller graveyards had previously been closed, including Hen Dy Cwrdd in 1858. There was therefore, a need for a public cemetery and for the Nonconformists to have an equal voice in its management of the cemeteries.

In 1875 Henry Richard M.P. wrote an article in support of Disestablishment and the question of chapel and church dragged on to the end of the 1890's. The Education Act of 1902 was a landmark in the relations between Church and Nonconformity and eventually there was a clear indication that the Nonconformists had at long last accepted the principle that the State should provide education. In the meantime the question of Disestablishment continued into the 1900's until the passing of the Welsh Church Act of 1914. This was the end of the main cause of disagreement between the Established Church and the Nonconformist Chapels and dissent in the Cynon Valley and of course Wales as a whole. Disestablishment received Royal Assent on 18th September 1914, but the Great War intervened and therefore postponed the implementation of the Act, which did not come into force until 1st April 1920, under the Premiership of Mr. David Lloyd George. It was also around this period and after, that the gradual decline in the Nonconformist Chapels began to emerge in the Cynon Valley and the rest of Wales and membership began dwindling, leading to the closure of a vast number of chapels. Sadly this trend of decline has accelerated, more so since the 1960's and chapels are now being demolished at an alarming rate. This aspect of Chapel decline will be examined in chapter nine.

Chapter 3

AN ARCHITECTURAL STUDY

Page No.

(i) **Development of Chapel Architecture in the Locality 1700-1910.**   **192**

(ii) **The Architects and Designers.**   **198**

(iii) **The Builders.**   **201**

(iv) **The Grade Two Listed Chapel Buildings.**   **202**

(v) **Chapel Design Phases.**   **204**

"The chapels – despised by architects, ignored by guide books, too briefly mentioned by directories, these variegated conventicles are witnesses to the taste of industrial Britain. They try to ape nothing. They were anxious not to look like the Church which held them in contempt; nor like a house, for they were places of worship; nor like a theatre, for they were sacred piles. They succeeded in looking like what they are – chapels, so that the most observant traveller can tell a chapel from any other building on the street."

Extract from Nonconformist Architecture in "First and Last Loves" by John Betjeman, 1952.
Courtesy of John Murray, Publishers, London.

(i) Development of Chapel Architecture in the Locality 1700-1910

This chapter deals with the development of chapel architecture in the Cynon Valley and the architects, designers and builders of the period from 1700-1910. It concludes with a list of the grade two listed chapel buildings in the locality, and the various chapel design phases.

We have learnt from chapter two that the early Dissenters held their services and prayer meetings in primitive and secret conventicles in order to worship as guided by their conscience and beliefs. With the passing of the Toleration Act 1689 the Dissenters began meeting in converted barns, cow sheds, and old farm houses especially adapted for holding their services. By 1720 about fifty Meeting Houses had been established throughout Wales. These converted buildings were known as the Barn Type or Cottage Style early Meeting Houses of around 1680-1720 which was called the Conventicle Period and falls within the Primitive Phase of chapel design. They were designed basically as "Preaching Houses" and were plain and simple in external appearance, reflecting the style of the surrounding farmhouses, cottages and barns. The first chapel, Hen-Dy-Cwrdd Unitarian Chapel, Trecynon, established in 1751 met such a description of the cottage style chapel as we have read in the last chapter, and another example is the oldest surviving Nonconformist chapel of Maesyronnen Independent, converted from a barn in 1696. The cause of Ebenezer Welsh Independent Chapel, Trecynon commenced in a small cottage called "Tyr Capel" (Chapel House) licensed for worship in 1804. In his "History of Llanwynno", written in 1888, Rev. William Thomas (1843-1890), otherwise known famously as "Glanffrwd", gives an interesting description of the first Old Bethel chapel, Ynysybwl, built in 1786 and converted into two houses in 1880. The description of the old chapel is worthy of mention here in Glanffrwd's own words:

> **DID YOU KNOW?**
>
> The former spire of St. David's E.P., Aberdare taken down circa 1960 was 85 feet high. The spire of St Elvan's Church, Aberdare is over twice as high at 189 feet.

"The two houses on the hillock a little above the new chapel of the Calvinistic Methodists in Llanwynno still have an air of sanctity about them. Those two houses were the original chapel – the place of worship for many generations, a temple and a house of prayer, never consecrated by a bishop nor fashioned by any builder of note; indeed its only adornment was a coat of white-wash once a year on the walls, a bit of dark-blue paint at the corners, and occasionally a little mortar between the grey stones, just enough to keep the place dry. The interior walls were bare, except for the clock in front of the pulpit and a row of long nails along the side walls and back, on which men hung their hats. Like the outside, the inside walls were whitewashed. There was a row of seats along the back wall from end to end facing the pulpit, another row along the eastern wall and from the eastern door to the pulpit steps and from the other side of the pulpit to the other door and right to the fireplace. In a word, the seats were firmly fixed with their backs to the wall, with the Big Seat in the centre and two small seats, one on either side of the Big Seat. The seats were not numbered but known by the names of families in the parish, such as Mynachdy seat, Glog seat and Fanhaulog seat. There was also a bench with arms and back on which people could sit back to back. This was at the eastern end opposite the door. Then there was rather a long bench on the middle of the floor opposite the Big Seat and two others facing each other on either side of the fireplace. There was also a fixed bench around and outside the Big Seat, and those who sat on it had their backs to the Big Seat and the pulpit. This was a good place for those who did not wish to face the preacher, but for those who wished to listen in comfort it was purgatory.

There were also three windows at one end, and the pulpit was opposite the middle one; indeed, the inside sill was the pulpit seat. The pulpit therefore was right in the middle of the chapel facing the north wall with its row of seats, and the clock which was presented in my time, right opposite the pulpit on the plain whitewashed wall. At the back of the chapel there is a stone in the wall stating that the chapel was built in 1786. The cost was borne by the members and their friends, and although it was not a beautiful building, there were signs that the Spirit of God was with the people there and had blessed them with a beauty greater than that of grand architecture and fine walls, namely, the sanctification of souls. There was "hwyl" in the chapel, and at many meetings "the living Spirit" was felt. I have heard voices in song and praise hundreds of times between the walls of the old Fanhaulog Chapel. Many giants of the ministry preached here, pleading the forgiveness of sins through the blood of Jesus Christ, and making the place, "a House of God and a path to Heaven." Many souls were saved. There are, safe in Paradise tonight, many pilgrims who began their spiritual journey in the plain little chapel of Llanwynno. Their names are forgotten here, but they are safely enrolled in the Book of Life."

Glanffrwd also mentions an early Meeting-Place of Nonconformists who met at Rhyd Y Gwreiddyn ("source of the stream"). The first public worship in Ynysybwl is believed to have been held here in 1774. According to Methodistiaeth Cymru (Welsh Methodism), they met in this old cottage known as Ty-tan-wal ("the house under the wall") and located west of Fanheulog about one mile south west of Ynysybwl. About 30-45 met in this farm cottage where "they observed clear signs of God's presence among them and at times would begin to praise God with loud emotional cries."

The Barn Type style of Meeting House took the rectangular form of the domestic long wall façade where in most cases the position of the pulpit was located in the centre of the long wall and normally opposite the entrance doors. Alternatively the pulpit was at times placed between the entrance doors of the chapel with a window behind to give natural light for the preacher to read as in the case of Capel Pen-Rhiw which was converted from a barn in 1777 and re-erected at St. Fagans's Museum of Welsh Life in 1956. Seating consisted of deep wooden box pews with hinged doors in later designs. The floor comprised beaten earth often with straw. In later years stone slabs were used. Walls were random rubble local stone with white wash. Roofs were thatched and later replaced by stone and slate.

Gradually, towards the end of the "Barn Chapel" period of the 1700's new purpose built chapels appeared and chapel design took on a more permanent form. They were single storey structures without galleries and this design continued from the early 1800's up to around 1840 when the gable façade became more common. These earlier chapels were simple in design with little embellishment and were built in the local vernacular style. Many of those built in the Cynon Valley around 1840-60 resembled the colliery engine and winding houses which were more often than not located near the chapels. In these early designs, the classical architectural features had not yet been exploited or fully developed. They were simple straightforward buildings built of local stone with round-headed windows and doors. They were not as yet architect designed and many who designed and built the chapels around 1840 were often those who were responsible for erecting industrial buildings and the earlier designs associated with the local coal and iron works. Ministers themselves and local builders also "dabbled" in chapel design around this period. Some ministers had been carpenters or masons before entering the ministry and they used their skill and expertise in designing and drawing up plans of their chapels. In part (ii) of this chapter we will observe the local chapels designed by ministers and colliery engineers and it was not until the 1890's that local qualified practising architects and surveyors were first engaged in the design of Cynon Valley chapels.

Navigation Colliery, Mountain Ash. "The Navi". Opened 1855; closed 1940. Many chapels built in the Cynon Valley around 1840-1860 resembled the Colliery Engine and Winding Houses as seen in this photograph.

The earliest classic phase of chapel design had no pretence to architectural beauty or merit and their appearance was often plain and sombre. The façade had by now moved from the long or side wall to that of the gable-end, and the pulpit was moved from the side wall to the gable wall. This design also suited many sites in the locality as the chapels took up less expensive street frontage. Most architectural designs of merit were reserved for the front gable façade where some embellishment in dressed stonework was shown off to advantage. The sides or rear of the chapels were plainer comprising random stonework or render finish. This is borne out by an observer of the day who wrote:-

> *"The Trellwyn Methodists have built a church,*
> *The front looks like an Abbey,*
> *But thinking they can fool The Lord*
> *- They've built the back part shabby."*

"From "The Sand in the Glass", with acknowledgement to the author, Michael Llewellyn and to John Murray (Publishers) Ltd. 1943.

Growing industrialisation of the coal and railway industry led to an increased population in the Cynon Valley and a large influx of immigrants from England, Ireland and part of Wales seeking work in the

Poster of Centenary Services dated
September 1969, Providence,
Mountain Ash.

PROVIDENCE (E.C.) CHURCH

MOUNTAIN ASH

1869 CENTENARY SERVICES 1969

Wednesday, Sept. 17th

7 p.m.   SERVICE OF THANKSGIVING

CONDUCTED BY

Minister Rev. J. A. Hollyman

AND

Rev. Dr. W. T. Pennar Davies, B.A., B.Litt.

Sunday, Sept. 21st

11 a.m.   FAMILY SERVICE

6   EVENING WORSHIP

CONDUCTED BY

Mr. Hugh G. Powell

Talybont-on-Usk

PRYSE & SON, PRINTERS, MOUNTAIN ASH   Tel. 2791   AND AT GLYNNEATH   Tel. 349

growing industries. The boom in chapel building had begun by 1850 and together with the influence of various Religious Revivals chapel building progressed at a fast rate. By now, the classical period of chapel architecture was beginning to emerge.

The Religious Revivals of 1849 and 1859 led to growing congregations and a huge demand for new and larger Nonconformist Chapels. Many of the older existing chapels, some only barely twenty or thirty years old, were demolished to make way for a larger building or else the chapels were enlarged and in some cases a gallery added to increase capacity. The huge increase in chapel building continued after 1860 but levelled off around 1910. An example of events leading to the rebuilding of a chapel through increased membership is Providence English Congregational Chapel, Mountain Ash, built in 1869 and rebuilt 1911. The old chapel had reached a state of serious structural instability to the extent that the roof supporting tie beams had become unsafe and were gradually sinking. The unstable roof and imposed weight seriously affected the stability of the main walls, which consequently cracked and bulged outwards, making the building unsafe. The gallery had become increasingly full as a consequence of larger congregations resulting in the main walls and gallery spreading out and becoming extremely dangerous to the occupants and the public. The Chapel was therefore demolished and rebuilt in 1911 at a cost of £2,250-00p.

Rivalry and competition between the different denominations also led to an increase in the rate of chapel building, and splinter groups of "Mother-Daughter" chapels resulted in a duplication of each denomination. The early classic designs up to around 1850 were simple and often sombre and harsh in appearance, with little or no architectural embellishment, although the interiors of many early chapels of this period were fitted out with top class joinery and other features by skilled craftsmen. Some effort was made to enhance the external appearance particularly the front gable façade by the introduction of drip mouldings at first floor level and drip moulds around window and door openings. Pilasters were sometimes featured often raised and projecting from the main wall surface. Stone plaques depicting the names of the chapels were usually placed within the triangular upper portion of the gable called the "pediment", and these varied in shape, size and design.

After the Religious Revivals of 1849 and 1859 and the resulting increase in the erection of chapels, a more classical design was adopted involving the employment of professional architects. From the 1860's, chapel design had entered the "Classical Phase", whereby a mixture of designs were taken from neo-classical architectural features. These were copied from the past masters and found in the classical buildings of Italy, Greece and Rome. Qualified architects were quick to follow these designs by introducing classical pediments, pilasters, columns, cornices, drip courses and broken arches; the "Halo Arch" being an effective treatment of the upper gable façade. Experiments in the various arrangements and design of windows were carried out allowing scope to vary the front façade considerably. In addition, the use of dressed stone, stucco smooth lime mortar render, and rustication were popular features and gave scope to varying contrasting design treatment around window and door openings. The main aim during this period was to design chapels to maximise seating capacity and to meet the increasing demand for chapel building from 1860 onwards. The early vernacular designs of simple and plain appearance were by now gradually disappearing, to be replaced by a grander and more magnificent architectural expression following much bolder and enterprising classical themes. Design elements from different periods of architectural history were being employed and emphasis was concentrated on the front façade, whereas the side and rear elevations remained plain. Careful consideration was given by architects and designers to experiment in producing designs of good proportion and a pleasing image. The gable façade provided the opportunity to design many variations for window arrangements and positions as well as concentrating on the treatment of designs in the pediments, wherein name plaques and lettering and other features were usually positioned. The two-storey gable end façade with galleries became the accepted form of chapel design from around the 1860's. Architects and designers consulted specialist books, Journals and illustrated catalogues on chapel architecture where an assortment of well-tried classical designs had been followed. A rich variety of designs were concentrated totally on the front façade and architects copied and reproduced endless styles of classic architecture from different parts of Europe.

It can be said that the classical style of chapel architecture in the Cynon Valley and elsewhere throughout Wales had been firmly established by 1860. From 1860 up to around 1890 chapel design entered the "Golden Age of Classicism" wherein a mixture of designs and styles continued to be employed in a grand manner and concentrated mainly on the front gable façade. It was during the latter part of the nineteenth century that local craftsmen and artisans were much sought after. Masons, carpenters and joiners, roofers and slaters, painters, decorators and plasterers all contributed by exercising their expertise and highly developed skills. Many examples of stone cutting and shaping and high class joinery work can be seen in the chapels throughout the Cynon Valley. Many years of diligent apprenticeship training and learning were required to meet the high standards of skilled workmanship expected of each craftsman. By the close of the nineteenth century, scores of chapels adorned the local scene throughout the Cynon Valley from Ynysybwl in the south, to Penderyn in the north; some were

> ### MORE ON CHAPELS
>
> There are far more chapels in Wales than in the rest of Great Britain; they are a "National Emblem". The chief characteristics of the Welsh Chapel are a disregard of the established rules of design and proportion. They were "Preaching Houses", not a "Shrine". They were built as a result of The Great Religious Revivals of the past, and they represent pennies saved which might otherwise have been spent on drink, or smoking or gambling.

simple and plain, others were grand with ideas copied from the old masters. The "Palladian" window after the Italian Renaissance architect Andrea Palladio (1508-80), commonly known as "The Trinity Window", was a popular feature in the grander designs. Also copied from Italy was the "Halo Arch" where the arch breaks through the lower pediment, designed originally for the San Andrea Church in Mantua, Italy by Leon Battista Alberti (1404-72) in 1470. Both Palladio and Alberti stimulated interest in antique Roman architecture and pure classical style during the Italian Renaissance period. A brief note on Gothic Architecture; broadly speaking, this comprised the "Perpendicular style" including pointed, arched window and door openings, tracery work in window design and spires, and were normally for the English speaking chapels.

San Andrea Church, Mantua, Italy. Designed by Leon Battista Alberti (1404-72) in 1470. He stimulated interest in antique Roman architecture and pure classical style during the Italian Renaissance period. The "Halo Arch", shown in this photograph was copied in many of the chapel designs throughout Cynon Valley and elsewhere. The introduction of an arch across the face of the façade sometimes produced a discordant effect in the design. Refer to Chapel Ref. No.103 – Bethania C.M. Chapel, Aberdare for an almost identical appearance to the design of the San Andrea church of Alberti.

As the nineteenth century progressed chapel architecture entered a phase where the "Golden Age of Classicism" had been almost totally exhausted. The final phase of chapel design is commonly known as "The Decadent" or "Eccentric Years", and also described as "The Debasement Phase". This phase covers the late nineteenth century period to early twentieth century up to around 1910. Chapel building more or less came to a stop following the Religious Revival of 1904-05 and had virtually halted by the outbreak of the 1914-18 Great War. The

CHAPEL GALLERY HAS NO SUPPORT!

The gallery of Soar Welsh Independent Chapel, Penderyn, unusually has no pillar supports as found in other chapels. The gallery is cantilevered in its support and is the only one of its type in the Cynon Valley.

classic themes had been well tried out by the late nineteenth century but in the Final Phase architects became more daring in their expression of Neo-classical design features. Such an approach led to eccentric ideas and ostentatious designs. A mixture of bizarre designs led to a general deterioration in the standard. Excessive use of materials including bricks, slates, ceramics and terracotta produced a heavy decadent style in chapel architecture. The use of Art Nouveau and Baroque styles almost at random and without due thought produced a strange and eccentric style. The Classic design phase of former years had been exhaustively explored and "over designed" by the turn of the twentieth century. The Classic Phase and Decadent Phase however, also encouraged more lavish interiors, beautiful ceiling designs and central roses; ornate elevated pulpits, galleries and grand imposing organ casings.

How was the building and rebuilding of the chapels financed? How did members raise the money to build these grand edifices? This was done by setting up building funds and raising money from bazaars, concerts, singing festivals, raffles, tea parties, lantern lectures and through bank loans. The coal owners also helped towards the building costs by contributing generously. We are told of donations of a dram of coal given to each miner to help towards the cost. However, many chapels fell into debt which took many years to clear in most cases. Financial help sometimes came their way from the philanthropists of the period including Samuel Morley M.P. (1809-1886). Mr Morley did his best to promote the building of chapels in the 1860-70's and volunteered to help that work in Wales by offering to give ten shillings (50 pence) each for 10,000 sittings provided each respective chapel was erected within five years. Within six weeks during the late 1860's the foundation stones of no less than six new chapels had been laid in the locality and it was not long before the entire £5,000 had been claimed. In addition to fund raising and generous contributions from outside the chapel, the financial responsibility often fell on the members themselves who were expected whenever possible to contribute generously. They also helped in other more practical ways in the voluntary employment of their talents, and members who were skilled in masonry or carpentry work and other trades, would help in the construction of their chapels out of a generous "labour of love".

(ii) The Architects and Designers

Over the years, Cynon Valley chapels have been designed by a variety of individuals including colliery engineers who designed the engine and winding houses, municipal engineers and surveyors, builders and craftsmen, ministers and chapel members. It was not until the early 1890's that the majority of qualified professional architects were first engaged and commissioned in the design of chapels in the locality; this is notwithstanding the fact that the Royal Institute of British Architects was founded in 1837 and the Architectural Association in 1847. A number of professional architects' practices in Aberdare and Mountain Ash designed dozens of chapels throughout the Cynon Valley, particularly from 1890 to 1912, as will be seen later in the text. A number of notable ministers extended their talents to designing chapels from as early as 1829 up to 1894, but after this period professional architects took over from the amateur designers as chapel design entered a more classical phase. Much of their work can be seen repeated here and there in other chapel designs and in some cases architects copied each other, exchanging design ideas and themes throughout the locality. Broadly speaking, the architects designed classical chapels for the Welsh Nonconformist congregations whilst the Gothic and Perpendicular style was generally used for the English-speaking Nonconformist congregations and the Established Church. It is reputed that the great engineer Isambard Kingdom Brunel (1806-1859) designed a Wesleyan chapel in Merthyr Tydfil in 1853 to replace one which had been demolished in order to make way for the Taff Vale Railway Station in 1841. Legend has it that the new chapel was designed on the spot by Brunel and was probably the only chapel he designed in Wales. It is worth noting that the preacher and chapel designer Rev. William Jones of Ton Pentre (died 1907) who trained as a carpenter before entering the ministry, is said to have designed over 200 chapels in different parts of Wales during the late nineteenth century. Most of the classical chapels of the late nineteenth and early twentieth century were however designed in the "Grand Classical Style" by professional architects.

Fortunately, original plans of Cynon Valley chapels have survived from the period 1872 to 1931. A total of forty-one drawings covering seventeen chapels in the Miskin to Mountain Ash localities were donated to the Cynon Valley Museum by the then Cynon Valley Borough Council in 1996. The earlier plans dated 1872-1890 were drawn in black ink on inferior thin tracing paper which over the past 120 years have become brittle with age and require expert restorative care. The later plans of 1890 to 1912 were prepared on thicker tracing cloth, while others were drawn on a canvas-backed heavy cartridge paper. Many of the drawings have been meticulously colour washed. All the drawings have been photographed by the author and are in his private collection covering all chapels in the Cynon Valley. The old drawings show very little annotation and what notes are indicated describe drains, ventilation and damp courses. It appears that architects in most cases prepared a written specification covering all trades and aspects of work and materials used. Here are examples of notes on the older drawings, pre 1900.

"All floors to be ventilated; slate damp proof courses to all walls; drains under buildings to be embedded in concrete; vents to be carried 2 feet (600mm) above eaves; vent stacks to be 4 inches (100mm). "Air Grates" to be fixed at damp course; 6 inch (150mm) glazed ware drain pipes laid to true falls. All walls to have D.P.C. as per Regulation no.17 (as at 1899); drain ventilators to be carried clear of all doors and window openings".

Most of the drawings were prepared to a scale of one inch representing eight feet (1:96 metric scale).

All plans required approval by the Local Board. In the surveyors' report of the Mountain Ash Local Board there appeared the following confirmation of approval on the 13th November 1869 for Providence English Congregational Chapel, Mountain Ash:-

"I beg to report that I have received plans of a Congregational Chapel to be built in Union Square (now Union Street), Mountain Ash to which I do not see any objection.

I am, Gentlemen
Your Obedient Servant
S.O. Harpour, Surveyor"

The chapel which took only seven months to build cost £850 and left a debt of £450. It was demolished in 1911 and rebuilt in 1912.

The architects' fees appeared quite reasonable:-

In 1860	Chapel cost £800;	fees £27 (3.2%)
In 1904	Chapel cost £2043;	fees £74 (3.7%)
In 1912	Chapel cost £2250;	fees £90 (4%)
In 1912	Chapel cost £883;	fees £45 (5%)

The following is a list of professional architects and other designers including surveyors, engineers, ministers and chapel members who have been involved in the design of fifty-two chapels (out of a total of 180 recorded) throughout the Cynon Valley from 1829 to 1931. The designers' names are in alphabetical order followed by the respective chapel reference number and date.

A.E. Alder. 42/1931
David Bevan, Hirwaun. 161/1857
W. Douglas Blessley (architect). 111/1877
    Also designed the Great Western Hotel, Cardiff (1876) and the Prince of Wales Theatre, Cardiff (1878).
Edward Davies, Aberdare. 72/1938
Thomas Davies. 104/1859

Evan Griffiths (1824-1899), Aberdare. 103/1853, 116/1876.

Also designed chapels in the Rhondda and at Taffs Well, and The Temperance Hall, Aberdare, built in 1858 by Phillip Rees, (now the Palladium Bingo Hall).

Evan Griffiths (Junior). 129/1862

S.O. Harpour (engineer and surveyor), Mountain Ash. 60/1869

Rev. Evan Harris, Merthyr. 144/1856

Rev. Joseph Harrison. 127/1829

Mr. Henton, Aberdare. 28/1905

Herbert Jenkins, surveyor, Mountain Ash. 48/1880

Mr Evan Jones. 117/1860

Thomas Joseph. 104/1852; 119/1864; 130/1852

He was a colliery engineer from Hirwaun who came to Aberdare to open a new colliery.

Rev. William Lewis, Aberdare. 96/1858; 151/1840

Also designed other Baptist Chapels near the Cynon Valley.

Tom W. Millar, M.S.A., architect, Mountain Ash. 35/1903; 37/1907; 43/1904; 58/1901; 60/1912; 63/1904; 131/1905.

He was also a conductor of the Mountain Ash Orchestral Society and an accomplished pianist and organist; often performed recitals in local chapels. Mr Millar was also a local councillor and designed the huge Pavilion, Mountain Ash. Built in 1901, it was the venue for the 1905 and 1946 National Eisteddfods.

Morgan and Elford, architects, Aberdare and Mountain Ash. 55/1901; 56/1893; 59/1905; 62/1927.

Also designed the enlarged Workmen's Institute and Public Hall, Penrhiwceiber in 1900; alteration of St Winifred's Church in Wales, Penrhiwceiber in 1911 (built 1882-83), Free Library and Public Hall, Trecynon in 1902. Charles Henry Elford died in 1934 and is buried at Nolton Cemetery, Bridgend.

Rev. B. Owen, Minister of Zoar Chapel, Merthyr Tydfil. 97/1858; 115/1856.

H.J. Paull, architect, Cardiff. 108/1860.

W.S.Rampling (Aberdare surveyor). 109/1858; 115/1859.

Owen Morris Roberts, Portmadoc, Gwynedd. 127/1902.

Rev. Dr. Roberts, Pontypool. 6/1889; 12/1894.

Thomas Roderick (1854-1922), Clifton St., Aberdare. 15/1893; 18/1903; 30/1894; 36/1891; 49/1900; 84/1898; 85/1901; 91/1891; 101/1908; 103/1889; 113/1890; 124/1899; 133/1902; 138/1907; 162/1912.

Also designed Aberdare Girls School 1905-07; Cwmaman Institute 1891-92; Hope Welsh Presbyterian Chapel, High St., Merthyr Tydfil, 1892; Aberaman Public Hall and Free Library, and the conversion of the Temperance Hall to that of the New Theatre and Hippodrome, 1895. He was a member of Bethania Calvinistic Methodist Chapel, Aberdare. His sons Henry and Benjamin were architects in the business.

J. Llewellyn Smith. 116/1909.

Mr. Thomas of Glandwr. 144/1836.

Charles Thomas, Abertawe. 135/1902.

Rev. H. Thomas, Briton Ferry. 151/1867.

G.A. Treharne M.I.M.E. engineer and surveyor, Aberdare. 38/1903; 84/1898.

Thomas Roderick – Architect, Aberdare (b.1854 d.1922).

The names of architects appear on a few chapels and are inscribed on the Memorial Foundation Stones; these include T.W. Millar (refs. 35, 43, 63 and 131) and Thomas Roderick (ref. 30).

(iii) The Builders

Before the builders and building contractors came on to the chapel construction scene, stories abound of the pioneers of the earlier chapels who laboured voluntarily to build their places of worship. We are told of the men helping in their spare time after their normal days work. Everyone helped, including the ladies who assisted by gathering stones from nearby rivers carrying them on their heads in baskets or in their aprons. Farmers would help by allowing the use of their horse and carts to transport stones and other materials to the site. The builders engaged by contract to undertake the works would on occasions fail to complete the task and the faithful members, some of whom were craftsmen, would have to step in to finish the work. The cost of building the chapels is shown in chapter one for each respective chapel history where applicable.

> **PUBLICAN TO BUILD A CHAPEL**
>
> Some anxiety was felt by the members of the English Congregational Chapel at Abercynon, built 1886, about allowing the Publican, Mr Games, to build the chapel. Nevertheless work proceeded and Mr Games built the chapel for the price of £2150, with seating for 600.

The following is a list in alphabetical order of builders, mostly local, who built thirty five chapels of Cynon Valley out of a total of 180 recorded. Not forgetting those individuals who were "builders" in their own right and included the chapel members themselves, both tradesmen and non-tradesmen. The list of the chapel builders is followed by the respective chapel reference number and date.

D. Bevan, Hirwaun. 137/1867
Mr. Blackburn. 72/1938
Thomas Charles, Llandilo. 108/1860
David Davies, Trecynon. 124/1899
T.W. Davies, Mountain Ash. 31/1907; 38/1903; 43/1904; 60/1912
David Edwards, Trecynon. 101/1864
John Edwards, Carpenter, Gadlys. 117/1860
David Evans, Aberdare. 103/1853
F.W. Games, Abercynon. 15/1898. He also kept a public house.
D. Grier. 72/1858
David Harries, Mountain Ash. 51/1864. He was a member of Bryn Seion, Mountain Ash.
William Hodges, Mountain Ash. 60/1869
Howell Brothers, Navigation (Abercynon). 12/1894
Charles Jenkins & Sons, Porth. 6/1889
Dan Jones, Foundry Road, Hirwaun (died 1940). 156/1905; 157/1906; 162/1912; also an undertaker.
Jones Brothers, Barry. 59/1905; 63/1904; 135/1902
Jones Brothers, Penydarren, Merthyr. 101/1908
David Jones, Mason, Gadlys. 117/1860
John Jones, Gwawr Cottage, Godreaman. 84/1898
Messrs. Jones & Morris. 115/1856
James Lee, Manchester. 154/1900
Mr. Lewis, Pontypridd. 17/1897
Harry Llewellyn, Aberaman. 39a/ 1884
Frank Miles, Mountain Ash. 58/1901
David Morgan, Treorky. 83/1862
John Morgan, Clifton Street, Aberdare. 103/1889; 125/1896; 138/1875
J. Morgan & Son. 125/1896
Morgan Shon Morgan, Penywaun. 127/1811
Price, Penarth. 28/1905

Samuel Parker, Abernant. 121/1860

D. Rees, Trecynon 131/1905

W. Rees 115/1859; also built The Temperance Hall, Aberdare.

Abraham Richards. 104/1859

John Richards and Thomas Phillip Richards, Penywaun. 127/1811

Simon Richards, Aberdare. 116/1867

Thomas Roberts, Abernant. 121/1860

Mr. Rossiter (S.R.G.) Contractor, Hirwaun. 155/1986

J. Llewellyn Smith. 116/1909

Mr. Spratt, Tonypandy. 17/1905

Michael Thomas, Graig Street, Aberdare. 113/1890

William Brothers, Cribinddu Farm, Ynysybwl. 5/1888; 10/1890; (William and Edward Williams – they were also Deacons of Jerusalem, Ynysybwl).

Surprisingly only two chapels have the builder's name engraved in stone on a plaque, namely D. Grier, Aberaman – English Wesleyan Methodist Chapel at Mason Street, Aberaman, built in 1858, and T. W. Davies, engraved on one of the Foundation Memorial Stones of Hope Primitive Methodist Chapel, Penrhiwceiber, built in 1907.

(iv) The Grade Two Listed Chapel Buildings.

The Secretary of State for Wales is required to compile lists of buildings of special architectural or historic interest; the lists are constantly under revision for all local authority areas. The principles of selection for the lists are drawn up by an expert committee of architects, antiquarians and historians. All buildings built before 1700, which survive in anything like their original condition, qualify for listing, as do most buildings between 1700 and 1840. Between 1840 and 1914 only buildings of definite quality and character qualify. Selected buildings built after 1914 may also be listed.

Grade 1 – These are buildings of exceptional interest.

Grade II* – These are particularly important buildings of more than special interest.

Grade II – These are buildings of special interest, which warrant every effort being made to preserve them. Most listed chapels are in this grade.

It is an offence to demolish, alter or extend a listed building without listed building consent and the penalty can be a fine or imprisonment, or both.

Information on Listed Buildings can be found at: – CADW – Welsh Historic Monuments, Cathays Park, Cardiff, CF10 3NQ. Note: The Welsh word CADW translates – "To maintain or preserve".

The following is a list of the Grade Two listed chapels in the Cynon Valley based on the report produced by CADW as at autumn 2004. The chapel name is followed by the chapel reference number. A total of eighteen chapels are shown as listed throughout the Cynon Valley from Penrhiwceiber up to Hirwaun. Twenty-five buildings are listed altogether; these include the main chapel buildings, halls, Sunday schools, and vestries. There is however, a marked absence of listed chapels within the lower part of the Cynon Valley. The majority of those listed are concentrated around the central areas of the valley.

ABERAMAN
  Saron Welsh Independent – 77
ABERCWMBOI
  Bethesda Welsh Baptist – 68
ABERDARE
  English Wesleyan Methodist -107
  Siloa Welsh Independent – 113
  Hall attached to Siloa Chapel – 113
  Calfaria Welsh Baptist – 104
  Hall attached to Calfaria – 104

Trinity Welsh Presbyterian – 116
Hall attached to Trinity – 116
Bethania Calvinistic Methodist – 103
Sunday school attached to Bethania – 103
ROBERTSTOWN
Salem Welsh Congregational – 122
Vestry attached to Salem – 122
TRECYNON
Hen-Dy-Cwrdd Unitarian – 129
Heol Y Felin Welsh Baptist – 130
Hall attached to Heol Y Felin – 130
Ebenezer Welsh Independent –127
Bryn Sion English Baptist (now Carmel E.B.) – 124
GADLYS
Bethel Welsh Congregational –117
Gadlys Welsh Baptist –119
HIRWAUN
Nebo Welsh Independent –150
PENDERYN
Siloa Welsh Baptist –161
MOUNTAIN ASH
Noddfa (Elim) Pentecostal Chapel (Grade II*) –59
Bethania Welsh Independent –48
PENRHIWCEIBER
Carmel Welsh Independent – 48
OTHER NOTES – (CHURCH IN WALES)
St John The Baptist Parish Church (Founded 1189), Aberdare – Grade II*
St Elvan's Church, Aberdare – Grade II*
St Fagan's Church, Trecynon – Grade II
Church of St Cynog, Penderyn – Grade II
St Margaret's Church, Mountain Ash – Grade II
St James' Church, Llwydcoed – Grade II

WHICH ARE THE LARGEST CHAPELS IN THE CYNON VALLEY?

Saron W.I., Aberaman is the largest chapel in Cynon Valley with seating capacity of 900 plus a few more seats, and is reputed to have a small number of seats more than others in this seating category; out of 180 chapels listed, only four have a seating capacity for 900, viz –

Saron W.I., Aberaman (900 + a few!)
Calvaria W.B., Abercynon
Siloa W.Cong., Aberdare
Ebenezer W.I., Trecynon
The next largest chapels in the Cynon Valley range from 800 to 850 seats, viz –
Rhos W.B., Mountain Ash – 850
Calvaria W.B., Aberdare – 840
Hermon W.C.M., Penrhiwceiber – 800
Carmel C.M., Trecynon – 800
Heol-Y-Felin W.B., Trecynon – 800
Nebo W.I., Hirwaun – 800

The ten chapels listed above are amongst the largest built in the Valley. There are numerous in the 500 to 700 range, and rather less between 200 and 500.

(v) Chapel Design Phases

It is difficult to accurately define various design phases to correspond to particular dates, however, the following gives and approximate guide to the relevant phases of chapel design in the locality.

(A) 1600-1690 – Conventicle Period; Dissenters meet in secret, remote places, in barns and cottages; the Period of Persecution until the passing of the 1689 Act of Toleration.

(B) 1690-1800 – Primitive Phase; the "Barn Chapel" period, small Meeting Houses for services and worship assume a simple domestic cottage-like appearance. Some barns and cottages are converted and registered as licensed places of worship.

(C) 1800-1820 – Early Sub-classical Phase; purpose built chapels emerge on the scene, simple and plain in appearance.

(D) 1820-1850 – Long Side-Wall design changes to the one or two storey gable end façade; Classical Phase. The "Golden Age" of classicism begins. Designs carried out mainly by engineers or surveyors, and by amateur designers such as craftsmen, builders, ministers and chapel members. Architects not yet commissioned.

(E) 1850-1890 – Early Post-classical Phase. The "Golden Age" of classic chapel design continues. Professional architects are commissioned to design chapels frequently adopting neo-classical features copied from the past such as use of pediments, columns or pilasters, cornices, drip moulds and balustrade parapets, and a variety of window designs and arrangements.

(F) 1890-1914 – The Final Phase in chapel design and building. The Post Classical Period involving eccentric designs. Also referred to as the Debasement or Decadent Period leading to a general deterioration in the standards of design. Earlier classical phases continue but in a more irregular, excessive and eccentric form with peculiar mixes of designs from all periods of architecture. Professional architects continue to be engaged on chapel design but building came to a virtual stop in 1914 up to the outbreak of the First World War.

Detail of Column Capital, Tabernacle, Ynysybwl.

Plaque for the hard of hearing, Tabernacle, Ynysybwl.

Cast Iron balcony (gallery) balustrade detail. Moriah, Abercynon.

Ceiling of Bethel Chapel, Gadlys.
(Doug Williams)

Pulpit and organ console, Moriah, Abercynon.

Ceiling, Moriah, Abercynon.

Interior view from rear gallery, Carmel, Penrhiwceiber.

Pulpit, Carmel, Penrhiwceiber.

Stairs to pulpit, Carmel, Penrhiwceiber.

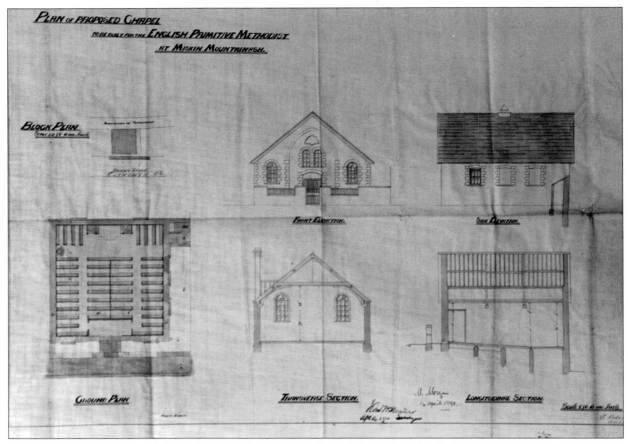

Original colour-washed drawing on linen cloth, 1890. Bethesda, Miskin.

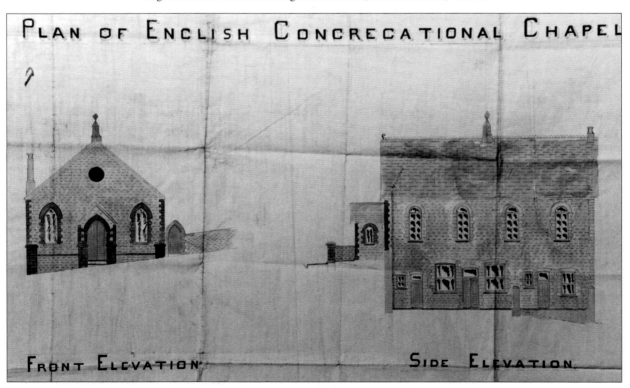

Original colour-washed drawing on linen cloth. 1903. Canaan, Miskin.

209

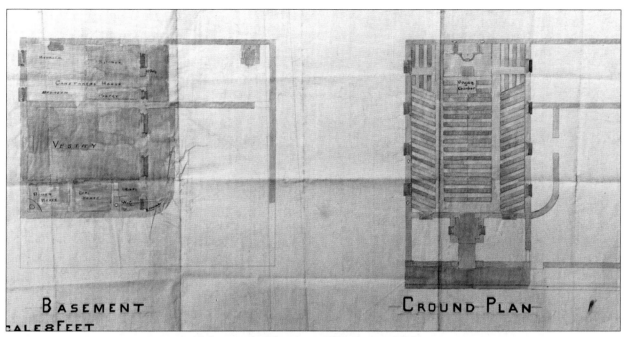

Colour-washed drawings, 1903. Canaan, Miskin.

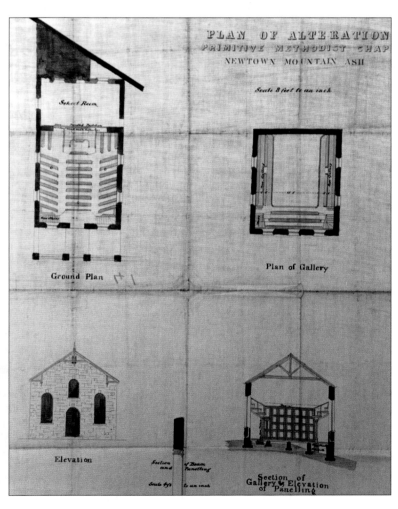

Original colour-washed drawings on linen
cloth, Zion, Newtown circa 1890.

Interior, Mount Pisgah, Miskin.

Window detail at rear gallery position, Zion, Newtown.

Pulpit and arched stencilled inscription, Bethania, Mountain Ash.

Ceiling rose, Bethania, Mountain Ash.

Ceiling panel, Bethania, Mountain Ash.

Pulpit, Bethania, Mountain Ash.

Oval shaped gallery, Noddfa (Elim) Mountain Ash.

Pulpit, Noddfa, (Elim), Mountain Ash.

The colourful and ornate ceiling, Noddfa (Elim), Mountain Ash.

Coloured stained glass window over rear gallery, Soar, Mountain Ash.

Ceiling rose, Noddfa (Elim), Mountain Ash.

214

Ceiling rose, Salem, Robertstown.

Interior view from the pulpit, Ebenezer, Trecynon.

Ceiling detail, Bryn Sion (Carmel), Trecynon.

215

Gallery balustrade, Ebenezer, Trecynon..

Pulpit, Ebenezer, Trecynon.

The intricate ceiling rose, Ebenezer, Trecynon.

Pew detail (pitch pine), English Wesleyan Chapel, Trecynon.

Pulpit and organ, Noddfa, Trecynon.

Gallery (balcony) Balustrade detail, Noddfa, Trecynon.

Ceiling rose, Siloh, Trecynon.

Interior view from rear gallery, Heol-Y-Felin, Trecynon.

Ceiling Rose, Green Street English Wesleyan Chapel, Aberdare.

Pulpit and organ, Nebo Newydd, Cwmdare.

Pulpit, Nebo, Hirwaun.

Ceiling rose, Ramoth, Hirwaun.

Ceiling Rose, Green Street E.W., Aberdare.

Piped organ, built in 1910 by Norman & Beard
of London and Norwich (cost £650), Carmel,
Penrhiwceiber.

Harmonium made by D.W. Karn Co. Ltd,
Woodstock, Canada. Penuel,
Penrhiwceiber.

Harmonium circa 1885,English Baptist Chapel,
Cefnpennar.

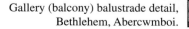

Gallery (balcony) balustrade detail,
Bethlehem, Abercwmboi.

Chapter 4

THE CHAPELS INTERNALLY

		Page No.
(i)	**Introduction**	**221**
(ii)	**Pulpits**	**222**
(iii	**Pews**	**223**
(iv)	**Galleries**	**223**
(v)	**Floors; Walls; Ceilings**	**224**
(vi)	**Windows and Glazing**	**225**
(vii)	**Organs**	**226**
(viii)	**Heating and Lighting**	**230**
(ix)	**Clocks**	**231**
(x)	**Chairs**	**232**
(xi)	**Sunday School Banners and Marches**	**232**
(xii)	**Miscellaneous**	**234**

"Whosoever thou art that
enterest this chapel,
Remember it is the House of God.
Be reverent,
Be silent,
Be thoughtful
And leave it not without a prayer
To God
For thyself,
For those who minister,
And for those who worship here."

(1912 Welcome notice displayed in the entrance vestibule of Providence
English Congregational chapel, Mountain Ash.)

(i) Introduction

Let us now take a look inside our chapels and observe the rich ornamentation of content and interior design; the highly skilled workmanship in the elaborately carved pulpits and pews and the magnificent pipe organs with their serried rows of pipes encased in beautifully carved wooden casing. Glance upwards and note the impressive galleries and balustrading and the ceilings with their delicate plaster central roses, which have a sculptured quality that makes them exceptionally attractive. There is also a vast selection of memorabilia and artefacts of all descriptions; there is so much richness to be seen .... right here in The Cynon Valley.

The early chapel interiors were simple and stark with a few wooden benches and a large table and chair at the front for the minister. The eighteenth century Meeting Houses were normally of long wall design with the pulpit in the centre of the long side wall. Later from the early nineteenth century the gable dominated the appearance of almost every chapel and became the main front façade and entrance; they accommodated anything between 100 and 250 worshippers and were normally single storey with no gallery. Decoration and embellishment was kept to a minimum. Later, as chapels became larger through increased membership and increased finance, more attention was given to the interior finishing, decoration, furniture and fixtures. The internal layout of the chapels in the locality and generally elsewhere is basically similar in design, with a front entrance lobby, porch or vestibule, a staircase left and right leading to the gallery. Where galleries are provided the seating accommodates 500 to 900 worshippers. Immediately we enter the front doors of the chapel we arrive in the lobby with a porch screen and doors leading to left and right aisles with pews positioned left, centre and right. The pulpit is at the far end with the Set Fawr (Big Seat) for the Deacons. The position of the pipe organ, where installed, is behind the pulpit or to the side of the pulpit in the gallery area, or located in front of the Set Fawr area with the organ chamber and pipes located out of sight behind the pulpit. There is usually a Sunday school, hall or vestry and a small kitchen at the rear or side of the chapel with a side entrance. A small anti-room is often provided for the Minister and Deacons, directly accessible to the main chapel area. There are however several variations in layouts and not every chapel has a gallery. The example given above is the most common found in a two-storey chapel in the Cynon Valley.

(ii) Pulpits

The pulpit is certainly the most elaborate interior furniture feature and main focus of attention in Nonconformist chapel design. It is usually centrally positioned opposite the main entrance doors and elevated above the communion table and Set Fawr area. The lofty position of the pulpit creates an imposing and intimate feeling and atmosphere in bringing the minister and congregation together. The minister can be seen from any seat in the chapel and with the use of slender gallery supports, an unobstructed view of the pulpit is provided. A large Bible with ornate brass clasps invariably lies on a stand in front of the preacher. In his 1984 book *"Welsh Chapels"*, Professor Anthony Jones mentions the elevated pulpits from where the preacher took command like a captain on the bridge of his ship, and he also tells us of a *"three-decker"* pulpit that was so high that some visiting ministers refused to ascend *"the perilous perch"*, choosing instead to speak from the safety of the Big Seat. Professor A. Jones also mentions the early pulpits as being simple boxes called "Preaching Tubs". In front of the pulpit at ground level or slightly higher and raised is the Set Fawr reserved for Deacons, Elders and visiting dignitaries, being a pew seating arrangement or chairs situated around the large Communion Table. This enclosed area also doubled up for Sunday school concerts and anniversaries when a makeshift stage was erected below the pulpit. From circa 1830, when the long wall façade became a design feature of the past, and chapels became larger, the pulpit was invariably positioned on the gable wall opposite the front entrance doors. In the older chapels entrance doors are sometimes found on the same wall as the pulpit, but in most cases the entrance and pulpit are on opposite walls. Therefore, the gable wall with its entrance became the main façade and from the 1830's it dominated the external appearance of almost every chapel in the Cynon Valley. Access to the raised pulpit is normally by a short staircase on each side. They are beautifully made with fine ornate carving and joinery work of a high standard. The employment of skilled craftsmanship is revealed at its best in this part of chapel furniture and is created to satisfy both the eye and the spirit. It is *"furniture as architecture"* and with highly polished mahogany, or varnished pitch pine inset with exquisite tracery panel work, elaborate fine mouldings and ornamental carving. In due course as finance permitted, mahogany and oak were sometimes used and took the place of pine usually for the pulpit joinery. However, the use of varnished and polished pine is the most common timber found throughout the locality. In some cases good quality pine and deal were comb-stained and varnished to give the effect of more expensive mahogany or oak finish at a much cheaper price. Not all pulpits are grand or ornate; some comprise simple lecterns positioned at ground level within front and side rails with simply designed fronts, whilst others have attractive wrought iron balustrading. To complete this section on pulpits I quote an example of a most distasteful conversion to an alternative use of chapel furniture, nothing short of ecclesiastical vandalism, in that of a grand old pulpit being shipped to the U.S.A. and re-modelled to form a drinks and cocktail bar area!

(iii) Pews

The pews of the eighteenth century chapels were usually simple makeshift crude benches often without backs and with no pretence to providing comfort or luxury through long services and sermons. The later pews were somewhat more "comfortable" with backs and often made of oak, later to be replaced by mahogany and polished-varnished pitch pine. They were solidly built and made to last for years. Pew arrangements comprise two main types, open pew arrangement and enclosed or "box" type with small doors. The latter are sometimes referred to as "pen-pews" and are allocated with numbered plaques. The open pews have oval or round shaped enamelled number plates fixed to the side of the end pew of each row. In some chapels pews have a central division. The pews of the nineteenth century are often polished, comb-stained varnished pine and are examples of fine furniture at its very best. Joinery embellishments vary considerably and some are quite plain without elaborate detailing. Pews in the galleries are generally plain in design and not so elaborate as those found at the lower chapel area. Dressings to pews include brass umbrella stands and cast iron hooks with a shallow tray drip bowl below to contain water from the umbrella. Backs of pews often have circular metal bracket holders for accommodating communion wine glasses and a narrow shelf for hymnbooks. The author came across an unusual feature found in Tabernacle W.I., Ynysybwl where on the end of pew number nineteen is a plaque that reads, *"Fitted seat for the hard-of-hearing. To adjust volume turn knob at base of handle. Ardente Acoustic Laboratories Ltd., England."* Pews come in all shapes and designs; square-ended, elbowed with arm rests, "Y"-shaped, rounded tops, bevelled splayed sides; some have attractive foliage embellishments whilst some are quite plain. Seating in Sunday Schools/Vestries comprises fixed oak or pine benches. A clever seating design is to be seen at Bethania W.I., Mountain Ash, where there are "tip-up" seats which double up as a bench and desk type table. Pew layouts are arranged so that all seats face the pulpit; in some chapels however, the side pews are splayed towards the pulpit for a better view of the preacher. Around the early 1900's some chapel members reserved their particular seats through payment of "Pew Rents" and pew collectors were duly appointed. Through the pew rent system anyone desirous of obtaining a seat for personal use by subscription of pew rent was to formally to apply for this privilege. Nameplates indicated which seat or seats were rented and often a complete row would be taken up by a family. Pew rents were abolished in many chapels in the 1920-30's. Alas, some chapels, which are still active, have ripped out their pews and replaced them with modern removable chairs for versatility of use of the main chapel area. Also, through the plight of chapel closure, particularly since the 1950-60's, pews and pulpits have been broken up and dismantled. In some cases they are sold and end up in homes or else are re-used for some other good and useful purpose. Pews are wonderful – albeit that they are not the most comfortable of seating furniture! There is nothing more pleasing to the eye than pitch pine darkened and mellowed to a rich golden colour through age. The smell of well-waxed polished pews is something one rarely forgets. Pews have symmetry, elegance, solidity and fine detail, be it simple or elaborate. They come in all shapes and lengths and are made from the best wood, by the best craftsmen and are made to last forever!

(iv) Galleries

As a result of Religious Revivals throughout the years chapel membership increased particularly following the 1859 Revival; consequently raked galleries or balconies as they are sometimes called, with tiered seating overlooking the main chapel interior space were added or included in the design to accommodate the swelling numbers of worshippers. The gallery is reached by staircases usually located left and right of the porch or vestibule area. The gallery is an important element in chapel layout and design and is supported by slim cast iron columns, which were made at the local iron foundry works at Gadlys,

Abernant and Hirwaun. These supports were made less frequently out of stone or wood. The columns are encrusted with decorative bases and ornate Corinthian capitals and some are attractively fluted; many are beautifully decorated in different colours and some have splendid stencil artwork. The slim circular pillars usually about four inches (100mm) in diameter are ideal as they allow the congregation a clear, unobstructed view of the preacher and pulpit. They vary from eight to twelve feet in spacing depending on the size of the gallery area they support. Many designs have been employed in the front balustrading of galleries; some are boarded in fine joinery and panel work whilst others have intricate open wrought iron designs forged into decorative patterns. In the two-storey chapels the gallery is usually "U" shaped in plan and located on three sides. Some, however, completely surround the four walls of the chapel interior as can be seen in Noddfa (Elim) P.C., Mountain Ash, while others have galleries on one or two sides only. Whatever their arrangement they offer a clear view of the preacher from every seat. A chapel with 900 seats provides about 500 seats on the ground floor and 400 in the gallery.

The following was reported in 1907 in The Aberdare Leader: -

> *"A pleasing feature on Sunday evenings in the chapels of our valley is the number of young men and women who fill the galleries".*

When the chapels were full the galleries were usually occupied by the younger members leaving the ground floor pews for the older folk who not only reserved their particular seats through subscription of pew rents, but also supposedly did not particularly want to negotiate the stairs to the gallery.

Striking examples of open wrought iron balustrading can be seen in Calfaria W.B., Aberdare, where the intricately designed balustrades are decorated in gold with the lower half shaped to a half curve and bowed with a hint of foliage and feather-like shapes in the design. Other fine examples are at Noddfa W.B., Trecynon; Bethlehem W.I., Abercwmboi; Moriah E.B., Abercynon. Mount Pisgah E.B., Miskin, is regrettably demolished but had a wonderful wrought iron balustrade to the gallery. The wooden balustrade panels at Highland Place Un., Aberdare, have unusual carving designs in what appears to be of Greek influence. Solid wood panelled balustrades are found in the majority of Cynon Valley chapels and are beautifully varnished and stained with comb-grain finish. The wooden gallery balustrading at Ebenezer W.I., Trecynon is a superb example and surrounds all four sides of the chapel and is of a high standard of workmanship as is the entire interior. The wooden panel work at Heol-Y-Felin W.B. is extremely attractive and also surrounds all four sides. The gallery at Noddfa (Elim) P.C., Mountain Ash, is most unusual being oval or elliptical in plan shape.

At Rhigos, the three-sided gallery at Calfaria W.I. terminates in an unusual curved fashion on the long wall side of the chapel. A rare feature exists at Soar W.I., Hirwaun, where the entire three-sided galley is cantilevered with no supporting pillars and is the only one of its kind in the Cynon Valley. Not all galleries are imposing or large; some, like Mount Pleasant E.Cong., Hirwaun, are quite modest and small having just a one-sided rear gallery with organ console taking up the entire centre area.

(v) Floors; Walls; Ceilings.

Floors

In the early Primitive Design stage, floors were earth covered with straw. Later stone slabs were used (flagstones) and laid on well-compacted soil or clay and some were covered with earthenware tiles. In later years the main chapel area normally comprised timber boarding or hardwood blocks. Some have tiles using Victorian patent stone whilst many front entrance lobbies and some aisles have ceramic tiles of elaborate design and attractive colours.

Walls

Most external main stonewalls are two feet to two and a half feet thick; the first floor walls are usually reduced in thickness. Earlier chapels are finished in lime mortar or plain plaster render and decorated in lime wash. Some chapels have vertical or diagonal designed timber board panelling above the seating area at ground and gallery levels terminating at window sill level. Timber panelling is also seen behind pulpits and the walls above are frequently ornamented with splendid classical pilasters, moulded arches and stencilled decorative artwork, often incorporating scriptured texts. A common feature behind the pulpit area is the use of a semi-circular arch or the less used pointed Gothic arch, terminating in ornate corbels. A recessed area behind the pulpit with arch and/or pilasters is also to be seen. Fully panelled boarded areas often extend the full width of the wall behind the pulpit. A number of chapels are finished in plain stone Ashlar blocks with unpainted finish and flush painted joints. A delightful example of an elaborate internal wall treatment can be seen behind the pulpit at Bryn Sion (Carmel) E.B., Trecynon, where embellishments include fluted pilasters with Corinthian capitals all beautifully decorated. Stone, marble or brass memorial plaques are featured on the interior walls of several chapels throughout the valley. At Nebo W.I., Hirwaun, the wall behind the pulpit features three projecting semi-circular plaster moulded arches terminating on elaborate scrolled corbels and attractively painted in dark and light blue and white.

CEILINGS

Along with fine joinery work found in pulpits, pews and grand pipe organ casings, the ceilings too are regarded as one of the main architectural features of a chapel. They are richly ornamented in the form of handsome ceiling roses highlighted by colourful and intricate plasterwork designs in delicate colours making them exceptionally appealing and attractive to the eye. Many ceilings are covered in high class joinery with polished or stained boards often arranged in attractive designed layouts. The elaborate patterns of the plasterwork were designed by artists and specialists. Italian plasterers were brought over to work and prefabricated designs were found in illustrated catalogues. Light pendants are to be seen in many chapels suspended from these wonderful ceiling roses. Some ceilings are left plain particularly in vestries and school rooms. The ceiling at Noddfa (Elim) P.C., Mountain Ash is striking in appearance with two large, splendid ceiling roses lavishly decorated in blue, gold, and yellow. There are sections of ornate moulded panels incorporating four smaller ceiling roses. This chapel is Grade Two listed and the ceiling is one of the most outstanding and finest in the Cynon Valley. Bryn Sion (Carmel) E.B., Trecynon falls in the same category being one of the most impressive ceilings in the locality, with panel work in rich mouldings, exquisite cornice work and an ornate ceiling rose. Bethania W.I., Mountain Ash has a magnificent and lavish ceiling with several attractive roses and deep ornamented ceiling coving all richly decorated. Ebenezer W.I., Trecynon has large ceiling roses with delicate and graceful designs which are repeated in the smaller square perimeter panels. Calvaria W.B., Aberdare also has an imposing ceiling with impressive roses surrounded by a square frame panel, all decorated in a multitude of colours. Other ceilings worthy of mention are at the following chapels: – Bethania W.B., Abercwmboi; Bethlehem W.I., Abercwmboi; Libanus C.M., Abercwmboi; Saron W.I., Aberaman; Sion W.B., Cwmaman; Bethania C.M., Aberdare; English Wesleyan, Aberdare; Bethel W.B., Abernant; Salem W. Cong., Robertstown; Nebo Newydd W.B., Cwmdare; Calfaria W.I., Rhigos; Ramoth W.B., Hirwaun; Heol-y-Felin W.B., Trecynon; Tabernacle W.I., Ynysybwl, and Moriah E.B., Abercynon.

(vi) Windows and Glazing

Windows particularly in the front façade come in a multitude of designs and fenestration arrangements, from very simple with just two windows, up to as many as eleven in the front façade alone. They are normally sliding sash and are square, rectangular, rounded or square tops, geometrical, Gothic with pointed arches. Others are small and tall, bull-eye, wheel windows, plain or intricate with delicate tracery work and rose type designs. Some are found grouped together as in central trio or triple arranged windows known as the "Trinity Window", the centre window normally being larger than those they flank each side. There are even windows found in the pediment area of some chapels with a name plaque squeezed in for good measure! Some groupings of windows are repetitive and can include as many as five or six windows with round or horizontal tops positioned together on ground and first floors of a façade. Some are quite impressive being positioned within a large "Halo" type arch; others are surrounded by moulded arches and pilasters. Windows in the side elevations are usually rectangular sliding sash with no embellishments whatsoever.

Glazing is normally plain but coloured leaded lights are found in some chapels where the designs do not portray biblical or religious scenes but rather have hints of attractive floral and foliage shapes in the design. Ffrwd chapel in Mountain Ash has rectangular tall windows entirely glazed with small square panes coloured green, red, blue and yellow. Most Gothic type windows are found in English Congregational, Primitive Methodist and Presbyterian chapels. Providence E. Cong., Mountain Ash has one large Gothic window in attractive tracery work and coloured leaded lights. However, stained glass is rarely used, as it is too expensive to purchase and replace. Glazing is normally one eighth of an inch thick (3mm) rolled glass. Porch screens contain attractive glazing designs in coloured, engraved or etched glass; these were supplied by the same firms that produced glass for the public houses of the period. The windows at Ebenezer W.I., Trecynon, are quite elaborate having moulded pilasters with ornate capitals and arch surrounds while others including Trinity E.B., Cwmaman, have only two plain round headed windows. Some facades have large windows with massive rusticated voussoirs as can be seen at Soar W.I., Mountain Ash. The variation in window design and fenestration is endless and range from very simple to "over-the-top" eccentric arrangements. The examples given are but a small selection found throughout the Cynon Valley. The scope and variety of designs and arrangements can be studied in more detail by referring to the drawings in Chapter One and photographs shown throughout this book.

(vii) Organs

From around 1880-90 the small harmonium organs with their charming unique sound, single or double manual keyboard and fine joinery casework were replaced by the larger pipe organs with two or three manuals and pedal organ. Many Cynon Valley chapels installed new grand pipe organs around 1900-1915. However, their Founders did not build Welsh chapels of the early 1800's with pipe organs, and congregations sang unaccompanied prior to the introduction of harmoniums or pipe organs. The early pioneer members of Nonconformist chapels objected to the use of *"modern machines"* or any such man-made device in the worship of God and organs were therefore frowned upon and not generally accepted until towards the end of the nineteenth century. Small harmonium organs were however commonly used circa 1880-90 and some as early as 1860 as in Bethesda W.I., Abernant which was provided with a harmonium made in 1855 by Alexandre Pere et Fils of Paris, and supplied by Harmston & Co. of Aberdare and Pontypool. The opposition to organs is further borne out by the story of a wealthy friend who once offered a pipe organ to Jerusalem W.P. chapel, Ynysybwl as a gift, but to his great disappointment and surprise it was refused by the Deacons who believed, *"The devil would be able to come in and enter the chapel through the organ pipes"!!*

Grand pipe organs became common at the turn of the twentieth century and their position within the chapel varied:-

> (i)   The organ console detached and placed on the floor in front of the pulpit and Set Fawr, facing the preacher with the pipes located in the organ chamber behind the pulpit.
> (ii) Organ console, organ pipes and chamber completely behind the pulpit on a higher level with the organist's back to the preacher and congregation.
> (iii) Organ console located in the gallery at the side opposite the pulpit with organ chamber behind and organist's back to the preacher.
> (iv) An unusual location where organ and console are opposite the pulpit positioned centre in the rear gallery.

Some critics argue that the central positions of these fine instruments located behind the preacher somewhat distracts from the appearance and focal point of the pulpit. However, if the pulpit is the main centre of attraction as one enters a chapel, worshippers and visitors must surely be impressed by the striking appearance of the grand pipe organ with their imposing rows of serried pipes decorated in attractive coloured stencilled artwork and enclosed in high class varnished and polished joinery casing, often of Gothic design.

Let us now examine the working and operation of a harmonium organ and the much larger grand pipe organ. The harmonium organ is a type of reed organ patented in 1842 by the French instrument maker Alexande F. Debain (1809-77). The name has been widely associated and used for reed organs in general, over the years. Air from pedal operated bellows causes the reeds to vibrate; a lever-action knee swell device is used to influence dynamics. The harmonium was widely adopted in the U.S.A., Canada and Great Britain in the 1850-1900's as a home and church instrument. The larger pipe organ is an

On 10th March 1904, the opening of the new grand pipe organ took place at Bethania C.M., Aberdare. The organ cost was £585. Two Grand Recitals were performed by E.T. Davies F.R.C.O. of Dowlais and Miss L Teify Davies, Contralto, and Mr Lloyd Chandos, Tenor.

> Reserved Seat – four shillings (20 pence)
> First Seats – half-a-crown (12.5 pence)
> Second Seats – one shilling (5p)
> Limited numbers

instrument in which air is fed by bellows, into a large wind chest. It is released under pressure into metal or wooden pipes of various lengths and bores, by the action of keys operated by the player's fingers and/or feet. The ranking of pipes, which vary in pitch, volume and timbre according to their length, material, width of bore, and the method by which air is made to vibrate in them, are brought into action by means of operating draw knobs or stops. Players can select registration, or a combination of stops, appropriate to the music they wish to play. Most chapel pipe organs have two manual keyboards; some have three but rarely four, along with Great and Swell organs. Couples may be used enabling pipes belonging to one keyboard to be sounded on another. Keyboard manuals generally range from fifty eight to sixty one notes; the pedal organ normally has a thirty note radiating concave pedal board in hardwood and contains the largest bass pipes of eight to sixteen feet tall.

Pipes are lead and pure tin alloy, wood and zinc and can vary from about two feet to sixteen feet tall. The pipe organ is tuned by the use of metal sleeves at the top of each non-reed pipe and tuning knives and brass cone tools. The cone opens the pipe to sharpen and cone in to flatten. The white keys are made out of ivory and black keys are of ebony hard dark wood. Inside the spacious organ chamber which is generally behind the pulpit, is located the quiet electric operated motor to serve the large bellows. In earlier days, the bellows were filled with air by operating by hand a large wooden lever about eight feet long. It took considerable effort to keep the bellows full, particularly during lengthy concerts or hymns with numerous long verses! The organist would know when the air in the bellows was about to expire by a small lead pendulum on a piece of string attached to the bellows and conveniently located at the side casing of the keyboard/console, in view of the organist. If the lead weight was raised to a given mark on the consul cheek casing, more air was needed and the organ blower, who was positioned in the organ chamber, was called upon to work harder by the organist giving a signal of discreetly tapping his foot on the pedal board. The official chapel Organ Blower was an important post and the appointment was decided by the Deacons. It seems that this gratis post was repeatedly difficult to fill – as difficult as that of filling the organ bellows I hasten to add!!

The operating action of the organ is called *"The Tubular Exhaust Pneumatic Action with built in stop key console"*. The balance swell pedal operated by foot works the swell shutter louvers for the desired volume and expression. In early days, pipe organs were hand blown and later assisted by hydraulic pressure from the water mains supply Today they are operated by electricity but have a back up of hand blowing in the event of electric mains failure. Harmonium organs work by foot operating a pedal to fill the bellows; these organs are made of oak or mahogany and have around 15 stops and usually one manual keyboard. Most pipe organs contain around 750 to 800 pipes. The pipe organ at Ebenezer W.I., Trecynon has 794 pipes, two manuals, 21 stops, and was installed in 1938. The former organ at Providence E.Cong., Mountain Ash had 734 pipes and two keyboards. The larger organs number up to 1500 pipes and the English Wesleyan Chapel, Aberdare which is one of the largest organs in The Cynon Valley

"Organist fails to turn up for an Aberdare Wedding Service"
– October 2002 –

..... so, one of the guests had a brilliant idea and decided instead to play The Wedding March on his mobile telephone! However, the timing of the march was much faster than expected, and the Bride and father were forced to almost run down the aisle to keep up with the music!

with over 1500 pipes was rebuilt in 1993 at a cost of £20,000. In contrast, the organ at St Paul's Cathedral, London, renovated and installed over one hundred years ago is five times bigger having 7500 pipes and is meticulously tuned by an expert no less than twenty five times a year. The 150-ton organ at the Royal Albert Hall, London is even larger with 9779 pipes measuring a total of nine miles!

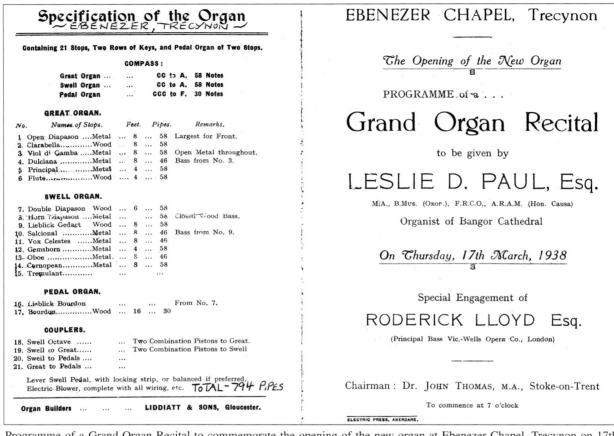

Programme of a Grand Organ Recital to commemorate the opening of the new organ at Ebenezer Chapel, Trecynon on 17th March 1938. The Programme also shows in detail, the Specification of The Organ containing 21 stops, two rows of keys, pedal organ, and 794 pipes.   *(Programme courtesy of Mr Eirwyn Davies, Organist of Ebenezer Chapel)*

When a new organ was provided or an existing one rebuilt, special Dedication Services and concerts were held in recognition and proceeds were allocated to the "New Organ Fund". Many other fund-raising efforts and events were carried out to help meet the cost of installation. The cost of providing and installing a new pipe organ during 1900-1915 varies from £350 to £500, whilst a larger organ of 1900-1905 cost up to £850. The more modest harmonium organ could be purchased for around £20 in the 1880's. Upon the closure and demolition of a chapel it is sadly inevitable that pipe organs also disappear at the same time. Some however are dismantled and donated to another chapel. Over one hundred years ago harmonium organs were being imported from manufacturers in Canada, U.S.A., France and Germany. Ironically, more than a century later the opposite is happening whereby grand pipe organs in good working order are being dismantled and are being exported to places including Holland, Norway and Denmark. The cost of

HIDING INSIDE AN ORGAN PIPE!

The Royal Albert Hall in London has a massive pipe organ, recently renovated. During the early years of the 20th Century, when the Suffragette movement were actively campaigning for votes for women, one enterprising lady decided to conceal herself with a megaphone inside one of the larger pipes of the organ, from where she hoped to broadcast her message loudly and clearly, disrupting a forthcoming event in the process. Unfortunately for her, the caretaker took his dog with him on his rounds of the building, and the dog gave her away by barking loudly at the base of the pipe, having detected her presence. Needless to say she was extricated and ejected from the building!

dismantling and rebuilding far exceeds the amount for purchasing these fine instruments. It seems that enthusiastic foreigners realise only too well the pure inimitable tone that only a grand pipe organ can produce and are therefore picking them up at bargain prices. If only the organs, like the chapels themselves, could be saved and remain in use where they belong rather than being sold to buyers abroad ...... if only!

There now follows a list of pipe organ builders, manufacturers, and suppliers of harmonium organs. The chapel reference number is given, followed by the organ builders or supplier.

> **BEWARE OF THE MICE!**
>
> The Canadian Harmonium at Siloam Welsh Baptist Chapel, Penderyn, patented 24th February 1887, has "Mouse-Proof pedals"!

Ref. 9   – Harmonium by W.W.D.M. & Co., Scranton, Virginia, U.S.A.

Ref. 17   – Piano made by the British manufacturing Co. Ltd., London; Supplied by Phillips, Aberdare.

Ref. 28   – Two manual harmonium by P.H.J. Trayser of Stuttgart.

Ref. 29   – Pipe organ built by Norman and Beard Ltd. of London and Norwich, 1910. Cost £650.

Ref. 34   – Harmonium built by D.W. Karn Co. Ltd., Woodstock, Canada; Supplied by Harmstons Ltd. of High Street, Aberdare (established 1887) and Abertillery.

Ref. 36   – Harmonium made by Cuelph, Ontario, Canada.

Ref. 47   – Canadian Harmonium.

Ref. 48   – Harmonium by Bell Piano and Organ Co., Cuelph, Ontario, Canada.

Ref. 55   – Pipe organ built by W.C. Vowles, Bristol.

Ref. 60   – Pipe organ built 1912 by Blackett and Howden, Newcastle-upon-Tyne and Cardiff; cost £352; 734 pipes; taken over by Hill-Norman & Beard Ltd., Norwich.

Ref. 63   – Pipe organ built 1904 by Messrs. Martin and Coate of Oxford.

Ref. 74   – Harmonium by H. Christophe of Paris – Manufacturer of harmoniums for chapels and salons; Bronze Medallist – Universal Exposition, Paris. 13 stops; single manual; five octaves.

Ref. 85   – "University" organ; two manual; 17 stops; five octaves; by Dale Forty of London and High Street, Cardiff.

Ref. 85   – Pipe organ donated by chapel Ref. 61. Formerly operated by water-driven pump.

Ref. 91   – Harmonium by Alexandre Pere and Fils, Paris; 2 manual; 20 stops.

Ref. 93   – Harmonium by D.W. Karn Co. Ltd., Woodstock, Canada; Single manual; 10 stops.

Ref. 97   – Harmonium supplied by Harmston & Co., Piano & Organ Merchants, Aberdare; Single manual; 20 stops; made by H.Christophe & Etienne, Chaperon Succe, Paris. Grand Prix Medal Winners in the Universal Exposition.

Ref. 97   – Pipe organ built by Norman and Beard of London & Norwich, 1909.

Ref. 103 – Pipe organ built and installed 1904; two manuals and pedal organ. Built by Norman Beard Ltd., Norwich.

Ref.107   – Original pipe organ built circa 1880 by Peter Conacher, Huddersfield. Rebuilt early 1900's by Mr. A.E. Harmston, Aberdare (he was organist at Ref.107, 1891-1916). Organ rebuilt in 1993, by Roger. D. Taylor of Burrington, Near Bristol and his colleague Neil Hoskin (at a cost of £20,000). Three manual; taken from Trinity Methodist Chapel, Risca; contains over 1500 stops; one of the largest in the Cynon Valley.

Ref. 107 – Harmonium by D.W. Karn Co. Ltd., Woodstock, Canada; five and a half octaves; 9 stops.

Ref.113   – Pipe organ built and installed in 1890 by Peter Conache, Huddersfield.

Ref.115   – Pipe organ built 1891 by Messrs. Thompson & Shackell, Cardiff.

Ref. 120 – Harmonium by Kelly & Co., London; Prize Medal, London, 1885.

Ref.121   – Harmonium made in 1885 by Alexandre Pere et Fils, Paris; supplied by Harmston & Co., Pontypool and Aberdare.

Ref. 127 – Pipe organ rebuilt in 1938 by Liddiatt and Sons, Gloucester.

Ref.128   – Harmonium by D.W. Karn Co. Ltd., Woodstock, Canada; Single manual; 21 stops, London and Hamburg.

Ref.128   – Harmonium by W.W. Putman & Co., Staunton, Virginia, U.S.A. five and a half octaves; 10 stops.

Ref.130   – Pipe organ built by Gray & Davison, 370 Euston Road, London. Located high in the gallery behind and above pulpit.

Ref. 133 – Harmonium by Estey Organ Co., Brattleboro, Vermont, U.S.A. 13 stops; single manual; five and a half octaves.

Ref.138 – "Selma Lincoln" electric organ (replicates a reed instrument). Single manual; 5 octaves; 6 stops. Supplied by Victor Freed, 11th Dec. 1955.

Ref.138 – Pipe organ built circa 1910-15 by Blackett & Howden; reconstructed in 1977 by Morgan & Lloyd Organ Builders, Aberdare. 21 stops; 2 manual; five octaves; takes up almost whole width of the chapel.

Ref.147 – Harmonium by Estey Organ Co., Battleboro, Vermont, U.S.A. Supplied by R.J. Heath & Sons; 14 stops; single manual.

Ref.156 – Harmonium by Bridgeport Organ Co., Bridgeport, Connecticut, U.S.A., 16 stops; single manual; five and a half octaves.

Ref. 161 – Harmonium by W. Bell, Cuelph, Ontario, Canada. Note the "Mouse-Proof Pedals", patented 24th February 1887.

John Davies, member of Gadlys W.B., Gadlys ("Pendar"), informs us that Ben Phillips of Canon Street, Aberdare was a supplier of musical instruments in the 1870-80's and was inventor of The Cheffonier Organ Cabinet and Harmonium Lockers. He supplied musical instruments to many of the older chapels in the locality. He was the first organist of Bethel W.B., Gadlys and self-taught. At Bethania Welsh Independent Chapel, Mountain Ash, can be seen a remarkable and unusual keyboard instrument called an "orgapian" made by E.W. Homes & Sons, Berkleyhead, and used in chapels in the 1890's. It is a combination of a wind organ (orga) and piano (pian) – hence the name "orgapian".

Advert dated 1912.

(viii) Heating and Lighting.

Candles were in use throughout the early to middle 1800's and in the late 1800's paraffin (kerosene) oil lamps and gas lamps became common. Many chapels were heated by coal-fired boilers but these were converted to gas in later years. Vestries and Schoolrooms were heated by freestanding open cast iron coal stoves usually positioned in the centre of the room with a metal flue. The stoves would sometimes smoke the room out if the wind blew in a certain direction, making it almost impossible to see the preacher at the pulpit; however, the stoves were quite effective in emitting radiant heat. Today some chapels are equipped with overhead electric heaters fixed to the fronts of the balconies; expensive to run and not aesthetically pleasing. Electricity was introduced to the Cynon Valley around 1897 and at the time was considered *"a technical miracle"*. In the same year the local newspaper reported – *"Incandescent lights are now in places of worship throughout the district;"* and *""The motor car is now giving an up to date appearance in the locality"*. During the Second World War blackouts were common and necessary in chapels, school rooms and elsewhere. One evening during the First World War in 1916 the chapel lights failed in the valley and candles had to be lit. It was emphasised (humorously) that the cause of the failure was not due to a Zeppelin raid, but rather by the fusing of the wires!

In his "History of Mountain Ash, written in 1896, William Bevan tells us, *"In the absence of artificial light the nights could often be pitch black, and when street lighting by means of gas was introduced into the towns in 1897 the local people were ready to believe that they then lived in one of the chief cities of the country. Prior to the arrival of gas, the chapels and shops were lit by means of oil lamps and candles, and when the oil was poor and inferior in quality conditions would be very unpleasant and inconvenient. Occasionally, the light in chapels was so poor that the preacher would struggle to read his notes, and if he was reading his sermon he would have to pretend to cough frequently in order to pause and assist matters. The lighting conditions were also very similar in the collieries both underground and on the surface."*

W.W. Price M.A., the notable local historian tell us that in the 1840's, lighting of the E.W.M. Chapel, Green Street, Aberdare was given by mould candles with snuffers. The pair of snuffers provided for the pulpit cost 3/6d (17.5p) whilst those in the body of the chapel cost ten pence each (about 4p).

Gas was introduced into the locality in 1887 when the Local Boards of Health of the districts took over the Gas Works in order to provide light to the chapels and churches, around the collieries, the offices, shops, dwelling houses, the streets and business premises. Today, in an effort to save on heat loss, some chapels have fixed a suspended grid system and draped either polythene sheets or fixed special ceiling tiles at balcony level, to the complete detriment of the overall appearance of the chapel. Redundant oil and gas lamp fittings fixed to walls can still be seen today in some chapels throughout the locality.

(ix) Clocks

Almost every chapel and vestry/schoolroom has a clock. They are to be seen in all shapes and sizes and are beautifully designed and made in high-class wooden casings of mahogany, oak or walnut. Some are quite plain and ordinary looking with simple circular casework; some clocks have elaborate glass or solid casework accommodating the pendulum mechanism and most faces have Roman numerals. More unusual types have the numerals one to twelve replaced by letters depicting a short biblical text or phrase, e.g. the twelve letters DILY-W(CH)-YR-OEN (translated, "Follow the Lamb"), other faces have the twelve letters CRED YR EFE(NG)YL (translated, "Believe in the Gospel"), and "JESUS SAVES" with numbers 3 and 9 with a square dot. The usual position in the chapel is for the clock to be displayed on the balustrade of the rear gallery in full view of the preacher where he may be constantly reminded of the time and to ensure his sermons do not become too long! Many clocks were presented on behalf of a group some being members of a Sunday School, or by individuals and were made and purchased locally.

The following is a list of local clock makers and suppliers. The Reference Number of each chapel is shown followed by details of the clocks: -

Ref. 7   – Rhodd Gan Mr & Mrs Bevan, presented by W.C. Davies, Mountain Ash.
Ref. 48   – Rhodd Yr Ysgol Sabbothol, presented by Thomas Evans, Aberdare.
Ref 84   – Presented by Miss C.M. Rowlands and Miss A. Davies. Supplier – Thomas & Co., Aberdare.
Ref. 85   – D. Thomas, Aberdare. Numerals read "CRED YR EFE(NG)YL". Trans: "Believe in the Gospel."
Ref. 85   – Alfred Lea, 18 Commercial Street, Aberdare.
Ref. 97   – Thomas Jenkins, Merthyr. Rhodd Yr Ysgolheigion Sabbothol.
Ref. 101   – Numerals read – "JESUS SAVES" with numerals 3 and 9 shown in square blocks.
Ref. 103   – Rhodd Yr Ysgol Sabbothol dated 1853, Thomas Evans, Aberdare.
Ref. 107   – F Eschle, Aberdare.
Ref. 121   – Thomas & Co., Aberdare.
Ref.124   – Rhodd Yr Ysgol Sul. Simmonds, Aberdare.
Ref.128   – Presented by W.C.Davies, Mountain Ash.
Ref.131   – Rhoddedig Gan Y Plant. Runge, Aberdare. Numerals read – "DILYN W(CH) YR OEN", translated: "Follow the Lamb."
Ref.131   – B Jones & Sons, 19 Canon Street, Aberdare. "Stanward – half hour strike."
Ref.150   – "Nebo" – David Bevan, Herwain (i.e. Hirwaun).
Ref 157   – Thomas & Co., Aberdare.
Ref 162   – Thomas & Co., Aberdare

(x) Chairs

Commemorative or Memorial chairs were made to celebrate special occasions including local Eisteddfodau, whilst some were donated by family or chapel members in memory of a loved one. A number of them have survived and date from around 1890-1910. They are beautifully carved by skilful wood carvers and joiners and usually are made of oak.

The following is a list giving the chapel reference number followed by details of the chairs:

Ref. 8   – "Eisteddfod Frehnol Cwir Yn er eyn". "Oenedlaithol Cymru A Laddo Adeddir". Eisteddfod chair, Caernarfon 1906.
Ref. 29   – Y Ydl (?) Cadair, Gwent.
Ref. 77   – "Eisteddfod Gadeirol Peniel".
Ref. 91   – Photo No. 1030 (A.V. Jones Collection), no description shown.
Ref. 124   – Photo No. 1509 (A.V. Jones Collection), no description shown.

(xi) Sunday School Banners and Marches

These were used on special occasions in Sunday School Parades and Marches and also hung or displayed in the chapel or vestry room, and behind the pulpit during other special events including Sunday School anniversaries and concerts. They varied in size and some measured up to six feet wide by nine feet high, and were painted in oil on pure silk. They are very colourful with scrolls bearing a text and usually the name of the Sunday school and chapel and show biblical scenes and such events. A number of banners have been donated to the Cynon Valley Museum where some are on display. A notable maker of silk banners for chapels, Trade Unions and Friendly Societies etc., was George Tutill of 83 City Road, London. He set up business there in the late 1800's and made several banners for the chapels of the Cynon Valley. Other makers of silk banners were

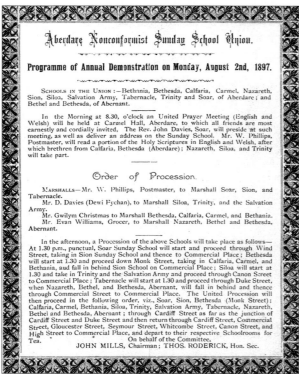

Programme of Annual Demonstration, 2nd August 1897 describing in detail, the Order of Procession for the various Sunday schools in the Union.

Advertisement for Sunday School Banner, 1907.
Courtesy of John Harvey, Author of "The Art of Piety", 1995.
National Library of Wales and University of Wales Press, Cardiff.

E. Riley & Co., Leeds during the early 1900's and Keesey of Birmingham in the early 1800's. During the processions and marches the Sunday school scholars would proudly display and carry their banners through the streets. Marshals were duly appointed and The Order of the Procession was meticulously timed and organised. Annual demonstrations and marches were held and many chapel Sunday Schools took part. The following programme of such a demonstration by the Aberdare Nonconformist Sunday School Union is shown below and took part on Monday, August 2nd 1897.

A Sunday school summer demonstration and annual tea party was held in Mountain Ash in August 1876; the children paraded the streets carrying banners and flags, bearing mottos indicative of the occasion. Choirs of children sang a selection of music and afterwards they retired to the vestry where a good supply of tea and cake was provided. The *"Aberdare Times"* 1867 reported one of these special occasions following a Sunday school anniversary of the local chapels in which 900 children, including teachers, formed a procession and marched through the streets to Duffryn House. The report is as follows:

> *"The children partook of tea under the shade of the noble trees. Lord and Lady Aberdare, and members of his lordship's family exerted themselves to the utmost to make the Sunday School children happy. They attended to the young ones and indulged in various amusements including the laying on of a number of swings suspended from the tree branches."*

A similar treat and event was reported following a Sunday school anniversary and procession in 1877:

> *"The children were regaled with tea and cake at The Workmens' Hall, Mountain Ash, and in the evening at the same place, a very pleasant entertainment, got up for their gratification, came off."*

Procession by members of Bethel,
Abernant, circa 1930.

Procession – Sunday School Banner carried by members of
Carmel, Trecynon. 1932.

The children and teachers of Zion English Baptist Sunday School, Hirwaun, circa 1920.

Sunday School and Banner – English Congregational Chapel, Abercynon, circa 1905.

Teachers and Sunday school children of Christ Church English Baptist Church, Gadlys, carrying the Church Banner through Aberdare Park, circa 1970.

(xii) Miscellaneous

PRESENTATION TROWELS

The laying of the Foundation Stone of a chapel was an important ceremonial event and included special meetings, marches and speeches by V.I.P.'s and guest of honour. Prominent people including M.P.'s and local businessmen were invited to perform the task of laying the stone, which was usually witnessed by a large gathering. An engraved silver trowel was presented to the layer who may also have donated a large sum of money to the "cause". The ceremony was followed by a luncheon and several speeches took place either in another local chapel close by or else in a hired room of a Public House. The Aberdare Times reported such an occasion on the laying of the Foundation Stone of Providence English Congregational Chapel in September 1869. This is the report:

> "After being presented with a handsome silver trowel by the Rev. Daniel Jones, Mr Samuel Morley Esq., M.P. gracefully gave thanks and then proceeded to lay the stone. After deftly arranging the mortar with the silver trowel and gently lowering the stone into its place he proudly expressed that he had great pleasure in declaring the stone duly laid."

CHINA WARE

Attractive teapots, plates, cups, mugs, saucers and jugs were manufactured by the thousand during the nineteenth and early twentieth centuries, bearing the name and sometimes a picture of the chapel or minister. Many were made for commemorative events and were used as "best china" for special services, anniversaries and tea parties etc.

Chapter 5

THE CHAPELS EXTERNALLY

Page No.

(i) **Stone Name Plaques.**   **235**

(ii) **Styles of Plaque Lettering**   **237**

(iii) **Welsh to English Translations of Name Plaques.**   **237**

(iv) **Cynon Valley Chapel Names and Their Meanings**   **237**

(v) **External Memorial and Foundation Stones.**   **240**

(vi) **Art in Ironwork.**   **241**

(vii) **Burial Grounds and Graveyards.**   **242**

An architectural study of external design features of the chapels from Primitive Phase to the Golden Classical period has been dealt with in Chapter Three. We shall now examine other external aspects and characteristics of the chapels in our locality and their immediate surroundings.

> *"We love the Place, O God,*
> *Wherein Thine honour dwells;*
> *The joy of Thine abode*
> *   All earthly joy excels.*
>
> *It is the House of prayer*
> *Wherein Thy servants meet,*
> *And Thou, Oh Lord, art there,*
> *Thy chosen flock to greet.*

Extract from the hymn by William Bullock 1798-1874
Henry William Baker 1821-1877

(i) Stone Name Plaques
Stone Plaques depicting the name, denomination and dates are found on almost every chapel and Sunday school in the Cynon Valley. Some are in Welsh, others in English and some have brief descriptions whilst many give more detailed information. Some are so detailed they may be considered a brief history in themselves. Structural changes from window replacement to a total rebuild were usually commemorated by a plaque recording the date of the re-opening. Plaques come in all sorts of shapes, sizes and designs, and a variety of lettering styles. They are positioned in different locations on the front façade but the most common are those within the triangular space known as the pediment. They are found in a variety of shapes from plain to very ornate. The English Congregational chapel at Abercynon, and Bethany E.C., Godreaman have three leaf clover patterns known as "Trefoil". The most unusual and flamboyant were

those of the former Hermon W.C.M., and Bethesda E.B. chapels both at Penrhiwceiber but demolished in 1995 and 1996 respectively. Both these plaques reflected the eccentric and mixed style of architecture of the chapel. Other unusual plaques are found in the shape of wings or similar design as in Noddfa W.I., Godreaman (Ref: 86.) and Soar W.C.M., Cwmaman (Ref: 92.). Among the plainest is the circular plaque of the former chapel Trinity E.B., Cwmaman (Ref: 93.) which depicts merely the date "1908". A number of chapels have very simple small plaques including Salem W. Cong., Robertstown (Ref: 122.), while others are ornate with fine embellishments as in the blazing bible carved on the stone wall plaque over the front door of Bethania C.M. Aberdare (Ref: 103.). This chapel also has an attractive name plaque under a large arch above three grouped sash and circular windows. Trinity W.P., Aberdare (Ref: 116.) contains two ornate name plaques one within a bold and impressive arch, the other below and between two pilasters. Plaques also reflect the general chapel design as in Soar W.I., Mountain Ash (Ref: 63.) with a circular shaped plaque containing four radiating spokes or keystones copying the voussoirs of the half-rounded window and door heads. Generally, the older chapels around 1820-1860 have simpler rectangular designs, reflecting the sub-classical phase of architecture of that period.

"Wing"-shaped stone name plaque. Noddfa, Godreaman

Name plaque in raised lettering. Soar, Cwmaman.

The "Blazing Bible" carved in stone over the front door of Bethania, Aberdare.

Stone name plaque, Bethania, Aberdare.

The plaques are usually produced and no expense spared, from local pennant, sandstone or slate but rarely marble. In all cases the skill of the stone carver is evident. These gifted and patient artisans also carved headstones of graves on which their company's name was often engraved. Rarely, if at all, is the stone cutter's name found on chapel name plaques. Congregations and members were clearly proud of their name plaques. A number contain sparse information while others are adorned with details on the re-building, enlargement and renovation, etc. Sandstone and local stone have deteriorated through the effects of weather, frost and pollution resulting in spalling of the surface and large areas breaking away. A few name stones have been salvaged rather than falling to the mercy of the bulldozer and have been set aside or erected elsewhere. When a chapel is rebuilt, the original plaque is often located elsewhere on the chapel or on the ground adjacent.

(ii) Styles of Plaque Lettering.

Lettering of plaques usually reflect the particular period and style of a chapel and vary from lettering raised from the surface to that of the cut and chiselled type. The early chapels, around 1800-1830, have bold lettering and are normally block serified, unshaded. Around 1830-1850 they are generally heavily shaded sanserif and alternatively serified. The late classic period 1850-1870 has heavy block, close spacing and crude sanserif. Approaching post classic 1870-1910 the varied forms become freed from the surface and are spread across the façade often following the line of an arch. Many chapels were rebuilt more than once to accommodate increasing numbers either through denominational rivalry or through growing membership during Religious Revivals. Numerous examples display names and dates which give a "snapshot" of the history of the building and rebuilding of a chapel. They have become a design necessity and prominent hallmark of the nineteenth century chapel.

(iii) Welsh to English Translation of Name Plaques

The following are examples of Welsh to English translations of structural terms shown on name plaques:-

ADEILADWYD	Built
ADEILADAETH	Building
ADAIL; ADEILAD	Building
ADEILADU	Build (v.t.)
CORFFOLAETH	Build (n.)
HELAETHWYD	Extend or Enlarge
ADGYWEIRIWYD	Repaired or Renovated
ADNEWYDDWYD	Renovate or Repair
AILADEILADWYD	Rebuilt (Second Building)
	Ail = second

> **WELSH v. ENGLISH SPEAKING CHAPELS**
>
> Between 1751 and 2004 the number of Welsh and English speaking chapels built were as follows:-
>
> Welsh speaking = 105
> English speaking = 75

Here are a number of Welsh to English translations of denominations commonly found on name plaques:-

BEDYDDWYR	Baptist
BEDYDDIWR	Baptist
CAPEL Y BEDYDDWYR	Baptist Chapel
ANNIBYNNOL	Independent
CAPEL YR ANNIBYNWYR	Welsh Independent Chapel
ADDOLDY YR ANNIBYNWYR	Independent Place of Worship
TREFNYDDION	Methodist
METHODISTIAID CALFINAIDD	Calvinistic Methodist
CAPEL Y TREFNYDDION CALFINAIDD	Calvinistic Methodists
ADDOLDY Y TREFNYDDION CALFINAIDD	Calvinistic Methodist Place of Worship
CALFINIAD; CALFIYDD	Calvinist
CAPEL WESLEAID/WESLIAD	Wesleyan Chapel
EGLWYS Y WESLEYAID	Wesleyan Church
YSGOL SABBOTHOL	Sunday School
YSGOLDY Y BEDYDDWYR	Baptist School

(iv) Cynon Valley Chapel Names and Their Meanings

ABERNANT-Y-GROES UCHAF   Mouth of the River Nant –
Groes = Cross; Uchaf = Upper

BABELL	Tabernacle
BETHANIA	"House of Ananiah" or "House of Prayer"
BETHANY	Town on the east slopes of the Mount of Olives, near Jerusalem. At Bethany, Jesus raised Lazarus from the dead. Here, the Ascension took place. Also – "House of Figs"

BETHEL	An ancient town near Jerusalem; the place where the dream of Jacob occurred. Also "Bethuel" – "House of God"
BETHESDA	A pool in Jerusalem reputed to have healing powers, where a paralysed man was healed by Jesus.
BETHLEHEM	Town on the west bank of the River Jordan, near Jerusalem; birthplace of Jesus and early home of King David. In 326A.D. the Church of the Nativity was built over the grotto said to be the birthplace of Jesus. Hebrew – "House of Bread".
BEULAH	Name given to Palestine after the Exile, when it was "re-peopled" and restored to God's favour. From the Land of Beulah; "Land of Heavenly Joy", also Hebrew for "married. Also, the marriage or bonding of the faith with The Lord.
BRYNGOLWG	Hill view
BRYN SEION	After Mount Zion
BRYN SION (ZION)	Sion Hill – on which the city of Jerusalem stands.
CALFARIA	Calvary
CALVARIA	From the Latin calvus – bald – skull; the place just outside the walls of Jerusalem where Jesus was crucified. Also called Golgotha – place of the skull.
CANA wine.	Town in Galilee where Jesus performed his first miracle by changing water into
CANAAN	Ancient region between the River Jordan and the Mediterranean. The promised land of the Israelites.
CARMEL	After Mount Carmel, Israel
EBENEZER	Name given by Samuel to a stone set up to commemorate a victory of Israel over the Philistines. Hebrew for "stone of help". A place of several confrontations between the Israelites and Philistines in the time of Samuel.
ELIM	The refreshing oasis of seventy palm trees and twelve wells or water springs, of potable water which was the second camp of the wandering Israelites. An oasis; the fountain and provider of spirituality and faith. Also translation – "Red Sea" – on the coast of the Gulf of Suez. Also "Terebinths Green Oaks" Greek – Terebinth = "Turpentine Mediterranean tree"
EMMANUEL	A variant spelling of Immanuel. From the Hebrew – "God with us". The child whose birth was foretold by Isaiah, and who in Christian tradition is identified with Jesus.
FFRWD	Stream or brook.
GOBAITH	Hope
GWAWR	Lord; king ; or dawn
HEBRON	City on the west bank of the Jordan. "Place of the Covenant". Also "City of Refuge". One of the oldest cities in the world, built 1730 B.C. A religious centre of Islam. The home of Abraham.
HEN DY CWRDD	The old Meeting House
HEOL-Y-FELIN	Mill Street (Trecynon)
HERMON	After Mount Hermon on the border between Lebanon and S.W. Syria.
HOREB	In the Hebrew Bible a mountain thought to be Mount Sinai (N.E. Egypt) where Moses received the Law from God, and God made a covenant with Israel by giving Moses the Ten Commandments on tablets of stone. Mount Sinah – Sinah = "Bush" or "Dry, desert-like"; Horeb = "The mountain of God".
JERUSALEM	Capital of Israel situated in the Judean hills. The Holy City of the Jews, Christians and Muslims.
LIBANUS	After Lebanon? Country west of Egypt; near Cyrene.
MORIAH	After "Mount Moriah". The district where Abraham, the father of Isaac and the

founder of the Hebrew people, prepared to sacrifice his son, by God's command. The hill on which the threshing floor of Ornan purchased by David was situated. This became the site of Solomon's Temple; identified with the hill on which the Temple of Jerusalem is built.

MOUNT PISGAH	The mountain slopes to the north east of the Dead Sea, from one of which – Mount Nebo – Moses viewed Canaan
MOUNT ZION	The hill on which the City of Jerusalem stands.
NAZARETH	Lower Galilee, North Israel; home of Jesus in his youth. After the Latin nazaraeus – to consecrate
NEBO	After Mount Nebo in Jerusalem. A mountain 12 miles east of Jordan. Place of Moses' death. Town on the slope of Mount Nebo of Judah.
NODDFA	Refuge; shelter.
PENUEL	The place on the picturesque Jabbok – River Jordan, where Jacob wrestled with a stranger and obtained an Angelic Blessing. Also – "Face of God" – Place where Jacob meets God in a wrestling match, thus winning God's Blessing by force and receiving the name Israel.

> **FANCY THAT! – A PENNY WELL-SPENT!**
>
> Penuel Welsh Baptist (Ysgoldy Beddyddwr – Baptist School), Cwmbach, was built in 1906. In 1975 Penuel was converted into a house, and named "Penny Well Spent!" Penuel = Penny well.

Also – Fortified tower of this highland position is mentioned in the Book of Judges. Hebrew = "Peniel".

PROVIDENCE	The belief that all things are ultimately ordered and governed by God towards a purpose; the belief in the trustworthiness, goodness and power of God.
RAMOTH	Hebrew = "Ramah". Isolated town near the Syrian border. Ramoth was "assigned" to Gad in the early occupation of Palestine. "City or town of refuge for Gad" or "heights". Situated west of the Jordan.
RHOS	Moor; pasture; meadow or marsh
SALEM	An Old Testament name for Jerusalem. Hebrew = Shalem; "Safe and Sound". Identified by Jewish tradition with Jerusalem by the Byzantines with Salem.
SARON	A level piece of rich fertile land in Canaan which in time became eroded to nothing more than a wilderness. The plain of Sharon. Also the Rose of Sharon is mentioned in the Old Testament.
SEILOH	After the town Shiloh in central ancient Palestine in
SILOA	Canaan. At one time sheltered the Ark of the Covenant
SILOH	until captured by the Philistines.
SILOAM	After the pool in Jerusalem where Jesus cured a man of his blindness. Also "Shiloah" = "Sent". In the land of Canaan, north of Bethel. The Pool of Shiloah of Siloam, south east of Jerusalem.
SION	After Sion Hill, on which the city of Jerusalem stands. After Mount Zion.
SOAR	After "Zoar" – one of the five cities of the plain on the east side of the Red Sea. Ruled by a king whom Chedorlaomer defeated. Also, the name of the small city that Lot and his family sought refuge after their ordeals at Sodom, when Lot's wife unwisely looked back at the forsaken place.
TABERNACLE	Tent; Old Testament – the portable sanctuary in the form of a tent in which the ancient Israelites carried the Ark of the Covenant.
TRINITY	The union of three persons; The Father, Son and Holy Ghost in one Godhead.
YNYSBOETH	"hot, burnt river-meadow" Ynys = meadow, pasture on the banks of a river or stream. Poeth = hot; burned; pungent; inflamed.

YNYSLWYD   Grey field; grey meadow
                  Ynys = river meadow; Lwyd or llwyd = grey or brown,
                  Also llwyd = holy.
ZION – (SION)   After Mount Zion – the hill on which the city of Jerusalem stands. In Hebrew it
                  probably means fortress or rock.

Thanks to Deric John, Tom Evans and Geoffrey Evans, for their help in compiling some of these chapel names and their meanings.

(v) External Memorial and Foundation Stones

These are usually found grouped together at the lower position under the ground floor windows. However some are located at a higher level either between ground and first floor windows or above the upper windows. They are laid and built into the main front external wall to commemorate the opening or rebuilding of a chapel and are inscribed with the names of individuals from all walks of life. They include ministers, J.P.s, doctors, solicitors, M.P.s, architects, engineers, surveyors, business men, military heroes and members and officers of the chapels. Here is a small selection of well-known dignitaries of past days whose names appear on memorial stones: -

> **THE NAMING OF TRECYNON**
>
> Rev. William Edwards, minister of Ebenezer W.I., 1844-1884 was responsible for the name "Trecynon", replacing "Heol-Y-Felin". The Local Authority wanted suggestions for the naming of the growing suburb.

Lord Mayor of Cardiff
Sir W. Reardon Smith, Cardiff
Gwilym Jones, Solicitor, Mountain Ash
R. Corey Esq. and John Corey, Cardiff
D.A. Thomas M.P. (1907). Later Viscount Rhondda
Alderman R.W. Jones M.D. (1907)
Tom. W. Millar, Architect, Mountain Ash
Isaac George Esq. High Constable of Aberdare and Miskin Higher (1904)
E.M. Hann Esq. "The Oaklands", Aberdare (1909) (b.1850 d. 1931)
Rees Llewellyn, C.S. Bwllfa House, Cwmdare (1906)
Miss. F Marian Harrison, Maesgwyn Tce., Cwmdare – later to be Lady Marian Williams
Dame Phyllis Harrison, "Harrisonville", Cwmdare
W.M. Llewellyn Esq., M.E., D.C., Bwllfa House, Cwmdare (1916).

The names of local dignitaries around 1880-1916 were usually shown on the Memorial and Foundation Stones because they had contributed towards the chapel "cause" or funds, or had served faithfully as an officer.

All the plaques are of local stone or slate and rectangular in shape, and have chiselled-carved lettering. As with name plaques the same carvers worked on the Memorial Stones. Prior to laying a Memorial Stone, a service was held and an engraved silver commemorative trowel was presented to the layer. The Memorial Stones of a number of demolished chapels have been saved and set aside, e.g. the stones at the Dare Valley Country Park built into the external walls of the Accommodation Block and Information Centre. Although a difficult task, every effort should be made to preserve, record or at least photograph all of the stones when a chapel is demolished; by doing this a small part of our chapel heritage will have been saved. The largest number of external memorial stones on a front façade is thirty-eight at the former Noddfa W.B. chapel, Trecynon, Ref: 131(converted to a dwelling house in 2002); Zion E.B., Ynysybwl (Ref: 10.) has sixteen and Ffrwd W.B., Mountain Ash (Ref: 55.) has twelve stones. Most chapels contain up to around six, whilst there are several that have no memorial stones whatsoever.

> **HIDDEN TREASURE**
>
> At Trinity W.P., Aberdare, the Foundation Memorial Stone was laid in October 1867; underneath this stone a casket of white marble was deposited containing coins of the realm dated 1867, plus copies of newspapers and periodicals of that year (e.g. copies of "Gwladgarw").

(vi) Art in Ironwork

Original nineteenth and twentieth century wrought ironwork and cast ironwork can be seen in many chapel forecourts, side boundary railings and gates, and are usually painted black; tops or finials are sometimes gold, white or silver and have "barley twist" or "fleur-de-lis" ornamentation and floriated cap designs. Some have survived around 150 years or more, but a large number were dismantled and taken out during both World Wars and melted down to be used for producing military hardware towards the war effort. The ironwork was made and forged by local foundries at Llwycoed, Abernant, Gadlys, Aberaman, Hirwaun, Dowlais and Merthyr Tydfil. Names include Fothergill, Scale, Guest, Waynes, Hill, Bacon, Homfray, and Crawshay. Cast iron is hard and brittle and made in a mould to the shape required. It could be used to produce complex shapes such as intricate door brackets and being strong in compression it was also used in internal gallery column supports. The capitals of these columns were expertly cast into attractive designs. Wrought iron is ductile and strong in tension and can therefore be forged into decorative patterns or rolled into bars, as found in boundary railings, gates, internal pulpit rails and gallery balustrading.

Detail of iron finial to railing of chapel boundary. Typical of many throughout Cynon Valley

Ornamental cast iron door bracket, Highland Place Unitarian Church, Aberdare.

Finial detail of chapel railings.

(vii) Burial Grounds and Grave Yards

The local Health Boards of Aberdare and Mountain Ash were established in 1854 and 1867 respectively. Prior to the opening of seven public cemeteries by these local Health Boards, and later the local councils, between 1860 and 1936, interment took place in the burial grounds within the curtilage and boundaries of the chapels. The earliest burial ground in the Cynon Valley is at St John's Parish Church, Aberdare (founded 1189). The earliest memorial headstone known here bears the date of 1685. At this burial ground an Order of Council dated 10th June 1864 prohibited burials except for vaults and walled graves constructed before 5th May 1864. They had to be free from water, and each coffin had to be embedded in charcoal and separately enclosed in masonry or brickwork, properly cemented. The oldest graveyard belonging to a Nonconformist chapel is at Hen-Dy-Cwrdd, Trecynon, where the first burial was that of a young child in 1797. This burial ground closed on 17th April 1858. Today it is in quite a dilapidated state and many headstones have been damaged and overturned. They have also deteriorated through age, decay and pollution. However, recent efforts have been made to tidy up the area. Fortunately, the renowned local historian William Watkin Price (1863-1967) carried out a survey and record of all the headstones here in the 1960's and he listed the details making reference to a plan he prepared of the burial ground. In 1994 the Cynon Valley Council carried out a similar survey of the burial ground at Abernant-y-Groes Uchaf Unitarian Chapel, Cwmbach (Ref: 94.). The graves here date from 1845 to 1860. At Salem W.Cong., Robertstown (Ref: 122.) the last burial was in 1883. Prior to 1866, in addition to the old burial ground at the Parish Church of St John, many residents from the lower end of the valley were buried at the graveyards at Llanfabon and the Parish Church of Llanwonno.

In the early 1850's there were sixteen Nonconformist Chapels in the Cynon Valley with burial grounds attached, all in close proximity to dwelling houses. These, together with references, are as follows:-

        Abernant-y-Groes Uchaf, Un., Cwmbach – Ref: 94.
        Bethania C.M., Aberdare – Ref: 103.
        Bethel (old) W.C.M. – Ref. 144.
        Calfaria W.B., Aberdare – Ref: 104.
        Carmel E.B., Aberdare – Ref: 105.
        Ebenezer W.I., Trecynon – Ref:127.
        Gwawr W.B., Aberaman – Ref: 73.
        Hen-Dy-Cwrdd Un., Trecynon – Ref: 129.
        Heol-y-Felin W.B., Trecynon – Ref: 130.
        Nebo W.I., Hirwaun – Ref: 150.
        Ramoth W.B., Hirwaun – Ref: 151.
        Salem W.Cong., Robertstown – Ref: 122.
        Saron W.I., Aberaman – Ref: 76.
        Siloa W.Cong., Aberdare – Ref: 113.
        Siloam W.B., Penderyn – Ref: 161.
        Soar W.W.M., Hirwaun – Ref: 152.

In addition there are several burial grounds throughout the Cynon Valley attached to the Established Church in Wales.

Writing of the old burial ground at St John's Parish Church, Aberdare; in 1853, the vicar, Rev. John Griffiths stated: – *"There is now very little space in this ground unoccupied. The graves now are always dug six feet deep which has not always been the case. Paupers' graves were formerly dug four and a half feet deep. We have buried as many as three in a single grave but the majority of graves contain only one body. The soil is clay and usually damp. Until the ground was drained last year (1852) there was so much water in the soil that the coffins were often floating in it. The drainage is not very complete."*

During the 1850's the question of providing additional burial accommodation had engaged the attention of Rev. John Griffiths for some time, and meetings on the subject were held to resolve the growing problem. In the early 1850's Rev. Thomas Price, minister of Carmel W.B. Chapel, Aberdare (Ref: 105.), stated that the old burial ground of his chapel was first used in 1812, and that by 1853 it had become full. The Rammell Report of 1853 confirmed that Nonconformist chapel burial grounds were nearly full. The public health danger was very great at a time of epidemic disease including small-pox and typhus 1846-53 and particularly the deadly and highly contagious cholera epidemic which made its dreaded appearance in the district in the summer of 1849. This was during a period when weather records indicate a period of drought, and when cholera victims were buried in large numbers close to the peoples' houses. This gave rise to contamination of wells and other sources of drinking water, which led to further outbreaks. Sources of water supply dwindled and the people were driven to take it from contaminated wells and "spouts". The first cholera victim was William Morgan of Penywaun who was buried at St John's churchyard on the 13th June 1849. The burial grounds of Soar, Bethel, Nebo and Ramoth, Hirwaun, are filled with the victims of the cholera epidemic of 1849.

The serious situation of over-crowded burial grounds in the 1850's eventually led to the provision of the following seven public cemeteries in the Cynon Valley between 1860 and 1936: -

Aberdare 1860	
Aberffrwd, Mountain Ash (Caegarw)	1866 (see note below)
Ynysybwl	1896
Abercynon	1901
Maes-yr-Arian	1908 (see note below)
Bryn-y-Gaer, Hirwaun	1914
Rhigos (Community Council)	1936

The land of Aberffrwd Cemetery (3 acres), was given by the Right Hon. John Bruce Pryce, Lord Aberdare.

Maes-yr-Arian Cemetery was so called after a "Field of Silver"; old silver coins were discovered there about 1850 in the wall of a field, which bears the name Maes-yr-Arian, or "The Field of Coins", containing thirty-six Elizabethan Shillings. Around 1908, a farmer ploughing in another field a little way up the valley saw something shining in the soil and stooping down he picked up three nobles of the reign of King Edward IV (reigned 1461-70 & 1471-83), three groats and a silver penny. They were gold coins in splendid condition with the mint gloss still upon them.

During the 1880's poverty was prevalent throughout the district. Some families would gather together in a cemetery to dig graves. Everyone helped and on completion would receive a ticket for which they would be paid one shilling (5p) at the local Town Hall.

It is not within the scope of this chapter to outline details of the hundreds of headstones throughout the burial grounds of our chapels or the Established Churches in Wales which contain the names of prominent men and women who have brought great fame to the Cynon Valley through their talents and enterprise. Time spent in searching these out would surely reveal the many great past pioneers and founders of so many good and worthwhile causes, not only in religious fields but also in countless other secular circles. However, members of The Glamorgan Family History Society and other local enthusiastic researchers are known to be currently engaged in listing burial head stone details in public cemeteries throughout the Valley. It would be interesting to know if this worthwhile voluntary work is being developed and progressed in respect of our Nonconformist chapel burial grounds. Such invaluable records allow us to build up a picture of the past social life and history of the locality from unique primary sources. It helps us to broaden our awareness of the talented people of our valley as well as the not so well known, and it gives us the opportunity to take a brief glimpse into the lives of our local folk and culture and to be for ever proud and grateful to them for providing our rich local heritage.

244

Ceiling rose, Bethlehem, Abercwmboi.

Detail of column capital, Bethlehem, Abercwmboi.

Enclosed box type pews with door. Libanus, Aberaman.

The organ at Bethel, Gadlys.
(Doug Williams)

Ceiling rose, Libanus, Aberaman.

Ceiling rose, Saron, Aberaman.

Interior during demolition. Inscription translated "Thine Kingdom Come" Bethania, Cwmbach. 1995.

Interior during demolition, Bethania, Cwmbach.

Interior as seen from the pulpit of the largest chapel in the Cynon Valley, with over 900 seats, Saron, Aberaman.

Ceiling rose, Sion, Cwmaman.

Pew detail, Ebenezer, Cwmbach.

Stained glass leaded panels of vestibule doors, Saron,
Aberaman.

Pulpit and stairs in classical design, Bethania, Aberdare.

Ceiling rose in delicate and intricate plasterwork, Bethania, Aberdare.

Ceiling rose and panel, Calvaria, Aberdare.

Gallery (balcony) balustrade in gold coloured wrought iron, Calvaria, Aberdare.

Interior from the rear gallery, Green Street E.W. Chapel, Aberdare.

Pew detail, Green Street E.W. Chapel, Aberdare.

Gallery (balcony) support in stencilled artwork, Siloa, Aberdare.

Ceiling rose, Bethel, Abernant.

Interior as viewed from the pulpit, Trinity, Aberdare.

Interior from the pulpit, with large Bible. Bethesda, Abernant.

Detail of organ casing and stencilled artwork to the pipes, Gwawr, Godreaman.

Detail of casing and pipes, uppermost section of organ, Gwawr, Godreaman.

The organ at Gwawr, Godreaman, donated by Rhos, Mountain Ash in 1975. It was operated by water driven pumps when at Rhos Chapel.

Plaque on harmonium organ. The organ was supplied by Harmston & Co. Aberdare. Bryn Seion W.I. , Cwmbach.

Plaque, harmonium organ, Bryn Seion W.I., Cwmbach

Harmonium organ made by D.W. Karn & Co. Ltd., of Woodstock, Canada. Trinity, Cwmaman.

Pulpit and organ, Green Street E.W. Chapel, Aberdare.

254

Harmonium organ, Green Street E.W. Chapel, Aberdare.

Organ and console, Highland Place Uniterian, Aberdare.

Organ at Siloa, Aberdare.

Harmonium organ made by Estey Organ Co., Battleboro.
Vemont, U.S.A. Siloh, Trecynon.

Interior as viewed from the rear of Trinity Chapel, Aberdare.

Interior of Ebenezer, Trecynon, as seen from the rear gallery.

Harmonium organ made by W Bell, Cuelph, Ontario, Canada, 1887 – Siloam, Penderyn

Detail of 'mouse-proof' pedal of harmonium organ, patented 24/2/1887. Siloam, Penderyn.

Front cover of Souvenir Bazaar Programme dated October 1912. – Siloa, Aberdare.

John Elias (1774 – 1841)
preaching circa 1830.
(National Library Wales)

"The Rivals –
Church &
Chapel"
contemporary
post-card.
*Courtesy of Kevin
Adams 1904 Ltd.*

Clock located on rear balcony balustrade at Tabernacle, Ynysybwl.

China ware, typical of many items seen in
Cynon Valley chapels. Tabernacle, Ynysybwl.

Eisteddfod chair in oak, Caernarfon, 1906. Tabernacle, Ynysybwl.

259

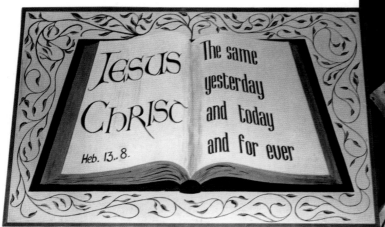

Decorative artwork on the front interior wall
of Bryngolwg E.F.C.

(Mission Hall), Miskin.

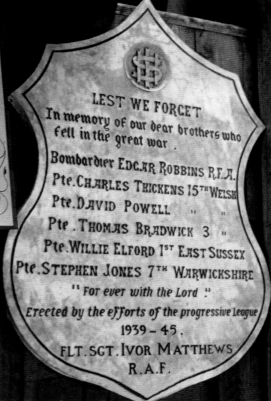

Marble Memorial Plaque – 1939-1945 Great War. Mount
Pisgah Chapel, Miskin.

Fine bone china commemorative 'Love Mug' dated 1882. Zion P.M. Chapel, Newtown.

Chapter 6

CHAPEL – A WAY OF LIFE

		Page No.
(i)	**Introduction**	**260**
(ii)	**Ministers; Preaching; Sermons; Salaries.**	**262**
(iii)	**Officers and Members; their roles and duties.**	**270**
(iv)	**Chapel Rules and Discipline**	**281**
(v)	**Temperance and Abstinence**	**283**
(vi)	**Music and Singing in Chapel**	**285**
(vii)	**War and Poverty**	**288**

"The chapels made life bearable and meaningful to thousands of people, both through their means of grace and through their character as social and cultural centres. The debt of the communities thrown up by the Industrial Revolution to the Welsh Chapels is incalculable."

With acknowledgement to
Canon E.T. Davies

"Religion in The Industrial Revolution in South Wales" (1966).

(i) Introduction

During the nineteenth and twentieth centuries, the chapels of the Cynon Valley and elsewhere throughout the neighbouring towns of South Wales played a central role within the locality and influenced the religious life of the mining communities. They were not only places of worship and fellowship but served also as educational, social and recreational centres throughout the week. The chapel was, and still is to this day, above all a product of the people and dominated the scene and lives of folk throughout the Valley. The fellowship of our chapels and their members had a powerful effect over the education and lives of the community, and was a source of great strength for the support and advancement of the Welsh Language. In the nineteenth century the majority of our chapels were Welsh speaking. They provided a place for people to participate in a wide range of educational and cultural interests including singing, music and concerts; Eisteddfodau and Gymanfa Ganu, drama and literature; lectures and debates; history and art and much more besides. Such influence continues albeit on a diminished scale. Before Foster's Education Act 1870, many of those who could not afford State Education were taught the three "R's" as well as Religious Education and Bible Studies in the Sunday schools. Prior to 1870 the Government took very little responsibility for education and schools. Day schools ("British Schools") were set up by the Nonconformist chapels. The Iron and Coal Companies also supported the Day Schools financially by deducting money from wages to pay for the education. The 1870 Education Act enabled Primary Schools to be set up and run by Local School Boards paid out of the Rates; this was a welcome introduction to the education system where Day Schools run by the Sunday schools were becoming inadequate to meet the demand. Canon Jenkins, Vicar of Aberdare, proposed a resolution in a Public Meeting which was duly carried, to adopt the Education Act of 1870. Consequently, in March 1871 the first School Board was formed in the Parish of Aberdare.

Sunday was undoubtedly a day for the best suit, best dress and family walks and other simple and pleasurable pursuits, but above all the Sabbath was a day for rest and worship, and the chapels were regularly attended. Often members would have to arrive at their places of worship up to one hour before services commenced to be sure of a seat. Sunday lunch or dinner would be prepared the day before to devote the Sabbath to chapel services which for many was considered the highlight of the week. These architecturally impressive grey-stoned buildings were often the largest in the locality, only overshadowed by the colliery engine and winding houses and large Workmen's Institutes scattered around the valley. Throughout the 1800's and early 1900's the Cynon Valley population comprised a high proportion of chapel-goers including members and visitors known as "listeners" or "gwrandawyr". These were the casual attendees or non-regulars, who were not full chapel members and usually occupied the seats in the gallery. People felt a need to attend a place of worship for fellowship and for devotional, educational and social reasons. Furthermore, chapel was a place where many could retreat from the poor and often miserable existence of industrial life in the nineteenth century.

> **ROMAN CATHOLICISM**
>
> Shortly after 1850 it was estimated that there were about 300 Catholics at Aberdare and about 200 more in Hirwaun. Services were conducted in the Long Room of the Horse and Groom Public House. Their Priest was a Father Muldoone.

In the late 1800's, the chapels established Friendly Societies to collect contributions from members, to be expended on the poor and needy in times of illness, old age and family bereavement. In these difficult years the soup kitchens distributed up to 100 gallons of soup each day, three days a week, to those in need. Many members gave their voluntary help to this cause, and the Chapel vestries were made readily available. Food and soup was often paid out of the Colliers' wages at a donation of up to three old pence each week. During this period, poverty in the valley and elsewhere was prevalent. Street begging was known to occur, and some children walked about with no shoes. The Poor Law was in operation, and Vagrancy Relief was made available through the Workhouses, which were governed by the Board of Guardians, and was partly intended to assist in "The Relief of Tramps". Vagrants at times attended Chapel services but often took a back seat. The idea of wearing one's Sunday best was accordingly overlooked on occasions. To enter the Workhouse through sickness or want was a fate to be avoided at all costs. Life here for a local unfortunate was a terrible experience, and paupers did not on the whole live long. However, in the midst of poverty, weariness and despair, there was always the spiritual comfort of the Chapel, where one could pray and listen to eloquent sermons – a place of worship and solace in days of difficulties and hardship for so many during this period.

Chapel was the centre of much activity where friendships were formed and cultivated, and where self-made fun and recreation gave a firm foundation and positive outlook on life; a place of refuge and prayer, a place to rest at stressful times and to simply meditate. During the period 1850 to 1900 chapels appeared in abundance as they catered for an expanding and newly industrialised population. Proportionately there were more Chapels in South Wales than any other part of Great Britain, and in the Cynon Valley alone over 150 were built during these years. By the late nineteenth century Nonconformity in the Valley had become a predominant force and the erection of Chapels continued at a prodigious rate through to the early 1900's when it then slowed down considerably. After the 1904-05 Religious Revival very few Chapels were erected and by the 1914-18 War, building work came to a virtual halt. "Chapel" is still a way of life but only for the minority. Social habits and the attraction of modern secular interests have changed peoples' attitude towards attending a place of worship. In South Wales this has led to diminishing congregations and the closure and demolition of many of our chapels. Since 1914, 56 have been demolished to date (2004), 11 are vacant, 50 converted to other uses and 63 remain active. Another Revival is perhaps too much to expect as we enter the twenty-first century. However, some awakening is necessary to halt the decline and thus avert the inevitable disappearance of further chapels in our valley. The closure of chapels is occurring at an alarming rate and

> **CHAPEL STATISTICS**
>
> In Calvaria Welsh Baptist, Monk St. between 1845-1915, 2250 were received into baptism; there were 1200 scholars in the Sunday school with 131 teachers, in 1863; between 1845-1888, 3847 were received into membership; Rev. Dr. Price baptised 1596 in the 40 years between 1886 and 1926.

with it a unique cultural existence is fast fading away. Only 35% of a total of 180 remain open and active for worship, whilst 31% have been demolished; 28% have been converted to an alternative use and 6% remain vacant. "Chapel – A Way of Life" may one day be just a memory as future generations emerge.

(ii) Ministers; Preaching; Sermons; Salaries

The members and officers who make a chapel function are numerous and each has a useful and important role to fulfil. The responsibility of the Minister or Pastor as leader is varied, from advising his congregation and members in good and bad times, and offering spiritual guidance, and in being their comfort and councillor in times of strife. In addition the Minister officiates at christenings and Baptisms, Weddings and funerals, and the all-important duty of visiting the sick and lonely and bereaved. He is at all times available to his congregation and ready to extend his hand of friendship to both young and old.

The Sermon, of course, plays an important part in the order of worship. In bygone days preaching the Message would often last from half an hour to two hours or more. During his sermon the Preacher would display eloquent rhetoric and above all would introduce that wonderful description of expression in Welsh oratory – "THE HWYL". The following is an apt description of that special quality of mood and grandiloquence common alone to the Welsh Preacher.

> **WHEN SERMONS WERE LONG**
> Rev. William Edwards, ordained at Ebenezer W.I., Trecynon in 1844 regularly preached for well over two hours to his congregation on Sunday evenings.

"THE HWYL"

"In bygone days it was usual for the Welsh preacher in the peroration of his sermon to enter into what is called in Welsh – "The Hwyl", which is a special form of impassioned utterance half-way between speech and song, and so rhythmical and emotional that sense gives way entirely to sound. A Welsh preacher in the Hwyl would not shrink from the most grotesque and bizarre effects; a simple appeal for funds for the mission field would become an elaborate play with the musical value of the words shilling, Patagonia and Timbuctoo, it was formal notification that he had become possessed of the living Word, that the afflatus had descended upon him; he spoke as if with the gift of tongues but the tongue was Welsh embellished with the most striking and esoteric words which happened to fit in with whatever rhythmical scheme that the preacher was pursuing at the moment."

> **A LABOUR OF LOVE**
> In 1817 the salary of the Rev. Joseph Harrison of Ebenezer W.I., Trecynon ranged from ten shillings (50 pence) to thirty shillings (£1.50) per month, depending on the amounts collected in the offertory plate.

*From – "A Bundle of Sensations"
– Goronwy Rees (Fellow of
All Saints Oxford University;
One time Principal, Aberystwyth University).*

Courtesy of Chalto & Windis, 1960.

Sundays were days set aside from normal activities, when famous and charismatic Preachers visited the town and attracted great crowds; many queued for hours to ensure a seat at such services and sermons often lasted for several hours. It has been said that unless a Welsh Preacher could act, he would never become a good preacher. This was borne out by many actions performed in the pulpit; occasionally the preacher was seen striking the Bible with his fist until the sacred Book was almost battered and his knuckles sore. In addition, he would raise the pitch of his voice as high as the top note of the smallest flute Chapel pipe organ, and sometimes leap into the air – almost out of the pulpit! This gesticulation and "Bible-punching" was performed to retain the

> **PAID ENOUGH ?**
> In 1848 visiting Preachers received three shillings (15p) each Sunday evening service. Lay Preachers ("callers") received one shilling, seven pence (8p) per Sunday.

attention of the Congregation – probably with the object of getting the sleepy ones in the pews out of their slumbers!

Nowadays, preachers are rarely open to criticism of the content and delivery of their sermons whereas in earlier times, particularly around the 1860-70's, they were subject to regular assessment and commentary. A considerable volume of Chapel news and events appeared in The Aberdare Times, and the outspoken views of readers were often published. Such accounts appeared under the appropriate heading of – "Our Ministers, Our Chapels, and The People". The following reports written by local Chapel observers illustrate the opinions and general attitudes towards some of the local Ministers. One observer wrote:

"Our Ministers scarcely ever visit the members of their various Chapels and rarely visit the members of their congregations. How often therefore do they visit those wholly spiritually unconcerned?"

(Aberdare Times, 1869.)

A further critic wrote the following concerning the quality of sermons:

"The majority of sermons these days contain but very little of the subject matter necessary to the convincing of a hardened sinner of the error of his ways. They also prove an appalling deficiency of the knowledge of human nature possessed by our Ministers, and they no longer strongly prove a great want of earnestness on the part of the Ministers. In short, what we have today are mere conventional sermons. We have not the burning zeal of the past generation, and indeed the very zeal is altered, for in these days it means nothing but bigotry; all the zeal we see now used is for the propagation of the different "ISMS". There is now no plain practical scriptural lessons, no earnest appealing, but rather begging applause by the relating of meaningless tales, which are as evanescent in their effect as they are shallow in Christian philosophy. It is to me (the letter writer), quite a relish, an enjoyment beyond all comparison, to read some of the sermons of the old diviners (of the early 1800's); Oh! – what sweetness, what plainless. What meekness, and what simplicity. Yet what earnest vigour that pervades the whole".

(Aberdare Times, 1869)

The Ministers of this period were therefore subjected to criticism which probably led to some improvement, as members could easily consider worshipping elsewhere, since there was an abundance of Chapels in the valley. Towards the end of 1869 an observer criticised the local Minister for talking too much and not doing enough! According to one Chapel critic, there appeared too much preaching and too little working! Furthermore, it was said that scores of Ministers were not properly prepared for their work, and that the style and subjects of sermons and teaching were not very convincing. The observer stated:-

"It behoved the Ministers to be men of higher literary attainments than the commonality" –

and advised them to take a more active part in moral works and to attend exclusively to their own creeds and sects. He further commented that the Ministers were producing sermons of stormy verbosity and unnecessarily speaking themselves hoarse in the effort of making an impression on the congregation! Some critics of the day demanded sermons and teaching in the plainest rudiments of geography, for ideas of the Creation of the Universe and its Laws appeared to be limited, for they were never taught. Teaching during weekday evenings was suggested, and it was hinted that if the teacher or Minister possessed sufficient knowledge of various subjects for tuition, and had anything like a pleasant way of conveying his knowledge, then he need not fear the want of an audience. It was advised that Reading Rooms and cultural entertainments should have their active support. In short, anything and everything should be the work of the Minister, as man could then, through adequate tuition, not only in religion, but also in all things that have a moral aspect. The observer concluded:

> A note in the chapel records of a dinner by Unitarian Ministers –
>
> To David Llewellyn, Y Bryn Hyfryd, 25th October 1833 –
> To Dinner, 11 ministers at two shillings (10p) per head = £1.2.0d (£1.10p)
> 4 Quarts of Ale at 6 pence (2.5p) per quart = Two shillings (10p).

"The more man's mind is expanded in generalities, the more capable is he of thoroughly undertaking that which pertains to his immorality, and the better will sermons be appreciated".

(Aberdare Times)

These selected extracts from the Aberdare Times of 1869-71 are just a few of the many that were featured. They illustrate the opinions and feelings towards the Ministers, whose tasks were made more difficult through such challenges and criticism, in what was at the time an expanding and growing Chapel revival.

The Ministers and Preachers were not only subject to criticism but also to advice! Here is an account found in the Mountain Ash Almanac of 1902 under the heading "Advice to Preachers".

> CHAPELS IN "THE ICE AGE"
>
> Inclement weather did not intervene with open-air baptisms. In 1900 the minister of Carmel E.B., Aberdare, Rev. Thomas Jones (1873-1905) baptised a young girl in the River Cynon, and ice on the river had to be broken! Rev. T. Jones baptised 1200 people during his 32 year ministry at Carmel.

"It would be a good thing if some divines would take home to themselves the advice given them by the late Mr Spurgeon:
Mind your figures of speech are not cracked. Don't talk like the brother who said – "I fly from star to star, from cherry-beam to cherry-beam."
"Get amongst your people, or somebody may be saying of you as one old lady said of her minister, that he was invisible all the week and incomprehensible on Sundays.
Shun all affection in the pulpit and mind you never get into the "goody-goody" style. One of this sort said – "I was reading this morning in dear Hebrews".
Mind the theme of your sermon suits yourself. A beardless boy should not preach from – "I have been young and now am old'."

Sermons could be long and last a couple of hours. A preacher noted for his dry, long and monotonous sermons commented during his address – *"I don't mind you looking at your watches at all, but when you put them to your ears I get quite irritated!"*

Rev. William Edwards, minister of Ebenezer W.Cong., Trecynon, was known for his long sermons and often preached for up to two and a half hours to his congregation on Sunday evenings. Some preachers impressed the congregation by actually looking up frequently at their hearers and not being completely tied to their notes, whilst others were totally dependent on notes for most of the sermon. An elderly lady was once asked her opinion of a certain preacher tied to his notes, she remarked – *"He reminds me of a crow in a field, two pecks and a look up!"* It was in this respect that there were claimed to be too many "crows" finding their way into the pulpit!

Preaching did not only occur inside the chapels but sometimes in the open air. The local press reported the uncleanliness of the streets on Sundays, following high-spirited events the previous night, so it was claimed. However, this did not appear to distract the unfavourable

> COLD CONVERTS
>
> In the early 1880's many Ynysybwl Welsh Baptist converts were baptised in the River Clydach, and at times ice had to be broken before baptism could proceed.

practice of "street preaching". The chairman of the Local Board drew attention to the obstruction caused by enthusiastic persons preaching and singing in the public streets. One member of the Board however, had this to say:

"They are doing some good here; one of the worst persons in Mountain Ash has become quite a reformed character." – (Aberdare Times 1869).

We have seen in a previous chapter how ministers were involved in so many activities of chapel life, outside the duties of preaching sermons and how in the early days this included designing and supervising the erection of chapels. In 1866 one minister got rather carried away in the most unusual and craftiest of ways. Professor Anthony Jones writes of a Wesleyan Chapel in Merthyr Tydfil (built 1866) which was built larger than intended. In order to increase the dimensions of his chapel, the minister visited the site one night and moved the builders' markers!

Let us now briefly examine the salaries received by the ministers throughout various periods. Around 1815-30, it seems that congregations did not believe in high wages for ministers. Rev. Dafydd Jones and Rev. Joseph Harrison, ministers of Ebenezer W.Cong., Trecynon (Ref. 127) 1813-15, and 1817-35 respectively, were paid only ten shillings (50p) per month; twenty shillings (£1) to thirty shillings (£1.50) per month was considered high wages and the amount the minister received depended on the amounts collected in the offertory plate. In 1848 preachers received three shillings (15p) per Sunday, whilst visiting Lay Preachers or "Callers" received one shilling seven pence (8p) per Sunday. Remuneration to preachers at Old Gobaith C.M., Cwmdare (Ref. 138) was half a crown (12 and a half pence) for a Sunday evening service. However in 1868 insufficient collection was raised for the preacher, Ebenezer Pugh. His remuneration was accordingly enhanced by the most unconventional of means by his receiving of a goose from a nearby member's holding! By 1863 salaries had risen, but not by much. Rev. W. Williams, minister of Bethlehem W.I., Abercwmboi (Ref. 69) received £4 per month which was less than a collier's wage; in 1865-70 a skilled worker received £6 per month and in 1871 a collier earned one pound five shillings (£1.25) per week. Ministers also received additional expenses on top of their earnings; visiting Ministers preaching in 1830 at Carmel C.M., Trecynon (Ref.125), who travelled on horseback to the chapel were paid £1-15s-0d (£1.75) in providing hay for the horse; seven shillings and six pence (37p) to the ostler for taking

> **MOTHER SHEPHERD (B.1836 D. 1930)**
> Affectionately known as "Woman of the Valleys". Born 1836 at Talywain, Monmouthshire, Nee – Pamela Morgan. Came to Aberdare in 1878 and lived at "The Nook", East Avenue, Gadlys, Aberdare. Became a Captain in The Salvation Army. Was sent from Salvation Army headquarters in 1878 because of her knowledge and love of the Welsh language. She opened the Mission Hall at Pentwyn Bach, Trecynon and became actively associated in Aberdare and the neighbourhood with Women's Guilds in various chapels, sewing guilds and temperance groups. She later became a Probation officer. She died in February 1930 aged 94. Her funeral was on 1st March; the procession from Trinity W.P., Aberdare, numbered around 700 mourners. Her meetings in the town were so large they had to be held in The Temperance Hall (built 1858), the largest hall in Aberdare with seating for 1500 people. Mother Shepherd was well known for the Welsh National Costume she frequently wore with great pride.

care of them, and other sums for tobacco and pipes. The horses were kept in a small stable situated at the rear of the chapel. It appears that much more money was expended on the horses, ostler and tobacco than was given to the minister, who probably received only about two shillings (10p) per service. In 1833 the chapel accounts records show details of expenses for dinner attended by a visiting Unitarian Minister at Hen-Dy-Cwrdd, Unitarian Chapel, Trecynon. The records indicate – *"To dinner at two shillings (10p) per head; Ale at five pence (2p) per quart."* Presumably the provision of ale was well before Temperance and Total Abstinence Societies came into being! In 1890 a minister at Mountain Ash resigned over conflicting reports, dissension and confusion over the salary, commenting – *"I have taken the definite step of resignation rather than see any split in the membership of the chapel."* There must have been heated discussions over the salary issue leading to such a drastic action as that of resignation. By 1915 the ministers' stipend had risen to around £10 per month; 1934 – £14 per month; 1944 – about £20 per month; 1970 – £60 per month. Salaries varied from one chapel to another; some low some high. Bethel W.Cong., Gadlys, was known to pay their minister about £25 a month in the early 1920's, and this was considered a high salary. In 1941, the minister's salary was around £15 per month for a chapel in Mountain Ash; rent of a terrace house was eleven shillings (55p) per week with outside W.C. but no bathroom. However, the low wages at this time meant little to the minister who commented – *"Salary is low but we are never the less happy, for houses and material things count for nothing in our lives."* Many a minister exercised generosity towards his fellow man, and some were known to conduct weddings and funerals free of charge.

Rev. Thomas Humphreys, Sion Cwmaman from 1868-1910. Died in 1911 aged 72.

Memorial plaque - Rev. Thomas Humphreys b.1839, d.1911. Minister at Sion, Cwmdare for 42 years (1868-1910).

Rev. William Harris (right). Minister of Noddfa W.B., Trecynon. Circa 1910.

Rev. Rees Jenkin Jones M.A., Hen-Dy-Cwrdd, Trecynon. 1864-72.

Rev. R Ivor Parry M.A. (b.1908 d. 1975), Siloa, Aberdare 1933-65.

David Watkin Jones - Dafydd Morganwg (b.1832 d.1905). Poet, Geologist and Historian. Born in Merthyr; lived most of his life in Hirwaun. Wrote "The History of Glamorgan" – "Hanes Morganwg" - Published in Welsh in 1874.

Minister and Deacons in the pulpit and set fawr of Bethesda, Penrhiwceiber, 1905.

Rev. E R Dennis, Hen-dy-Cwrdd, 1916 until his death in 1949

Rev. David Owen Davies, ("D.O."), Elim, Cwmdare. 1961 – 81.

William John Evans (1866-1947). Organist and Choirmaster at Siloa, Aberdare, 1886-1937. A notable musician who conducted almost 1000 Singing Festivals. He was father of the late Ivor L. Evans, one time Principal of The University College, Aberystwyth. (See also Chapter 8 vii).

Rev. Glaslyn D. Bowen. Trinity, Aberdare 1966 – 92.

Centre – Rev. Henry Jones, Cwmbach, and prominent members of Nazareth and Bethania, Aberdare.

Rev. Dr. David Price, Siloa, Aberdare 1843-78. Founder of Siloa.

Rev. Jean S. Wilkinson, Providence, Mountain Ash 1957-64; taken in 1957 during a visit to David Prosser's Farm at Gelli Wrgan, near Llanwonno. The first lady English Congregational Minister in the Cynon Valley.

Photographs by courtesy of "Illustrated", November 1957.

Rev. David Silyn Evans, Siloa, Aberdare, 1880-1930 (50 years).

Rev. Dr. Thomas Price (b.1820 d.1888), Carmel ("Penpound"), Aberdare and Calvaria, Aberdare 1846-1888.

Rev. John Griffiths, Vicar of Aberdare 1846-59.

Rev. Jonah Morgan (b.1814 d.1888),
Bryn Seion, Cwmbach 1856-88.

Rev. W. Samlet Davies, Horeb,
Llwycoed, 1871 up to his death in 1923
(52 years).
Jean John and Russell John.

Rev. Daniel Jones, Soar, Llwycoed,
1876 until his death in 1898.
Jean John and Russell John.

Rev. William Aerwyn Jones, Nebo,
Cwmdare, 1909 until his death in 1951.
C.V.H.S.

Rev. D. Jacob Davies, Highland Place,
Aberdare, 1945-57 (d.1974).
Courtesy of Rev. Eric Jones.

Rev. R. Ivor Parry M.A. (b.1908
d.1975), Siloa, Aberdare, 1933-65.
C.V.H.S.

Rev. Margam Jones, Moriah, Llwycoed
for over 20 years. A renowned poet and
philosopher.
Jean John.

Rev. James Griffiths, Calvaria,
Aberdare 1890-1930.

Rev. J.Grawys Jones. Ebenezer,
Trecynon, 1885-1925.

Rev. Glannant Jones, Saron, Aberaman
1931-73.

Rev. H. P. Jenkins, Saron, Aberaman,
1893-1922.

Rev. R. Rowlands, Saron, Aberaman,
1864-91.

Rev. William Edwards, Ebenezer,
Trecynon, 1843-84.

Rev. Benjamin Lewis, Ebenezer,
Trecynon.

Rev. D. Herbert Davies B.A., B.D.,
Calvaria, Aberdare, 1932-47.

Rev. E. J. Williams, Noddfa, Ynysybwl,
circa 1900.

Rev. Huw Roberts, B.A., Noddfa,
Ynysybwl.

Rev. William Barker-Jones, Noddfa,
Ynysybwl, 1891-95.

Ministers of Tabernacle, Aberdare. Left to Right: Rev. T. M. Jeffreys 1914-20, Rev. E.R. Davies 1922-30, Rev. Percy Thomas 1936-40.

| Rev. D. Teify Davies, Bethel, Hirwaun, 1916-43. (A fine Baritone singer). | Rev. W. Josiah Williams, Bethel, Hirwaun, 1866-1912. | Rev. Bleddyn Cynwyn Davies, Salem, Robertstown, 1931. |

(iii) Officers and Members – Their Roles and Duties

THE CHAPEL DEACON:

Firstly let us study in detail the duties of the Deacon of a typical Nonconformist Chapel exercising independence and autonomy, and managing its own affairs without external means of governing. The Deacon was often a powerful and prominent public man in the locality. In bygone days they could be seen sitting each Sunday in the "Big Seat", starched-wing collared and black sober-suited with their bowler hats at their side.

> *"Gods on show, and hard straight faced, lost only when the public praying comes! Righteous men displaying their gold watch-chains on their black waist-coats."*
>
> *(From National Library of Wales Journal 1979-80, Vol. XXI)*

The trustworthy Deacons of the past came from various walks of life and to be a Chapel Deacon often led to promotion in their employment. They played an important role in Chapel life, not only on Sundays but also throughout the week. They were considered to be the reliable link and pillars of strength between the members and the Minister. Visitations to sick members were also high on their list of duties. These faithful and stalwart servants took part in many important decision-making aspects of chapel activity where autonomy and independence was exercised, as well as performing the most humble of tasks. These ranged from the lighting of the chapel boiler on cold Saturday nights ready for the Sunday Service, to the pumping of the organ bellows, and carrying out of minor repairs to the chapel fabric. They performed such duties with little or no complaint. Some excelled in the art of lay preaching and others became faithful chapel officers using in some instances their occupational gifts and talents for the "Cause". They provided practical help in building up and maintaining the morale and life of the chapel, and possessed an enthusiastic capacity for chapel work. Above all, they were people with foresight and tact, whose wisdom in practical affairs, finance and building organisation ensured the success of the chapel's administration. They were generous-hearted, thinking always of the good of others in the chapel, and they placed before all else the care and well-being of its members in a sympathetic manner. It is probably true to say that a chapel is living and effective when the leadership comes from the Diaconate. After all, ministers often come and go but the Diaconate are permanent with an

> **Notable members and personalities of Hen-Dy-Cwrdd Unitarian Chapel, Trecynon**
>
> (a) Griffith Rhys Jones, - "Caradog" (b.1834 d.1897), conductor of the famous "Cor Mawr" choir; in 1872-73 he led the South Wales Choral Union to victory in the Crystal Palace Challenge Cup in London. A statue stands in Victoria Square, in his memory.
>
> (b) Rhys Hopkin Rhys – A regular attender and member at Hen-Dy-Cwrdd during the 1800's, (b.1819 d.1899); blinded by a gun-cotton accident in 1847, he was a leading figure and was largely responsible for the creation of Aberdare (Dumfries) Park, opened 16th July 1869, cost £6300. He was also instrumental in the improvement of the waste and sewage system in the town.
>
> (c) Thomas Dafydd Llewellyn
>   (Llewellyn Alaw – 1828-79)
>   He gave the Welsh Nation an early glimpse of The National Anthem (see ch.8 vii)
>
> (d) Rev. E.R. Dennis (1882-1949)
>   Founder of the Little Theatre, Aberdare 1931; formerly an engine shed
>   Minister of Hen Dy Cwrdd 1916 – 1949
>
> (e) William Watkin Price (1873-1967)
>   Local historian
>
> (f) Evan Thomas
>   Inventor of the Safety Lamp
>
> (g) Sir D.R. Llewellyn (1879 – 1940)
>   Mine owner – Bwllfa

intimate knowledge of the chapel and the local neighbourhood situation. They attended chapel regularly and were loyal servants in assisting and helping the minister and ready to cooperate with fellow members in their work for Christ, the chapel and the community in general.

The minister, as the accepted leader was also the Chairman of the Diaconate, and Deacons' meetings were held in private and were confidential. Matters covered were not discussed outside the meeting. Deacons had to be flexible and ready to accept new methods and ideas, to be forward-looking with a "ready-to-experiment" attitude. They were elected to see that the chapel does its job effectively. Deacons discussed financial matters relating to the chapel and the care and maintenance of the building. Teamwork was all-important and they organised fund-raising and appeals for financial help where and when needed. They also ensured the maintenance and remuneration of the Minister and Lay preachers. Every chapel member was eligible for election, by a voting procedure. They had responsibility for building and contents insurance matters and, where applicable, a manse. They took care of chapel deeds, Minute Books of meetings and other records, and all other legal documents, and ensured these were kept in a safe place. Trusteeship was reviewed from time to time and the Deacons kept in touch with fellow members who had been transferred to another chapel or had left the district. The well-being of our chapels depends on the leadership and advice of Ministers and Deacons; Chapels grow in strength and witness under their guidance and direction. The foregoing notes outlining the duties of a chapel Deacon are applicable in the case of a Nonconformist Chapel exercising autonomy and self-governing independence from outside sources, the Congregationalists or Independents being a denomination following such administration and control.

Deacons, Tabernacle, Ynysybwl, circa 1900.

Rev. Jean S. Wilkinson, Minister
1957-64 and Deacons, Providence,
Mountain Ash 1957.

Minister and Deacons of Providence.
Taken in February 1986. (Left to
Right) Alan Jones (the author),
Mervyn Bradwick, Mrs. Elizabeth
James. Rev. David Pennells (Min.
1984-1986), Nev. Lukey-Davies,
Austin Clift, Mrs.Maralyn Jones,
Jeffrey Milton. (Absent – Mrs Megan
Coslett, Bob Demery)

Deacons – Blaenoriad, Eglwys
Annibynol, Soar, Penderyn.
Doug Williams.

Deacons and Members, Cynon Valley chapel, name unknown.

Minister and Deacons, Bethesda, Penrhiwceiber 1905.

Minister and Deacons at opening of Bethesda, Penrhiwceiber, 1905.

Minister, Rev. D Teify Davies (1916-43) and Deacons, Bethel, Hirwaun 1923.

60 years after their great triumph at the Crystal Palace, local historian Mr. John Davies suggested a reunion of the survivors of Caradog's "Cor Mawr", which was held at Bethel Chapel, Gadlys on the 17th July 1933. Some of them are seen in this group taken outside the Chapel with the organisers in the back row, who are (L. to R.) W. H. Templeman, John Davies, Glen George, W. R. Evans and J. L. Rowlands. On the left is The Rev. Daniel Harries, Bethel.

Minister and Deacons, Nebo, Hirwaun, circa 1930. Minister front row centre is Rev. Efonwy Hughes.
Doug Williams.

Minister Mr. D.J. Anthony, third from left (front) and Deacons, Noddfa, Ynysybwl.
Stephen Thomas.

Minister and Deacons, Tabernacle, Ynysybwl.

The first Minister Rev. R.O. Evans (1888-89) and Deacons, Tablernacle, Ynysybwl.

Deacons, Calvaria, Aberdare, circa 1912.

Deacons and Minister, Calvaria, Aberdare, 1912. Minister – front row, centre – Rev. James Griffiths.

Minister and Deacons of Calvaria, Aberdare, 1926. Minister – front row centre, Rev. James Griffiths.

Ministers and officials 1900-1913, Tabernacle, Aberdare. Minister Rev. J. Morgan Jones, 1902-13.

Minister and Deacons, Hen-Dy-Cwrdd, Trecynon 1951. Minister front row centre – Rev. D Jacob Davies.

Deacons, Siloa, Aberdare 1933. Front row centre – William John Evans, organist and choirmaster, 1886-1937

Deacons – Calvaria, Aberdare, 1951. Minister – front row centre – Rev. Huw D. Thomas.

Minister and Deacons, Sion, Cwmaman, 1925.
Doug Williams.

SECRETARIES AND TREASURERS

The chapel secretary's work covers administration, correspondence and recording the Minutes of chapel and Deacons' Meetings. The Treasurer is responsible for all financial matters relating to the running of the chapel including Records of Account of income and outgoings and reporting the same to the Annual Chapel Meeting. He is also responsible for the payment of bills, repairs, insurance etc., and the recording of members' weekly contributions. The Fabric Secretary deals with the care, repair and maintenance of the chapel building and internal fabric and organises funds to cover some repair costs. Often, the Fabric Secretary is a tradesman or craftsman well versed in repair and general building work matters.

> **CHAPEL DAMAGED BY ENEMY ACTION!**
>
> Bethania Welsh Baptist Chapel, Cwmbach (built 1858; demolished 1995) was severely damaged by enemy war action/bombing on 30th May 1941; the vestry was completely destroyed. Tragically, four residents living nearby were killed. The chapel was restored and renovated 1950-51.

SUNDAY SCHOOL SUPERINTENDENTS AND TEACHERS

The Sunday School became the nucleus from which new chapels were born. It was common for a group from one chapel to establish a Sunday School in an area which in time became a new "Cause". Sunday Schools provided a basic training in Bible Study, the three "R's" and music, especially Tonic Solfa, and the richness of the musical life of the chapel was impressive. The Sunday Schools were the powerhouse of Welsh Nonconformity. The strength and importance of Welsh in Sunday School was significant as this fostered and preserved the Welsh language. During the nineteenth century up to ten or twenty Sunday School teachers would be on the roll looking after as many as 200 children. The oversight of this was the responsibility of the Sunday School superintendent who guided and supervised the Sunday School teachers. Brownies, girl guides, cubs, scouts and life brigades etc., all played an active role in chapel life and took part in the services.

Sunday school teachers, Horeb, Lwydcoed, 1928. Jean John.

Teachers and children of the Sunday school at New Road, Ynysybwl, circa 1950.   *Stephen Thomas.*

Aberaman Ecclesia (Christadelphian), Gwawr Street, circa 1917. Founded in 1863; the oldest in the Cynon Valley. (See Ref. 39A and 39B). Back row – third from right – William Pugh, fourth from right – John Marshall, founder members.

Group outside the English Wesleyan Chapel, Llewellyn St., Trecynon. The Sunday school building (built 1905) is under construction awaiting a roof covering.

CARETAKERS

The caretaker is one of the most important jobs in chapel work but is a post that not too many people volunteer to undertake. Those who do look after the chapel as caretakers often avail themselves voluntarily and the work can be a "labour of love" for many years. Where remuneration is made this is quite small e.g. in 1847 a caretaker's wage was just one shilling (5p) per week, rising to six shillings per week in 1912. The following outlines the duties of a chapel caretaker of a typical chapel in 1912.

> *"The Caretaker shall be appointed after the vacancy is announced. The wage is £1-5-0d (£1.25) per lunar month paid by the Chapel Treasurer, after each Communion Service.*
>
> *The Chapel and Vestry shall be cleaned throughout, once a month. Seats, pulpit, organ and bench, and pews shall be dusted regularly each week, with clean dusters.*
>
> *Stair rods, umbrella stands and door knobs shall be regularly cleaned and the brass shall be polished. The Caretaker shall be responsible for preserving the Communion Set, Books, Bibles, Table Cloth and Mourning Ribbons. The chapel shall provide cleaning utensils, but not soap, polish and dusters.*
>
> *The Caretaker shall open either Chapel or Vestry in time for meetings and/or Services, and shall ensure that no access is allowed to the chapel or Minister's/Deacon's Room, during the week, unless special permission has been obtained from The Deacons. Heating and Lighting shall be laid on before each Service and/or meeting".*

THE SISTER-HOOD

Their main function is as follows:-

1. Fellowship and to meet together on a regular meeting basis.
2. To raise money for Chapel Funds.
3. To organise Sales of Work and "Bring and Buy" Sales.
4. Sale of Christmas cards and gifts.
5. To invite visiting Speakers for Lecture Evenings.
6. To arrange needle-work or embroidery classes and other such skilled craft work.

Sewing Class, Ramoth, Hirwaun 1909-1910.

Deacons and Sisterhood, Bethel, Rock Terrace, Old Ynysybwl, 1915.
Stephen Thomas.

(iv) Chapel Rules and Discipline
The title of this section may imply to the reader a somewhat authoritarian and formidable content. On the contrary, discipline in chapel life had a lighter side reflecting not so much serious misdemeanours but rather minor occurrences and amusing stories.

FIDGETING, TALKING AND GIGGLING
Disciplinary procedures were exercised in a local chapel and the following resolution was passed in the early 1900's:-

> *"That in order to bring about a more reverent atmosphere in the chapel worship, Stewards shall be appointed each week to sit among the children to stop them chatting and fidgeting."*

A situation familiar to this day when young children and indeed adults find it perhaps difficult to sit through long sermons – nothing changes!

Further similar discipline was exercised which necessitated an entry in the Chapel Minute Book, as follows: -

> *"That to maintain order in the gallery, two members and one of the Deacons in the lobby shall station themselves in the gallery for that purpose."*

One wonders if this action was intended for the adults as well as the children. Being congregated high up in the gallery would appear to tempt fidgeting without being noticed. Another remark was made and minuted:-

> *"The Diaconate to approach members concerning the occasional lack of reverence during services and Sunday School teachers to impress on the scholars the necessity for silence throughout the services."*

In 1880, the local press reported an occurrence concerning annoyance to the preacher under the heading – *"We Want More Reverence."* It was reported that preachers at some chapels were forced to stop their sermons at times owing to talking and uncontrollable giggling of some members of the congregation. Perhaps unknown to the preacher he may well have said something amusing! There is also the unusual story of a minister who observed the congregations' attention wandering during his sermon, whereupon he produced a set of balls and proceeded to perform an impromptu juggling act from the pulpit. This strange spectacle naturally took the congregation by surprise. After a while the minister sternly declared, *"Since most of you appear to be completely uninterested in what I have to say to you this evening I just as well resort to alternative entertainment and see if this works!"* (Aberdare Almanac 1890).

SLEEPING IN CHAPEL.
Falling asleep in chapel attracted comments. The Rev. J. D. Williams of Cardiff delivered a notable sermon at a Cwmbach Chapel on the "Eternal Punishment of the Ungodly." In spite of the rousing nature of the meeting there were some who were inattentive. At a joint meeting of Trecynon Chapels in 1885 a complaint was made that many of the congregation were seen dozing during the long sermon! A suggestion that they should be fined was rejected.

Positive measures were taken to prevent members sleeping during services and sermons. It is related of one John Rudge that in April 1725 he bequeathed to a chapel in Shropshire twenty shillings each year that a poor man might be employed to go about the chapel during the sermon to keep the people awake. This duty was also sometimes performed by the Deacons who, with a long stick, went around the chapel, and if any of the congregation were asleep, tapped them on the head! (Aberdare Almanac Dec. 1903).

Sleeping in chapel appears to have been a common occurrence for many past generations. Here is an extract from a poem on "Boyhood Memories" by N. T. Harrington, 1830.

> *"Ah let me enter, once again, the pew where the child nodded as the sermon grew:*
> *Scene of soft slumbers! I remember now the chiding finger; and the frowning brow of stern reprovers, when the ardent June flung through the glowing aisles of the drawing noon."*

Sleeping, giggling, fidgeting and chatting; this indeed presents a somewhat bemusing picture of chapel life, and whilst not to be condoned it never the less reflects the light-hearted, human side of minor misdemeanours that required some reprimanding comment or disciplinary action.

COUGHING IN CHAPEL.

A further annoying problem was reported in The Aberdare Times in 1887 under the heading, "Coughing in Chapel", the tone of which was probably intended to be of a serious nature –

> *"Coughing in chapel has become a roughness of manner, and a great annoyance to the preacher and to their neighbours in the pews. One cough seems to "suggest" another, and the preacher has to shout against a sort of platoon fire from the pews!"* -

Congregations were accordingly politely and discreetly requested by the Deacons, at a convenient time during the singing of a hymn, to exercise control over their bouts of coughing or else leave the service until matters improved.

CHAPEL ATTENDANCE

Poor chapel attendance did not go unnoticed. In a meeting on 5th August 1857 at Tabernacle English Congregation Chapel, Aberdare (Ref. 115), the following resolution was passed and entered into the Minute Book:

> *"Members absent for two consecutive months from both the meetings of the chapel and the celebration of The Lord's Supper, or from either one or the other, without assigning a sufficient reason by either word of mouth or letter, shall, except under special circumstances be considered as no longer members of this chapel."*

This strict ruling would be difficult to uphold today. However, the Christian reputations of such members were duly investigated and the merit of the case determined by a majority of the votes of the members present at the Chapel Meeting.

A similar disciplinary approach was exercised at Nazareth E.B., Mountain Ash (Ref. 58). The rules of the chapel stated that the suspension of members was automatic when three consecutive Communion Services were missed. Members were reinstated upon application to the Monthly Chapel Meeting. This was the "Court of the Chapel". All matters however trivial or serious were reported and discussed at the meetings. Attendance at weeknight meetings for worship was left to the members' discretion, whereby –

Members of the
congregation during a
service at Zion, Ynysybwl,
circa.1930.
Stephen Thomas.

"they should make it a matter of conscience to attend with as much regularity as possible". Whilst on the subject of chapel attendance, Rev. T.M. Lloyd, minister of Jerusalem W.P., Ynysybwl (Ref. 5) (1925-31), spoke of a member who did not attend chapel on a regular basis and who was referred to as "Johnny Fortnight". In order to maintain regular chapel attendances, Rev. T.M. Lloyd followed rigid and precise procedures. He believed that travelling on a train or bus on a Sunday was a sin, so his visiting preaching engagements were all conducted within walking distance of the Chapel, otherwise he would travel on Saturday evening and return home on Monday morning.

One particular preacher could not help but express his outspoken views on chapel attendance in a witty manner. The visiting preacher at Nazareth W.B., Abercynon (Ref. 19) commented on the sparse attendance of the morning services by saying that the members were like "black-pats" – which only came out at night! Whether this comment helped to boost numbers in attendance or just merely brought a wry smile to members is not known.

STRICTER DISCIPLINE

I shall conclude this section on Chapel Rules and Discipline by referring to the stricter aspect of Rules of Conduct. The late Rev. Ivor Parry tells us that in 1855 a notable feature of chapel life was the stern and austere measures taken to enforce discipline. The chief misdemeanours punishable by excommunication were:-

a) Intemperance.
b) Keeping Licensed Premises.
c) Theft.

Other prohibited acts were:-

1) to cut the hair short and part it down the side.
2) to wear any emblems belonging to the Ivorites or Oddfellows in Chapel.
3) to work on Communion Sunday.
4) to attend Sunday Funerals.
5) to marry a non-believer.
6) to wander from chapel to chapel "to the neglect of their own congregation".

Those guilty of these misdemeanours had to stand in the aisle during the administration of Holy Communion and had to seek readmission into the chapel fellowship at a weeknight meeting. The idea behind excommunication was that the chapel was a community of believers whose actions should measure up to their professions of faith. The code of chapel discipline, however, made no provision for the more covert sins of pride, avarice and cruelty etc.

(v) Temperance and Abstinence.

This section deals with the many categories of temperance requiring some action to be taken in matters relating to forbearance, moderation, restraint, prohibition, self-control, self-denial, self-discipline, sobriety, teetotalism and non-indulgence. Several societies were formed to encourage members to "Take the Pledge" and abstain from alcohol, tobacco and gambling. Sport, particularly on Sundays, was also frowned upon. The Band of Hope Pledge attracted many young people from an early age to adulthood, the emphasis being on restraint and self-discipline. Drinking and smoking were considered social evils and abstention was to be encouraged at all times. Even to this day there is an all-out effort being made by Government and others to ban smoking in public areas and to prohibit the drinking of alcohol on the streets. In the 1860's the chapels were at the forefront of The Temperance Movement, for they saw alcohol, public houses and drunkenness as a great nuisance and evil which undermined the Christian way of life.

Temperance Societies and Movements were formed including, Band of Hope; Rechabites, Good Templars, Temperance Associations; and Societies of Total Abstinence. They all encouraged people to "Take the Pledge" and promise to abstain from the evils and temptations of the "forbidden fruit".

"In a meeting of The Mountain Ash Local Board in February, 1870, a discussion took place on *"The Sale of Liquors on Sunday"*, in which the Rev. Daniel Jones stated that he had heard of the matter before. *"The opening of Public Houses on Sunday was a crying evil"* he said – *"for on that day most workmen had their weeks wages in their pockets and were idle, and did not know what to do with themselves, it was very natural for them to go to Public Houses where there was company with whom to chat"*

(Aberdare Times).

A Canvass and Survey was held in Mountain Ash in 1878 on householders on the question of stopping the sale of intoxicating liquor on Sundays. The survey attracted local press coverage. A total of 941 householders were interviewed out of which only 65 were against stopping the sale on the Sabbath. Forty-two remained neutral. Out of 465 colliers, only 12 voted "against". Not surprisingly three Publicans voted "for" and five "against". All seven Ministers interviewed voted to stop sales. The canvass led to the campaign which saw the closing of public houses in Wales on Sundays by the passing of the Welsh Sunday Closing Act of 1881.

The Temperance Society was very active during the late 1800's and they reported that monies spent on intoxicating liquors was almost twice as great as the total paid for bread, and nearly four times as much spent on butter and cheese; four and a half times as much was spent on alcohol as milk. The Society advised that if quiet streets and loving homes were to be the norm, with children properly fed and clothed, the Chapels should promote social gatherings for tea drinking, reading, reciting and singing! The issue of Sunday Closing was in full debate in 1880 and the Nonconformist Ministers decided to support the Temperance Movement for securing the closure of public houses on Sundays in South Wales, and to obtain signatures from petitioners. The Temperance Movement naturally had much to say in this matter and in 1881 Sunday Closure became law.

Innkeepers as well as their customers were open to criticism. In a meeting of the Welsh Independents held at Tredegar, the following was reported in 1905 under the heading of "Drinkers should be refused Admittance to Chapel."

"We believe that the chapels who refuse membership to Innkeepers are correct. If it is right to say this, then it is right also to do the same with drinkers. We maintain that if selling drink renders a man unsuitable for chapel membership, then buying it should do the same."

The South Wales Temperance Association held its meeting at Bethania Chapel, Mountain Ash, in June, 1893. Included in this conference was the presentation of an able paper written by Mr. William Bevan, Providence Deacon and Trustee, entitled – "The best Way of Attracting Young men from the Public Houses". His view was that special and increased attention should be given to the homes of the workmen; they should be made as cheerful as possible and books and papers should be made readily available. He also encouraged attendances at reading rooms and public baths. In the 1860's "The Mutual Improvement Society of Young Men" was formed; this enabled tuition in the "Three R's" and other subjects, along with setting up lecture and debate meetings. Mr. Bevan was a well known figure in the town and a prolific writer on local and chapel history. He delivered many lectures at Providence E.Cong., Mountain Ash, (Ref.60), and other local chapels, covering a variety of subjects, and wrote (in Welsh) the winning Essay of The Easter Eisteddfod in 1896, on "The History of Mountain Ash". – (Translated by A.V. Jones and published in 1990).

In 1894, a meeting of the newly formed "Temperance Society of Total Abstinence" was held in Providence, E. Cong., there being 57 adults and 50 children in attendance. The Society was separate from other similar temperance organisations already active, and was the third to be formed in Mountain Ash. The first was Duffryn Street Chapel in 1892 with 164 adults and 90 children, and the second was Newtown Primitive Methodist Chapel in 1893, with 45

CHAPEL IN A TELEVISION DRAMA SETTING
Bryn Seion Welsh Independent Chapel Cwmbach was used as a setting in a television drama in the early 1990's. This caused controversy among local residents because the script involved drug use etc. This chapel closed in December 1999 and as at 2004 is partially demolished.

adults and 57 children. Others were soon to follow. For non-members of the Society, there was always "Harvest Ale" available at one shilling (5p) a gallon!

William Bevan tells us that during the last six months of 1895, ninety-six people in Mountain Ash were fined in the Court for drunkenness, and the total fines and costs reached £82, which equated to about fourteen shillings (70p) a month for every public house. In 1896 there were nineteen pubs in Mountain Ash.

Attitudes towards temperance also had an effect on sporting activities and other leisure pursuits. The practice of certain local rugby clubs in obtaining licences to establish facilities for Sunday drinking and to conduct lotteries was seriously frowned upon by the chapels. The Aberdare Leader reported in 1954 that every effort should be made to restrain the use of these destructive pursuits deploring the formation of licensed clubs in direct association with rugby football clubs. It was added that the Welsh Rugby Union should exercise some restraint on Sundays and seek to maintain the Sabbath tradition. Furthermore, the press revealed that accidents and deaths on the road continued at a high rate and that a considerable number of them were due to the effects of alcohol. Sadly this problem continues today (2004), exactly fifty years on from this period. Much earlier however, measures were taken in sporting circles to encourage temperance and abstention from alcohol; in 1879, the Mountain Ash Temperance Football Club was formed and was limited to players who were teetotallers!

In 1861 The Aberdare Times was "severely shocked" to report about practices of breaking the Sabbath by men passing their time away playing "pitch and toss". It was thought those in question could not have been aware of the "brutalising effects upon their minds", inflicted by this game.

Strong opinions were expressed by some critics regarding the holding of fairs in Mountain Ash which were claimed to cause a nuisance. In 1871, the Local board discussed the holding of fairs and stalls in Oxford Street. Deacon Mr John Griffiths said that the noise interfered with the Board Meetings held in The Workman's Hall. He added, *"Fairs are quite unnecessary in Mountain Ash, they do no good to the place and take much money away; they leave nothing behind worth looking at. They are also the cause of great immorality and interfere with the traffic by blocking up the roads"*. Incidentally, the Workman's Hall referred to was built in 1864 at a cost of £1000, and demolished in 1904 to make way for the Council Town Hall and offices built at a cost of £5000.

The stern Methodists had something to say on the playing of ball games on the Sabbath. An inscription on the walls of the little Baptist Chapel at Llanfair Discoed in Gwent reads:

> *"Whoever here on Sunday*
> *Will practice playing at ball,*
> *It may be before Monday*
> *The Devil will Have You All."*

(vi) Music and Singing in Chapel

The Nonconformist members of our chapels are, by tradition, renowned for their wonderful singing, mixing melody with harmony with a deep feeling of expression and hwyl. Indeed we may boldly say,

> *"Before anyone did anything worthwhile, the Nonconformists sang everything with hwyl!"*
>
> (A.V. Jones – 2004)

Many readers will remember the chapels full with as many as 500 to 900 present, when the Gymanfa Ganu (Singing Festivals) were popular. An interesting account relating to "Singing in Chapel" was written on the opening of Bryn Seion W.I., Cwmbach (Ref. 97) on 10th may 1858. The report is as follows:-

> *"Choirs from several local chapels sang exceedingly well with sweetness and purity, and they took pleasure from listening to each other and from their style and desire to please others and not themselves; such simplicity and beauty! Young men are giving their money and donations and their voices to help religion rather than destroying themselves through following shallow things. It was*

easy to see from the distant choirs, that singing is quickly being perfected in our Valley and our chapels – they are becoming more conscious of artistry and becoming more simple whilst rising in feeling of the heart!"

In marked contrast, over thirty years later the contrary was reported in 1890 by "The Singing Association":-

"Congregational singing in places of worship in our locality is most wearisome, and the most dragging singing that ever tortured human ears. If Ministers and Deacons of our Chapels neglect singing, they neglect a means towards bringing in the people who still linger in such crowds outside our chapel doors"

From *"History of Providence Chapel, Mountain Ash"*
By A.V. Jones – 1987

The Association therefore set about in earnest to encourage and promote the improvement of singing in the chapels. Wonderful Cantatas and Concerts were performed in chapels throughout the Cynon Valley by acclaimed choirs, often supported by notable orchestras. Such an event was reported in the local press in 1914:

"The Cantata at Salem W.Cong., Robertstown,(Ref. 122) was admirably produced and the singing throughout was sweet and melodious. The choir did excellently and sang with expression and was commendable, each part giving abundant proof of careful training. Proceeds amounted to £18-5-2p towards chapel funds."

Later in 1932, Salem choir performed "The Passion of The Cross". It was reported that,

"The choir and artists gave the work a sympathetic and intelligent treatment that made the performance a very pleasing one."

Some musical occasions albeit outside the chapel, were not without humorous treatment. In 1873 two American Evangelists and Hymnodists, Dwight Lyman Moody (1873-1899) and Ira David Sankey (1840-1908), came to Britain to preach and sing the Gospel. During one of Moody and Sankey's revivalist campaigns a comedian at a Musical Hall would say, *"I feel rather Moody"*, to which his joking partner would reply,

"and I feel rather Sankey-monious!"
(from Aberdare Almanac 1880).

Many chapels could boast of famous choirs, musicians and orchestras, guided by talented conductors, choirmasters and precentors; Ebenezer, Trecynon; Bethania, Aberdare; Siloa, Aberdare; Bethania, Mountain Ash; to mention only a few. The devotion and artistic brilliance of these accomplished musicians will always be at the forefront of the musical life of our Chapels.

Choir Officials and Committee, Ebenezer Choral Society, 1999. Taken to celebrate the 150th Anniversary of the Choral Society, 1849-1999 held at Ebenezer Chapel Trecynon.

Dafydd John (1823-1894). Conductor and Precentor at Ebenezer, Trecynon for over forty years. (See also Chapter 8 vii).

Ebenezer Orchestra, Trecynon, circa. 1930.
Elfed Bowen

Orchestra (Cynon Valley Chapel –unknown) circa. 1910.

Ebenezer Orchestra, Trecynon, and Llwydcoed Brass Band. Taken during a concert to celebrate the opening of the new organ at Ebenezer Chapel, 1938.
Doug Williams.

Orchestra, circa. 1904, Ebenezer, Trecynon. Conductor – W.E. Thomas, seated in centre of front row; to his left is Rev. Grawys Jones, minister 1885-1925.
Elfed Bowen.

(vii) War and Poverty

The period following the 1914-18 War was generally considered to be the beginning of the decline of Nonconformist Chapels in the locality and elsewhere. Not only had chapel building come to a halt but also a continuing decrease in chapel membership numbers was being experienced. By the end of the 1939-45 War numbers had diminished considerably, continuing well into the 1950-60's and thereafter.

> **FANCY THAT**
>
> During the Second World War, The Pavilion, Mountain Ash, was used for storing large quantities of food. Men were paid three shillings (15p) a night to stand guard.

During 1939 six out of eleven Nonconformist Chapels in Mountain Ash were without a Minister and a similar situation existed throughout the locality. Two terrible wars and the twenty-one uneasy years of unemployment and poverty between 1918-39, undoubtedly had a disastrous and deteriorating effect on the religious life in Wales. Even the Great Religious Revival of 1904-05 did not stem the eventual decline. Not long after this period many chapels were experiencing debts and financial difficulties throughout the depression years and the General Strike, and up to 1929. The trade depression during the War years and early 1920's affected the entire community and took its toll on chapel finances and falling membership. A Minister expressed his regret at the Great Trade Depression which had taken place in cycles during 1920-29, but he remarked, *"Trade in the Spiritual World need never be slack!* Throughout these difficult years there were long queues at Labour Exchanges, soup kitchens were set up and hunger marches held.

Soup kitchen – Group outside Bryngolwg Mission Hall – 1926.

Soup kitchen organisers and helpers – Bryngolwg, Miskin 1921.

Soup kitchen, chapel in Trecynon,
circa. 1900.

Brass Memorial Plaque,
First World War,
Trinity, Aberdare.

> DID YOU KNOW?
>
> American G.I. soldiers, mostly black, worshipped at Elim English Wesleyan Chapel, Perthcelyn, (formerly The Primitive Methodist Mission Room, built 1931; demolished 1952). The soldiers were based at Lletty Turner Field where they had their training camp and canvas tents. They remained there for about six months until "D-Day" in June 1944.

During the war years 1914-18, thousands of our Cynon Valley young men were called up for active service in France and Belgium. As many as forty-seven young men between 16-18 years of age from Bethesda W.B., Abercwmboi (Ref.68) went to the First World War in 1914. The position was similar throughout the chapels of the valley and too many youngsters falsified their ages to eagerly engage themselves as conscripts. Those fortunate to return home on leave were greeted with an Evening Tea Party called a "Soiree", and gifts were presented to these gallant young soldiers of our locality. The chapels needed to be insured against air-raid, blinds were provided to comply with the blackout restrictions and leading members of chapels were called into military service. There remained signs of poverty in the town during the early years of the First World War, and to assist those in need, a "Poor Fund" was set up by the Chapels. The War began in August 1914, and young members of many chapels, some only 17 years old, left to serve their country. Many Belgian refugees entered the valley and special funds were set up to help those in need. Clothes were distributed to the poor and unemployed and donations were given towards the "Poor Children's Boot Fund". Throughout the War, parcels of "good things" were despatched to those who were prisoners of war in Germany.

In January 1918, Rev. James Jones, Minister of Elim W.Cong., Cwmdare (Ref. 135), was dismissed by the congregation for expounding political references into his sermon and for preaching against the war. The Aberdare Leader commented, *"It comes as rather a shock even in these days for a minister to be dismissed for preaching peace. However, no minister ought to take advantage of his pulpit to attack his political opponents"*.

Several batches of our gallant lads were released from Germany in the spring of 1919, where many had been prisoners of war for up to four years. Through demobilisation, men gradually found their way back into their former employment and returned to the chapels. In June 1919, a "Peace Sunday" was held, in memory of those who sacrificed their lives in the Great War. Later in the year, Lord Aberdare made a handsome gift of the plot of land now known as the "Peace Park" to the Mountain Ash Council, and this was opened to mark the end of the war.

During the Second World War, Chapels made several efforts to raise funds for "Comfort for his Majesty's Forces". Furthermore iron boundary railings of many chapels were taken down and removed to be smelted down as part of the War Effort for ammunition and military arms, and to add to the scrap iron which was in short supply. Following the outbreak of the war on the 3rd September 1939, hundreds of evacuees came to the Cynon Valley from all parts of the Country, particularly Kent, Essex and the Midlands and the heavily bombed areas of London, Birmingham and Coventry. The evacuees were seen with their small cases of belongings, Gas Masks and identification labels around their necks. Chapels and Churches gave a warm welcome to these youngsters and made them feel at home. In July 1944, thousands of evacuees arrived in Cynon Valley from London, which was being heavily bombed. Throughout the war the use of chapel vestries was made available free of charge as voluntary-run social centres for members of the armed services. Notices were displayed, *That in the event of an air-raid, the service is to terminate, a hymn announced, and those wishing to leave the chapel should do so quietly and orderly*".

Because of the absence of street lighting during "black-outs", white lines were painted on the pavement kerbs to assist pedestrians in the dark. The necessity for blackout facilities was a common occurrence during the early war years, and "Fire Watches" were systematically organised in a rota manner. Chapels and vestries required blacking out each night to enable the holding of Fire Guard and Fire Watch lectures.

Many Peace meetings and pre-wartime talks had taken place before the outbreak of the War. The topic of one discussion in 1938 was, "Is War Inevitable?" A year later on the 18th July 1939, leading up to the start of the war, large gatherings met at the site of the first Nonconformist Chapel in the district, at Cwm-y-Glo near Merthyr, to pray for peace. During the war, special efforts were made to assist the Red Cross and Mercantile Marine Society, and collections were made. The Red Cross parcels sent by the chapels to soldiers and prisoners of war were of great help. Christmas cards were sent to members in the Forces and the cost was met out of the "War Comforts Fund" which was established in most chapels throughout the war to help the poor and needy. In addition ministers drafted personal letters to chapel members in H.M. Forces. The chapels also contributed towards the W.V.S. Information Bureaux, and religious services were held in connection with *The Cessation of Hostilities in The European Theatre of War*". A Welcome Home Fund was formed in the summer of 1944 toward greeting the members of various chapels who were soon to be demobbed from H.M. Forces. They were greeted upon release, and a Welcome home Meeting and Party, was arranged for those, who by God's mercy, had safely returned home. Upon return from overseas they received the handshake of "Welcome Home", plus a present of ten shillings (50p).

During the war, American soldiers (G.I.'s) used the chapel vestries and they also paraded at morning services. Some readers may remember their camps and tents at the Lletty Turner Fields near Newtown, Mountain Ash. The soldiers used the vestries for rest and a place where they could settle down to write letters home to their loved ones. Vestries were made available for the storage of tinned food and flour. During June 1941, when the Duffryn Infants School, Mountain Ash was bombed by enemy action, the chapel vestries were used until the new Duffryn Infants School was opened in June 1949. Soon after the end of the war it was decided that the tenancy and renting of chapel vestries be terminated. The Chapel Unions of various denominations continued to request finance for chapels damaged by war. One such chapel was Bethania Welsh Baptist, Cwmbach (Ref.96), which was damaged by enemy action on 30th May 1941. Tragically, four people were killed nearby.

The Great Wars had affected the chapels both spiritually and financially. Membership also declined and many chapels were left with debts which in most cases took several years to clear. However, the "baby-boom" of the middle 1940's into the 1950's contributed to thriving activity in the Sunday Schools, but by the 1960-70's through to the present date, numbers in both the adult membership and Sunday Schools continued to rapidly decline.

Chapter 7

RELIGIOUS REVIVALS

		Page No.
(i)	**Introduction**	**291**
(ii)	**Early Religious Revivals, 1620-1884**	**292**
(iii)	**The 1859 Welsh Revival**	**295**
(iv)	**Profile of the Welsh Revivalist – Evan Roberts (1878-1951)**	**299**
(v)	**The 1904-1905 Welsh Revival in the Cynon Valley**	**307**
(vi)	**Services Held Below Ground**	**311**
(vii	**Quotes from the "Converted"**	**313**
(viii)	**Effects of The Revival on Various Addictions and Secular Attractions**	**314**
(ix)	**Religious Mania and Hypnotism**	**316**
(x)	**The Role of the Press**	**317**

"This remarkable upheaval seems to be rocking Welsh Life like a great earthquake."
David Lloyd George (1863-1945) December 1904.

"This is The Lord's Doing; it is marvellous in our eyes."
Rev. J.L. Jenkins, Minister of Trinity Welsh Presbyterian Chapel, Aberdare. January 1905

"A Revival is similar to letting out the contents of a reservoir. When all the contents have run out, it must have time to fill before another outpouring is possible."
Rev. D.M. Phillips, M.A., Ph.D. Tylorstown, 1906.

(i) Introduction

"By Revival we mean an awakening among the people to their spiritual state; a renewed and more active attention to religion. Such an awakening is often accompanied by great exhilaration which is often mistaken for the thing itself. Whenever there is a genuine revival there is a change of habits among those who are affected by it. The more lasting the change, the greater is its reality. Mere spasms of emotion and temporary excitement do not necessarily imply a revival. One has to distinguish between what is false and what is real between the superficial and the lasting. The criterion by which we are to judge, is the permanent effect."
Rev. J. Vyrnwy Morgan, D.D. 1909

For almost four hundred years many Religious Revivals, large and small, have taken place throughout Wales, and elsewhere, each having a different approach and effect. Some revivals were solemn in their theological context, whilst others were full of rejoicing mixed with fanatical excitement taken to emotional excess. A minority however passed off quietly and peacefully. The effects of poverty and disease, led to outbreaks of revival, as people turned to the spiritual comfort and refuge of the chapel. Whatever form they followed, revivals brought about great increases in chapel worship and activity, and consequently thousands of people of all denominations were affected and many converted. However, such excitement had an opposite effect on some who took the change too seriously and fell victims to religious mania, and ended up in asylums. Revivals throughout the ages led to the practice of Temperance and pledges of abstinence, and to a general improvement in the quality of life. Many folk changed their ways, leading to a decline in drunkenness, thieving, and gambling, and those affected by the change returned to God, The Bible and the chapel, as both adults and children came under the powerful spell of the "message". The enthusiasm often became contagious and confessions of awful sins were reported and heard on every side expressing a strong desire to lead a better and different life.

As we will learn later in section (ii) of this chapter, many Revivals had taken place since the middle of the eighteenth century. However, the Great 1904-1905 Religious Revival started by the Evangelist and Revivalist Evan Roberts (1878-1951) of Loughor, near Swansea, was the largest and last widespread movement of its kind in Wales. To a certain extent it gave the Welsh nation a vision of its spiritual need and shortcomings. It was considered in its day to be a "last ditch" effort to save religion from being engulfed by

Evan Roberts, The Revivalist – 1904.

other social organisations and new secular interests and attractions taking place outside the chapels. There was no mistaking the superhuman character of the 1904-05 Revival; it was a sudden and general break with the past. Some claimed it was short-lived, and whilst it was certainly remarkable in its day, the effervescent effort was not long lasting and many lost their initial yearning and enthusiasm within months. At the height of the 1904-05 Revival, amidst the excitement and passion some soon became doubtful, and wondered whether or not the Revival was – *"A real resolution of character or merely a glorious riot of the emotions." – (Aberdare Leader, 1905)*. Within less than three years the intensity of the last Great Religious Revival had burned itself out, and simply fizzled away. It effectively came to a halt by the summer of 1907.

(ii) Early Religious Revivals, 1620-1884

It is difficult to furnish the exact number and dates of past Revivals. However in this section we shall study the major revivals that took place in Wales from 1620 up to 1884. The famous 1859 and 1904-05 Revivals are dealt with in detail in Sections (iii) and (v) of this chapter, respectively. The power and influence of the many revivals throughout the ages was enormous, and a profoundly wonderful and unique experience. They were all different in many ways, being inspired through the events of several social problems and circumstances, but the outcome was generally that of an unadulterated blessing and success, resulting in many thousands being converted and received into chapel membership.

Past Revivals

1620-30. A Revival led by Vicar Pritchard at Llandovery and District, and extending to St. David's, Pembrokeshire, filled every church on the route to overflowing. Full of fervour and song it brought about a better moral condition of the people. It also helped to bring about the publication of the first popular edition of the Welsh Bible.

1735. The preaching of the notable Welsh Calvinistic Methodist, Howell Harris (1714-73) of Trefecca Uchaf, Powys, was the immediate cause of the 1735 Religious Revival in Wales, although Griffith Jones (1683-1761) of Llanddowror, near St. Clears, was the precursor of this movement. He was also the pioneer of the famous Circulating Schools for both young and old. Between them, Harris and Jones gave birth to the Welsh Nonconformity of the eighteenth century. Harris, although a layman all his life, had a wonderful gift of natural oratory and was a most impressive and charismatic preacher. Almost simultaneously with the Breconshire Movement occurred that of the Llangeitho Revival. Harris felt himself endued with the power after taking Holy Communion at Talgarth Church on Easter Day 1735. Daniel Rowland (1713-90) also became involved in the movement at Llangeitho Church, near Tregaron, Cardiganshire. It was said that this Revival was more spiritual and general in character compared with other Revivals. In a few years time no fewer than ten ordained clergymen were engaged in the work of preaching the Gospel and spreading the Revival in Wales. The celebrated William Williams of Pantycelyn (1716-91), the great hymnist who wrote over one thousand hymns, was also active in this movement. During this period, the Wesleyan Methodist Church was founded in 1739, beginning with open-air preaching.

1762-63. The "Great Revival". Prime figures were ordinary people from among all dissenters and nonconformists. The Movement originated at Llangeitho and was led by eminent Revivalist and Preacher Daniel Rowland.

1785-87. A Theological Revival.

1791-92. During the latter half of the eighteenth century, several Revivals were witnessed, but they were all more or less local. Seven Revivals, it is said, broke out in Howell Harris' time at Llangeitho alone. The most remarkable of the awakenings was that which occurred during the last decade of the eighteenth century (1791-92), and was a very powerful upheaval producing marked effects upon thousands of people.

1790-94. A period involving Missionary Revivals influenced by the French Revolution. Richard Price, Morgan John Rhys and Rev. Thomas Evans (1764-1833), (Tomos Glyn Cothi), played a prominent role during this movement and held sympathy for the Revolution links. Rev. T. Evans was minister at Hen-Dy-Cwrdd Unitarian Chapel, Trecynon (Ref. 129) from 1811 to his death in 1833. He was also a politician and prolific hymn writer.

1806-09. A Practical Revival led by John Elias (1774-1841) of Abererch, near Pwllheli, who was known also as "The Prince of Preachers". This Revival was especially touching and emotional, and reached out to children and the Sunday School.

1811-14. A Revival characterised by the rejoicing and "jumping with joy" reminiscent of the late eighteenth century Revivals. During this period, in 1811, the Welsh Calvinistic Methodist connection was set up.

John Elias (b.1774 d. 1841), during the Religious Revivals 1806 to 1832.

1814-15. Theological and Spiritual Revival commenced by Christmas Evans (1766-1838) of Llandysul.

1817-22. The "Beddgelert" (Gwynedd) Revival; local in its effect but intensive and spiritual. It lasted over five years.

1828-29. The Great Rejoicing Revival. Inspired out of rural and industrial poverty, the unemployed, the depressed and the discontented.

1829. This Revival had a widespread effect. It was said – *"There was much leaping with joy and loud praising. Women removed their bonnets and shawls in participating. There was an old small table which was leapt upon by exultant worshippers; its stability was a source of concern for the more modest and conservative of those present, but nevertheless it held firm."* The 1829 Revival first broke out locally at Ebenezer Welsh Congregational Chapel, Trecynon (Ref. 127), and was the first large scale Revival of its kind to occur in the Cynon Valley.

John Elias during the Revivals 1806-32.
By courtesy of National Library of Wales.

1831-32. The Cholera Revival – the most solemn of all revivals, and the most sudden in its occurrence. Its leader was John Elias (1774-1841) of Abererch (near Pwllheli). As the terrible cholera epidemic spread and the death toll rose, fear gripped the locality forcing people to turn to the refuge of the chapels which quickly filled, and those in search of salvation were converted.

1837. The Temperance Revival. Hardened drinkers in areas of heavy industry and mining were influenced by this Revival and this led to pledges of abstinence in large numbers.

1839-43. A peaceful and quiet revival with a practical bias largely owing to the preaching of Rev. John Jones of Talysarn, Gwynedd, a celebrated Calvinistic Methodist. This revival brought about a healthier atmosphere both in morals and in theology. The chapels of North Wales were visited by a religious convulsion in 1839 and 1840, followed by South Wales in 1841, 1842 and 1843. However, it so transpired that the period from the end of 1843 was – *"A season of almost universal declension."* – (Quote by Dr. T. Rees of Swansea).

1849. The 1849 South Wales "Cholera Revival" was noted for its fierceness, and for the number of its back-sliders, and the suddenness with which they lapsed after the disappearance of the epidemic. The terrible visitation of cholera was principally the means of arousing people's attention in 1849. From 26th May to 18th July 1849 there were no less than 1670 cholera cases in the Parish of Aberdare alone; 632 died and masses turned to religion. From 27th May to 30th December 1849 over 200 members were received into chapel membership in the valleys, including over 100 on one particular Sunday. It will be noticed that the Revivals of 1829 to 1849 were largely inspired by social problems including disease, poor health standards, and unemployment and wide spread poverty. Over 9,000 converts were added to 67 Independent Chapels in South Wales in only three months during the Summer of 1849, and some 1200-1500 converts were received into membership in Merthyr Tydfil during the year.

<u>1859.</u> See Section (iii) of this chapter for a detailed study of the 1859 Religious Revival, in which Humphrey Jones (1832-1895) and Rev. David Morgan (1814-1883) played a prominent role. This Revival was more general in its scope and effect than previously experienced. The interval between 1859 and 1904-05 witnessed many Revivals from time to time throughout the locality and Wales in general. The 1859 Revival also encouraged an increased interest in the Welsh language.

<u>1866.</u> A Revival arising from the Cholera outbreak in Tredegar.

<u>1868.</u> A Revival led by Rev. David (Dafydd) Morgan ("Ysbyty-Ystwyth").

<u>1875.</u> Rev. John Richard Hughes and Richard Owen, both of Anglesey were the leading revivalists during this period.

<u>1875-77.</u> At Rhymney, Brynmawr and other parts of Monmouthshire strong waves of revival took place. They were generally of a shorter duration than previously witnessed and occurred among adults and older people. It compared well with the 1904-05 Revival for preaching, intensity of feeling, open air gatherings, sincerity, courage and passion for the salvation of sinners. It led to large numbers being converted and received into chapel membership.

<u>1879.</u> A fervent revival; particularly prominent among the Baptists. Many new converts received. In a total of nine chapels in Aberdare, 540 converts were baptised and 139 were restored to membership during this period.

<u>1882-84.</u> The Revival led by the Rev. Richard Owen (1839-87), one of the most genuine, powerful and God-sent Revivalists that Wales ever witnessed. His Revival "tent" was filled each night to overflowing and his preaching was so powerful that hardened sinners groaned and wept.

Rev. Richard Owen (1839-1887), leader of the Revival 1882-84.

<u>1904-05.</u> The last of the major Revivals. The "Great Evan Roberts Revival" is dealt with in detail in Section (v) of this chapter, and primarily covers the extraordinary events witnessed throughout the Cynon Valley. It was a period of fanatical excitement and extreme emotional excess; a movement of momentous proportions having a district message for the chapels and the age, both social and religious, and also extending worldwide.

(iii) The 1859 Welsh Revival

In terms of religious fervour this was the greatest shaking of the heavens and the earth the nineteenth century ever knew and experienced – that of the glorious 1859 Religious Revival. It began in North Cardiganshire and was mainly theological in form, content and doctrinal intent. The pioneer of this Revival was the Welsh Wesleyan Methodist Humphrey Jones (1832-95) of Tre'r-ddol, near Talybont, Cardiganshire. In 1854, before the outbreak of the revival, Jones sailed to America and ministered there at The Episcopal Church in New York State. E. Isaac wrote in 1930 that Jones returned to Wales from America in 1858, where he had witnessed the breaking out of a powerful awakening that had taken place in New York State in 1857. When he returned home Jones became the main means of kindling a religious awakening throughout the principality, promptly

> **THE SALVATION ARMY IN THE 1880'S**
>
> "They parade the streets for hours during the evenings, and conduct rather long public meetings. They sing, pray, speak with much enthusiasm and strength, and continue to do so hand in hand with 40 or 50 applicants for salvation and then they kneel in front of the "Penitential Bench". They are almost the only people to be seen in the locality reading The Bible on the train or in the streets."
>
> *From "Baner ac Amseran Cymru" (Transaltion) – 1888*

spreading the good news of the American Revival around North Cardiganshire. Thus the seeds were sown for a fresh Welsh Revival. Special local meetings and prayer services soon took place and in due time, much of Cardiganshire was deeply aroused. Eventually the adjoining counties and the whole of Wales felt the strange new power that was at work. Humphrey Jones, like Evan Roberts was laid aside and became ill in the midst of his labours; he too suffered from mental exhaustion and depression due to hard work, hectic excitement and passion of the Revival. Like Roberts, he also observed strict silence and prayer sessions for considerable periods at a time. He died at Chilton, U.S.A., in 1895 and is buried at Brant, Wisconsin. A tablet was unveiled in his memory in September 1933. Another notable preacher who also hailed from Cardiganshire was the Revivalist, David (Dafydd) Morgan (1815-83), of "Ysbyty Ystwyth". He came into contact with Humphrey Jones, and like Jones he did much work in spreading the revival message around Wales. Morgan was a carpenter by trade before becoming the minister of Maesglas Calvinistic Methodist Chapel at Ysbyty Ystwyth, in 1868. Within a few months of the revival in Cardiganshire, in the summer of 1858, the message of awakening spread to the Cynon Valley and neighbouring districts, but it was a while before the Revival took a positive hold in the locality.

Rev. Humphrey Jones (1832-1895).

Rev. David (Dafydd) Morgan (1815-1883), during the 1859 Revival.

Rev. Humphrey Jones (1832-1895)

Rev. David (Dafydd) Morgan (1815-1883).

Early in 1859, at services in Ebenezer W.I., Trecynon, Siloa W. Cong., Aberdare and Saron W.I., Aberaman, reports reached the ministers and members of a powerful religious revival in South Wales, and soon Ebenezer W.I. became the centre of revival activity in the Cynon Valley. The Rev. John Davies, the minister of Saron W.I., Aberaman, confirmed that the older members of Ebenezer Chapel, who had witnessed the famous Revival of 1829, thirty years earlier, encouraged the Movement. Rev. William Edwards, minister of Ebenezer Chapel from 1844 to 1884, broke the news to his congregation of the 1859 revival activity in Cardiganshire and joyous scenes were thereafter witnessed in Trecynon, and later at Hirwaun and Aberaman. The news soon spread throughout the Cynon Valley. Large congregations wept with joy and many of those deemed to be sinners by members or others were converted. The Revival ultimately led to a quick and massive increase in chapel building throughout the Cynon Valley and in adjoining localities. During the period 1858-60, twenty-eight new chapels were built in the Cynon Valley. From 1850-70 a total of 56 chapels were erected which represents 31 per cent of the total of 180 throughout the area. This was the busiest period of chapel building work.

People flocked to the chapels in numbers never seen before. Ministers and deacons became concerned at times as their congregation remained worshipping within the chapels until almost daybreak and it was difficult to persuade them to leave and go to their homes. Special prayer meetings were held in some chapels and also in various collieries before the start of the shift. The Temperance Movement became increasingly active during this period. The Temperance Hall, designed by Evan Griffiths, was erected at Aberdare in 1858 at a cost of over £3000, with 1500 seating capacity. It was financed by the local Temperance Society and supported by David Davis and David Williams (Alaw Goch) – coal owners, and H.A. Bruce, M.P., (b.1815 d.1895 –later became First Baron Aberdare of Dyffryn). Geoffrey Evans tells us that in 1895, The Temperance Hall became The New Theatre and Hippodrome and in 1918 it was renamed The Palladium Cinema. It is now (2004) a Bingo centre. People abandoned theatres, taverns and Music Halls in order to be part of the revivalist congregations. Taverns were forced to close through lack of trade and rugby clubs cancelled their fixtures, leading to many players being received into chapel membership. The cause of temperance and social purity was given a powerful stimulus and the social and religious life of the Cynon Valley and elsewhere, was altogether lifted on to a higher plane.

The year 1859 was indeed a memorable year for the Great National Revival throughout Wales, and the Movement kept stirring for some eighteen months or more. Such was the immense fervour and increase in chapel membership that a member commented – *"The walls of the chapels are shaking with great praise and song."* In South Wales, it was estimated that as many as 110,000 new members were received in 1859. Preaching with incredible enthusiasm reached such a high pitch that the crowded congregations broke into spontaneous prayer and praise making further preaching impossible. Meetings frequently continued from 6.00p.m.to10.00p.m.and sometimes into the late night and early hours of the morning. Hundreds of penitents expressed their intentions of joining the chapels, and over 300 alone joined Ebenezer W.I., Trecynon in the early months of 1859. T. Rees tells us that at one service, fifty six converts were made at Ebenezer, and at Saron W.I., Aberaman, fifty new members were admitted every month for four consecutive months. The huge increase in Saron's membership at first presented few problems as this chapel had been enlarged in 1856 to provide seating capacity for a little over 900, making it the largest chapel ever built in the Cynon Valley. Revival Meetings lasted anything up to five hours each, without a break. The Revival Meeting of Welsh Independent held at Siloa W.I., Aberdare, on 5th July 1859, commenced with prayer at 6a.m. and 8a.m. Two preachers spoke at a meeting at 10a.m., there then followed a young people's prayer meeting at 1p.m., and a public meeting in the afternoon. An evening service was at 6.30p.m., followed by scenes of extraordinary religious fervour which carried on until 10.30p.m., resulting in forty converts being received at the "Penitential Bench". Sermons often lasted two to three hours without a break. At Nebo W.I., Hirwaun, in March 1859, a meeting of the Independent Association was held, the results of which gave a great impetus to the Revival Movement. Many new converts were received throughout Hirwaun and the upper reaches of the Valley. Further down the valley, the monthly meetings of Independents of the Aberdare Valley were held throughout 1859 at Bethania W.Cong., Mountain Ash, and often went on from 10.30a.m. to 11p.m. (over twelve hours!) –

without a break! William Bevan, a Deacon and member of Bethania Chapel (later of Providence E.Cong) and manager of the Deep Duffryn Colliery, witnessed these meetings and tells us – *"There were scores if not hundreds of people in the street outside Bethania Chapel all afternoon, unable to gain access into the Meeting. Some were praying, others shouting; some sang hymns whilst others lamented in spiritual meditation."* Hundreds were received into membership, and it reached such high numbers that the old first Bethania Chapel, Mountain Ash, built in 1854 had to be rebuilt completely during 1859, at a cost of £950, with seating for 750. The 1859 Revival resulted in the enlargement and erection of many new chapels throughout the Cynon Valley, and a general revival of interest in the Welsh language. Twenty-five new chapels were built in the locality during the period 1859-60. Rev. Owen Jones of Dowlais was instrumental in spreading the message effectively through the Welsh language. Rev. John Davies spoke of worshippers at Saron W.I., Aberaman, rising from their seats during the middle of a sermon and jumping with uncontrollable joy. Around 1400 new members were added to the Welsh Independent Chapels in the Aberdare parish within the first six months of 1859. The Nonconformist chapels were not the only places of religious worship to be affected by the 1859 Revival. The established church was also very much caught up in the enthusiastic movement and in April 1859 over 200 people were confirmed in the Aberdare parish by the vicar Father John Griffiths of St Elvan's, and vicar Father David Davies of St. John's. Spontaneous prayer meetings and a zeal for the conversion of the irreligious were the leading features of the 1859 Revival. Many meetings continued until daybreak and were sometimes held in the open air, either because the chapels were too full, or as an attempt to attract non-members or casual "hearers" (gwrandawyr), with a view to them becoming new converts or members. Anybody prayed or gave out a hymn and meetings generally terminated, not through rigid time limits, but rather owing to the sheer physical exhaustion of the revivalists. Many were carried out of the chapels in a state of frenzy and fatigue, unable to move hand or foot. Physical manifestations of euphoria were very well marked, and people often became delirious and frantic, giving vent to their emotions by jumping and shouting – "Hosannah" and "Hallelujah", and such exclamations.

The Rev. David Silyn Evans, minister of Siloa W.Cong., Aberdare, from 1880-1930, an incredible 50 years, said of the 1859 Revival – *"Peoples' fears were greatly played upon in the 1859 Revival, whereas the keynote of the later 1904-05 Revival was that of the Love of God."* As we have read in Section (ii) of this chapter, many revivals were witnessed throughout the locality during 1859 up to the last revival of 1904-05. In the 1859 movement there was an emphasis on preaching and the salvation of sinners, and such was the power and influence of this and other revivals that thousands changed their ways and became converted and followed the Temperance and Abstinence movements and societies throughout the locality.

I shall conclude this section on a musical note! The 1859 Revival also marked a new era in the history of Welsh sacred music. That date saw a revival quite as much in congregational singing as in religion. The introduction of the "tonic sol-fa" system is also coincidental with the year 1859, and it was during the latter half of the nineteenth century that the great Singing Festivals (Gymanfa Ganu) began properly to be the great power in Welsh religious circles. Since this period and well into the 1900's music was of paramount importance in Welsh chapels, and sacred song was powerfully stimulated from outside by the eisteddfod and festivals of concert and singing. A master of song of the period Dr. Joseph Parry (1841-1903), of Merthyr Tydfil, once observed – *"The next Revival in Wales will be a singing revival."* The remark was founded upon knowledge of the national character and experience of the period around 1850-1900. Indeed, events around this time established its correctness, and the Gymanfa Ganu became hugely successful and attracted enormous numbers into the chapels not only up to 1900 but also into the first half of the twentieth century. Regretfully from about 1950 onwards, the Gymanfa Ganu fell into decline as chapels gradually began to close and disappear from the local scene. However, it is satisfying to know that the tradition of the Gymanfa Ganu still continues in some chapels albeit on a reduced scale.

Somewhat smaller revivals took place after 1859 but the next Great Religious Revival was that of 1904-05. Led by Evan Roberts, it was the last major revival of its kind to be witnessed in the Cynon Valley and throughout Wales. This shall be studied in Section (v) of this chapter.

(iv) Profile of The Welsh Revivalist – Evan Roberts (1878-1951).

How befitting it is on this the Centenary of the Welsh Revival of 1904-05, to be studying a profile of the great revivalist and evangelist, Evan Roberts. It is equally appropriate to mention here the close connection of Evan Roberts with the Cynon Valley, particularly the association with Trecynon where on the 13th to 15th of November 1904, he conducted his first Revival Meeting outside his hometown of Loughor. He later held services and prayer meetings throughout the Cynon Valley where hundreds of converts were received. Mountain Ash too, can be

Evan Roberts during the Revival 1904-05.

justifiably proud of its link with Evan Roberts, as it was here that he lived, worked, worshipped and preached for four months from August to December 1899.

Evan Roberts was born at Island House, Bwlchymynydd, near Loughor on 8th June 1878. He was brought up in a religious and humble Welsh-speaking background and was baptised at Moriah Calvinistic Methodist Chapel, Loughor, and named Evan John Roberts. His middle name was scarcely heard and he was known simply as Evan Roberts. His parents, Henry and Hannah Roberts, brought up fourteen children and Evan was their ninth child born, but only eight had survived over the years up to 1906. He commenced school in 1883 aged five years. In March 1889 his father met with a mining accident and consequently Roberts left school barely twelve years of age and started work in Mountain Colliery, Loughor, as a door boy earning five shillings a week. In 1894, aged 16 years, he undertook work as a coal cutter working a heading. The following year he became employed at Blaengarw Colliery for six weeks and then returned to Loughor where he worked from 1895 to 1898 at Broad Oak Colliery. During this time an underground explosion occurred killing five colliers, but fortunately Roberts was not hurt. Soon after, work began to slow down at the colliery resulting in his journeying to Mountain Ash to seek work in the thriving coal industry then evident in the town. There, he was employed underground at Deep Duffryn Colliery (opened 1855; closed 1980), for four months from the end of August to end of December 1899. During his stay at Mountain Ash, he became a member of Bethlehem Calvinistic Methodist Chapel, Pryce Street, (Ref.49) – (Built 1857; Rebuilt 1900; Demolished 1980). He probably chose Bethlehem Chapel because the denomination – Welsh Calvinistic Methodist, was the same as that of his hometown chapel Moriah, and also because of the close proximity of his work place and lodgings. (Evan Roberts returned to Bethlehem Chapel on 21st November 1904 while visiting the South Wales Valleys during the official "First Journey" of his Revival Meetings.) Here, he preached and gave several talks and was very active in the work of the chapel. He lived as a guest in the home of William Lloyd and his wife, Draper and Outfitter, Emlyn House, Oxford Street, Mountain Ash. Mr Lloyd was a well known Deacon and member of Bethlehem Chapel. While there, Roberts gave up his time to reading, poetry and studying the Bible, and here produced a notable poetical composition – "A Sacrifice For Thy Sake", and

other work of like nature. He frequently wrote letters home in the form of poetry. At the end of December 1899 he returned home and found employment at Broad Oak Colliery where he received good wages and stayed until September 1902. He then gave up working on the coalface and began to learn the trade of blacksmith; he was now aged twenty-four. He was employed at

TRECYNON ON THE RELIGIOUS REVIVAL MAP 1904-05

Bryn Sion English Baptist Chapel (Carmel E.B.), Mill Street, Trecynon, was the first chapel in Cynon Valley to be visited on 13th November 1904 by the great Evangelist and Revivalist, Evan Roberts (1878-1951) during the Religious Revival in Wales 1904-05,

Forest Colliery, Pontardulais, four miles from his home, and worked with his uncle (his mother's brother). He was fifteen months learning the trade of blacksmith from September 1902 to December 1903. Whilst at Pontardulais he attended weekly meetings at Libanus C.M. chapel and every Saturday evening he returned to his home at Bwlchymynydd. Soon he was able to shoe horses and whilst doing so would often sing hymns. He always kept a Bible in the blacksmith shop and at break-times and every possible opportunity he would read from the Holy Scripture.

In the book – "Evan Roberts The Great Welsh Revivalist and His Work" (published 1906), the author, Rev. D. M. Phillips M.A., Ph.D., of Tylorstown, writes, *"Throughout 1903, Evan Roberts became increasingly anxious to finish work and become a Preacher, and was almost constantly engaged in the habit of prayer. He regarded the period 13 to 26 years of age as rich in his history of preparing him for his future preaching vocation and Revival work."* He became a member of Moriah C.M. chapel, Loughor at thirteen years of age in 1891, and by fifteen Roberts became a Sunday school teacher, superintendent and secretary. He was brought up amidst strongly religious beliefs, and the influence of his home life and his deepening religious convictions led him eventually to the Christian ministry. At the end of 1903 he openly declared his wish to become a preacher thus fulfilling a desire and passion which had lasted the past ten to twelve years. He was advised to enter Newcastle Emlyn Preparatory School for Ministers, and on 17th December 1903 he favoured preaching as a vocation. He finished work as a blacksmith and left the colliery at Pontardulais never to return there again; soon after he delivered his first sermon at his home chapel, Moriah C.M.

Evan Roberts commenced his "trial" or probation on 3rd January 1904, and preached in several local chapels. His "test" was successful and he was urged to prepare for the provincial examinations to become a candidate for the Ministry. The examination was held on 16th August 1904 at Pontrhyd-y-fen, a few miles from Port Talbot. He came eighth out of fourteen students and was now free to enter a school to prepare for the Trevecca College Examination. However, as the time drew nigh for the opening of the school at Newcastle Emlyn in September 1904, he became undecided about his immediate future. Should he do away with school and examinations and go out to preach and work for the Master instead, which he felt was his true calling in life? Doubts were creeping in. After entering the school at Newcastle Emlyn on 13th September 1904, matters became worse for him. He began experiencing difficulties at concentrating and learning as a student at the school and confessed that his only need and wish at this time was to study and read the Bible. He felt that school was hindering his calling to become a preacher. From 16th August to the end of October 1904 were memorable weeks in his

Evan Roberts, circa. 1904.

C.V.H.S.

life and his inward struggle would eventually give birth to the means of a mighty Revival. The appearance of the revivalist in Evan Roberts was not sudden but was the result of his lifetime struggle, a lonely and long process of agonising torment and vexation of spirit.

During September and October 1904 he attended prayer meetings at Newcastle Emlyn and was invited to join a religious conference at Blaenannerch where he met with his friend Sydney Evans. His teacher at the school forever strove to get Roberts back to his studies to draw him out of himself and his strange moods of indecision and settle his doubts and thus concentrate his mind on his schooling; but to no avail! His only wish now was to give up school and immediately become a preacher. By October 1904, there was no further hope of getting Roberts back to school at Newcastle Emlyn. The Convention held the year previous in 1903 at New Quay, South Cardiganshire, under the leadership of Joseph Jenkins (1859-1929) had great influence on the development of Roberts as a Revivalist. From the age of thirteen to twenty-six through constant prayer he was set on becoming a preacher and revivalist. Rev. Joseph Jenkins, in collaboration with Rev. John Thickens (1864-1952), was foremost in wanting a Revival and around December 1903 to January 1904 there was an intense spiritual tone beckoning a religious awakening. The Rev. J. Thickens (later of London) was then (1903) a pastor at Aberaeron. A "Divine Fire" began to take a firm hold on the members at the Calvinistic Methodist Chapel at New Quay, and Rev. Joseph Jenkins continued to preach there. By January 1904 the "fire" soon spread to Blaenannerch, Newcastle Emlyn, Capel Drindod and Twrgwyn. In a conference held at Blaenannerch in September 1904, Roberts was filled with the Holy Spirit. He said, *"I prayed for a Revival for thirteen years."* Many prayer meetings were held around this time and on 29th September 1904 Roberts decided not to continue with schoolwork. On 1st October 1904 he became full of the idea of going through Wales on a Mission Tour. He was greatly affected spiritually by the meetings and services held at Newcastle Emlyn and Blaenannerch. He said at this time, *"The Revival is coming."*

Evan Roberts became influenced by the sense of spiritual power at these meetings, and felt his immediate calling was to go out and preach the Gospel and seek converts. These meetings became the catalyst of great things that were about to happen. The seeds were sown for a great religious awakening within the locality, and this was henceforth to change Roberts' life forever. Early in October 1904, prayer meetings continued and Roberts had a longing that the "fire" should reach Loughor. At this time of inward struggle some thought that Roberts' mind was becoming unbalanced and impaired. In October 1904 when he left Newcastle Emlyn and Blaenannerch, Roberts became engaged in excessively long prayer sessions and people feared for his health. On 31st October he left Newcastle Emlyn by train for his home at Loughor to work amongst the young people of Moriah Chapel. Here he gave his first Revival

MISS MARY DAVIES
(Gorseinon).

MISS ANNIE DAVIES
(Maesteg).

MISS S. A. JONES
(Nantymoel).

MISS MARY DAVIES
(Gorseinon).

MR. EVAN ROBERTS
(Loughor).

MISS LIVINIA HOCKER
(Gorseinon).

MISS MAGGIE DAVIES
(Maesteg).

MISS PRISCILLA WATKINS
(Gorseinon).

MISS ANNIE M. REES
(Gorseinon).

THE REVIVALIST AND SOME OF THE YOUNG LADY EVANGELISTS.

Courtesy of The Western Mail & Echo Ltd. 1904

Evan Roberts and his assistant Evangelists, 1904.

Lady Evangelist, Miss Annie Davies of Maesteg.
Accompanied Evan Roberts during the 1904-05 Revival.
By permission of Llyfrgell Genedlaethol Cymru.
The National Library of Wales Aberystwyth

Sermon. His preaching was attended by extraordinary results. Very soon, large crowds flocked to hear him and were moved to tears. He underwent a series of remarkable psychic experiences which eventually led him to become the central figure of the Welsh Religious Revival of 1904-05. It must be noted however, although Roberts was the driving force behind The Movement, he was not its author or originator as the Revival had been active in New Quay and elsewhere around 1902-03, over two years before the Loughor outbreak. Roberts now began conducting informal services, regular prayer meetings and Bible classes in his own Moriah Chapel and others nearby. Owing to his energetic preaching style these meetings soon attracted large numbers and there was witnessed a pronounced showing of spiritual conversion. It was not too long before Roberts was accompanied and assisted by a number of lady evangelists, among them the sisters Miss Maggie and Miss Annie Davies of Maesteg, and Miss S.S. Jones of Nantymoel. His brother Dan and his friend Sydney Evans also gave admirable support. Between them they began circulating local chapels in the Loughor district. By his winsome and attractive ways of addressing his congregation, Roberts soon attracted numbers by the thousand.

The period 31st October to 12th November 1904 was considered to be – *"The Break of Dawn of The Revival at Lougher."* – (Quote by Rev. D.M. Phillips). Such a fortnight had never been known in the history of Wales since the 1859 Revival. It was described as being thirteen wonderful days full of spiritual power. During early November 1904 Roberts attended several prayer and revival meetings throughout the district of Loughor and neighbouring towns, attended by his lady evangelist assistants, and many new converts were made. On 4th November 1904 Roberts said– *"We are on the eve of a great Revival, the greatest Wales has ever seen."* On 5th and 6th November, large congregations met at Moriah Chapel where Roberts preached until 11.30 p.m. A power was gradually taking hold of the people of Loughor. The second week of November was called – *"The Second Week of The Revival Dawn at Loughor"*, and Roberts referred to it as – *"The Week of Direct Prayer."* On 7th November services at Moriah Chapel continued throughout the night to 3.00 a.m., and on 8th November until 4.00 a.m.!! The spiritual power was intense and affected all who attended. Some thought that Roberts was becoming insane through excessive worship and over-work. However, one of the older members of Moriah Chapel commented – *"I saw many like him in the 1859 Revival, hence there is no reason to fear anything."* On 10th November 1904, The Western Mail reported the headlines – *"A Wonderful Preacher – Great Crowds of People Draw on Loughor. Congregations Stay till 2.00 a.m. in the Morning."* On 11th and 12th November Moriah Chapel was again full to overflowing, with many ministers from other chapels attending; the services continued through the night until 5.00 a.m. the following morning!!

The first public intimation that something unusual was afoot was the above report of The Western Mail on 10th November, stating that a remarkable religious revival was taking place, and for some days Evan Roberts had been causing surprise with his extraordinary orations. The press reported that the Loughor revival had commenced and that – *"Evan Roberts had now set the heather on fire"*. The Western Mail further reported scenes that took place at Brynteg Chapel, Loughor on 11th November. The meeting began at 7.00 p.m. and without a break continued until 4.30 a.m. the following morning! The Loughor movement bore all the works of a genuine and spontaneous religious revival, as anyone who tested it by the light of past awakenings in Wales might have seen. Of the Revival, Roberts explained that the intensity of its occurrence was attributable to the presence of The Holy Spirit and he believed Wales was on the eve of one of the greatest revivals ever experienced. Throughout November and December 1904 and well into 1905, the Revival made rapid progress and Roberts went from place to place, mainly in the Glamorgan industrial areas, exhorting the people to, *"Heed the Divine Will"*. He was in great demand and many ministers were now asking Roberts to preach at their chapels.

"Showers of Blessing in Wales" – June 1905.
Courtesy of Western Mail & Echo Ltd.

We now come to an important and memorable event held at Cynon Valley; a "chance out of the blue" which placed the locality firmly on the Religious Revival map. On 11th November 1904, the minister of Bryn Sion C.M. Chapel, now Carmel E.B., Trecynon, the Rev. John Morgan, knowing of Evan Roberts' recent success at Loughor, wrote to Roberts' minister at Moriah Chapel inviting Evan Roberts to preach at Bryn Sion Chapel due to a visiting minister not turning up for the Sunday Service. Roberts replied by telegram accepting the invitation to preach at Trecynon on Sunday 13th November 1904 and thus the first official "First Journey" of Evan Roberts "the Revivalist" commenced. By a chance invitation Bryn Sion C.M. Chapel became the first chapel visited by Roberts outside his hometown of Loughor. This is surely an auspicious and memorable event to record, and one of which the people of Trecynon and Cynon Valley may by justifiably proud. On 14th and 15th November, by invitation, Roberts extended his visit at Trecynon and remained there to preach at Ebenezer W.Cong. Chapel, where remarkable scenes were witnessed. Meetings followed in the coming days and weeks throughout the Cynon Valley and the chapels became densely packed with worshippers hours before Roberts was due to attend. Sounds of congregational singing could be heard far into the night and early hours of the following morning. In the months following, Evan Roberts underwent an exhaustive schedule of meetings throughout the South Wales Valleys eventually reaching the rest of Wales, Liverpool and the North of England.

Evan Roberts was described as a young man of striking appearance, distinguished looking with an intellectual air and expressive, piercing eyes. The Rev. D.M. Phillips mentions that some referred to him as "the boy preacher", because he looked so young for his twenty-six years. It was said that he appeared to have had no great gifts of speech or oratory and was not a man of commanding personality. – *"He simply talks, pleads, exhorts, explaining and telling his own story simply and winningly, and smilingly invites."* (Western Mail 1905). However his magnetic power over people was simply inexplicable. His words were few and simple, and there was no particular planned order of service in his meetings. His manner was perfectly natural and unassuming, and above all his warm and winsome smile was irresistible and captivating. Rev. J. Vyrnwy Morgan D.D., wrote in 1909, *"His joyous smile is that of a man in whom there is no guile".* Roberts himself said, *"The three most important things in dealing with people are smile, voice and hand; and sometimes in greeting to use two hands, but not always. There is a great deal in a smile – more than is thought by half the world."* His silence too worked wonders at times and his presence sent a thrill through a vast concourse of people of all ages, of both sexes and of almost every temperament. It was further commented in the press, *"The Revival Meetings are really indescribable, and to visit them is to feel and realise the presence and Truth of God; the Movement is beyond criticism. It works for good, and what works for good should have the support of all."* A young man in one of the local meetings commented, *"We have plenty of better speakers and possibly abler men, but they do not seem to be imbued with the same power as he wields in drawing immense crowds and keeping them altogether."* Evan Roberts had a complex character; it was said that he was elusive; – *"The moment we touch him, he eludes us; he is here and he is gone!" He left a priceless legacy for the Nation; a Revival that gave him a name and a fame which have tested the dual claims of both ambition and aspiration."* (Western Mail). He was indeed an ideal spiritual leader and an inspired revivalist. Rev. J. Vyrnwy Morgan writes, *"For a brief period, Roberts loomed largely in the imagination of the people who were moved more by the mystery of the man rather than by his "Cause". Many were indebted to him as the symbol of the Revival, for the one ray of heavenly light that had fallen upon their souls and the all-genial glow of hope that had entered their homes; homes that for many weary years had been darkened by sin and unbelief. Some felt he repelled and quenched rather than inflamed the revival."* Roberts impressed his personality on every meeting. Unfortunately at times he could be moody, erratic and critical. This was one of the tragedies of the revival and his view of human nature was considered by some to be unkind and often unjust. To illustrate this point I quote the following which appeared in The Aberdare Leader in April 1905 – *"At Ebenezer W.I. Chapel, Trecynon, Evan Roberts told a Calvinistic Methodist minister who sat next to him in the pulpit that the place was full of devils and that he could not remain, at the same time advising that the meeting should be brought to a close. Roberts left and went on to Bryn Sion Chapel, Trecynon, only to make a similar complaint, namely that Bryn Sion likewise was full of devils. An aged Christian man in the gallery called out in Holy anger – "Art thou a Prophet?"* Many occasions arose elsewhere when Roberts said within five minutes of his appearance, that the Holy Spirit was not present. When they sang they were told by Roberts that they did not sing with sincerity.

Furthermore, in one instance he said that three hundred hypocrites were marring the effect of a certain hymn that was being sung. Such was the moody and critical nature of the man at times.

However he remained a wonder and a mystery to thousands; he was moved more by his emotions than by his intellect or ideas. He was not considered a particularly fluent speaker and often preached in broken sentences. People said that he had a clairvoyant's face. *There is something in his face that mesmerises the people; none can play the hypocrite in his presence,"* (Western Mail). Some believed he could read their thoughts and their past life like a page in a book. Some thought he had the powers of life and death. Many sought the opportunity of coming into physical contact

Evan Roberts, circa. 1904.

Evan Roberts aged 27, in 1905.

with him that they might partake of his virtue. Some rubbed his hat with the sleeve of their coat and said that the dust that fell was "Holy Dust".

The personality of Evan Roberts was surrounded with clouds of marvel and even of miracle itself. Amongst this ecstatic activity and immense popularity, there was however a dark and serious side to the Revival. In February 1905 his life took a sudden turn for the worse; rumour was circulating that already he was becoming mentally unstable; he was suffering from over-work and nervous exhaustion and needed a long rest. He went into seclusion and stayed at a friend's home, that of a Mr. and Mrs. Penn-Lewis of Leicester. The Revival continued and was very much in progress during this time, but Roberts showed signs of continuing ill-health. He ceased to attend meetings and went deeper into depression and seclusion. After declining hundreds of requests for interviews he eventually told the Western Mail that he was no longer equal to the strain of facing an audience and that his time henceforth would be devoted to private prayer. He would sometimes pray from 1.00 a.m. for four or five hours at a time, engaged in private, intimate talking with God.

On 1st February 1905, the Western Mail published a letter written by the Rev. Peter Price B.A., (1864-1940), Minister of Bethania W. Cong. Chapel, Dowlais. The letter expressed condemnation of Evan Roberts saying that his Movement was a mockery and a blasphemous travesty of the real thing. Price accused Roberts of exhibitionism and commented that the Revival was a bogus sham. He claimed that there were scores of young colliers in Dowlais with whom Roberts was not to be compared either in intellectual capabilities or spiritual power. People said, *"Evan Roberts is led by the Holy Spirit."* Price commented, *"No, quite to the contrary; judging from his behaviour and talk, The Holy Spirit is led by Evan Roberts!"* Later in June 1906 there was witnessed a remarkable outburst of religious fervour in a North Wales Chapel where Rev. Peter Price was refused occupation of the pulpit owing to his attack and criticism of Roberts the previous year. In February 1905, there were protests of Price's scathing criticism and sympathetic comments were received from many of Roberts' followers. On the other hand, many agreed with Price and condemned Roberts' style and approach to the Revival. The Peter Price controversy was a turning point in the 1904-05 Revival and affected Roberts enormously. However, he kept silent on the issue and did not make any public or written response. Furthermore, in addition to Price other sceptics said that the Revival was a sham and a mockery.

Some children did not take to Roberts; they were at times frightened of him. They did not like his contortions and some rushed out of the chapels and ran home in fear and

Rev. Peter Price B.A. (1864-1940). Minister of Bethania W.Cong., Dowlais.

astonishment. Indeed, even at the start of the Movement there were reports of fear, – *"Exhortations and Horrors of Hell!"* Roberts stated, *"If men are not burnt by the Revival "fire" in this life, they will be burnt by everlasting fire in the next life!"* Some converts were so much afflicted by such fearsome remarks that they became mentally disturbed and, in extreme cases, a small number even took their own lives or were admitted to the asylum suffering from acute religious mania. Gradually, the Revival began to die down as Roberts' health continued to deteriorate through nervous exhaustion. September 1905 was a month of struggle for Roberts; he had reached a state of exhaustion by now and his influence waned as the revivalists and followers began to dwindle and lose interest. By October 1905 it was said that, *"his soul was agitated and restless and he was suffering greatly from mental depression and physical exhaustion"*, (Western Mail). By the end of January 1906 he confessed to being, *"quite run down and needing to take it slowly"*. He continued his seclusion and observed strict silence for considerable periods at a time. Most of his time around this difficult period was spent in prolonged periods of private prayer. During these trying and strenuous day and night vigils, Roberts had little time to sleep, eat or drink. By March 1906 it was reported that Roberts needed much rest, and he therefore continued to recuperate at his friend's home, at Leicester where a slow recovery transpired over many months. However, he did manage to attend meetings occasionally and in the middle of April 1906 he attended a Convention at Bangor. Further meetings took place at Porth in June 1906, and the following month he attended a Keswick Convention.

When the First World War broke out in 1914, Evan Roberts was thirty-six years old. During the War he was called up for service three times but was rejected each occasion due to his poor health. In 1920 he gave out a "message" to the Welsh People when he spoke unexpectedly at a convention at the Tabernacle, Cardiff. Eifion Evans tells us (1969) that in November 1928 Roberts returned to Loughor to attend his father's funeral and whilst there took part in prayer meetings. In February 1930 he visited Pontardulais and attended public meetings of the Calvinistic Methodist General Assembly. From 1930 to 1951 he resided as a guest with his friends Mr. and Mrs. Oswald Williams of Rhiwbina and at times attended the Park End Presbyterian Church of Wales, Cardiff, where he occasionally spoke at week-night devotional meetings.

Evan Roberts (b.1878 d.1951) taken in his late sixties.
Brynmor Jones Collection.

Memorial plaque outside Moriah Chapel, Lougher - unveiled in 1953.

Evan Roberts was a phenomenon; his great influence and success cannot be attributed to anything but his goodness and the fact that the Holy Spirit was always with him. The Western Mail writes, *"He was a man who had experienced stranger things than fall to the rest of us. In his youth he seemed to hold a Nation in the palm of his hand, and after many years of near silence and retirement he still retained much of his magnetic personality and that idealism and fervour that characterised his work during the height of the Revival. In his day he endured severe mental and physical strain, but his religious conviction remained firm to the end."* He never truly recovered his health completely after the stress of the Revival campaign and on 29th January 1951 he died in a Cardiff Nursing Home aged 72. He is buried in the family burial place in the cemetery at his beloved Moriah Chapel, Loughor. He never married and in his will he left his entire estate to his friends at Rhiwbina. A memorial to his honour and memory, situated at the front of Moriah Chapel, was unveiled in 1953.

A wax cylinder recording of Evan Robert's voice during a Revival Address was discovered in 2002, and has recently been expertly enhanced in digitised form, and restored by The National Screen and Sound Archive of The National Library of Wales, Aberystwyth. The Address took place on 18th January 1905 at a chapel in Tredegar and was recorded by a local ironmonger on an early phonograph device. The recording is the only known surviving recording of Evan Robert's voice during the 1904-05 Revival.

(v) The 1904-05 Welsh Revival in The Cynon Valley

The publication of this book in November 2004 coincided exactly with the Centenary of the outbreak of the famous Religious Revival of 1904-05, which broke out in Loughor in the first weeks of November 1904, and was led by the great Evangelist and Revivalist Evan Roberts (1878-1951). People were awakened as if out of a deep sleep. It shook the whole nation from centre to circumference and occurred suddenly and without warning of any kind and spread rapidly throughout the Cynon Valley and the rest of Wales. Many of the older folk compared it with the power and effects of the Great 1859 Revival, (see Section (iii)). People thronged the chapels day and night and were packed in far beyond the registered capacity of such buildings, without any decrease for months on end. In the larger chapels, up to a thousand or more were in attendance sitting in the aisles and every available space, including the steps of the pulpit. The Revival was heard in chapels, houses and even the coalmines. It was a fearfully glorious and remarkable sight, an awe-inspiring spectacle which can never be erased from the memory. Many recalled the frenzies, quaking, contortions and extravagances of Revivalists of the extreme type, and the lurid details of the life in hell, which they gave. Men, women and children came under the "spell" of the "Message". Big grown-up men unblushingly cried aloud in public for salvation, and it is not surprising that some folk fainted and collapsed in the excitement. The 1904-05 Revival was the last of the Great Religious Revivals, and was dominated by working class youth and by women. Remarkable scenes of religious ecstasy and human emotion were witnessed with strong men weeping and groaning; women cried and sobbed, bursting spontaneously into prayer and sacred song. Prayer meetings carried on into the early hours of the morning and people danced joyfully in the streets without inhibition; there was indeed much praying, singing, shouting and rejoicing. The Revival affected the children too as they prayed during their playtime periods and also held meetings of their own in private houses, in barns and in some instances even in empty pigsties!

Service during the 1904-05 Revival.
Kevin Adams and Emyr Jones 1904 Ltd.

Rev. J Vyrnwy Morgan wrote in 1909, *"The Revival was short-lived, but nevertheless remarkable. It shone with such brilliance and intensity that those who experienced it thought it impossible that it could ever end; but it did, after a little less than three years, around the summer of 1907. Many did not want the Revival to last too long as the tension was seen to be too great to bear. The Revival gave the Welsh Nation a vision of its need, but the vision was not long lasting and passed away before its fruits were fully realised. Many lost their enthusiasm within months."* It was said that the Revival was not suitably organised and controlled and not directed into the proper channel. However, with ever increasing momentum the Movement advanced throughout 1904-07, creating unprecedented excitement among the chapels and the secular institutions outside. In every chapel, every man, every convert, and in every gathering there was something fresh, unexpected and surprising. Numbers swelled in most chapels throughout the Revival and consequently many were enlarged or rebuilt to accommodate the increased membership. During the period 1903-07, 20 new chapels were built in the Cynon Valley as a result of the Revival. A breakdown of these figures is as follows; 1903 = 4 new chapels built; 1904 = 2; 1905 = 5; 1906 = 6; 1907 = 3. This chapel building activity was the last to be seen in the locality. From 1910 there was a gradual decline in chapel attendances and membership, and an almost complete halt in the erection of new chapels. From the 1940's –50's, numbers decreased dramatically and dozens of chapels were closing their doors leading eventually to demolition. This aspect of decline is covered in chapter nine.

Let us now examine in detail the period immediately before the outbreak of the Revival. We have seen in section (iv) of this chapter that Evan Roberts was undoubtedly the central figure in this revival, but he was not its originator, much less its conceiver; neither was Loughor the birthplace of the movement. Rev. J. Vyrnwy Morgan wrote in 1909, *"The truth is that from nearly two years before the Revival broke out, the flame of awakening was ablaze in Cardiganshire in 1902, especially at New Quay, before Evan Roberts was even heard of."* The newspapers of South Wales, particularly The Western Mail, were instrumental in eventually bringing it to public recognition. The spirit of the Revival had been in the air for months and even years before it broke out in Loughor, in the first weeks of November 1904. It had actually manifested itself in various places including Tonypandy, Treharris, Dowlais, Cilfynydd, Penrhiwceiber and other places, but was most notable at New Quay, Cardiganshire, under the leadership of Rev. Joseph Jenkins (1859-1929). Conventions and prayer meetings had been held in New Quay in autumn of 1903 and early in January 1904, thus creating a new spiritual atmosphere. Rev. D.M. Phillips tells us that rumblings of the coming storm were also heard in the spring of 1904 and the nation seemed as if it was preparing for a great awakening and lamentation. The Revival had been ignited and awakened after years of spiritual slumber by the enthusiastic youth of New Quay, Cardiganshire, and in particular by a young woman of about twenty years of age, namely Miss Florrie Evans who whole-heartedly and openly testified her love for Jesus at Tabernacle Calvinistic Methodist Chapel, New Quay, during February 1904. Henceforth, the floodgates were opened for the breaking out and a mighty awakening of the Spirit of God throughout Wales. Meetings continued throughout September 1904 both at New Quay and Newcastle Emlyn. After these meetings Evan Roberts returned to his home in Loughor and began holding regular prayer meetings at his own chapel Moriah W. Calvinistic Methodist, and soon he was attracting large gatherings. The Western Mail was the first to publish, on 10th November 1904, the start of these Revival Meetings. Evan Roberts appeared at the psychological moment and through his meetings, in the early weeks of November 1904 at Loughor, he at once became the recognised symbol of the Revival. – (Extracts from Rev. D.M. Phillips).

We shall now turn to the Cynon Valley and examine the extraordinary Revival scenes witnessed in the chapels throughout the period 1904-05. Trecynon was the first place visited by Evan Roberts outside his hometown of Loughor, where the revival had broken out in the first weeks of November 1904. The Revival reached Trecynon on 13th November 1904, starting with services held at Bryn Sion Calvinistic Methodist Chapel (now Carmel English Baptist) and within days the movement spread extensively up and down the Cynon Valley. The minister and members of Ebenezer W.I. had read of the work of grace taking place in Loughor and Mr. Roberts accepted an invitation to preach at Ebenezer W.I. on 14th November. The Western Mail covered the event in detail and is quoted here – *"Upon arrival, the service commenced quietly; there were many empty pews and a coldness in the atmosphere which boded ill for a successful meeting. Some half dozen small groups of miners and their wives and sons were gathered together for a weekly prayer meeting. Suddenly, five young ladies from Loughor who accompanied Roberts walked up the aisle and seated themselves in the "Set Fawr" and started singing; the early coldness was already beginning to thaw under the influence of the singing when Roberts took his seat beneath the pulpit. The chapel by this time was filling rapidly and more hymns were sang as Roberts walked up and down the aisle swinging his arms and clapping his hands, whilst at times he gave a short sharp spring off his right foot and smiled joyously upon the people around him. He talked of the 1859 Revival and said there would be a perpetual revival if men would only keep their hearts open instead of closing them to every influence. He spoke for an hour and a quarter in a quiet, confident style and there was no doubting his absolute sincerity and conviction. During that memorable night at Ebenezer W.I. Chapel, Trecynon, on 14th Nov. 1904 many men and women broke forth in prayer and song, and a meeting which had opened so coldly was in a white heat of religious enthusiasm before the last word had been said."*

On the first day of the Revival reaching Ebenezer, Trecynon, on 14th November, two old pilgrims, who had never forgotten the Revival of 1859-60, suddenly sprung to their feet at a prayer meeting, and, with arms uplifted, shouted: *"Here it comes! – old '59!"* There was no name for it, only the equation of an old hallowed memory of the great Revival of 1859. (Quote by H. Elvet Lewis, 1906).

The following day, 15th November, The Western Mail reported on the services, again held at Ebenezer W.I. on a second visit by Roberts and the five young singing evangelists. Ebenezer W.I. was well known in connection with Edward Morgan's Revival in 1859, and although Aberdare did not appear in Nov. 1904 to have joined Trecynon there was no doubt that before the week was out, similar services would extend also to Aberdare and the rest of the Cynon Valley. The Prayer meetings at Ebenezer on 15th November lasted from 10.00 a.m. to 1.15 p.m., and men stayed away from work in order to attend.

People who had come long distances the previous day remained in the village overnight in order to join the meeting. There was an evening meeting too, from 7.00 p.m. The chapel was packed to overflowing with much hearty singing and a brief address from Evan Roberts. In time even the pulpit of the chapel was filled, as well as the pews and gallery, and the aisles. Mr Roberts once more declared that the Revival was indeed coming. The services went on for fourteen hours without a break; no one bothered about the clock as hours passed like minutes. The amount of time spent in worship troubled some ministers to the extent that some attempts were made to abbreviate the services to not more than one hour at a time. A notice was displayed in one local chapel stating, *"Brief and Bright Services Held Here"*.

Into the chapels surged endless crowds and enthusiasm was contagious. Rev. David Silyn Evans (b.1850 d.1930), minister of Siloa W.Cong., Aberdare for an incredible fifty years (1880-1930), was always buoyant and youthful in spirit but at the time of the Revival he seemed to be endowed with seven times his accustomed energy. His chapel was kept open daily for services so that miners on the night shift could attend. A similar tribute was paid also to James Griffiths, minister of Calvaria W. Baptist,

Mother Shepherd (1836-1930) (Pamela Morgan), of Talywain, Monmouth. Sent from Salvation Army H.Q. in 1878 because of her knowledge and love of the Welsh language. In 1908 she opened a Mission Hall at Pentwyn-bach, Trecynon. In 1916 she received a public presentation on her 80th birthday in recognition of her work with the Salvation Army and community.

Aberdare (1889-1930), whose chapel was always full. Chapels were crammed to suffocation even on weeknights, with souls crying for mercy and being led into the vestry, helpless under the power of The Holy Spirit. Mother Shepherd (1836-1930), of the Salvation Army, was the heroine of many revival campaigns and she threw herself into the movement with characteristic zest, and revelled in the Revival. Into the Lodging Houses went the revivalist groups to sing and pray. Young women beautifully dressed, knelt with vagrants and tramps of the road who had casually turned in for a night's lodging. As the young people knelt among the rubbish on dirty, dusty floors, they prayed for these destitute wanderers. The unkempt rooms of the lodging house seemed to be filled with the Glory of God.

On 21st November 1904, at 10.00 a.m., Evan Roberts arrived in Mountain Ash. Large throngs of people gathered at the Mountain Ash Taff Vale Railway Station to welcome the young revivalist and his lady supporters, and to accompany him at once to Bethlehem W.C.M. The chapel was quickly crowded to its utmost capacity with much repeated hymn singing. Mr Roberts spoke in a deep voice of the history of the Revival and the manifestations of religious awakening which was traversing South Wales. In Aberdare, a dozen great meetings had been held since 13th November 1904. At Trecynon and Aberdare the Revival had increased in power during the week and the communion service at Siloa W.Cong. on 20th November was described as being the most impressive ever known to have been held in that chapel within the memory of anyone present. At Heol-y-Felyn W.B., Trecynon, on 27th November, between 90-100 adults were publicly baptised by immersion, and at Abercynon and Matthewstown the large gatherings held on 21st and 22nd November were inspiring in their fervour. Moving Revival Services were also held at Bethel W.I., Miskin; Rhos Chapel, Mountain Ash; Duffryn Street Chapel, Bethania and Providence – Mountain Ash, and the newly opened (1902) Hebron W.Cong. Chapel, Ynysboeth. Worshippers were so moved by the prayers that they rose to their feet and shouted joyously. Meanwhile people were singing the Gospel in the streets of Mountain Ash, and services were being held until 11.00 p.m. in the many full chapels. The Western Mail reported that a couple of days later on 23rd November, at Mountain Ash and Abercynon, services were even being held on the platforms of the railway stations while people were waiting for their trains to depart homeward bound. On the same day, a meeting was held at Jerusalem W.P., Ynysybwl; the chapel was crowded from pulpit to doors, along the aisles, in the entrance lobby, on the pulpit stairs, and even outside the chapel. Mr Roberts delivered an impressive address. Services were also held this day at the newly built English Wesleyan Chapel at Thompson Street, Ynysybwl (opened 1903). Extraordinary scenes of religious fervour and news from neighbouring districts continued to show that the tide of the Revival was still rising. From morning until late at night meetings were again held at Jerusalem W.P., Ynysybwl on 24th November and the chapel was full even before Evan Roberts arrived. Meanwhile at Abercynon the converts now numbered three hundred. Further away in Cilfynydd Roberts held meetings on 25th November, and scores of converts were added to the local chapels. Similar enthusiastic meetings continued throughout November and December 1904 and well into the beginning of 1905. By now the Revival was at its peak.

When Evan Roberts was resting at his home in Loughor, his brother Dan would hold meetings in his absence. Such an occasion was the 9th March 1905 when Dan Roberts visited Noddfa Baptist Chapel, Ynysybwl. The chapel was full and an overflow meeting was held at the English Wesleyan Chapel, Thompson Street. At Hirwaun on 18th January 1905, Evan Roberts preached to a full congregation at Tabernacle W. Cong. Chapel. In the evening a stirring service of prayer and song was witnessed by almost one thousand worshippers at Ramoth W.B. Chapel. Trainloads from Aberdare attended these services as well as people from the locality. The following day on the 19th January, Roberts conducted meetings at Nebo W.I. and Bethel C.M., Hirwaun. Much singing and prayer took place and a large gathering outside the chapel joined in and stood for three hours in the freezing cold with snow and ice on the ground. The pulpit was full of ministers, some of them sat with closed eyes, others knelt in silent prayer, whilst one or two prayed aloud. Some of the congregation were looking down into the "Big Seat" watching converts coming in one by one and casting themselves on the floor in agony and

> **THE 1904-05 RELIGIOUS REVIVAL**
>
> Day by day the trains are choked with visitors from the neighbouring valleys. The result is that these little chapels are utterly inadequate; there was much excitement, and many faintings.

remorse. At 6.30 p.m. the meeting at Nebo W.I., Hirwaun broke up, and people left for a 7.00 p.m. meeting to be held in a larger chapel. They literally ran from one chapel to the other in order to ensure a seat. From 8th November to 31st December 1904, around 80,000 converts had been registered in chapels throughout South Wales and Monmouthshire. The vicar of St. Margaret's Church in Wales, Mountain Ash prayed to God that the Revival would also extend to the Established Church, and the vicar of St. Elvan's Church, Aberdare said there was a need for a revival and hoped that much good would accrue from the present one. Numbers of new confirmations increased considerably throughout the Established Churches of Cynon Valley during the Revival period and after.

The Western Mail continued extensive coverage of the Movement and reported that many were carried away during the storm and excitement of the Revival. Thousands of well-ordered and God-fearing men and women found their life a treadmill grind for existence. For a pittance they had to work from early morning to late at night, to provide what was necessary for the physical comfort of those who depended upon them. Life was difficult when one toiled and sweated for so little recompense. Men, who had been regarded as either too old or too wicked to be saved, surrendered fully and absolutely and through the Revival became useful citizens and consistent and faithful chapel members. Rev. J.Vyrnwy Morgan tells us that the Revival found many ministers unprepared, and without any knowledge of coping with it. They had not been trained to bear the burden of lost souls on their hearts, because their education had been in another direction. It was not a part of their College curriculum to be taught, *"that he that winneth souls is wise"*, (Western Mail). This most urgent of all teaching was usually left to the chances of the "after-life".

Progress of the Revival from its start early in November 1904 to the end of January 1905 was simply phenomenal. Prior to the Revival only frivolous amusement would satisfy the spirit of the age but now, the Spirit had been sanctified and utilized to a better purpose. In this three month period around seven thousand converts per week were recorded and eighty thousand converts were reported during the period 1904-05. This figure represents about one tenth of the population of Wales at this time. The cause of Temperance and social purity was given a powerful stimulus, and singing festivals began to be a major part of Welsh religious life. The Revival continued up to the summer of 1907, when it then came to a halt. During this period after the Revival, there was a decrease of around 20,000 members in the four main larger Nonconformist denominations in Wales. By 1912 three quarters of the original 80,000 converts gained (about 60,000) had fallen away. Chapel membership decreased rapidly in the years immediately before the 1914-18 War, leading to cynicism and doubts as to the real value of the Revival

Baptism at Hirwaun, circa 1910.

(vi) Services Held Below Ground.

Throughout South Wales, underground prayer meetings were being held as early as 1858, before the 1859 Revival had broken out in North Cardiganshire. Such services held below ground were encouraged and organised locally by the notable coal owner David Davis Jnr. (b.1821 d.1884) of Maesyffynon, (son of David Davis, Blaengwawr, b.1797 d.1866), who employed several thousands of men at his Aberaman and Blaengwawr collieries. Davis, an active Wesleyan Methodist, attended the underground services with his workmen and managers. Much later, during the 1904-05 Revival, on 1st December 1904, The Western Mail reported a service held 450 feet below the surface at Nantymelyn Colliery, Cwmdare, the property of the Bwllfa and Merthyr Collieries (Limited), whose managing director was Councillor Rees Llewellyn. He had given permission for a Western Mail reporter to descend the shaft in order to see the effects of the 1904-05 Revival underground. Mr. Edward Pugh, a staunch Methodist was then the colliery manager, and was the reporter's guide on this occasion. The workmen on the night shift had gone down half an hour earlier than usual so as not to interfere with the operations of the pit. Seventy yards from the bottom of the shaft, in the stables, the reporter and his guide came to the prayer meeting. A script from the Bible was being read to about eighty colliers. *"The reader stood erect amongst the group, reading in a dim fantastic light that danced with the swinging lamps and vanished softly into surrounding darkness,"* (Western Mail quote). The reporter tells us that a number of lamps were attached to a heavy post closely wedged to support the roof, and around the impressive figure, Bible in hand, the colliers grouped themselves. The "stable" of the pit had been transformed into a "temple" as the men prayed and read from the scriptures and sang hymns. Such was the simple service held underground by rugged men, honest, earnest and plain. Some of the colliers were in the characteristic stooping posture; others were half reclined against the side of the road heading with their lamps fastened to their pockets, whilst others stood in the middle of the passage. Earnest, strong men all of them with faces that bore the scars of the underground toiler and downcast eyes that seemed to be "the home of silent prayer". Strong frames quivered with a new emotion. The reporter continued, *"What must the thoughts of these men have been as the words of the Gospel fell on their ears in this underground "temple" with the perils of their occupation crowding around them? If the minds of men are moulded by environment, surely they could be subjected to no more impressive experience than this."* After the reading of the scripture they sang a hymn which must have penetrated through the whole of the workings of the colliery. The Western Mail reporter writes, *"It echoed along the low roofs and the narrow walls, and when the last echoes were dying away, ever so far off, it seemed a supplicatory voice broke our ears. One of the colliers was speaking – "it is not enough to pray," he said, in Welsh, "because if we do not also watch, the promises which we make in our prayers will remain unfulfilled."* Such was the simple service held underground by these rugged men. It was kept up until the moment came for commencing the night's work, and not once, but many times God's blessing was asked for the honest and proper execution of the work. The reporter stepped into the cage to return to the surface, followed by the haunting echoes of a hymn. His report appeared in The Western Mail on 1st December 1904 and is reproduced here with their kind permission.

Service underground during the Religious Revival 1904-05.

Courtesy of the Western Mail & Echo Ltd.

Service underground at Nant Y Melin Colliery, Cwmdare, December 1904.

Courtesy of the Western Mail & Echo Ltd.

The Revival even had its effect on the pit horses working underground. So revolutionary was the change in the hearts of some of these swearing hauliers that the horses were bewildered and almost ceased work altogether. The Aberdare Leader reported that singing was heard from the beginning to the end of the shift. Instead of the customary lunge with the steel sprag, there was a friendly pat! At meal times underground the miners had opportunity to open their hearts. The pit ponies were completely confused! Rev. J Vyrnwy Morgan writes, *"The people, Lord, do not understand the strange things that are happening, neither do the horses that are down the pit."* They could no longer understand the miners' instructions because of the absence of crude swearing and loud, sharp curses. At Cwmaman colliery, trams and ventilation doors had been covered in religious texts written mainly in Welsh, and colliers sang hymns on their way to the colliery and again after their days work when they returned home. Many made their way to the chapels, clothes and faces covered in coal dust. The chapels were kept open almost continuously to allow the colliers to attend worship before going to work and again after they finished the shift. No doubt this special arrangement also extended to other workers in other employment. In his book "The Welsh Revival of 1904", (published 1969), Eifion Evans writes of the social impact resulting from the conversions amongst the miners. The colliery managers saw a marked change in the workmen. The Revival had made them better colliers and had brought about an improvement in attendance at the workplace. Furthermore the beneficial effects were evident in industrial relations, and through the Revival and changing attitudes, disputes were more readily resolved.

(vii) Quotes From The "Converted".

I shall open this section with a quote from Evan Roberts given in March 1906 whilst visiting the United Independent Chapel at Penygroes, Carmarthenshire. Crowds followed him into the chapel where he gave a short address, remarking, *"That God who filled eternity could surely fill a meeting for two hours, why could not every heart be filled with the Spirit of God? It is not because of God's inability but because of man himself."* A minute later Roberts told the congregation that the Devil had whispered a verse into his ear and that he could not go on with the meeting. (Aberdare Leader, March 1906).

In his book "The Welsh Religious Revival 1904-05", the Rev. J Vyrnwy Morgan compiled the following selection of quotes and prayers uttered by converts during the Revival:

A Confession
> *"Lord forgive me for going to the public house from the chapel meeting the other night, and forgive the grey-haired old Deacons who were there like myself. Thou knowest who they are, but I shall never mention their names!"*

Another convert prayed –
> *"I thank Thee for snatching me from the jaws of evil. Satan is busy; oh, the old devil! What a sneak he is. If he were here now I would strike him!"*

While uttering this last sentence the convert assumed the attitude of a pugilist.

A young collier's prayer –
> *"Blessed be Thy Name Lord for descending the coal pit to look for me. Some of the old men accompanied me home last night, and when I entered the house my little boy ran into my arms and exclaimed, "Dada, I love Jesus." – Glory be to God for the change in me!"*

In the Aberdare valley, a quaint old collier made a strange request through prayer –
> *"Almighty Father, I am afraid of the devil; he is after me everywhere. Send him to Merthyr for a pair of clogs that I may hear his footsteps when he comes near me."*

At Tonypandy, a man in the chapel gallery shouted out that he was going to heaven there and then, whereupon a well known character in the district who felt annoyed, called out –
> *"If you are going to Heaven, then go; but please go quietly!"*

At Bala, a youth prayed –

> *"Give me a clean heart Lord. It is time for Christmas boxes now. Give me a Christmas box. I have a blank leaf in my life. Give me a Christmas box from the white page of the new year."*

Another convert's prayer –

> *"Thou Lord dost receive all kinds of people. The King of England will not permit any man to enlist as a soldier in the British Army unless he is five feet, nine inches tall, and has so much breast-measure. But Thou accept everybody – fathers and mothers, young and old, rich and poor alike."*

AN IMPROVEMENT.
FATHER CHRISTMAS : This is very different to how I found you last year, Thomas. Who can I thank for it ?
CONVERTED COLLIER : God, and Evan Roberts !

Courtesy of the Western Mail & Echo Ltd. 1904.

A housewife prayed –

> *"We pray Thee, dear Jesus, to send Thy clean and Holy Spirit to us in this place, and may we do some Spring-cleaning in the house that we may be ready to receive him, for He will not come into a very dirty house."*

A man prayed for forgiveness –

> *"Lord forgive me and my old friend for neglecting other services of Thy House for so long at a time, and for going up the mountain to play cards, pitch-and-toss, and drink beer on Sunday. Now I give my heart to Thee and I give my life. Lord bless me and keep me."*

A confession by a businessman –

> *"Lord forgive me for overcharging my fellow man by £313."*

These selection of prayers and confessions are typical of many uttered during the 1904-05 Revival, seeking salvation and forgiveness.

> *"They are simple, beautiful and childlike, full of unconscious humour and even of deplorable ignorance, yet they are overflowing with earnestness, trust in God, and a zeal against evil as a personality."*

(Quote by Rev. J Vyrnwy Morgan 1909)

(viii) Effects of the Revival on Various Addictions and Secular Attractions.

We have already given attention to the various effects of Revivals that have taken place through the ages, and how these influenced and changed people, and eventually led them to the practice of temperance and pledges of abstinence. The change brought about a general improvement in the quality of life as people became converted and expressed a strong desire to change their ways and henceforth lead a better and different life. There is no doubt that bygone revivals satisfied the ideals of many people who previously had succumbed to addiction and bad habits. As in any age the immoderate or excessive craving for obsessions such as drinking, smoking, gambling or even theft and foul language, has alas been a part of society's shortcomings and temptations since time began. Through the Revivals there was a marked decline in such harmful addictions and stories abound of many folk surrendering to these compulsions and turning to God and the chapel for salvation and redemption.

Through the Revivals unbelievers were converted, drunkards, thieves and gamblers were saved and many thousands reclaimed to respectability and honourable citizenship. Thousands of families now found pleasure and happiness in their homes for the first time in their lives and their children were clothed and fed and cherished as they never were before. Workmen became more satisfied with their wages and surroundings. Confessions of awful sins were heard on every side. Theatres and public houses were in distress for lack of patronage and trade and seven police courts throughout various districts had clean sheets and were idle. In five weeks 20,000 conversions were recorded and some weeks later the number was presumed to be 50,000. In the eight months following the onset of the 1904-05 Revival, 150,000 had made applications for chapel membership in Wales. Theatre going in Aberdare dropped dramatically and newspaper reports told the country how talented actors and actresses failed to draw the crowds. Sport too was affected and some football matches had to be cancelled and fixtures changed. The Mountain Ash Temperance Football Club was formed in 1879 through the effects of the religious revival of that year and the team was limited to players who were teetotallers. Returning to the 1904-05 Revival, dance halls in many places were completely deserted. The women deliberately cut up their expensive dresses of which they had once been so proud, thus making sure that they would not succumb to any temptations and return to the dance floor. Cases of disorderly conduct and drunkenness were reported by the police as being very small. Police records show that in February 1905, when the Revival was at its peak, the total number of cases for drunkenness and disorderly conduct for Merthyr, Aberdare, Abercynon and Mountain Ash was 212. The Rev. J. Vyrnwy Morgan informs us that convictions for drunkenness in Glamorgan before and following the 1904-05 Revival was as follows:- 1902 – 9298; 1903 – 10528; 1904 – 10282; 1905 – 8164; 1906 – 5490; 1907 – 5615. It is clear from these figures that the cause of temperance and abstinence had been strengthened by the Revival. Many of the worst characters in the district were converted. Eifion Evans (1969), tells us that, *"Some folk on the way to the billiard room, public house, and theatre etc., upon hearing singing in the chapels, felt an urge to enter and join in."* Pubs, beer clubs and tap rooms became deserted whilst the chapels were full to capacity and great marches and processions by the various Temperance and Band of Hope groups were held through town and village streets. Shopkeepers closed their doors early in order to get a seat in the chapels and colliers attended chapels for worship in their working clothes straight after their shift. Even the Public Houses were given over to discussion on the Revival. Sales of Bibles soared and chapels were enlarged or completely rebuilt to accommodate the increased numbers of converts. Public Houses became empty and takings drastically reduced and rough folk ceased from using foul language; policemen had a quiet, easy time! After one particular Temperance Society meeting, fifty men gathered and threw their pipes on the ground and trampled on them while others discarded pouches of cigarettes and tobacco. Smoking clubs were empty and hundreds took the pledge of totally giving up the habit. Stories were told of hardened drinkers pouring gallons of alcohol in the gullies and drains and not surprisingly the brewery companies complained that they had lost around seventy-five per cent of their trade. Drunks, thieves and prizefighters were now on God's side and turning to the chapels by the hundreds. Political meetings were held, but in districts where the spirit of the Revival was strong, political leaders became Revivalists. Lectures had become a complete failure and at one University College the students felt a sudden impulse and held prayer meetings instead of attending lectures.

Impromptu open-air services were held in the market place, the square or the street corner. Sometimes passengers would go into the railway station and after purchasing their train tickets would crowd the railway compartments singing and praying. This enthusiasm was however not always welcomed by some fellow travellers. In the meantime,

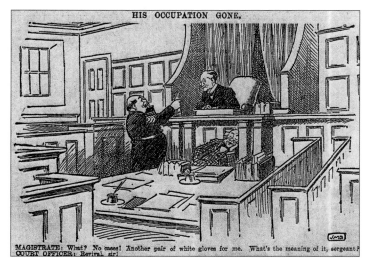

HIS OCCUPATION GONE.

MAGISTRATE: What? No cases! Another pair of white gloves for me. What's the meaning of it, sergeant?
COURT OFFICER: Revival, sir!

Courtesy of the Western Mail & Echo Ltd. 1904.

arrangements were in hand for the holding of the Royal National Eisteddfod of Wales, to be held at Mountain Ash. The Aberdare Leader reported the following in January 1905 – *"Will the Revival injure the Mountain Ash National Eisteddfod?"* Reports and discussions took place early in 1905 and questions were being put forward as to whether or not the Eisteddfod should be abandoned so as not to impede the Revival. The discussions continued for several weeks but fortunately, as we all know, the event was successfully held between 7th and 11th August 1905 and an average of 10,000 attended each day.

(ix) Religious Mania and Hypnotism

(a) RELIGIOUS MANIA

There was great rejoicing and activity during the Revivals of bygone years. But such spiritual excitement had an opposite and adverse effect on some people who became obsessed with the frenzy of these Revivals. They took the conversion and change too seriously and consequently fell victim to acute religious mania and mental illness through excess and over-indulgence in religious and theological matters, and sadly some ended up mentally insane. Sad stories are told of individuals obsessed with the religious fervour to such an extent that they became extremely depressed and unstable and some poor souls even took their own lives. One such tragedy occurred during the 1904-05 Revival when a young man became so hallucinated and depressed that he committed suicide by leaping off Brunel's Gamlin viaduct that once existed near the present day Dare Valley Country Park. During Revival Meetings converts worked themselves up to a delirious frenzy and became so wildly excited that they would perform the oddest and most irrational of actions, some quite dangerous. A report was written in the local press of a young man running through the streets at night half naked, his Bible in his hand and proclaiming passages from the scriptures. A young man in the chapel gallery was reported to have balanced precariously on top of the balcony balustrade in an attempt to leap into the pulpit to reach the preacher. The Aberdare Leader reported in December 1904 an occurrence at Soar W.C.M. Chapel, Cwmaman, where a lady worshipper unexpectedly ascended the pulpit and spoke for half an hour. After several attempts it took four men to remove her from the pulpit. The local press wrote of a young man at Elim W.Cong. Chapel, Cwmdare, who rushed up the steps of the pulpit, pushed aside the minister, opened the bible and commenced to read a portion of the scriptures, and make strange declarations. In the coming months he continued with these irrational actions and eventually the poor man was admitted to Bridgend Asylum suffering from religious mania. It was reported that he had pre-occupied himself with too much absorption in theological matters which ultimately unhinged his mind. These few examples of such sad events are sufficient to quote here, and illustrate only too well the extreme manic actions carried out by some unfortunate individuals, many of whom, sadly, were admitted to the lunatic asylum.

(b) HYPNOTISM

What prompted these unfortunate people to perform such extreme actions? It has been argued and extensively reported in the local press that some people were easily affected by the manner in which the 1904-05 Revival Meetings were conducted. In the Aberdare Leader of April 1905 it was claimed that Evan Roberts mesmerised his congregation. A statement appeared in the press by Dr. Walford Bodie, an eminent psychiatrist of the period, under the heading, *"Is Evan Roberts a Hypnotist? Does he mesmerize his congregation?"* The local press reported the following – *"Evan Roberts is claimed to be a hypnotist of great power. He seems to possess the ability to mesmerise; the air of mystery which he assumes gives him his extraordinary control over his audience. He approaches and affects them by first throwing himself into a hypnotic state which is accounted for by his silence and concentration while on the platform, and is indicated by the exhausted condition into which he subsequently falls."*

Some were of the opinion that he was grossly abusing a gift that was never intended for the coercion of fellow-beings and worshippers. The local press further reported – *"If Evan Roberts, in throwing himself into these hypnotic trances, does so without intention, then he is a monomaniac. If he does so intentionally then the case is even worse. By constantly applying hypnotic suggestions to sensitive mediums of the persons of weak will, he is doing them a great injury, and not helping the cause of religion one bit."*

In December 1904, Rev. R. Roberts, minister of Ebenezer C.M. Chapel, Cwmbach, commented, *"It has been said that this mighty Movement is due to the personal magnetism of Evan Roberts and that it is a "conversion by hypnotism."* Roberts retaliated by saying that he did not consider himself an inspired prophet or a magnetic preacher, and he became anxious at reading such newspaper reports which spoke of his so-called "personal magnetism". – *"There is nothing in it. It is not my magnetism, it is the magnetism of The Holy Spirit drawing all men to him."* The opinion of Dr. W. Morris, a Baptist minister at Treorchy, was in accord with Roberts' comments in that he was speaking on a spiritual plane and not a scientific one. Notwithstanding the controversial issues surrounding this argument, the "magnetic" power of Evan Roberts over people was inexplicable. The question of hypnotism over his audience was widely discussed and gave rise for concern as to the possibility that some individuals may have been prone to some form of hypnotism or mesmerism. Deliberations on this complex subject are better left to those qualified in this specialised field of study.

(x) The Role of The Press

The success of the 1904-05 Religious Revival in Wales was largely the result of wide press coverage and publicity, particularly by the Western Mail and Aberdare Leader. The Western Mail illustrated pamphlets Number 1 to 6 published between November 1904 and May 1905 featured the Revival prominently and extensively covered the Cynon Valley area and elsewhere. The press was a mighty power in every direction, and it did its part in bringing the Revival and the Revivalist to the notice of the country and wider afield throughout the world. The periods November 1904 to March 1905 were very busy months in the Revival and the newspapers reported in considerable detail the events which occurred in the many Nonconformist chapels of Cynon Valley and elsewhere throughout Wales. Without doubt the press gave the Revival a powerful impetus by its thorough coverage, the first report of which appeared in The Western Mail on 10th November 1904 – *"A remarkable Religious Revival is now taking place at Loughor. For some days a young man named Evan Roberts has been causing surprise by his extraordinary orations."*

As the Revival spread, coverage in the Western Mail and Aberdare Leader also continued, and Evan Roberts soon became the topic of conversation among all classes and sects including those in the coffee taverns and tap rooms of the public houses. In one respect the Revival of 1904-05 differed from its predecessors in as much that it took place in the limelight of widely reported newspaper publicity. No sooner had the Movement started it quickly spread and was known throughout Wales. During the Revival, the Western Mail commented that Wales was passing through a new and strange experience, and that the newspapers were being devoted extensively to reporting the proceedings. In the view of some critics, so successfully did they do their journalistic work that the Revival was described somewhat irreverently as, *"A Newspaper Revival"*. The Western Mail agreed that it had been the means of making the new Movement known throughout the land, but the Revival, by its own inherent force, would have covered the country independently of any help from any newspapers. The first public reference to the Revival appeared in the Western Mail on 10th November 1904, under the heading, *"A Wonderful Preacher – Great Crowds of People Drawn to Loughor – Congregation Stay Till Half Past Two In The Morning."* See Sections (iv) and (v) of this chapter.

The press worked the sentimentality of the Revival for all that it was worth, and it was a harvest-time for publishers and journalists. Rev. J. Vyrnwy Morgan commented, *"The real thing was taken up by the press of South Wales. Matters were taken up and boomed by the newspapers. It has gradually deteriorated into an orgy of singing and praying like a pagan feast. Quaint utterances and gesticulations in the press is indisputable evidence of the transforming nature of The Holy Spirit."*

The Rev. D.M. Phillips of Tylorstown writes in 1906, *"Since the Movement commenced nothing grieved him* (Evan Roberts) *more than an occasional exaggeration in the newspapers of his importance as a force in the Revival. In his opinion, that takes the glory that should be given to God alone."*

The said importance given to him by the newspaper reporters was due to the opinion and idea they had formed of Evan Roberts' sincerity and goodness. The press remained complimentary in their remarks towards Roberts. There was hardly any daily newspaper or periodical in England and Wales that had not published long articles on Evan Roberts and the Revival.

Courtesy of the Western Mail & Echo Ltd. 1904.

Courtesy of the Western Mail & Echo Ltd. 1904.

Courtesy of the Western Mail & Echo Ltd. 1905.

The Cynon Valley History Society acknowledges and thanks the Western Mail and Celtic Newspapers Ltd. (extracts from Aberdare Leader) for their kind permission to quote from their newspapers throughout the contents of this chapter.

The Lords' Prayer carved delicately in wood, Noddfa (Elim) Mountain Ash.

Decorative artwork located behind the pulpit on the internal wall at the English Baptist Chapel, Cefnpennar.

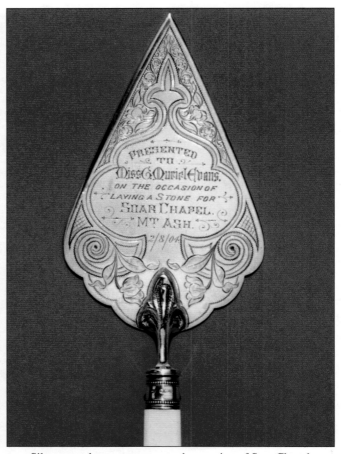

Silver presentation trowel at the opening of Bethany, Godreaman, August 1898.

Silver trowel to commemorate the opening of Soar Chapel, Mountain Ash, August 1904.

Courtesy of John Jackson, Ilkley, West Yorkshire.

China jug with inscription, Bethany, Godreaman.

Travelling Communion Set, Bethany, Godreaman.

Clock at Gwawr, Godreaman. Inscription reads "Cred Yr Efengyl"(Believe in the Gospel).

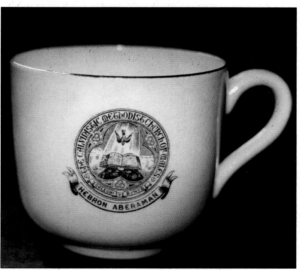

China cup inscribed (translated) "The Living Light" Gwawr W.B. (formerly Hebron W.C.M), Godreaman.

Eisteddfod Chair (not inscribed) in oak, Sion, Cwmaman.

China jug. Bryn Seion W.I. Chapel, Cwmbach.

Clock positioned on balustrade of rear gallery, Ebenezer,
Cwmbach.

China jug dated 1876, Calvaria, Aberdare.

Courtesy of the late John Vaughan Davies, Cwmdare (died 9th July 2004).
A close friend and neighbour of the author.

Clock donated by the Sunday School, dated 1855. Bethania, Aberdare.

Marble Memorial Stone. Highland Place Unitarian
Church, Aberdare.

Brass Memorial Plaque – 1939-1945 World War. Trinity, Aberdare.

Marble Memorial Plaque for Rev. D. Silyn Evans, Minister of Siloa, Aberdare for 50 years (1880 – 1930)

China plate dated 1914. Manufactured for a special bazaar. Bryn Sion (Carmel), Trecynon.

China teapot. Bethesda, Abernant.

Roll of Honour – The Great war 1914 – 1918. Carmel (was Bryn Sion), Trecynon.

Marble Memorial – Rev. J. Grawys Jones, Minister of Ebenezer, Trecynon, 1885 – 1925.

Marble Memorial Plaque – Rev. William Edwards (b.1812 – d.1884). Minister of Ebenezer, Trecynon, 1844 – 1884.

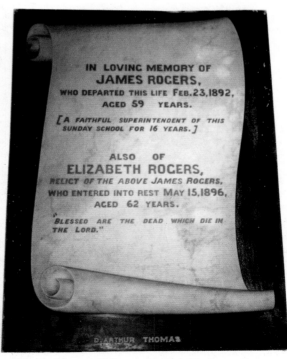

Marble Memorial Plaque – English Wesleyan Chapel, Trecynon.

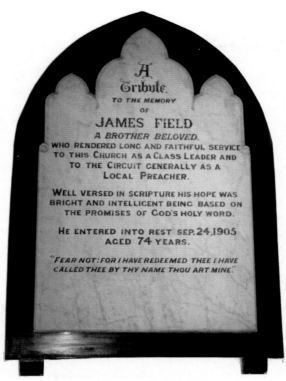

Marble Memorial Plaque – English Wesleyan Chapel, Trecynon.

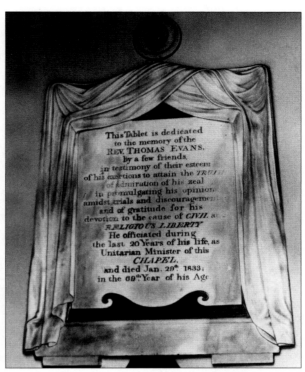

Marble Memorial Plaque – Rev. Thomas Evans (b.1764 – d.1833). Minister of Hen-Dy-Cwrdd, Trecynon, 1813 – 1833.

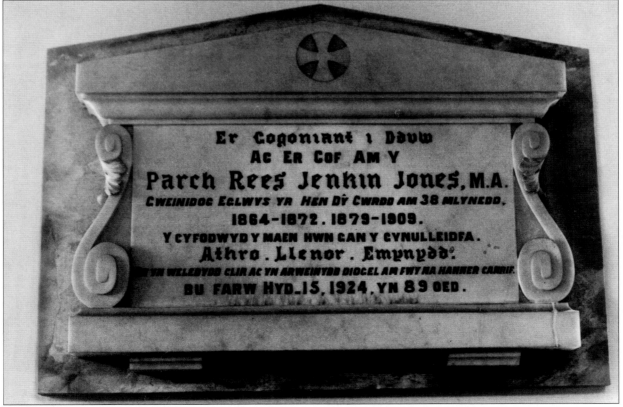

Marble Memorial Plaque – Rev. Rees Jenkin Jones (b.1835 – d.1924). Minister of Hen-Dy-Cwrdd, Trecynon 1864 to 72 and 1879 to 1909.

328

Marble Memorial Plaque dated 1905, of Owen Harris, a member and Deacon of Heol-Y-Felin, Trecynon, for thirty years.

329

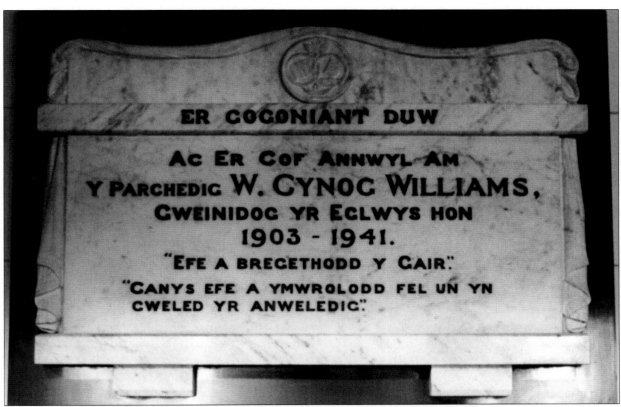

Marble Memorial Plaque – Rev. W. Cynog Williams, Minister of Heol-Y-Felin, Trecynon, 1903 – 1941.

Clock positioned on balustrade of rear gallery, presented to the chapel by the Sunday School children. The clock face reads "Dilynwch-Yr-Oen" Trans: "Follow The Lamb". Noddfa, Trecynon.

Minister's chair – Noddfa, Trecynon.

Clock with pendulum case – Noddfa, Trecynon.

China jug and teapot set – Noddfa, Trecynon.

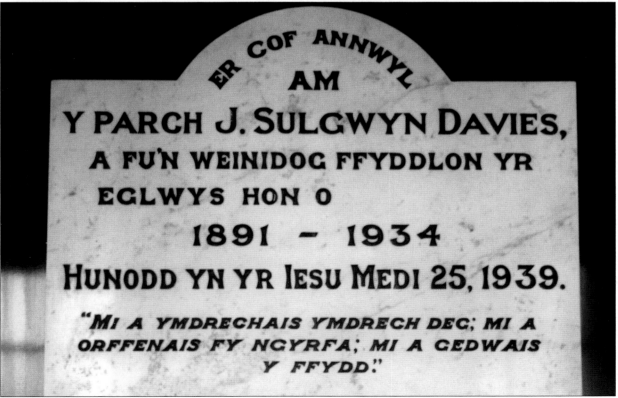

ER COF ANNWYL
AM
Y PARCH J. SULGWYN DAVIES,
A FU'N WEINIDOG FFYDDLON YR
EGLWYS HON O
1891 – 1934
HUNODD YN YR IESU MEDI 25, 1939.
"MI A YMDRECHAIS YMDRECH DEG; MI A
ORFFENAIS FY NGYRFA; MI A GEDWAIS
Y FFYDD."

Marble Memorial Plaque – Rev. J. Sulgwyn Davies, minister of Siloh, Trecynon 1891 – 1934 (died 1939). Lower inscription (translated) reads – "I made a fair effort; I completed my task; I kept the faith."

332

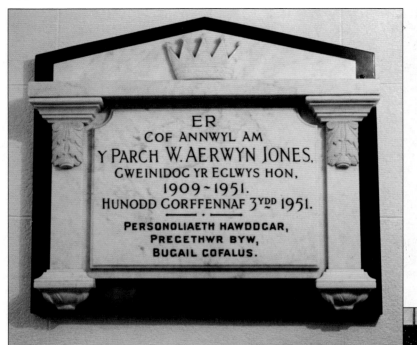

Marble Memorial Plaque – Rev. William Aerwyn Jones ("Jones Nebo"). Minister of Nebo, Cwmdare from 1909 until his death in 1951. Lower inscription translated reads; "A gentle person, a lively preacher, a caring shepherd."

Marble Memorial Plaque – Rev. William Samlet Davies (b.1841 – d. 1923) Minister of Horeb, Llwydcoed, 1871 – 1923.

China cup and saucer, Tabernacle, Abercynon.

China sugar bowl, Bethel, Trecynon.

China jug, Bryn Sion (now Carmel), Trecynon.

China teapot, dated 1891, Bethania, Aberdare.

Gold Medal, front and reverse, issued at the time of the Temperance Movement circa 1900, a pledge to abstinence – "Virtue – Sobriety – Brotherhood – Fortitude" Issued to James Williams (1859 – 1927), formerly of Glan Road, Gadlys, member of Bethel W.I. chapel Trecynon, Deacon and Precentor, Bardic name "Cynonydd". Maternal Grandfather of C.V.H.S. committee member Elfed Bowen, Plasdraw.

Courtesy of Elfed Bowen.

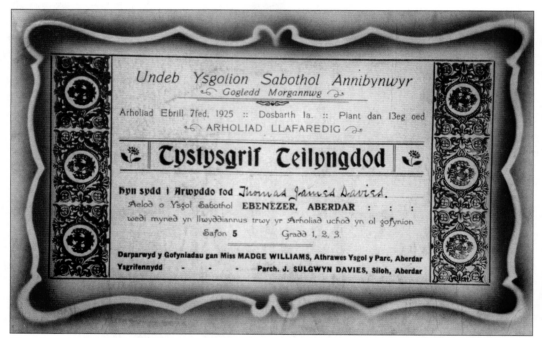

The above is an example of certificates awarded by Sunday Schools. The schools were well organised, teaching basically Biblical Knowledge, dealing with religious matters and supplementary general education; their influence at peak was immense. Falling attendance and chapel closures resulted in far fewer schools and pupils, with great decline or demise of accompanying activities.

Certificate provided by Mr. Eirwyn Davies, organist of Ebenezer Chapel, and brother of the above. Translation by Mrs. Eirlys Hatton, chapel secretary.

Certificate of Merit – 1925. Translation;

UNION OF WELSH CONGREGATIONAL SUNDAY SCHOOLS
North Glamorgan.
Examination April 7th. 1925.   Class 1A. Children under 13 yrs. Old.
Oral Examination
CERTIFICATE OF MERIT
This is to certify that   *Thomas James Davies*
Member of Ebenezer Sunday School, Aberdare.
Was successful in passing the above Examination in accordance with the requirements
Standard 5   Grades 1, 2, 3.
Questions prepared by Miss Madge Williams, Teacher at Park School, Aberdare
Secretary - - - - - -Rev. J. Sulgwyn Davies, Siloh, Aberdare.

Chapter 8

RECREATION AND ENTERTAINMENT

		Page No.
(i)	**Introduction**	**335**
	INSIDE PURSUITS	
(ii)	**Penny Readings**	337
(iii)	**Magic Lantern Slide Shows**	337
(iv)	**Lectures, Talks and Debates**	337
(v)	**Tea Meetings and Parties**	337
(vi)	**Bachelors' Knife and Fork Teas**	338
(vii)	**Music, Singing and Drama**	339
(viii)	**Band of Hope**	343
(ix)	**Bazaars, Sales of Work and Jumble Sales**	345
(x)	**Various Guilds, Groups and Clubs**	347
	OUTSIDE PURSUITS	
(xi)	**Trips to the Sea Side**	348
(xii)	**Charabanc Outings**	350
(xiii)	**Boat Trips on the Aberdare Canal**	352
(xiv)	**Outings to the Countryside**	353
(xv)	**Marching Processions**	354

*"Secular leisure-time pursuits
became a rival to religion,
As religion set itself up
as a rival to leisure-time pursuits."*
William Pickering

(i) Introduction

The quotation by William Pickering suggests rivalry between chapel activities and recreation and outside secular attractions. Let us examine this quotation more closely. Could the chapels be considered as "rivals" to secular leisure time pursuits? Over the years the chapels have certainly had plenty to offer by way of recreation and entertainment. Most of the pursuits whether of an indoor or outdoor kind, were simple and largely self-made fun where the talents of adults and children were used to the fullest. This helped considerably in fostering a close fellowship and companionship among members and friends. In the case of secular attractions these generally comprised events involving organised entertainment found in places such as Music Halls, theatres and clubs, etc. If there was so-called rivalry present then the chapels coped admirably in this "competition". The chapels have not only been places of worship, they have been the centre of countless social gatherings, recreation and entertainment, and also a means of providing community education for much of the population of the Cynon Valley. The chapels provided the many types of recreation and fellowship throughout the week and there was always something worthwhile going on to suit all tastes and ages. The chapels grew out of social groupings of the gathering together of people of all ages attracted by the many indoor and outdoor activities which were properly arranged and efficiently supervised. Such events attracted the members and became largely a sociable means of keeping the congregation together and maintaining a growing membership. The chapels had much to offer and at one time would have been considered as "rivals" to the secular leisure-time pursuits. Some groups including the Band of Hope and Temperance Societies viewed some secular attractions as harmful distractions and they therefore attempted to lure people away from the public houses, smoking rooms, gambling places, clubs and dance halls, and even sporting activities. In the 1940's for example, the chapels lodged a protest on the Council's decision to open cinemas on a Sunday. In the same period the chapels also opposed the opening of swimming baths on the Sabbath, claiming that they were causes of deterioration in chapel and Sunday school attendances. The reply was – *"The chapels should do something to make themselves more attractive in order to draw the children and adults to the chapels, and not the pool!" (Aberdare Leader, 1944)*.

Can secular attractions be considered as a rival to chapel recreation and entertainment? A change in the cultural habits and moral standards of today's society has in some instances affected the chapels. Simple social pursuits provided by the chapels have in many ways been taken over by outside secular attractions and a change of life style, despite the attempts of the chapels to change matters. The popularity and relaxation of outside attractions cannot be ignored. as well as necessary commitments. Clubs, cinemas, sport, spectator or participator, television, gardening, D.I.Y., weekend hobbies and perhaps trips by car to the coast, have all kept some people away from the chapels. Also the so-called "modern" practice of "retail therapy" otherwise known as "shopping for pleasure" (the "shop till you drop" syndrome) has probably enticed some people away from the chapels. Employment and shift-work is also a contributory factor for some who unavoidably have to work on Sunday. During the 1880's a sermon was delivered in a local chapel denouncing the clubs, billiard rooms and other so-called secular "evils" which abounded in the town and were generally preferred by the youthful portion of the congregation. The sermon also alluded to the unpleasantness and confinement showered upon the youth of the locality engaged as shop assistants by the "bad habit" of late shopping. The Aberdare Leader reported, *"The sooner this pernicious habit is uprooted the better, and the removal of late shopping will alleviate the suffering and confer a special boon upon a great number of the community."* A situation arose a century later in 1986 when the controversial topic of Sunday shopping underwent similar examination and criticism by the chapels, as did the new licensing laws on the Sunday opening of public houses which have been the subject of countless debates and arguments over the years.

Rivalry supposedly continues to this present day. Despite the words of the last lines of Pickering's quotation, the decline in chapel membership and the closure of chapels over the years plainly indicates that secular attractions and modern leisure-time pursuits have successfully *"become a rival to religion"*. Nevertheless, let us now take a look at the countless worthwhile activities engaged in by the chapels in bygone years; but before doing so, I quote here the words of a minister who once said from the pulpit, *"If you are too busy for God, you are too busy. Everyone should have time for God no matter how busy they are!"*

> ### BLOODY ACRE
>
> Sion Welsh Baptist Chapel, Cwmaman was built in 1859 on a site known locally as "Bloody Acre" or "Bloody Spot". It was so called after its previous use as a venue for cock-fighting. Miners from the Rhondda Valley, Merthyr and Aberdare collieries visited the site for their regular Sunday cock-fights.

INSIDE PURSUITS

(ii) Penny Readings

Usually held in the vestry or schoolroom, Penny Readings were a simple yet effective and highly popular form of entertainment, and as the heading implies each paid a penny (less than half a new pence) as an entrance fee. Volunteers were asked to perform and usually a programme was made available listing the performances to be held. Adjudicators were appointed for the competition which included the following items: – singing, poetry, prose-reading, scripture, tin-whistle, mouth organ, piano and violin solos. Some even exhibited their dancing and skipping skills. One of the most popular of events on the entertainment itinerary was that of recitation, both serious and humorous and these items did not lack a variety of entertainers. One "star turn" was the boy who was a born comedian who always ended his half-hour of hilarious reciting with his own masterpiece: - *"The thunder roared, the lightening flashed – and killed a pig in Mountain Ash!"* The lights of the vestry were switched quickly on and off to mimic the effect of lightning!

(iii) Magic Lantern Slide Shows

As with many events the proceeds of ticket sales augmented the chapel funds either to reduce the debt or to contribute towards a specific cause or improvement to the fabric of the building. The Magic Lantern shows were very popular and such simple pursuits brought much pleasure to young and old. The subject of slides varied from scenes of a biblical nature to general nature and geographical shows. The Lantern was also known as the "Phantasmagorian Magic Lantern" and it was popular around the late 1800's and early 1900's. The shows took place during Young People's weeknight meetings and similar occasions. The mechanical magic lantern worked with glass plate slides and the operation of a gas motor, and images were thrown on to a screen depicting pictures of an acceptable quality. Some images showed movement such as water falls, a train in motion, or a snowstorm and combined with sound effects from behind the screen the result to all present appeared to be wonderful. Often piano accompaniment added to the drama of the show.

(iv) Lectures, Talks and Debates

Lectures were often delivered by guest speakers or sometimes by the members themselves, illustrated by means of the Magic Lantern. Debates and discussions covered controversial topics such as: – *"The Sale of Liquors on Sunday"*, *"The Wisdom and Wonder of Creation"*, *"The Best Way of Attracting Young Men from the Public Houses"*, *"War and Afterwards"* (delivered in 1916), *"Should Bachelors be Taxed?"* *"Capital Punishment – For and Against"*. Mock trials were sometimes held and one of the Deacons would usually be appointed the presiding Judge; an apt appointment for some Deacons who with their strict and perhaps stern approach in matters would have made a very good Judge! An interesting debate took place in one of the local chapels on the topic, *"Was the Cynon Valley better in the pre 1914 era compared to the post 1914 years?"* This lively debate concluded that the latter period was the better!

(v) Tea Meetings and Parties

These were held on occasions and were often organised on a gigantic scale with 600-800 or sometimes as many as 1000 attending. They were arranged and co-ordinated with almost "military precision" with cake cutters, sandwich makers and tea brewers appointed. There was even an officially appointed helper to boil the water! Posters and handbills were circulated to members and to other chapels advertising the event, the proceeds of which helped to swell the funds or reduce debts. The children and adults gathered to meet and partake in these meetings and parties after marches and processions, and following Annual Summer Demonstrations. There were games and competitions for the children as well, either held in the vestry or a nearby field. New Year's Eve Suppers were always well attended after which the vestry was left open for games, or perhaps a lantern show, followed by a prayer meeting, to welcome in the New Year. In 1912, such a meeting incurred a sixpence (2½p) charge plus an extra two pennies (1p) if you chose meat sandwiches. Some Tea Parties included "Penny Bun" collections. As usual the children tucked in with enthusiasm and good appetites. The children's Annual Social Party was usually held in January when they enjoyed games and competitions and consumed large quantities of delectable pastries, jellies and trifles.

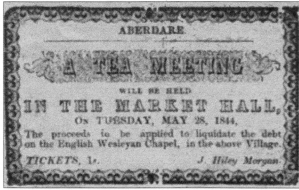

Ticket for a Tea Meeting for the English Wesleyan Chapel, Green Street, Aberdare, 1844.

Courtesy of Mrs Gwynyth Silvanus, Salisbury

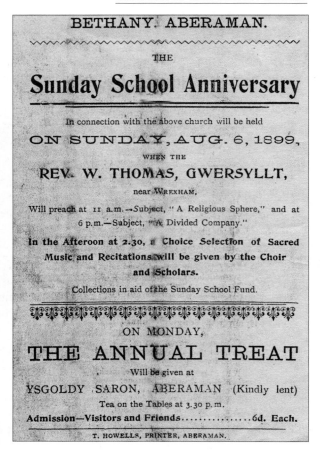

Poster advertising a Sunday School anniversary for Bethany, Aberaman, 1899.

The Sunday Schools were treated to Christmas Tea Parties, games and magic lantern entertainment Chapel members who were farmers or forestry workers supplied large Christmas trees which were decorated with Chinese lanterns and heavily laden with toys, dolls, sweets, chocolates and other presents and a good supply of fruit was also handed out to the children. The vestries were decorated with hand-made Christmas trimmings made by the members. After the tea, Santa Claus made his appearance to the great delight of the children. An amusing story was told by a local Minister regarding a persistent "gate crasher" of a Chapel Tea Meeting of the 1890's. It concerns a certain young local lad who frequently attended such meetings, and his failing in never knowing when to stop eating! At one such gathering he drank seventeen cups of tea with a corresponding quantity of cake, and bread and butter. Afterwards, he struggled up to the Minister and said, – *"I think I have been eating too much, and feel as white as a sheet; I think I shall have another cup of tea to put me right!"* This somewhat crafty lad did not belong to any particular chapel, and it seems was in the habit of dropping in just as he pleased to the various local tea meetings which were frequently held in most chapels at this time.

(vi) Bachelors' Knife and Fork Teas

Large gatherings were attracted by these popular events held and organised by the young people who were members of The Temperance Universal and Total Abstinence Society, Band of Hope and Young Peoples' Guild and Society. The teas were held in the chapel vestry with the aim of encouraging the temperance cause and were fashionable around the late nineteenth and early twentieth centuries. As many as five hundred or more attended the Tea which was often followed by entertainment, concerts and services of song. The functions were very well organised and meat carvers, cake cutters, bread and butter cutters, tea brewers and tray holders were duly appointed. In one particular Tea Meeting the official "tea brewer" was reported to have been rather lax in his duties when he served a weak brew of tea! There was much fuss and gossip over this, however, the excellent quality and blend of the tea, later amply compensated. The young ladies assisted in the Bachelors' Teas by decorating the tables with flowers, and the bachelors wore long, fancy, white starched aprons before setting about their serving and catering duties, and laying out the tables with crockery and cutlery. Doorkeepers, attendants and ticket collectors were officially appointed and the whole affair was organised with great efficiency. We may assume that many a courtship blossomed out

Bachelors' Tea Party, Siloa, Aberdare, held in May 1908. The proceedings ended with an evening concert of songs and recitations presided over by the Minister Rev. D. Silyn Evans.

of these social events, particularly if the bachelors caught the eyes of the ladies when displaying their domestic and catering skills with panache and efficiency!

(vii) Music, Singing and Drama

One of the most successful and celebrated musical events in the chapels was that of the Gymanfa Ganu – Singing Festival – accompanied by the organ or stringed orchestra and choir. Other chapels joined in and numbers sometimes exceeded one thousand in the larger chapels. The singing was full of passion, harmony and "hwyl". Singing has always featured prominently in the chapels, and the popularity of choral singing is maintained today by a number of well-known, thriving chapel choirs throughout the Cynon Valley. Choral Societies were set up, many of them as early as the 1850's and the locality was described at one time by Gareth Williams as, *"A musical hot-house."* In addition, the chapels performed concerts, Eisteddfodau, ambitious cantatas, magnificent Masses, organ recitals, and Operettas, along with competitions including solo instruments and singing. Music committees were formed to ensure that all-important professional touch to the performances. Children too took an active part in Anniversary Concerts and Services of Song. Drama also featured high in entertainment value and content, and excellent Drama Groups and Societies were set up displaying local talents and ambitious productions of high quality plays. These events were given the support of skilled stage-prop handy men and clever costume makers. Most chapels were fortunate in having their own enthusiastic "players" or actors, and dramas of all kinds were successfully performed, the proceeds helping to boost chapel funds.

(a) Notable Hymn Writers and Composers connected with the Cynon Valley
Over the past 150 years, the Cynon Valley has produced several talented hymnists and composers, a number of which includes the following: -

EVAN THOMAS DAVIES (1878-1969)
Davies lived in Plasdraw, Aberdare, 1943-1969. He was full-time Director of Music at Bangor University prior to 1943. Pioneered work on Welsh folk songs. Co-editor of *"the National Songs of Wales"* – 1959. Composer of *"Tydi a Rhoddaist"* – ("Thou Gavest") – a well known hymn popular with all choirs. A brilliant organist (F.R.C.O.), he inaugurated many chapel organs throughout England and Wales.

DAVID EVANS (1869-1944)
Singing Conductor/Precentor of Salem W. Cong. Chapel, Robertstown. Composed the tune *"Tre Salem"* to the words of William Williams of Pantycelyn. This well known hymn was sung in Communion Services.

WILLIAM JOHN EVANS (1866-1947)
A renowned organist and Choir Master at Siloa W. Cong. Chapel, Aberdare 1886-1937. A noted musician, he is said to have conducted almost 1000 Gymanfa Ganu (Singing Festivals) throughout Wales. He established an Aberdare Orchestra. Conductor of the famous Mountain Ash Male Voice Choir winning First Prize at Pontypridd Eisteddfod. Also victorious at The Albert Hall Eisteddfod, London. Co-editor of the Welsh Congregational Hymnal, which includes five of his own hymns, in particular the well known *"Rhys"* hymn. His son was Ivor L. Evans, one time Principal of University College, Aberystwyth.

DANIEL JAMES *("Gwyrosydd")* (1848-1920)
Born in Mynyddbach, Swansea. He was otherwise famously known as the Welsh Bard and Poet – *"Gwyrosydd,* and came to live at Caegarw, Mountain Ash, circa 1900, at the behest of the renowned local conductor Thomas Glyndwr Richards (1858-1935). He wrote the words of the famous *"Calon Lan"* the first public rendering of which was performed in circa 1910 at Bethania W.I. Chapel, Mountain Ash. John Hughes of Llansamlet put the words to music.

JAMES JAMES *("Iago Ap Ieuan")* 1832-1902)
Harpist and composer of the music for *"Hen Wlad Fy Nhadau"* – the National Anthem of Wales, composed in 1856, formerly known as *"Glan Rhondda"*. Born in 1832 at the *"Ancient Druid Inn"*, Argoed, kept by his father, in the parish of Bedwellty. He assisted his father in the weaving trade at Pontypridd, and later in 1873 became landlord of the *"Colliers Arms"*, Mountain Ash. His father, Evan James (1809-1878) was author of the words of *"Hen Wlad Fy Nhadau"*. James James lived in Mountain Ash from 1873 until his death in 1902 and is buried in Aberdare Cemetery. A plaque stands in his memory opposite *"The old Post Office"*, in High Street, Aberdare and is depicted bilingually carved on native slate in gold letters.

THOMAS DAFYDD LLEWELLYN *("Llewellyn Alaw")* (1828-79)
Harpest, and author of the first Parish History of Aberdare (1853) – "Gardd Aberdar". He gathered up the melody of "Hen Wlad Fy Nhadau" (1856) and included it under the title of "Glan Rhondda" in his unpublished collection of melodies, giving the Welsh people an early glimpse of their National Anthem. It was later harmonised and first published in "Gems of Welsh Melodies" in 1860. Later he became Landlord of the Harp Inn, Mountain Ash, where he died in 1879. He is buried in the graveyard of Hen Dy Cwrdd Unitarian Chapel, Trecynon, where he was a member for many years.

HENRY LLOYD *(Ap Hefin")* (1870-1946)
Poet and printer, he printed hundreds of popular songs, hymns and sheet music at his Printing Offices at Gloucester Street and Seymour Street, Aberdare. He was originally from Dolgellau, and came to Aberdare in 1891 as compositor in the offices of *"Y Darian"* Newspaper, and later at the Aberdare Leader. He established his printing business in 1893 and retired in 1940. He was an able poet and won the Chair in many Eisteddfodau. He wrote several hymns, including the well known *"I bob un sydd Fyddlon"* – ("To all who are faithful").

JOHN ROBERTS *(Ieuan Gwyllt)* (1822-1877)
A native of Cardiganshire, he came to Aberdare in 1858 as Editor of *"Y Gwladgarwr"*. During his brief stay in the town, he produced his famous collection of hymn tunes – some composed by himself – *"Llyfr Tonau"* – (Book of Hymn Tunes) – which transformed congregational singing in Wales. In 1859 at Bethania C.M. Chapel, Aberdare, as conductor he led what many consider to be the first Gymanfa Ganu in Wales. In the same year the Union of Denominational Community Hymn Singing was formed which was set up to encourage and improve the singing of hymns. By 1862 the Union was expanding considerably throughout the whole of Wales. In 1876, John Roberts translated and published the words of Ira D. Sankey's famous hymns from English into Welsh.

(b) Prominent Conductors, Choir Masters and Precentors of The Cynon Valley

DAVID EDWARD COLEMAN *("Eos Hefin" – "Summer Nightingale")* (1842-1892)
Also known affectionately as *"Coleman Bach"*. Prominent Conductor of Mountain Ash. Sectional

Conductor of the South Wales Choral Union which won Chief Choral Prize at Crystal Palace, London in 1872-73. Conductor of Bethania W. Cong. Chapel, Mountain Ash. Buried in Aberffrwd Cemetery.

HUGH ELLIS (1849-1939)
Lived in Alexandra Terrace, Mountain Ash. Conductor of the Mountain Ash United Male Voice Choir and member of Caradog's Choir 1872-73. Successful at many Eisteddfod contests. When he died in 1939 aged 89 at Allen Street, he was probably the oldest choir conductor in Wales. He is buried in Aberffrwd Cemetery.

DAFYDD JOHN (1823-1894)
Conductor and Choir Master of Ebenezer W.I. Chapel, Trecynon for over forty years. A cobbler by trade he was born in Cilgeran and came to Aberdare in 1849 largely due to the influence of Rosser Beynon. He became a member of Ebenezer Chapel and Choir Master and introduced a change in the manner of singing. He was the first to conduct Handel's Messiah in 1853, at Ebenezer. Sang with *"Caradog"* in the Crystal Palace and introduced Rosser Beynon's Hymn Book – *"Telyn Sion"*. Gymanfa Ganu became very popular with the United Chapels in 1887 at Hirwaun, Cwmdare and Llwydoed. Salem, Robertstown and Ebenezer, Trecynon combined under the baton of Dafydd John for many years.

W.H. JOHN
Conductor and Precentor for over sixty years at Bethel P.M Chapel, Cwmaman

GRIFFITHS RHYS JONES *("Caradog")* (1834-1897)
Brilliant violinist and Conductor of the South Wales Choral Union (*"Cor Mawr Caradog"*) comprising 500 voices which won the Chief Choral Prize at the Crystal Palace, London in 1872-73. Born at The Rose and Crown, Trecynon in 1834, he apprenticed as a blacksmith at Llwydcoed Ironworks, with his father. Appointed leader of Aberdare United Choir in 1858. Member of Hen Dy Cwrdd Un. Chapel, Trecynon. Died 4th December 1897 and buried at Aberdare Cemetery. On 10th July 1920 a bronze statue of Caradog was erected at Victoria Square, Aberdare, sculpted by Sir W. Gascombe John, R.A.

PROFESSOR TOM JONES
Conductor and organist 1891-1941 at Carmel E.B. Chapel, Aberdare.

W.H. JOHN
Conductor and Precentor for over sixty years at Bethel P.M Chapel, Cwmaman

JOSEPH REES
Well known Choir Master of Bethesda E.B. Chapel, Penrhiwceiber in the early 1900"'s

THOMAS GLYNDWR RICHARDS (1858-1935)
Born at Nantyffyllon, Maesteg in 1858. Conductor and Choir Master at Soar W.I. Chapel, Mountain Ash. Founder and conductor of the Mountain Ash Male Voice Choir which gave their first concert (87 in the choir) in London, November 1897. Leader of countless Gymanfa Ganu. In 1922 sang before the King at Buckingham Palace, and in 1908 performed in front of President and Mrs Roosevelt at The White House. Toured Canada, U.S.A., and U.K. many times. Died in 1935 aged 77 years and is buried at Maesyrarian Cemetery, Mountain Ash.

W.E. THOMAS
Conductor of the famous Ebenezer W.I. Chapel Orchestra, Trecynon during the late 1880's

(c) Prominent Organists

Notable chapel organists in Cynon Valley are covered in Chapter One. Many have served faithfully for up to and over fifty years, in the same chapel. A well known local organist who gave outstanding service was Edward Moses of Tabernacle E.Cong. Chapel, Aberdare, who served for an incredible sixty-five years – 1888-1953. He is the longest serving organist in one chapel, anywhere in the Cynon Valley.

Choir of English Calvinistic Chapel, Duffryn
Street, Mountain Ash, circa 1920. Mrs Clarice
Thomas is front row, second from left.

Poster for Sunday School Anniversary, 1923,
Zion Baptist Church, Hirwaun.

Juvenile choir, Tabernacle, Ynysybwl, 1897.
Conductor Mr G. Jones.

Minister, Deacons and choir, English Cong.,
Abercynon, circa. 1920.

Drama Group, Ebenezer,
Trecynon, circa. 1930.
(Elfed Bowen)

Programme for a Gymanfa Ganu (Singing Festival)
held at The National Eisteddfod of Wales, The Pavilion,
Aberdare, 6th-11th August 1956. Rev. John Roberts
(pictured), "Ieuan Gwyllt" (1822-77), conducted what
many consider to be the first Gymanfa Ganu in Wales,
at Bethania Chapel, Aberdare in 1859.

Ynysybwl Ladies Choir,
Presbyterian Church, Glyn
Street. Conductress since July
1992 – Mrs Joan Monk.
Accompanist – Mr Jason
Martin. Photo dated May 1997.

(viii) Band of Hope

One of the aims of the Movement was to instil practices of temperance and total abstinence in the youthful members of the congregation. The Temperance Society was formed around 1880 and endeavoured to denounce the consumption of alcohol and other harmful habits. The South Wales Temperance and Band of Hope Union was set up in the late nineteenth century and awarded Certificates of Merit to candidates who successfully prepared essays and lectures and "took the pledge" of total abstinence. The wording on the certificates was prepared by doctors and the Board of Education and included the following advice – *"Alcohol is not an aid to efficient work but always a hindrance." "Alcohol is not a stimulant but a narcotic drug." "Alcohol lowers the resistance of the body to disease"*. Not only alcohol was discouraged but smoking, gambling and some forms of secular entertainment were also frowned upon. The Band of Hope groups also did much good work organising concerts, teas, debates and lectures and they raised funds for the chapels in doing so. Other similar groups included the Mutual Improvement Society which was established in the chapels by young and older members around the 1870's and included such activities as lectures, debates, talks and Tea Meetings. They also had connections with the Temperance Movement.

Certificate awarded by
North Glamorgan
Welsh Congregational
Chapels' Union on
result of a Test. – 1925.
(Ebenezer Trecynon.)

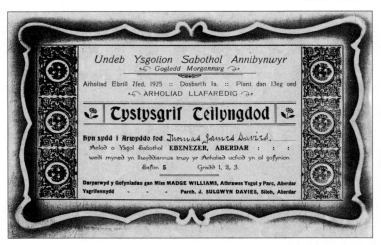

Certificate awarded by the Calvinistic Methodists' Sunday
school Union on result of a Test – 1912. (Gobaith, Cwmdare).

Tom Evans is currently (2004) a committee
member of The Cynon Valley History Society.
Tom Evans.

By courtesy of Mrs. Jean John, formerly of Llwydcoed.

The Band of Hope was a branch of the National Temperance Movement.
Jean John and Russell John.

(ix) Bazaars, Sales of Work and Jumble Sales

These were popular and efficient fund-raising events and greatly helped to swell chapel funds, reduce debts, and settle payment of various repair bills. They were often followed by teas at which up to 1000 people would be served. Successful bazaar and fund appeals often realised several hundreds of pounds, along with generous donations and contributions in addition to the proceeds of the actual bazaar. These events proved the determination of the chapel members in difficult times to survive and reduce debts. Large quantities of goods met with a ready sale and scores of stalls were set up and included a huge variety of goods and attractions. A list of the stalls included: – Drapery; fancy goods; flowers; fruit; slide shows; refreshments; art exhibitions; "laughing room"; ventriloquial entertainment; waxworks; remnants; books; cakes; toffee; sweets; ice-cream; well-wishers stall; sewing and pound stall; tasting stall; shooting gallery; photographic bureau; lucky dip and bran tub; china stall; dairy stall; slide shows; exhibition of newly designed weighing machines; museum and antique shows …… and much more!!!

The following officers were appointed to oversee the event: – President; Vice President; Treasurer; Secretary and Directors. The opening of the Grand Bazaar was often conducted by a prominent local dignitary who usually contributed a handsome donation, and bouquets were presented to the ladies by the young children. I recently came across a programme for a Grand Bazaar held in 1912 for Siloa Welsh Congregational Chapel, Aberdare. The event was held at the Intermediate School for Girls, Cwmbach Road, Aberdare, (now the Aberdare Girls' School). The object of the bazaar was to liquidate the debt of £670 remaining on the new vestry. The quotations referring to the various stalls are worthy of mention here: –

"They who give freely gather many smiles." Admission with luncheon – three shillings (15p). Admission with tea – one shilling (5p).

Women's Sewing Class -
"Great Business must be done today!"

17 Chapel Stalls -
"I do good business" – is our sole intent; so make your choice."
  (Merchant of Venice)

Fancy Stall -
"Shake out thy gold, and smiles of ladies fair shall be thy portion."
  (Shakespeare)

Sunday School Universal Stall –
"Come, walk up and purchase
with avidity.
Overcome your diffidence and
Natural timidity!"
  W.S. Gilbert

Flower and Fruit Stall –
"Look at them tenderly (the flowers)".
Sweet Stall –
"With the sweetest novelty your taste we please."

Book Stall –
"Some books are to be tasted, other to be swallowed and some few to be chewed and digested."

Refreshment Stall –
"Do not call a man happy till he's fed!"

Tea Room –
"The Best Sauce is hunger."
"Hunger is a sharp thorn
It can be extracted here,
– At The Tea Room!"

Cloakroom and Parcel Office –
"Hats, coats, sticks, umbrellas and parcels – in fact almost everything (except children!) may be left here at a charge of one penny each."

"When clouds are seen, wise men put on their cloaks."
(Shakespeare)

An advert at the Bazaar –
"For Good and Pure Temperance Drinks, try – Greenhalghs Stone Ginger Beer, Hop Bitters, Dandelion and Burdock. Obtained at 15 Glancynon Terrace, Aberaman."

In addition to the Grand bazaars smaller fund-raising events were organised including sales of work, prize draws, jumble sales, fetes and "bring and buy" sales; much the same as today, and all intended to raise necessary funds.

Programme and souvenir of Bazaar held at the Memorial Hall, Aberdare, 1909.

Front cover of a programme souvenir for a bazaar for Siloa, Aberdare, 1912.

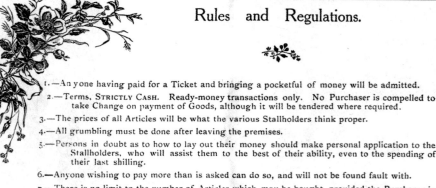

Rules and Regulations for the holding of a Bazaar in 1909, at Tabernacle, Aberdare.

(x) Various Guilds, Groups and Clubs

A list of these is as follows: -

> Young People's Guild; Young People's Society; Youth Club; Ladies Sewing Guild; Sister-hood; Teenage Club; Girl Guides; Brownies; Scout Troop; Cubs; Boys Own Group; Boys' Brigade; Life Boys; Young People's Christian Endeavour Group; Young People's Social Club; Friendship Club; Young People's Fellowship; Mothers' Guild.

The above groups played an important part in chapel life. They held concerts, lectures, debates, quizzes, drama, Bible classes, Eisteddfodau, Tea Meetings, lantern lectures, gramophone clubs and many other social events. They helped the chapel in many ways and contributed towards fund-raising programmes and chapel services.

Women's Society for Soldier's Parcels, Bethel, Gadlys. The Minister's wife Mrs Jacob is seated in the armchair. Circa. 1900.

Doug Williams

Horeb Bible Class, Llwydcoed, circa 1903. Mrs Rice Evans (centre) is the Teaching Instructor. The young lady standing second from the right is Ann Francis (Mrs Ann Davies).

Jean John and Russell John

Bible Class, Moriah, Lwydcoed, circa 1915. The teacher (centre) is Maggie Walters. Others in the photograph are – Annie Margaret Pugh (Walters), Mary Ann Davies (Owen), Annie Bronwen Morgan (Walters).
Courtesy of Jean and Russell John, and Mrs. Nesta Rees.

Sunday School Bible Class, Bethesda, Penrhiwceiber, 1964.

OUTSIDE PURSUITS

(xi) Trips to The Seaside

From as early as the 1860's the mode of transport to the seaside was by train/rail and horse drawn brake carriages. From around 1910 and into the 1920's the day-trippers journeyed by charabanc, and from the late 1920's they travelled by bus or coach. Travel by rail however, continued locally for over 100 years from around the 1860's to 1964 when the railways then closed as a result of The Beeching Report 1963. The Aberdare to Cardiff line re-opened in 1988. Annual outings included trips to Barry Island, Porthcawl, Mumbles, Langland Bay and Aberaeron. As many as six bus loads of children and adults journeyed to the seaside where the children enjoyed playing games on the sands, swimming or paddling in the sea, donkey rides, the fairground, making sand castles and indulging in the consumption of huge portions of toffee apples, candy floss, pop and the inevitable stick of rock. The Aberdare Leader reported the annual summer outing of a local chapel in July 1909 – *"Two hundred friends and children journeyed by rail to Barry Island. Through the kindness of the chapel officials, each tripper was provided with the "necessary" to purchase refreshments etc. Games and sports were indulged in on the sands and a happy day ended without mishap."*

The children looked forward for months and saved up for the annual seaside treat and for many it must have been the only holiday away from home. In August 1863, Tabernacle Chapel, Aberdare, took no less than 1,304 Sunday school scholars to Swansea by train. This was the first excursion ever to run from Aberdare by the Vale of Neath Railway line via Briton Ferry Road to Wind Street Swansea, then newly opened. It was reported that the excursion enabled Tabernacle Chapel to reduce their debt by £57.00. In 1879 a train excursion, Aberdare to Porthcawl, cost two shillings and six pence, or half-a-crown

> **SUNDAY SCHOOL SEASIDE OUTING**
>
> In August 1863, Tabernacle Chapel, Aberdare took 1304 Sunday school scholars to Swansea by train. An annual outing organised by Jerusalem W.B. Chapel, Penrhiwceiber in August 1905, took one and a half hours to travel by train to Aberaeron. In the early 1930's, 1700 trippers travelled to Porthcawl in two trains.

(12½p) return. An annual outing was organised in August 1905 by Jerusalem Welsh Baptist Chapel, Penrhiwceiber to Aberaeron, by train and the journey took one and a half hours. John F. Mear tells us in his book, "Aberdare Railways", published 1999, that two trains were required for the 1700 trippers travelling to Porthcawl on an annual chapel outing in the early 1930's. These pleasurable breaks were a means of escape for the working men and their families during the pre-war period depression, and for most folk was their only holiday during the year, all be it just for one day. John Mear further writes – *"They were a means of admission in spirit, if not in body, to the largely illusory world of the health-giving and relaxing holiday by the sea, where the ozone-laden Atlantic breezes reach Britain across almost four thousand miles of open sea, bringing the purest air it is possible to enjoy!"*

Much debate took place as to the date chosen for the outings, and if the weather turned out poor on the day there would be good-humoured uproar! The children were so excited the night before that they were unable to sleep, and were up at the crack of dawn with their buckets and spades at the ready. After their tiring day out, they simply "collapsed" and slept on the bus or train, all the way home.

Adults and Sunday School children of Zion, Ynysybwl, gathered together outside the chapel and ready to set off for their train outing to Barry Island. Circa. 1946.

Enid Williams.

(xii) Charabanc Outings

Char-a-banc, (French) – English translation, "wagon with seats". Definition – "A motor coach especially for sightseeing". The open-topped charabancs were in use around 1910 into the 1920's and could seat 20 to 25 passengers, or 30 with a "squeeze". They had solid rubber tyres and a canopy at the rear which could be raised to give

> **0 TO 12 M.P.H. IN TWO MINUTES**
> Charabancs of the 1920's were restricted to 12 miles an hour. They carried about 20 to 30 passengers. A trip to Barry Island took just over two hours.

protection in the rain. Their speed limit was restricted to 12 miles per hour and a trip to Barry Island would take around two and a half hours or perhaps more. Names of well-known local charabanc operators around 1915-1922 include: -

Gough's, Knight Street, Mountain Ash. "Napier" type charabancs, around 1914.
Dare Valley Motor & Engineering Co., Aberdare. First charabanc, July 1919.
J.M. Williams, Penderyn. "Dennis" charabancs 1922. His sole business was running a bus service from Aberdare to Penderyn.
Phillips, Mountain Ash, 1920.
Fred Mannings, Aberdare. First charabanc in 1921.
Stephen Probert, Aberdare. "Napier" charabanc, February 1920.
Leyshon Jones, Aberdare, 1920.
James Jones, Abercynon, 1920.
T.M. Evans, Abercynon, 1920.
Howell Davies, Abercynon, charabanc named "The Cynon Star", 1920.
Fred Williams, Aberdare, charabanc named "Happy Days", 1920.
Many charabancs were manufactured by Austin ("The Victory"), and Daimler; 20 to 25 seats.

The charabancs would be full to overflowing with children and adults and looking at the photographs of these it is a delight to see the joy and expectation of fun on the faces of the trippers. Popular destinations for a day out treat included trips to the sea-side and nearer home, a day out at Ystradfellte Caves, where the children enjoyed walking behind the falls and paddling or swimming in the pool; picnics and games were the order of the day. In 1884, The Aberdare Times reported – *"The choir of Nebo Chapel, Hirwaun, spent a most enjoyable day at Porthmawr, a picturesque spot a short distance from Ystradfellte; they travelled by waggonettes and traps and explored the caves. A luncheon picnic was enjoyed on the rocks at the mouth of one of the caves where the water falls over. Later they made their way to an adjoining field alongside the river and enjoyed games and sports."*

Seaside trips were also made by horse drawn carriage called "horse and brake" and Fred Mannings of Aberdare operated these as early as 1897. Around this period 1897-1900, the Aberdare Times reported – *"Motor cars are now giving an up-to-date appearance in the town."* After the charabancs of the 1920's buses and coaches became popular around the late 1920's and in time they became a competitive mode of transport to the trains which had been providing transport for the day-trippers as far back as the 1860's.

A chapel outing by charabanc to the seaside, circa 1920.

A day out treat by charabanc, circa.1920, ready to depart outside The George Hotel, 20 Commercial St., Aberdare (opened 1851, closed 1963). The charabanc is a "Dennis" make, and owned by the Dare Valley Motor Company formed in 1919.

A trip to the seaside by charabanc, circa 1920. Ready to depart from the "Square" in Cwmdare, outside the Dare Bakery.

Charabanc outing, Gough's , Mountain Ash. Circa 1914.

Before the days of the trams, public street transport meant horse-drawn cabs or omnibuses. Some omnibuses were double-decked but most were "Brakes" as shown in the photograph. In 1896 for example, there were 41 cabs and 63 omnibuses on the streets of Aberdare. In 1905 the number of licensed brakes was 128.

C.V.H.S.

(xiii) Boat Trips on The Aberdare Canal

Work commenced on constructing the Aberdare Canal at Abercynon in 1807 and within two years it reached Mountain Ash, and extended to Aberdare by the summer of 1812. The canal was 6¾ miles long and was constructed at a cost of £26,000. In his book *"The History of Mountain Ash, 1896"*, William Bevan writes – *"The building of the Canal was at first much against the feeling of the people, because of the fear of bringing strangers into the neighbourhood, and those anticipated thieves and all sorts of other bad influences; also because such intrusions would take away and sever parts of the land causing increasing difficulties in getting from one side of the valley to the other, and other such like inconveniences. The inhabitants thought it would be as well for the world to come to an end rather than to suffer such deprivations."* In addition to trade use transporting coal (Glamorganshire Canal) to the seaport of Cardiff, it also became a source of transport for leisure purposes when in the summer months it was used to carry Sunday School children for their annual outings. The Aberdare Canal joined the Glamorganshire Canal (Merthyr to Cardiff) at Abercynon. The latter canal began in 1790 and reached Abercynon in 1794 and Merthyr in 1795. In 1864 the Great Western Railway arrived and the canal trade began to suffer through the added competition of both the Taff Vale Railway (1846) branch line Abercynon to Aberdare, and the G.W.R. Consequently, the Aberdare canal closed in 1900 and in the early 1930's was eventually filled in. A new road (Cardiff Road) was officially opened in February 1933 following the old canal route from Aberdare to Abercynon.

A Sunday school treat for the children of Bethania, Mountain Ash, circa. 1900. The crowded boats made their way on the Aberdare Canal downstream from Ffrwd Bridge to Abercynon. In the background can be seen Wind Street (now Allen Street) and Bethania Street (now Phillip Street).

Glyn Davies.

Popular boat trips on the canal included rides from Aberdare to Mountain Ash and on to Abercynon. Hundreds of Sunday School children were taken by fleets of rowing boats so over-crowded one wonders how they ever kept afloat! Ian Wright tells us in his book "The Glamorganshire and Aberdare Canals" (pub. 2001) of the names given to the canal boats trading between Aberdare, Merthyr and Cardiff:- *"Awake"*, *"Perseverance"*, *"Providence"*, *"Comet"*, and finally the magnificent name – *"Fiery Dragon"*!

(xiv) Outings to the Countryside

In addition to local trips to Ystradfellte Caves, excursions were organised further afield to Caerphilly Castle and nearby beauty picnic spots and hillsides. Nearer home, following the Sunday School Summer Demonstration Parade in August 1876, around nine hundred children from the various chapels throughout Mountain Ash marched to Dyffryn House, the residence of Lord Aberdare, (demolished in 1986). Here they made their way to Dyffryn Grove, kindly lent for the day by Lord & Lady Aberdare; this field was also known as Dyffryn Field, situated near Dyffryn House. The Aberdare Times reported the occasion – *"The children partook of tea under the shade of the noble trees. Lord and Lady Aberdare, and members of his Lordship's family exerted themselves to the utmost to make the children happy. They attended to the young ones and indulged in various amusements including the laying on of a number of swings, suspended from the tree branches"* – (Aberdare Times 1876).

Sunday School treat, Ynysybwl, circa. 1900. – Aberdare Library.

Sunday School children also frequented the open fields adjoining Plasdraw where after tea parties they enjoyed playing games and sports organised by the teachers. Picnics and walks to Llanwonno were always popular, and sometimes a visit was made by Sunday School children and the youth clubs to Gelli Wrgan Farm, belonging to David Prosser (Deacon) and his wife who were members of Providence Chapel, Mountain Ash. Those were memorable occasions and wonderful treats, particularly the serving of tasty home-made bread and delicious farm milk. Readers from the lower end of our Valley will recall the annual Sports Day events held at the field of Lan Farm after the Sunday School anniversary. The children and adults took with them baskets of sandwiches and would be met by an ice-cream van. Nearby was a favourite beauty spot alongside the stream named "Nant Clydach" and known locally as "The Cwm" (Cwm Clydach), a popular spot for picnics and walks.

(xv) Marching Processions

The children paraded the streets singing hymns and proudly displaying their banners and were supervised by the Sunday School teachers. Afterwards, they would retire to the chapel vestry where a good supply of tea and cake was provided. Following a march and parade in Mountain Ash in 1871, The Aberdare Times reported – *"The children were regaled with tea and cake at The Workman's Hall (now the site of the present Town Hall), Mountain Ash, and in the evening at the same place, a very pleasant entertainment, got up for their gratification, came off." (Aberdare Times 1871)*

> **GRAND MARCHES**
>
> A Report – Green Street E.W.M. Chapel, Aberdare – In August 1880 the Annual Procession of Sunday schools took place; out of a total of 4500 scholars marching through the town, Green St. Chapel supplied 235 children;
>
> Trinity W.P., Aberdare – 250
> Sion E.W.M., Aberdare – 200
> Carmel E.B., Aberdare – 600

In May 1871, Whit Monday became the first Bank Holiday in Britain, when the shops were closed and collieries were at a standstill. The Sunday Schools of the Valley, Welsh and English, paraded the streets and enjoyed the annual fetes which were normally followed by a tea party in their respective vestries. During Queen Victoria's Jubilee in 1887, processions took place involving dozens of Sunday Schools and thousands of children throughout the locality. Afterwards, the usual tea party was provided and sports were indulged in; sometimes a firework display would be held too. The events of the August Bank Holiday of 1883 were reported in The Aberdare Times – *"Collieries ceased working and the busy trades throughout the locality paused to breathe. Sunday Schools turned out in procession with their banners and flags, and made the places resonant with sacred music."*

After marching in procession the children made their way to a nearby field and later were regaled with a plentiful supply of homemade buns, cake and refreshments. Groups of chapels joined together in the marches. One such procession held in Aberdare each August Bank Holiday involved at least ten chapels joining together at pre-determined locations and finally arriving at Aberdare Park where they sang hymns before returning to their own vestries for a tea party and games. The marches were always meticulously organised, and the streets were promenaded by two to three thousand Sunday School children. At the turn of the century the Annual Parade of Ynysybwl Sunday Schools gathered together and proceeded along the "Long Path" between new Road and The Square after which a picnic and games were held on lower "Gelli" or at the "Rec". Marches, processions and parades continued up to the 1950's and then came to a halt, due primarily to the continuing decline of numbers in the Sunday Schools.

Procession March, Sunday School teachers and children, Christ Church, Gadlys, circa 1950.

Annual Sunday School parade, circa 1919. The teachers and children are marching along the "Long Path" between New Road and The Square, Ynysybwl. The parade was usually followed by a picnic and sports day on the lower "Gelli" or the "Rec.", or at times on to Barry Island by Charabanc.

D. J. Rees.

Annual Sunday School Demonstration, forming up outside
Elim, Bwllfa Road, Cwmdare, circa 1910. Nebo Sunday
School in the background are gathering outside their chapel
to join Elim.

(John F. Mear)

Sunday School procession Elim, Cwmdare, marching
through Bwllfa Tce., circa 1910.

(Doug Williams.)

Young children of Nebo Sunday school, Cwmdare, marching
through Bwllfa Tce.

(Doug Williams.)

Sunday School march, Bryn Sion, C.M. (now Carmel E.B.),
Trecynon. Taken at Aberdare Park, circa 1910.

(Doug Williams.)

Procession by Carmel, Trecynon. Marching through
Aberdare Park, 1932.

(Doug Williams.)

Sunday School procession by Siloh, Trecynon. Taken at
Aberdare Park, circa 1910.

(Doug Williams.)

Procession passing through Bwllfa Road, Cwmdare, opposite
Elim. Further up the road can be seen the Sunday School of
Nebo, Cwmdare.

Chapter 9

THE CHAPELS IN A TIME OF CHANGE

		Page No.
(i)	**Introduction**	**356**
(ii)	**The Chapels – Past**	**356**
(iii)	**The Chapels – Present**	**360**
(iv)	**The Chapels – Future**	**362**

> *"O, abide with us, Blessed Lord, or otherwise we shall see many of our large and excellent chapels empty."*

> *John Elias of Abererch, 1822.*
> *"The Prince of Preachers" (b. 1774 d. 1841).*
> *Leader of the Religious Revivals, 1806-09; 1831-32.*

(i) Introduction

In Ecclesiastes, the Preacher teaches us the inevitability and necessity of "change" throughout our lives.

> *"To every thing there is a season and a time to every purpose under the heaven … – A time to break down, and a time to build up … – A time to cast away stones, and a time to gather stones together… – A time to keep and a time to cast away …"*

> *Ecclesiastes, ch.3, v.1.3.5.6.*

A parallel can be drawn from the above Old Testament reading. There is nothing more certain and obvious than the continuing change presently occurring in the chapels of the Cynon Valley from the beginning of a "cause" to its demise. A time to establish and build; a time of revival and decline; to close, abandon, change and convert, and eventually, when all else fails, to demolish. But, even demolition of the chapels is not the end as the perpetual cycle of change continues through the process of redevelopment of vacant sites and re-building yet again!

This chapter deals with the inevitability and process of "change", and examines the trend and rate of chapel building over the past 150 years and their eventual decline. We shall also study the present situation relating to the number of chapels still open for worship, those that have been converted to various alternative uses, and those chapels which have been demolished, leading to some form of redevelopment of the vacant sites. Tables illustrate the progress of both building and demolition of the chapels throughout their long history. The plight of our disappearing chapels is described and also the alternative uses for the empty buildings and vacant sites throughout our locality. Lastly, reference is made to relevant organisations and the advice they offer in attempting to save the best examples of chapels at risk, hopefully instilling interest and concern in us to continue our unique architectural heritage.

(ii) The Chapels – Past

Chapter two dealt with the earliest of the primitive conventicles and Meeting Houses of the seventeenth century and how, through the Toleration Act of 1689, the Dissenters or Nonconformists were allowed the freedom to build Licenced Meeting Houses for the purpose of worship. In 1751 the first Nonconformist

Chapel in the Cynon Valley, namely Hen-Dy-Cwrdd (The old Meeting House), Trecynon, was established and by circa. 1790-1810 chapels began to appear elsewhere in the locality. Through the expansion of the coal and rail industries and canal trade, and resulting population growth and the breaking out of various Religious Revivals, the rate of chapel building work increased enormously. This boom began in earnest by 1850 and continued into the remainder of the century at a considerable rate. By 1860 there were 67 Nonconformist chapels in the Cynon Valley and by 1900 the number shot up to reach 127 chapels. Over the next one hundred years, 1900-2000, a further 53 places of nonconformist worship were established. The final phase of chapel building is generally considered to be around the period 1890-1910, known in chapel architectural terms as "The Post Classical Period", involving various eccentric and mixed designs from different periods of classical architecture. By 1910-14, Nonconformist chapel building virtually came to a halt, apart from a number of Apostolic and Pentecostal "causes" being formed and various other denominations being reinstated; refer to chapter one – The Chapel Histories.

When were the chapels built? A statistical exercise shows us how, why and when the development of chapel building work has progressed in our locality since 1751. Current statistics (2004) reveal that 6,700 to 7,000 chapels have been built in Wales up to 1914. Around this time chapels were being erected at the rate of more than one a week. The 1851 Census states that there were just over twice as many Nonconformist chapels (2784) as Anglican Churches (1176) in Wales at that time. There were more chapels in South Wales alone than in any other part of Britain, and the Cynon Valley, Rhondda Valleys and Merthyr contributed immensely to the high numbers. Sadly, chapels are now closing at the alarming rate of about 1.6 a week. This loss has accelerated since the 1960's and increasingly so over the past thirty years. Even as far back as 1822 John Elias, preacher and revivalist of Abererch, expressed concern at the growing number of empty chapels appearing in his locality and elsewhere. Religious revivals took place throughout the early 1800's and membership numbers fluctuated during this period. However, the Great Revivals of 1829-1849 and particularly that of 1859 brought about a huge increase in converts, and chapel building consequently swelled considerably during this period and onwards. Tables illustrate the periods of chapel building on a large scale. In the Cynon Valley from 1751 to 1840 the rate of chapel building was slow with only fifteen erected. Through the combined effects of the expansion of industry and the Religious Revivals from the 1850's to 1904-05, the rate of chapel building increased and continued at a steady rate, the sharpest rise being between 1850-60 when forty chapels were erected representing 22 per cent of the total of 180 built. The following table shows the number of chapels erected in the Cynon Valley from 1751 to 2004.

WRITTEN IN "GININEN"
In 1900, the village of Hirwaun of nearly 5000 souls could now show four congregations, Methodists and Independents, full of worshippers and four Sunday schools of the brightest and most informed type that knew the Word of God as well as any Sunday school in any part of the Kingdom. (Author's note: there were in fact three Methodist and three Independent Chapels in Hirwaun in 1900).

In 1861 at Bethesda W.I., Abernant, lighting of the chapel changed from paraffin lamps to gas.

During the cholera epidemic in 1849 Ebenezer W.I., Trecynon received 139 new members between 27th May and 30th December 1849.

PERIOD	NUMBER OF CHAPELS BUILT
1751-1840	15
1841-1850	13
1851-1860	40
1861-1870	15
1871-1880	5
1881-1890	18
1891-1900	22
1901-1910	29
1911-1920	9
1921-1940	7
1941-2004	7
TOTAL NUMBER OF CHAPELS BUILT	**180**

The majority of chapels built between 1751 and 1890 catered for the Welsh-speaking population in the valley, but after this period an increasing number of English-speaking chapels were built. The following table shows the comparison of Welsh to English-speaking chapels erected in the Cynon Valley 1751-2004.

NUMBER OF CHAPELS BUILT		
PERIOD	WELSH SPEAKING	ENGLISH SPEAKING
1751-1840	14	0
1841-1850	9	4
1851-1860	34	6
1861-1870	9	6
1871-1880	2	3
1881-1890	8	10
1891-1900	11	11
1901-1910	13	16
1911-1920	1	8
1921-1930	2	4
1931-1940	0	2
1941-2004	2	5
TOTAL = 180	105	75

CHAPEL GHOSTS !

A local newspaper (Aberdare Leader?) reported that the ghosts of monks were seen in the basement of Saint David's E.P., Aberdare (Ref. 111) some time after its closure in 1952.

The table clearly reveals the overwhelming predominance of the erection of Welsh-speaking chapels built between 1751 and 1840 when 14 of these were erected but no English whatsoever. However, "competition" gradually emerged in the number of English-speaking chapels appearing from 1840 to 1890. By 1890, 76 Welsh-speaking chapels had been erected compared with 29 English-speaking. Between 1891 and 1910 there occurred a reversal in this trend when for the first time the number of Welsh-speaking chapels fell behind. From 1911 to 2004 the number of English-speaking chapels erected raced ahead with 19 English compared to only 5 Welsh. It is clear that the earlier chapels were largely Welsh speaking, but as English-speaking immigrants flocked to the valley to seek work in the expanding coal industry, there came a demand for more and more chapels to fulfil the needs of the increasing influx of the English-speaking population.

DID YOU KNOW?

The Jewish community in our locality once had a synagogue at Seymour Street, Aberdare.

A pawn shop at Oxford Street, Mountain Ash was first used for the weekly meetings of The Salvation Army in the 1870's. This became too small as numbers grew. They later held meetings in The Workmen's Hall (now site of the Town Hall), Mountain Ash. In 1886 they built their new Salvation Army Hall at Woodland Street, Mountain Ash (See Chapel Ref. No. 62). In 1879 their leader was Captain Emily Doyle.

Pew rents were abolished around 1916 - a regular source of income. It was taken over by the envelope system of donation.

Lower Perthcelyn was also known as "German Town", so named after German workmen who built the first houses there after the First World War around 1918-21. These included Dillington Terrace, Monmouth Street, and part of Glamorgan Street.

The site on which Bethesda English Baptist Chapel, Penrhiwceiber was built in 1884 was named by the Executors of Major V.H. Lee, after whom the nearby Lee Hotel - (demolished 2004) - was named. The chapel was demolished in 1996.

The Salvation Army's publication "The War Cry" first appeared on 27th December 1879.

The site of the large store "Wilkinsons" (formerly Tescos) was once occupied by the Tabernacle English Congregational Chapel, Aberdare, (built 1856; demolished 1973).

Out of the total of 180 chapels built, the three leading denominations (128) comprise 71% of the total, as shown in the following table: -

DENOMINATION	NUMBER OF CHAPELS BUILT	WELSH	ENGLISH	PERCENTAGE OF THE WHOLE
Baptist	47	30	17	26%
Independent/ Congregationalist	43	35	8	24%
Methodist	38	24	14	21%
Totals =	128	89	39	71%

Others include: –

Apostolic – 8; Mission Halls – 7; Pentecostal – 6; Salvation Army – 6; Primitive Methodist – 4; Gospel Halls – 4; Christadelphian – 3; Unitarians– 3; Others -11.

A CHAPEL SURROUNDED BY PUBS

The English Wesleyan Chapel at Green Street, Aberdare, was in the 1860's immediately surrounded by no less than six Public Houses! Namely –

Cross Keys, Green St., opened 1835; closed 1880
Angel Inn, 27 High St., opened 1848; closed 1892
Wellington Inn, Canon St., opened 1844; closed 1870
Mason's Arms, 51 High St., opened 1835; closed 1913
Forester's Arms, 23 High St., opened 1872; closed 1880
Green Dragon Inn, opened 1835; closed 1961 (now site of Aberdare Central Library)

The chapel is positioned between the former Cross Keys Public House and The Green Dragon Inn.

BURNT OFFERINGS!

The members of Carmel W.I., Penrhiwceiber held a special service in 1886 to commemorate the clearing of the Chapel debt. During the celebrations the paperwork relating to the financial debt details was placed on a silver tray and set on fire!

THE 1849 CHOLERA EPIDEMIC

In 1849 a serious outbreak of cholera swept hundreds to their ultimate graves throughout the mining districts, and consequently the people flocked to the chapels, the irreligious and ungodly, to make their peace with God and be saved from "The Wrath to Come"! Following the 1849 cholera outbreak, hundreds were converted and baptised.

A Religious Census was carried out in Aberdare in 1877. The result was as follows –

Out of 8271 inhabitants visited and interviewed, 7346 attended some place of worship (i.e.89%), whilst 753 did not (i.e. 9%), 2884 children attended Sunday school and 655 did not; 468 people said that they used to go to chapel but had ceased to do so. Out of 1753 houses visited only 61 were without a Bible; 31 house canvassers were refused information.

MORMON CHURCH AT ABERDARE WAS FORMERLY A PUBLIC HOUSE

The Mormon "Cause" at Aberdare commenced in 1844 at the Welsh Harp Inn, 5 Commercial Street, Aberdare. The Public House was opened in 1835 and closed in 1916. The site is now occupied by Woolworths Store, (see Chapel Ref. No. 177).

THE NICKY-NACKY (NICI-NACI)

Treaman Colliery was located behind Saron Ysgoldy W.I., Cardiff Road, Aberaman. The colliery was so named due to the noisy rattling of the pit rope over the head gear sheave, heard all over the village

CHAPEL WAS FORMERLY A PUBLIC HOUSE.

The Apostolic (Babell) Chapel at David Street, Trecynon, was formerly a Billiard Hall, and from 1867-1909 it was a Public House named "The Park View Inn", appropriately so named, as it faced The Aberdare Park.

(iii) The Chapels-Present
Unfortunately the twenty-first century statistics reveal a far bleaker picture compared to the hey-day of chapel building in the nineteenth century. The decline in chapels is reflected elsewhere throughout Wales and Great Britain. The closure and demolition of chapels have become extremely worrying and there appears to be no halt in this decline. The position of the 180 chapels built in the Cynon Valley since 1751 is as follows:-

THE POSITION AS AT AUTUMN 2004	NUMBER OF CHAPELS	PERCENTAGE
Active	63	35%
Vacant	11	6%
Converted	50	28%
Demolished	56	31%

Broadly speaking the figures can be summarised as follows: -
   Active – one third
   Vacant/Converted – one third
   Demolished – one third

Almost one third of chapels built have been demolished (56) out of a total of 180 over the past ninety years. The sharpest increase in the rate of demolition was between 1960 and 2000. In this forty-year period 45 chapels out of a total of 56 (79%) were demolished. The following table shows the number of chapels demolished since 1914.

PERIOD	NUMBER OF CHAPELS DEMOLISHED
1751-1914	NONE
1914-1950	6
1951-1960	4
1961-1970	8
1971-1980	9
1981-1990	10
1991-2000	15
2001-2004	4
TOTAL	**56 Chapels**

The worst period was 1995-98 when a total of twelve chapels were demolished. In Penrhiwceiber alone, four chapels were demolished within eighteen months during 1995-96.

CHAPEL ON TELEVISION

The demolition of Bethel Welsh Independent Chapel, Miskin (built 1903, demolished 1995) was featured in the H.T.V. documentary in 1995, directed by Hywel Davies, and entitled "On The Chapel Trail". Professor Anthony Jones presented and narrated the programme.

FAITH IN GOD, ON THE WANE?

In a National Poll of 10,000 people taken in February 2004, it was revealed that Britain has some of the lowest levels of belief and attendances at chapel or church. Only 46% said they have always believed in God, and only 21% attend religious services.

REDEVELOPMENT OF SITES AFTER DEMOLITION

To date (2004), out of the fifty-six chapels demolished, the sites of just under half of these (26), remain vacant and their future is uncertain. The remaining 30 vacant sites have been re-developed to various uses as follows: -

ALTERNATIVE USE OF VACANT SITES	NUMBER OF CHAPEL SITES
Vacant Sites	26
Housing Development	13
Flats	5
Bungalow	2
Open air/Amenity Areas	2
Meeting Hall	1
Doctor's Surgery/Medical Centre	1
Public Convenience/Open Area	1
Public Pay & Display Car Park	1
Large Store (Wilkinson's)	1
The Brethren	1
Chapels Re-built	2
Total	**56 sites**

Local authorities, building contractors and developers, private owners, chapel trustees, chapel unions etc. should ensure that vacant chapel sites are put to good use and not allowed to become overgrown, unkempt eye-sores and rubbish dumps. If they are not developed, other uses should be considered for the benefit of the community. For example, landscaped amenity areas with seating, play areas for children, and off-street car parking.

CONVERSION OF VACANT CHAPELS

A total of 50 vacant chapels (28%) out of a total of 180 built, have been converted to alternative uses. Most conversions have proved acceptable and visually pleasing but there are a small number where the chapels have been so altered as to render them incapable of recognition as a chapel externally or internally. The following table shows how the vacant chapels have been converted to an alternative use.

ALTERNATIVE USE THROUGH CONVERSION	NUMBER OF CHAPELS CONVERTED
Dwelling House	13
Flats	5
Bungalow	1
Builders' store/Workshop	6
Funeral Directors	3
Youth Club; Halls; Community Centre	4
Garage/Workshop	3
Mental Health Team	1
Day Nursery	1
Miscellaneous stores, etc.	13
Total number of chapels converted	**50**

Eleven chapels remain vacant and their future use remains uncertain. In the meantime they continue to deteriorate and are a constant source of concern through the incidence of vandalism and neglect. Thankfully, sixty-three chapels, just over a third (35%) remain active and open for worship. Some are thriving with up to sixty holding regularly attended services, whilst others are struggling to keep their doors open with just a handful of faithful members in attendance.

If the empty chapels throughout our locality cannot be saved or converted to some other use before demolition, they should at least be documented, measured and photographed internally and externally, plans prepared, and a data-base compiled. Professor Anthony Jones appropriately advises that the aim should be – *"Conservation by Documentation"*. The effort of the former Mid Glamorgan County Council Planning Department is an excellent example of survey and documentation work. During 1978-80, 600 chapels throughout Mid Glamorgan were surveyed and drawings prepared, 108 of these in the Cynon Valley. More of this type of work should be carried out and properly co-ordinated, or else we shall lose a great deal of information on our architectural heritage as more and more chapels are demolished. Many contain important architectural and historical features, and in the Cynon Valley eighteen chapels have received Listed Building Status. Unfortunately, too many chapels are empty and they continue to be vandalised as well as to deteriorate through neglect and the ravages of the weather and pollution. Some are in such a poor and dangerous structural condition that they have fallen beyond repair at a reasonable cost and eventually demolition seems the only course of action. The decline in chapels, particularly since the 1960's, is primarily due to the emergence of outside secular interests and the attraction of various recreation, sports and leisure activities. Ageing congregations with no youngsters to replace them has led to the decline in chapel attendances. Consequential lack of funds has regrettably led to the deterioration of the fabric of so many chapels, leading to their eventual closure and demolition. Professor Anthony Jones estimates that about 1.6 chapels are closing every week throughout Wales, resulting in a huge part of our local heritage being wiped out forever.

(iv) The Chapels – Future

It has been said – *"The only certainty in life is change"*.

Many say change, when it comes, is good, and that we should embrace it and look to the future with optimism and hope. There is no doubt that the chapels are going through a difficult period of change; all the more reason therefore, that every effort be made to save most and perhaps all of our chapels threatened with closure and demolition. Although this action is not always practical or possible, we should nevertheless attempt to save the best examples and ensure they are converted and put to good alternative use. Thankfully CADW – The Welsh Body responsible for looking after Historic Monuments of Wales – has been engaged over the past twenty years in inspecting and listing buildings of architectural interest and merit, thus ensuring that special permission be obtained from the local authority before altering or converting an empty chapel to alternative use. The ideal type of conversion would be for the purpose of a Community Meeting Hall or Centre, lecture or concert hall etc., just as the chapels, as religious auditoriums, were originally intended. When chapels are converted every effort should be made to execute the work in a professional and sympathetic manner in keeping with the existing design, and to retain as much of the external and internal features as is possible. Note the advice of CADW – *"Conservation and Conversion should go hand in hand."* The welsh word "CADW" translated is – "To maintain or preserve".

At all costs, the front elevation should not be altered. Fortunately, the majority of conversions throughout the Cynon Valley have kept the original front elevation intact and unaltered, and in many cases the appearance has been enhanced and improved through restoration, cosmetic repair, and tasteful re-decoration. Depending on the type and nature of conversion it is not always possible to keep and save chapel furniture including pews and pulpits etc., but with careful planning and design some architectural features can and should be saved and retained and incorporated into the overall conversion scheme. Ideally, qualified conservation architects, registered architects, and chartered surveyors should be consulted and engaged to ensure professional advice in this specialised type of design and conversion/conservation work.

Various organisations continue to carry out valuable work in ensuring and advising good design practice, conservation and documentation of chapels throughout Wales, including CADW; The Historic Building Council; The National Museum; and The National Library of Wales. The voluntary organisation CAPEL – The Chapels Heritage Society, founded in 1986, was formed to encourage the study and preservation of the nonconformist heritage of Wales, and to offer information and advice to chapel congregations on ways to maintain and preserve their buildings. CAPEL also advises the recording and studying of chapel architecture, and encourages trustees and members to safeguard their records and documents and to consider the sympathetic conversion of chapels no longer required for their original purpose. Private individuals and members of CAPEL are presently carrying out useful voluntary work in measuring and photographing the chapels in their locality, and collating records of various kinds. Furthermore with the help of the Welsh Religious Buildings Trust (WRBT), at Penygroes, Caernarfon, attention is given in assessing and assisting chapels in Wales under threat and in difficulty. Important and useful work is being carried out by the WRBT which is a registered charity with a view to rescuing, preserving and saving threatened chapels from closure and demolition. To assist in this important work, CAPEL has formed an Architectural Advisor's Section whereby professional conservation architects will investigate and advise when a major or historically important chapel is threatened. They also look into and offer advice on planning application details and proposals for such threatened and vacant chapels.

Libraries throughout the Cynon Valley contain excellent records and photographs of our nonconformist chapels including the W.W. Price and Rev. Ivor Parry Research Room (local history) at Aberdare Central Library and the local history collection at Mountain Ash. The Cynon Valley Museum contains excellent memorabilia, original drawings and photographs of chapels, and a good collection of chapel histories.

Documentation and recording information including the photographing of chapels externally and internally is absolutely essential. One individual in the Rhondda Valleys has filmed the chapels externally and internally on his camcorder as well as taking still images. In the Cynon Valley over the past 20 years, the author has collated three large volumes, comprising 2,300 photographs and 330 drawings and maps, covering the 180 chapels of the Cynon Valley, many of which are reproduced throughout this book. Further work can be done including consulting chapel records and minute books and referring to the many centenary booklets (Welsh and English), in the local libraries and in private collections. Valuable information can also be obtained from primary sources by interviewing the older members. Co-ordinated efforts are continuing through the various organisations to record and document most of the chapels throughout Wales. Chapel members can take part in this type of work by simply ensuring that relevant documents, deeds, registers, minute books, original drawings, photographs, memorabilia and centenary history booklets etc., are preserved and deposited in the local library research rooms, the Cynon Valley Museum, The Glamorgan Record Office, Cardiff, or the National Library of Wales, Aberystwyth.

THE CHAPELS – PAST, PRESENT AND FUTURE

A BRIEF SUMMARY

The Royal Commission on the Ancient and Historical Monuments of Wales (RCAHMW), Aberystwyth, in partnership with CAPEL, informs us that around 6,700 to 7,000 Nonconformist Chapels have been built in Wales up to 1915. The result of the RCAHMW Chapels Data-Base Recording Project can be consulted at their offices, or on-line through the internet on their COFLEIN Service on www.rcahmw.org.uk/coflein.

In the Cynon Valley, only a third of chapels remain active and open to worship today (2004), out of a total of 180 built since the year 1751. A third have been demolished, and the rest are vacant or have been converted to other use. In fifty years time, it is likely that only a handful of chapels will remain in our locality if the current trend of decline continues. An all-out effort should be made to raise awareness of this plight, and save the best examples of vacant and redundant chapels in our valley and the rest of Wales.

Rev. D.M. Phillips of Tylorstown once said in 1906:

> *"A Revival is similar to letting out the contents of a reservoir. When all the contents have run out, it must have time to fill before another outpouring is possible."*

The 'Reservoir of Revival' is indeed running out, and the decline in chapels sadly continues. Will the next fifty years avert this decline and enable the 'Reservoir' to replenish its supply of hope and goodness, and hence allow another Religious Revival outpouring? . . . Only time will tell!

To end this chapter here is a poem entitled: -

WHEN THE CHAPELS WERE FULL

Family and Friends gather to meet,
Arriving early to get a seat;
Preacher in pulpit and members in pews,
All are ready to hear The Good News.

Grand organ bellows with air swelling full,
Choristers eager to sing with great hwyl;
Faithful Deacons are in The Set Fawr,
The place is overflowing, at Capel Gwawr!

The Preacher delivers a fine stirring Sermon,
It's happening too, at Capel Hermon;
Collection plates with gifts overflow,
They shall reap, as surely they sow.

The Service is over, the people feel good,
They'd stay a lot longer, if only they could;
But along they go, their hearts full of cheer,
To homes of love, and the warmth they hold dear.

Alas – now the chapels are in decline,
Numbers decreasing through the passage of time;
Revival must come, this course to arrest,
As chapel and us, are put to The Test.

This Test to pass is the sure way forward,
For our sole duty is to please our Good Lord;
And once more the chapels soon will be,
Filled with praise again – just wait and see!

Alan Vernon Jones, February 2004.

. . . words of nostalgia and good times past; of hope for the future, for the chapels, for each one of us; and encouragement for our future generation on whom we rely to continue our fine local chapel heritage.

Illuminated Address dated 1909, to commemorate the services of Joseph Rees, Choirmaster, Bethesda, Penrhiwceiber.

366

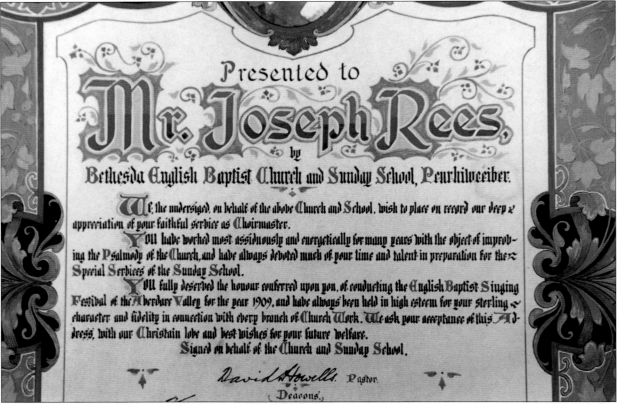

Enlarged detail – Illuminated Address (as previous details).

Certificate – Baptist Missionary Society.

Courtesy of Brinley Davies

The above is an example of the type of certificate awarded on passing a Tonic - Sol-Fa college examination. Jonah Bowen (1885-1950) was a member of Bethel Chapel, Trecynon. He worked for many years in Tower Colliery, Hirwaun, retiring as mechanic in 1949. The Tonic – Sol – Fa system of teaching singing was much used and resulted in high standards of singing in chapels and choirs.

Courtesy of Elfed Bowen (Son of Jonah Bowen.)

Certificate of Merit – Gordon Spencer, 1916.

Certificate of Merit – Maggie May Morgans, December 1915. Heol-Y-Felin, Trecynon.

Sunday School Certificate, awarded to William John Jones, Bethel, Hirwaun. Dated 1927.

Postcard dated 1911.

Sunday School banner – Bryn Sion (now Carmel), Trecynon. Established 1860

Banner – Temperance Union – 1898. Calvaria, Aberdare.

Banner of Carmel Sunday School, Trecynon. Formerly Bryn Sion.

Banner – Siloa, Aberdare.

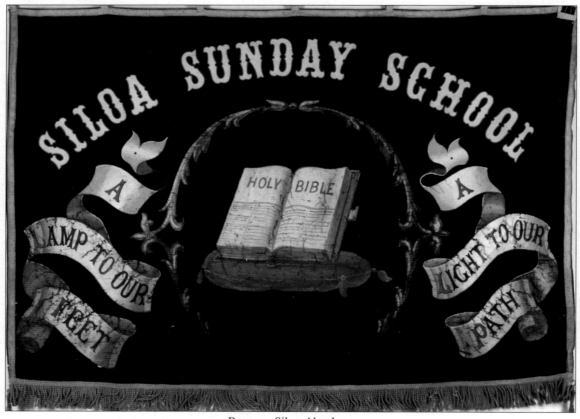

Banner – Siloa, Aberdare.

Sunday School banner, Carmel E.B., Aberdare. Dated 1840.

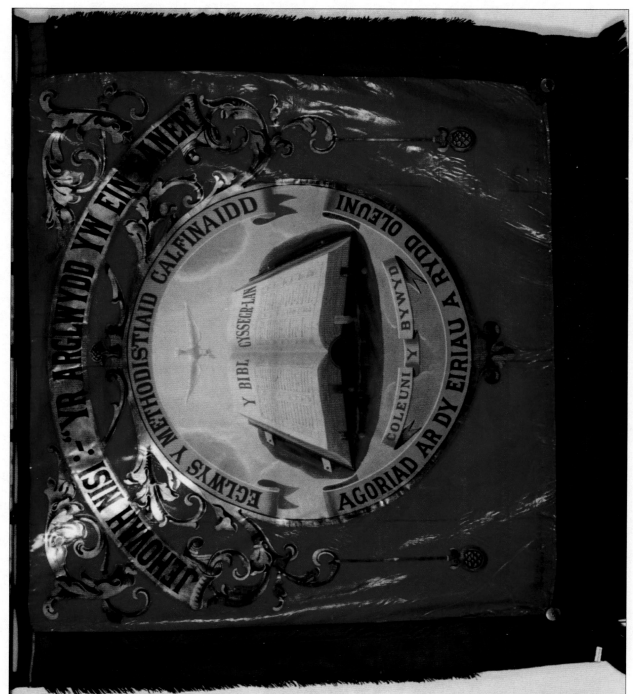

Banner – Bethania C.M., Aberdare.

Sunday School banner – Calvaria Welsh Baptist. Established 1807.

Banner – Cwmbach chapel, name unknown.

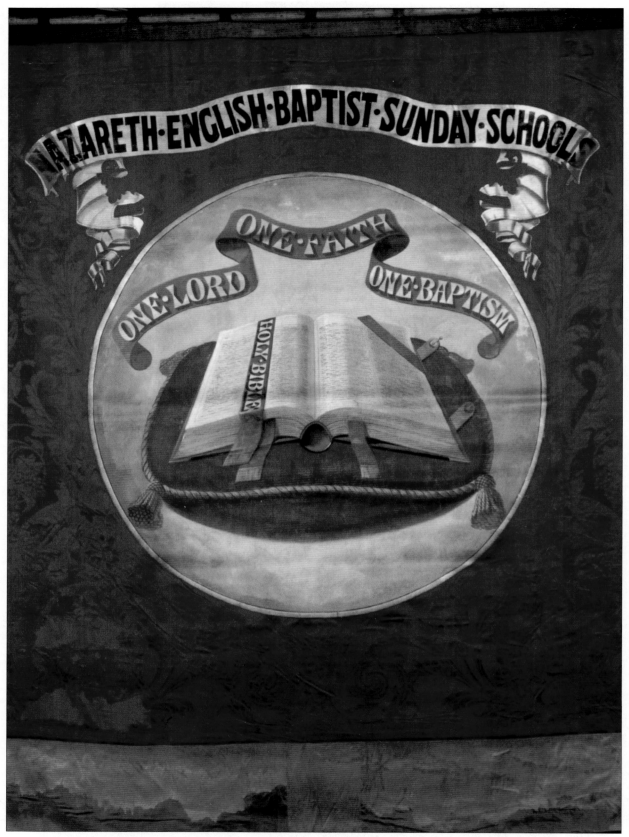

Sunday School banner – Nazareth E.B., Mountain Ash.

Sunday School banner – Carmel, Penrhiwceiber. This silk banner was made by George Tutill of City Road, London. Circa 1905.
Courtesy of Brian Davies, curator of Pontypridd Museum.

Sunday School banner – Noddfa W.B., Trecynon.

Sunday School banner – Siloh, Trecynon.

Sunday School banner – Bethel, Gadlys.

380

A. V. Jones.

Sunday School banner – Bethany, Godreaman.

NOTE: Photographs of the banners by courtesy of Cynon Valley Museum, except where otherwise credited.

Chapter 10

A COLLECTION OF TALES, POEMS AND FACTS

		Page No.
(i)	**Introduction**	**381**
(ii)	**Tales**	**381**
(iii)	**Poems**	**389**
(iv)	**Facts – "Figure It Out"**	**395**
(v)	**A Fond Farewell to The Chapels of Yesteryear**	**397**

"Stories and poems, we shall see,
Tell us much about you and me;
Facts and Tales are here to amuse,
"Figure It Out" – with numbers to peruse.

This chapter being the last,
Remembers the chapels of days long past;
Reliving events with fond regard,
Recalling happy times – not sad!

Alan Vernon Jones, March 2004

(i) Introduction

This last chapter contains what is intended to be a light-hearted and interesting collection of Tales, Poems, and Facts. The final section is given to a nostalgic and hopefully not too sad a "Farewell" to the chapels of yesteryear, when . . .

"All that remains are the distant happy memories faintly echoing from the decaying timbers and broken walls that once shook with passion, and trembled with the sweet harmonious strains of song and glorious praise!"

A.V. Jones, 2004

(ii) Tales

WOOING FROM THE PULPIT

Numberless anecdotes are told of the eccentricities and characteristic acts of Rev. Lorenzo Dow, the famous itinerant Methodist preacher. When he was a widower he said to the congregation one day at the close of his sermon –

"I am a candidate for matrimony; and if there is any woman here in the audience this evening who is willing to marry me, I would thank her to rise."

A woman rose very near the pulpit, and another in a distant part of the chapel. Rev. Dow paused a moment and then said –

"There are two. I think this one near me rose first; at any rate I will have her for my wife!"

This woman was in good standing in the community and possessed of considerable property and wealth. Very soon after, she became Mrs. Dow!

Local Almanac, January 1899

STAND UP, OR SIT DOWN?

    * <u>Announcement from church service leaflets, Michigan and New York, U.S.A.</u>

    * Hymn Number 326
        "Stand up, Stand up for Jesus!"

    * The congregation shall remain seated.
           Michigan Church Leaflet.

    * The congregation shall stand for Hymn Number 336, after which Dr. Fosdick will deliver his sermon, the subject being –"What are you Standing for?"
        New York Church Bulletin.

Extracts from "It Must Be True" by Denys Parson, 2002. Published by Ebury.
Used by permission of The Random House Group Limited, Northants.

AN INCIDENT CONCERNING GWAWR WELSH BAPTIST CHAPEL, ABERAMAN.

The Rev. David B Jones of Rhymni ("Dewi Elfed"), the newly ordained minister of Gwawr W.B., Aberaman, became a Mormon, as a result of which he was called to appear before the Baptist Association. He refused, claiming that the Association had no jurisdiction over him. Consequently, he was excommunicated in absentia. In the meantime Rev. David Jones had altered the Trust Deeds of the chapel in his favour; he deleted names from the original chapel deeds, including that of Rev. Dr. Thomas Price, Minister of Calvaria W.B., Aberdare, 1846-88. By this unscrupulous action the chapel fell into the hands of the Latter Day Saints (The Mormons). There followed a legal action culminating in the Assize Courts in 1851, when a verdict was arrived at in favour of the Baptist Association. To ensure that justice was done, Rev. Dr. Thomas Price with 2000 Baptist followers, marched to Gwawr Chapel together with the Law Officers. Rev. David Jones and one supporter locked themselves inside the chapel, but Dr. Price and one of his Deacons eventually gained access through a window. After a wild and exciting chase around the chapel galleries, Dr. Price forcibly ejected Rev. David Jones by literally booting him out of the front door of the chapel! By doing so, the chapel was re-gained and repossessed by the High Sheriff who, it was said, had no legal right to break down the door of the chapel. However, in the meantime Dr. Price had entered through a window instead to gain access and remove Rev. David Jones. The chapel was later re-instated and re-opened on 9th November 1851 under the auspices of the Baptist "Cause". Rev. David Jones later threatened to bring a case against Dr Price for assault but his bluff was called and the action was dropped.

Rev. Ivor Parry, 1965

A BUILDING IN THE CYNON VALLEY OVER 2000 YEARS OLD!

In his slide lecture on chapels of the Cynon Valley, Mr. Tom Evans of Abernant draws our attention to the similarity in appearance and design of Colliery Winding Engine Houses, and some of our local chapels. Mr Evans mentions an Engine House in Cwmdare bearing the name plaque "BC". This raised questions suggesting the building was erected in the year "Before Christ" and was therefore at least 2000 years old. However, it was later explained the letters "BC" referred to "Bwllfa Colliery"!

Tom Evans, 1997

OLD BETHEL C.M., YNYSYBWL (Built 1786)

In his book *"History of Llanwynno"*, written in 1888, Glanffrwd tells us that the great and notable Howell Harris (b.1714 d.1773) preached at Llanwonno and Ynysybwl before old Bethel C.M., Ynysybwl was built in 1786. The services were held at various places in the 1770's including *Ty-tan-wal"* (trans.

The house under the wall) located near Mynachdy, and there is no doubt that in this old farm house Howell Harris delivered powerful sermons. According to the old Welsh Methodists they met at Ty-tan-wal and – *"observed clear signs of God's presence among them. The congregation numbered 30 to 45 and were known to give rise to a "hwyl" and hearty thanksgiving and praise."*

"Glanffrwd", 1888

DEACON REBUKES THE WRONG MAN

To a young man who stood on the street corner peaceably smoking a large expensive cigar, approached the elderly chapel Deacon, teetotaller and impertinent reformer of immemorial legend.
"How many cigars a day do you smoke young man?" inquired the meddler in other peoples' affairs.
"Three," patiently replied the youth.
"How much do you pay for them?" continued the inquisitor.
"Six pence each."
"Don't you know Sir," continued the self-righteous sage, *"that if you would stop smoking and save up that money, by the time you are as old as I am, you might own that big building on the corner?"*
"Do you own it?" asked the smoker.
"No, I don't," replied the old Deacon.
"Well, I do," said the young man!

Local Almanac, June 1902

THREE LARGE HEAD STONES AND ONE SMALL ONE

Professor Anthony Jones, President of The Art Institute of Chicago, gave a slide lecture on "Welsh Chapels" on the 24th November 1995, at Ramoth Chapel, Hirwaun. One of his slides featured Llwyn Rhydowen Chapel, Cardiganshire, built 1834. One day, when he was looking around the chapel graveyard accompanied by the lady caretaker, his attention turned to three large ornate headstones adjacent to a much plainer and smaller one. He asked the caretaker who the deceased were. She answered, – *"The four headstones are of the Minister of this chapel and his three wives."* Professor A. Jones asked – *"Why are there three large headstones and one much smaller stone?"* The lady replied as if in a secret whisper – *"Oh, the smaller headstone is of his last wife; she was Church of England!"*

Professor Anthony Jones
Slide Lecture, 1995

MISSION HALL CATCHES FIRE AT CWMAMAN

The Mission Hall at Brynmair Road, Cwmaman was founded in 1920 by Rev. William Cooke, and built during the 1926 General Strike (See chapel Ref. No. 87). In November 1959, The Hall was seriously damaged by fire. Pastor Rev. Richard Henry Cook, then aged 66, rushed to save a smouldering Bible from the shelf of the pulpit. The fire broke out in the boiler room and severely damaged the pulpit and organ. One of the Elders, Mr. Ernest John Morris, 72, was very upset over this. Forty years of records and work were destroyed. The Hall had only recently been decorated in 1956 at a cost of £700. They continued the Meetings and services in the damaged Hall with canvas sheets for protection.

A.V. Jones, 2003

A DEACON'S COMPLAINT

A complaint and an apology were expressed in 1955 by deacon and farmer, Mr. David J. Prosser of Gelli Wrgan Farm, near Llanwonno. He experienced difficulty journeying to Providence E.Cong., Mountain Ash, by 6.00 p.m. on his tractor! His farm was in a remote part of the valley, and the journey to chapel was proving particularly awkward in manoeuvring his tractor through the busy streets, particularly at dusk. An application was therefore successfully made to the Public Bus Company to alter the scheduled bus times. The tractor was left behind at the farm, and a more comfortable mode of transport was made available, thus resolving the problem! For many years Mr. Prosser provided the chapel with a Christmas tree, kindly donated by the Forestry near his farm, and he delivered it on many occasions personally – in his tractor of course!

A.V. Jones, 1987

BRUNEL DESIGNS HIS FIRST AND ONLY CHAPEL

It is reputed that the great engineer, Isambard Kingdon Brunel (1806-1859), designed a Wesleyan Chapel in Merthyr Tydfil in 1853, to replace one which had been demolished in order to make way for the Taff Vale Railway Station in 1841. Legend has it that he designed the chapel on the spot and was probably the only known chapel he designed in Wales.

Professor Anthony Jones, Welsh Chapels, 1996

WHY WAS MONK STREET, ABERDARE, SO CALLED?

Monk Street was once known, many years ago, as *"Rhiw'r Mynych"* (trans: *"Monk's Hill"*), and used as a path by the Cistercian Monks who travelled from Maerdy (trans: *"Mary's House"*) to the old *"Grange"* or hermitage formerly situated at Plasdraw, and over the hill to the Cistercian Priories at Llantarnam, Margam and Penrhys. In 1860 there was not a single building above The Bird in Hand Public House, and from there one walked up between high hedges along a quiet country lane. Local legend suggests the *"Grange"*, or hermitage, at Plasdraw, was the site of a monastic cell. Furthermore, the tradition is that the Plasdraw site was dedicated to Saint Elvan. The ruins of the building are visible to this day.

Tom Evans and A.V. Jones, 2004

A NOTE ON BETHANIA W.I. CHAPEL, MOUNTAIN ASH

"Jones Llangollen" was a member with the Welsh Independents who met in the loft of Howel Thomas the Carpenter, Mountain Ash. In October 1852, during a Thanksgiving Service, the loft was quite full and the service lively. Consequently, the loft collapsed under the load and enthusiastic activity. Fortunately no one was hurt, but they had quite a fright. It was not long, therefore, before they set about the task of building a Chapel near the present Bethania in Philip Street. Work started in 1853 under the guidance of "Jones Llangollen", and when the building was only half built Rev. Jones resigned his position and emigrated to America, leaving the Chapel unfinished and also leaving his family behind in Mountain Ash. However the chapel was eventually completed in 1854.

A.V. Jones, 1987

REMINISCENCES BY D.T.ALEXANDER

Taken from a newspaper cutting dated 1904 –

"I remember that once a month on Sunday afternoons, Rev. Dr. Thomas Price (b.1820 d.1888) minister of Calvaria Welsh Baptist Chapel, Aberdare from 1846-1888, used to baptise his converts in the River Cynon, alongside the iron bridge at the bottom of Commercial Street, Aberdare. I have seen as many as 25 or 30 converts, men and women, on the same afternoon. On these occasions the whole of the Baptist community used to meet at the chapel and march in procession through the streets with the converts; the men converts being attired in long black robes, and the women in white. They marched through the streets from the chapel to the place of baptism singing hymns. As a matter of course, large crowds gathered on the river bank to witness the immersions."

D.T. Alexander

MINISTER BURIED ALIVE!

Rev. Thomas Evans (Tomos Glyn Cothi B.1764 d. 1833, ordained in 1794) was minister of Hen-Dy-Cwrdd, Un., Trecynon 1813-33. He was a native of Brechfa, Carmarthenshire and worked there as a weaver. He also wrote poetry and was a prolific hymn writer and author of one of the first English-Welsh dictionaries. He was a radical Reformer and during 1801-03 was imprisoned at Carmarthen for two years for allegedly publishing sedition and a song which the Government felt to be treasonable. He established a Magazine and caused agitation for political reform. He welcomed the French Revolution, 1789. He died in 1833, aged 69 and was buried on 29th January in Hen-Dy-Cwrdd chapel graveyard. Legend has it that 15 years later in 1848 when his grave was opened for the burial of his daughter, his skeleton was found to be lying face down; the position in which it had been laid to rest. Rumour was rife around Aberdare that the unfortunate man had been buried alive!

A.V. Jones 2002

A MINISTER'S LAST WORDS TO HIS CONGREGATION

In 1864, Rev. Hugh Hughes ("Huw Tegai") – Minister of Bethel W.Cong., Gadlys 1859 to 1864, was preaching in the pulpit one Sunday evening on the words – *"Blessed are they that die in The Lord."* Suddenly upon uttering these words he collapsed, and gasped what was to be his last words – *"Remember my Text".* Alas, three days later he sadly passed away.

A.V. Jones, 2002

HOUSE WAS A CHAPEL

Numbers 5,6,7 and 8 Tir Bach, Cwmbach, was formerly a chapel. No's 5,6,7 – the main chapel; no.8 – the rear vestry. During recent renovations a chapel bell was discovered hanging in the roof space of the present cottages. The chapel was called "Capel Lletty Shiencyn" from 1851 to 1864. In 1864 they moved to their new chapel, Ebenezer C.M. at Sion Terrace, Cwmbach (Chapel Ref. No. 101).

A.V. Jones, 2003

JOKES IN THE PULPIT

The famous Nasr-Eddin, the traditional Joe Miller of The Turks, three times fooled an assembly of true believers out of a sermon. The first time he ascended the pulpit he said – *"Oh, true believers, do you know what I am going to say?"* They replied, *"No"*, whereupon he asked – *"Of what use is it to preach to such ignoramuses?"* He then came down from the pulpit. The next time, when he asked the same question, they answered – *"Yes, we know"*, whereupon he said – *"Then it is useless for me to tell you,"* and he came down. The third time, having taken counsel together, the congregation prepared an answer which they thought would corner their joker-preacher, and said – *"Some of us know, and some don't";* whereupon the preacher promptly replied – *"Let those who know tell those who don't!"* – and once more he came down from the pulpit.

Local Almanac, June 1902

A FEAR OF HEIGHTS

From the elevated pulpits the preacher took command like a captain on the bridge of his ship. The "three-decker" pulpits were so high that some visiting ministers refused to ascend "the perilous perch", choosing instead to speak from the safety of the Set Fawr (Big Seat).

Professor Anthony Jones, Welsh Chapels, 1996

JOHNNY FORTNIGHT

Rev. T.M. Lloyd, minister of Jerusalem Welsh Presbyterian Chapel, Ynysybwl, spoke of a member who did not attend chapel on a regular basis, and who was referred to as "Johnny Fortnight"!

A.V. Jones 2003

SERVICES START ON TIME

An interesting account was published in the Aberdare Leader in August, 1931, under the heading of "Punctuality". A casual visitor to Providence E. Cong., Mountain Ash, was "staggered" to find that the services began punctually. As the Town Hall clock struck 11.00 a.m. Mr Gomer Lloyd Davies, Organist, began playing the introit, in time with the clock chimes, so it seemed. The visitor remarked that he had not yet attended a Chapel in town where a service commenced on time, some were 15 minutes late! Providence excelled in punctuality, and was in the news!

A.V. Jones, 1987

MINISTER IN JAIL!

Rev. Dr. Thomas Rees of Aberbargoed, Minister of Ebenezer W.I., Trecynon, 1840-44, received a "call" to Ebenezer in 1840 and the dramatic circumstances of his arrival are worthy of mention here. In addition to his ministry, Rev. T. Rees had kept a shop at Aberbargoed, and during the Chartist Riots he had issued large quantities of provisions on credit to the chartists and was subsequently unable to meet his financial obligations. As a result he spent a few days at the Debtors' Gaol at Cardiff, from which place he came straight to Ebenezer Chapel as their new minister.

A.V. Jones, 2000

"HIDDEN TREASURE"

The Foundation Memorial Stone of Bethlehem W.I., Abercwmboi was laid by David Davis of Maesyffynon in May 1859. Mr. Morgan Junior, Abercwmboi, placed two plates behind the foundation stone after placing a glass bottle underneath. Then a small boy, Edward John, placed half-a-crown (12_ pence) on the plate and "drew" one pound from Rev. William Edwards, Ebenezer, W.I., Trecynon. The boy then commenced "begging" from neighbours as no announcement of a collection had been made until £5 was obtained to follow the half-crown. The collection, which later received a contribution from every house nearby, raised £30.

A.V. Jones, 2002

JOHN WESLEY VISITS ABERDARE, 1749

On 6th April 1749, John Wesley the great Methodist Founder, visited Aberdare en route for an Evangelical Tour of Ireland. He travelled from Cardiff through the Vale of Glamorgan to Llantrisant on horseback, and over the mountain from Ynysybwl to Llanwonno and on to Aberdare. He tells us that he arrived in Aberdare – *"Just as the bell was ringing for burial at St. John's Church Yard."* John Wesley says he preached in the church to the mourners and then went on through the rain over the Brecknock Beacons. The great Evangelist visited Aberdare a second time on 20th March 1750. In his journal he writes – *"Expecting to preach at Aberdare, 16 Welsh! miles from Cardiff. I rode thither over the mountains, but we found no notice had been given of my visit. So, after resting an hour, I set out for Brecon."* It is unfortunate that Aberdare had not been ready for this second visit.

A.V. Jones

TITUS JONES OF LLANWONNO, BY "GLANFFRWD"

"Glanffrwd" of Llanwonno – Rev. William Thomas 1843-90, tells us that a preacher named Titus Jones also of Llanwonno, kept a school in his own house for many years during the 1860's. He was heard to say in a sermon on the evils of smoking tobacco – *"If God had intended you to smoke, he would have put a flue at the top of your head!"* His voice often rose during a sermon; it was a kind of squeaking tenor sound, and when he shouted as he often did, the effects were unpleasant in the extreme. He also frequently caught his hands on fire displaying the effects of hell to the Sunday school children!

Rev. William Thomas, "Glanffrwd", 1888

A CONVERTED DRUNK

"I have to thank God for sending the Salvation Army to the town. Since then, I have been a happy man. I would do anything, and go through fire and water for a beer; but Hallelujah! – now I have joined the Salvation Army, God has made me a new man. Not only that, but He has turned my home from a drunkard's home to a happy home; from a blaspheming home to a praying home. Hallelujah!"
This man is now our standard bearer. Lord Bless Him.

Woodland Street,
Mountain Ash, 1878

Refer to chapel reference number 62 for further details of the Salvation Army in the Cynon Valley.

A.V. Jones, 2003

WHY WAS GREEN FACH (near the Aberdare Central Library), SO CALLED?

The second Green Street English Wesleyan Chapel, Aberdare, built in 1859 during the Great Religious Revival, stands on ground once occupied by The Swan Inn, together with an adjacent shop and cottage. These were all burned down in September 1858 and the site was soon after purchased Freehold by the Methodists, for £266. The name of the chapel – Green Street E.W.M., is due to the fact that at one time there stood in front of the Green Dragon Inn (opened 1835; closed 1961) two cottages with a small green in the front; hence the name of the area was known as Green Fach (Little Green). One of the cottages was used by the vicar, Father David Davies of St. John's Church, Aberdare.

A.V. Jones, 2003

NOISE DISRUPTS CHAPEL SERVICES

In 1911 a cloud came over the Cause at Trinity W.P. Chapel, Aberdare, and the chapel was compelled, with great reluctance, to take out legal proceedings against the Empire Company Ltd., Aberdare. This action was for the removal of a gas engine the noise from which disturbed all meetings that were held in the lecture hall. The case was conducted successfully but the company later went into liquidation and the court costs fell upon the chapel. It was not until 1923 that this financial burden was lifted and paid off.

Rev. Glaslyn Bowen, (Minister 1966-92)

Noise of a different kind disrupted services in 1913 at Providence E.C. chapel, Mountain Ash. On behalf of the chapel the secretary was instructed to write to Mr Dan Bailey, secretary of the nearby Hibernian Club in Pryce Street, complaining of the disturbance caused by the Brass Band during their practice sessions which coincided with the Sunday evening services. The club respectfully changed the times of their practice session, and all ended well!

A.V. Jones, 2003

CONTROVERSIAL SUNDAY TRIPS TO THE SEASIDE

A Sunday train excursion to Barry Island was so popular that hundreds of adults and children took part. The result was that Sunday services at local places of worship were affected. It was decided therefore to hold a United Prayer Meeting in the locality on a Sunday morning just as the trippers would be passing nearby. The object of this assembly was to shame the excursionists, but it failed in its objective. One Sunday morning just after a packed train of almost 700 travellers had left the station, the Station Master, as he came up past the meeting, was stopped by one of the ministers who was taking part in the proceedings, and the following dialogue ensued: -

Minister: *"Do you know Sir that you have just booked hundreds of people to Hell on this Sabbath morning?"*

To this accusation the Station Master, with a twinkle in his eye, replied – *"Well, if I have there is a hope that they will all come back, as every one of them has a return ticket, which some of your folk wont be able to obtain when they go on their journey to that certain warm climate!"*

Reminiscences of William Rhys Jones, Cwmaman. 1946

DECEASED BECOMES AN EXPERT MUSICIAN

A local minister visited a friend whose husband had just passed away. Placing his hand on her shoulder he said –*"Do not weep dear sister for your beloved Tom, he is now in Heaven in a white gown among the angels playing hymns of glory on a Golden Harp."*

Looking up at the minister, the lady replied – *"That's very strange Reverend, he must have learned to play a harp very quickly as he couldn't even play a tin whistle here on earth. Furthermore, he wouldn't wear even a white shirt with me, but always insisted on having real Welsh flannel ones!"*

William Rhys Jones, 1946

DEACONS SHAME RELUCTANT GIVERS

Speaking to his Deacons prior to their going round the congregation to collect the Sunday offertory, the minister advised them in the hearing of all present to say – *"Thank you if during the collection a penny was put in the box; if they saw three pence, thank you very much, but if they saw a shilling or more to say loudly – Diolch yn fawr – Thank you ever so much!"*

A.V. Jones, 2003

IT'S HEAVEN FOR THOSE WITHOUT TEETH

During a Sunday service, a minister described the fate of those who would not be saved by saying there would be much weeping, wailing and gnashing of teeth in Hell. The effect on the mind of one child was somewhat amusing, as the little girl was heard to say – *"My dear Grand-Pa is bound to be in Heaven then, as he has left his false teeth behind and has no teeth to gnash with!"*

William Rhys Jones, 1946.

Stop-Tap Saves a Casual Drinker

During the 1904-05 Religious Revival, a revivalist shouted out to a man entering a Public House –

"There you go, starting on the road to damnation."

"No", replied the man, *"I am only going in for a pint."*

The revivalist answered – *"You are entering the gate to Hell, my brother."*

The man retaliated by saying – *"You need not worry friend if I am, because they will turn me out at ten o'clock when it is stop-tap!"*

A.V. Jones, 2002

The Prodigal Son Returns

A preacher known for his vivid and descriptive sermons was one day preaching on the story of The Prodigal Son. So graphically did he depict the return of The Prodigal Son, that when he pointed towards the front door of the chapel and said –*"Look, there he cometh through the door!"* – All the congregation turned their heads towards the door, carried away by his descriptive eloquence.

William Rhys Jones, 1946.

The Peg-Legged Preacher

It is not often that one hears of a minister of The Gospel with a wooden leg. The preacher, Rhys Davies who died circa 1850, however did have one. Few indeed must be those who can claim to have lost a leg or limb solely in the performance of their office as a Preacher. Rhys of The Wooden Leg was remembered in his village as having a hasty temper and, it was said, his tempestuous method of preaching was almost delivered at hurricane force. When in the pulpit his whole body shook, every part and every limb. He frothed at the mouth, he spat, he shouted, he jumped. Indeed he did most things that could be done within the confines of so narrow a stage. It was in one such emotional extreme while preaching with great passion in the pulpit, that he lost his leg. Gripped and possessed by the mounting rapture of a Revival Meeting in the 1840's he jumped high in his overwhelming joy, and whilst in the air performed a movement that no one not of the feline order, and certainly no human being with only two legs should permit himself to perform. He came down heavily and awkwardly on one of his legs and injured it, but he paid no attention to it at the time. It is doubtful whether he knew an injury had been received, for he had been spiritually lifted up to levels where pain is not felt. Neglected while he was in this state, his foot became swollen in his shoe with the result that when Rhys returned to the realm where legs mattered, it unfortunately had to be amputated. From that day on he carried for the rest of his life, evidence of the explosive power of the rapture which, like the blast of a bomb had hurled him sky-high in the pulpit.

Extract from *"Welsh Country Characters – Old Welsh Preachers."* D. Parry Jones, 1952.
Courtesy of The Fynnon Press, Cheshire.

Minister Almost Drowns Converts

In his enthusiasm and emotion a local minister of the 1860's got carried away while baptising members of his congregation in the nearby river. He immersed the converts not once or twice, but six or seven times, repeating the words of The Holy Scripture each time. The unfortunate converts became desperately breathless and near to drowning as the absent-minded minister held them under the water for long periods at a time.

A.V. Jones, 2003

The Bow and Arrow Preacher

H. V. Morton tells us that when John Elias (1774-1841) – "The Prince of Preachers", was preaching in the open air to a large gathering, he described how God let fly an arrow from his bow. So great was his emotional power that as he spoke the gathering parted to allow passage for the shaft!

With acknowledgement to H. V. Morton, 1932.

(iii) POEMS

CHAPEL.

Grey, stone-faced, gloomy,
No-Fun-Day, – Sunday,
-No laughing on Sunday.
- . . **CHAPEL!!**

Windows winking in the
setting sunlight,
double doors, wide open,
yawn a bible-boring invitation
to the solemn-faced and
sober-faithful,
talking quiet on the patient pavement.
- •   No laughing on Sunday,
- •   **CHAPEL!!**

Dafydd Morgans, (Deacon), shirt starched,
and false-teeth fitted, stands on the top step,
calloused hand half-raised in limpid welcome.
Brown-striped best suit, (-with waistcoat and tie!)
worn weekly for **CHAPEL, –** otherwise only for funerals!
Brown boots, polished shining, leather-laced and tied tidy.
•   No laughing on Sunday, – . . **CHAPEL!!**

Silent, sitting in the side-pews, – me,
sandwiched thin between Dai and Edith.
"No talking boy, or shifting your feet"!
Stand, when the non-conforming organ
bursts enthusiastic into painted praise!
Roof ringing with the hwyl of Chapel singing.
 No laughing on Sunday,. . **CHAPEL!!**

"Put the "sixpence-in-the-envelope"
into the collection box, – careful!"
"Close your book, – quiet!". – Service ended . . .
"Wait for the deacons to leave the "Set Fawr'," . . .
"Don't push!".
"Shake hands with the Minister, and say "Sir", nicely."
"Rush home quick and change your clothes!"
" – No laughing on Sunday, . . . **CHAPEL!!**

Escape at last,
to the living, warm, loving, sinful World outside,
and thank God
for six whole, unholy, laughing, fun-days, before
the next grey, stone-faced, gloomy, un-fun-day Sunday!
- No laughing on Sunday,
. . . CHAPEL!!

From *"Off on a Tangent"* by Brynmor Evans – 1999, – reproduced here with his kind permission.
Brynmor is currently (2004) Secretary of The Cynon Valley History Society.

Playing Ball Games on The Sabbath

"Whoever here on Sunday
Will Practice playing at ball,
It may be before Monday
The Devil will Have You All".

Inscription on the walls of the little Baptist Chapel at Llanfair Discoed, Gwent.

THE CHAPEL

A little aside from the main road,
becalmed in a last-century greyness,
there is the chapel, ugly, without the appeal
to the tourist to stop in his car
and visit it. The traffic goes by,
and the river goes by, and quick shadows
of clouds, too, and the chapel settles
a little deeper into the grass.

But here once on an evening like this,
in the darkness that was about
his hearers, a preacher caught fire
and burned steadily before them
with a strange light, so that they saw
the splendour of the barren mountains
about them and sang their amens
fiercely, narrow but saved
in a way that men are not now.

Poem by R. S. Thomas
From – *"Wales – An Anthology"*
With acknowledgement to Alice Thomas Ellis and William Collins & Co. Ltd., Publishers

TEN THOUSAND INSTANT CHRISTIANS

Welsh entertainer Max Boyce writes: -
"One of the great influences on the Welsh way of life has undoubtedly been the tradition of the
"Chapels". It is therefore sad to see their decline and sadder still to see them converted into bingo
halls and the like.

I remember one Rugby International in which we'd been singing the old Sunday school
favourites in the pubs of Cardiff all the morning: "Rwyn canu fel cana'r aderyn", "Draw draw yn
China". Then again at the ground it was Welsh hymns that rang from the terraces: "Cwm
Rhondda" and "Calon Lan".

It seemed strangely sad therefore that on the way back from the match we should pass a Chapel
with a sign outside which said "FOR SALE".

Seeing that sign influenced me to write this song."

When He sees the Hope & Anchor where we sang before the game,
Where "Cwm Rhondda" and "Delilah" first sounded both the same.
The bar was filled with singing, and the songs came on a tray.
And Saturday was Sunday; I wonder what He'll say?

When He sees the North Enclosure with its belly-full of ale,
And sees that male-voice flagon, sing to the twisted barrier-rail.
"Cwm Rhondda" and "Penmachno" – hymns of yesterday –
But only half-remembered, I wonder what He'll say.

When He sees those touch-line tenors, with their copies made of sand:
Ten thousand instant Christians, and the Glynneath Silver Band.
"Come on mun, Ref., for goodness sake, the ball was still in play,"
Ten thousand instant Christians, I wonder what He'll say.

When He sees that empty chapel with its locked and shuttered doors,
And sees that dusty Bible, cobweb-covered floors.
The numbers slowly dwindling, much fewer now each day:
Calfaria now a bingo-hall, I wonder what He'll say.

From – *"I Was There"* by Max Boyce, 1979
Reproduced with his kind permission.

ODE TO A NEW CHAPEL ORGAN
(Ebenezer Welsh Congregational Chapel, Trecynon 1938)

ORGAN NEWYDD, EBENEZER

Ebenezer! Eglwys annwyl,
Iddi nawr y canaf glod,
Am ei llwyddiant gyda'i gorchwyl
O gael Organ, oedd ei nôd,
Help fydd hwn i'r gynulleidfa
Gyda'i mawl i Achos Duw
Nes gwneud teimlad yr holl oedfa
Yn fwy gwresog ac yn fyw.

E. Treharne (Local bard)
(Verse 1 of 4)

TRANSLATED:

Ebenezer! Beloved chapel
Praises now to you we sing,
On obtaining a new organ
Greater fervour now we bring,
Faithful now are much assisted
In their praise of God's Great Cause,
Congregational expression
Warmer, livelier, without pause.

Rhown ein diolch i'r casgluddion
Am ei gwaith mewn modd diflino,
Mynd o gwmpas trwy bob tywydd
Dros ei Eglwys heb ddiffugio.

E. Treharne 1938

TRANSLATED:

Grateful thanks to fund collectors
Steadfast, constant and untiring,
Struggling out in stormy weather
Proud to follow chapel's bidding.

Translation (free) by Elfed Bowen

OUR HERITAGE

We welcome you this morning
 To join us in our praise –
And thanks for all "Moriah"
 Has done in bygone days.

We feel a cloud of witnesses
 Surround us, from the past,
For saintly men and women
 Set out to do a task.

They built, upon the hill, this Church
 A hundred years ago,
And since that time it's had its days
 Of happiness and woe.

But always, Lord, Thou hast been there
 Their Captain and their Guide
To help them keep – through all the years
 The Church doors open wide.

Not only past endeavours now
 But future hopes and plans
We would commit, both old and young
 To use us, through Thy hands.

And as the future years unfold
 To help us carry on
And follow in the steps of those
 Who to Thy home have gone.

So keep us true to Thee, O Lord
 And all the Church holds dear
For we are all Thy family
 However far or near.

Poem by Mrs. Flo Harris and reproduced here with her kind permission. The poem was written in 1993 to commemorate the Centenary of the beginning of The "Cause" of Moriah English Baptist Chapel, Abercynon. Mrs Harris is an Elder of the chapel and celebrates her 92nd birthday in November 2004.

HOW THE CHAPELS WERE BUILT

The Trellwyn Methodists have built a church,
The front looks like an Abbey,
But thinking they can fool the Lord
They've built the back part shabby.

From *"The Sand in The Glass"*, with acknowledgements to the author,
Michael Llewellyn, and to John Murray (Publishers) Ltd., 1943.

CAPEL CALVIN

There's holy holy people
They are in Capel bach –
They don't like surpliced choirs,
They don't like Sospan Fach.

They don't like Sunday concerts,
Or women playing ball,
They don't like William Parry much
Or Shakespeare at all.

They don't like beer or bishops,
Or pictures without texts,
They don't like any other
Of the Nonconformist sects.

And when they go to Heaven,
They won't like that too well,
For the music will be sweeter
Than the music played in Hell.

Poem by Idris Davies (1905-53)
From – *"Wales – An Anthology"*
with acknowledgement to Alice Thomas Ellis,
and William Collins & Co. Ltd., Publishers. 1991.

CHAPELS IN GLAMORGAN

Once there were Sundays when chapels were young,
And streets glowed with Sunday faces,
Old and young hymn-wise and carefree
Roamed to and fro The Holy Places.
Now, at street corners and between houses,
Chapels stand windowless and silent.
Nocturnal lights shatter their darkness,
And behind naked walls scattered glass
Lies buried in footprints of moss and memories.
They are falling one by one – obsolete
And broken they fall to Prosperity.
From – *"The Night's Prison"*, by Robert Morgan,
Welsh miner and schoolmaster, 1967.

With kind permission of Gomer Press, Llandysul, Ceredigion.

BAND OF HOPE & TEMPERANCE

"We are Temperance Children,
Dwelling midst the hills,
Working for our Master,
Doing all He wills.

To make the people sober
Is our one great aim,
We are always anxious,
Drunkards to reclaim."

Anon. (circa 1860)

(Sunday school teachers warned the children of the dangers of strong drink by singing songs about orphans crying for their drunken fathers.)

OLD WELSH CAROL
(verses 1 and 5 from 5)

Awn i Fethlem, bawb dan ganu
neidio, dawnsio a difyrru
i gael gweld ein Prynwr c'redig
aned heddiw, Dydd Nadolig.

Awn i Fethlem I gael gweled
y rhyfeddod mwya' wnaethped
gwneuthur Duw yn ddyn naturiol
i gael marw dros ei bobol.

TRANSLATED

To Bethlehem with dance and song
We journey as a joyous throng
To see and worship, if we may
Our Saviour born on Christmas day.

To Bethlehem, and there to see
The greatest wonder that could be
God is there, as baby small
To live, then die, to save us all.

Rhys Prichard 1579-1644
Translation (free) by Elfed Bowen

(iv) Facts – "FIGURE It Out".

1700 – The number of members Rev. Thomas Humphreys baptised between 1868 -1910. He was the minister of Sion W.B., Cwmaman for 42 years, and the longest serving at Sion. He died in 1911.

4 – Pounds per month was the salary received by Rev. Robert Owen, minister of Bethlehem W.I., Abercwmboi, in 1860.

38 – Memorial Foundation stones are located on the lower front façade of Noddfa W.B. Trecynon; they depict names of individuals from all professions and walks of life.

65 – The number of years Mr. Edward Moses was organist at Tabernacle E.C., Aberdare from 1888 up to his death in 1953. His services were carried out without remuneration; truly a "labour of love". The longest serving organist in one chapel anywhere in the valley, he kept a grocer shop on the corner of Cross Street, Aberdare

4500 – Sunday school scholars from various local chapels marched through Aberdare town proudly displaying their respective banners. This took place in August 1880 during the Annual Procession of Sunday Schools.

1500 – The number of pipes (approx.) contained in the pipe organ at Green Street E. W. M., Aberdare. One of the largest organs built in the Cynon Valley.

20000 – Pounds was the cost of rebuilding the above organ in 1993.

39 – Different categories of religious denominations exist throughout the Cynon Valley. (See appendix E).

117 – Is the number of years served by the first three ministers of Siloa W. Cong., Aberdare. Rev. Dr. David Price, 1843-78; Rev. David Silyn Evans, 1880-1930; Rev. Ivor Parry, 1933-65.

1751 – The year Hen-Dy-Cwrdd, Unitarian Chapel, Trecynon was founded. "The old Meeting House".

9000 – New converts were added to 67 Independent Chapels in South Wales in only three months during the summer of 1849 in the Religious Revival of that year.

110000 – The number of new members received during the Religious Revival 1859.

80000 – Converts were made during the Religious Revival 1904-05.

60000 – Is the number of converts out of the above 80000 that had fallen away by 1912, leading to a general decline in chapel membership during this period throughout Wales.

1000 – Up to this figure was the number of people attending Chapel Tea Meetings during the nineteenth and early twentieth centuries.

127 – Chapels were built between 1751 and 1900.

1689 – Was the year that Dissenters began holding meetings at the Cwm-y-Glo Conventicle, near Merthyr.

15 – Chapels were demolished throughout the Cynon Valley during 1991-2000.

1596 – The number of baptisms performed by Rev. Dr. Thomas Price, minister of Calvaria W. B., Aberdare during his ministry there 1846-88. He died in 1888, aged 68 years.

50 – Is the number of years served by Rev. David Silyn Evans (b.1850 d.1930) during his ministry at Siloa W. Cong., Aberdare from 1880 to1930.

2145 – Pounds was the staggering amount of debt finally cleared by unemployed members of Trinity W.P., Aberdare in 1934.

900 – The number of children in the Sunday School of Ramoth W.B., Hirwaun in 1904.

524 – Adult members were on the role at the above chapel during 1904. The huge numbers of both children and adults were as a result of the Religious Revival of 1904-05.

2975 – Pounds was the cost of rebuilding Bethel W.Cong., Gadlys in 1913. The chapel was demolished ninety years later in 2003.

52 – The number of years Rev. William Samlet Davies was minister at Horeb W.I., Llwydcoed, from 1871 to 1923. He died in 1923, aged 87 years.

3000 – Was the number of pounds debt cleared in 1947 at Noddfa W.B., Trecynon.

1774 – The year that Rev. William Thomas ("Glanffrwd") tells us the first public worship was held in Ynysybwl at a cottage named "Rhyd-Y-Gwreiddyn" (translated: "source of the stream). The cottage was located west of Fanheulog and about one mile south west of Ynysybwl, following the River Ffrwd.

1 – Shilling per week (5p) was a chapel caretaker's wage in 1847, rising to six shillings per week in 1912.

62 – The number of years Miss M.S. Jones was a Sunday School teacher at Moriah E.B., Abercynon, from 1922 to 1984.

50 – Is the exact number of years Handel Davies was organist at Carmel W.I., Penrhiwceiber from 1930 to 1980. He died in 1982.

900+ – The seating capacity of Saron W.I., Aberaman. At just over 900 seats this chapel is the largest in the Cynon Valley.

3 – Shillings (15p) was the amount received by a visiting preacher in 1848.

6 – Public Houses surrounded Green Street E.W.M. chapel, Aberdare in the 1850's.

34 – Percent of the total of chapels built in the Cynon Valley have been converted (50) or remain vacant (11).

1749 – The year that John Wesley the great Methodist founder, visited Aberdare.

1304 – Sunday School scholars belonging to Tabernacle E. Cong., Aberdare journeyed by train to Swansea Bay for the annual outing.

12 – Miles per hour was the maximum speed allowed for charabancs in the 1920's.

67 – The number of chapels built in the valley between 1751 and 1860.

56 – Chapels have been demolished out of a total of 180 built since 1751.

131 – Teachers taught 1200 Sunday School scholars at Calvaria W. B., Aberdare, in1863.

35 – Percent of chapels remain active and open for public worship throughout the Valley, i.e. 63 chapels out of a total of 180 as at Autumn 2004.

1642 – Was the year that Nonconformity in and around our locality began at Blaencanaid, located between Abernant and Heolgerrig, near Merthyr.

4 – Percent was the average fee of architects preparing chapel plans around 1904-1912. e.g. £90 fee to draw plans of Providence E. Cong., Mountain Ash for a building cost of £2250, built in 1912.

18 – Is the number of Grade II "Listed Buildings" throughout the Cynon Valley.

9770 – Pipes are contained in the 150 ton organ at The Royal Albert Hall, London. They measure a total of nine miles laid end to end.

16 – Burial grounds are attached to various Nonconformist chapels throughout the valley.

100 – The number pf gallons of soup distributed each day, three days a week to the poor at the Soup Kitchens during 1879.

10 – Pounds per month was the average salary of a minister in 1915.

1670 – The number of cholera cases in the Parish of Aberdare between 26th May and 18th July 1849. Out of these, 632 died.

12 – The number of hours a Meeting took place, 10.30 a.m. to 11.00 p.m. without a break at Bethania W.Cong., Mountain Ash, during   the 1859 Religious Revival.

253 – Is the number of years Nonconformity has been present in our Valley, i.e. 1751 to 2004

53 – Chapels were built in the Valley between 1900 to 2004.

105 – The number of Welsh-speaking chapels built in the Valley.

75 – The number of English-speaking chapels built in the Valley.

31 – Percent of the total of 180 chapels built have been demolished (i.e. 56)

6700 – Is the estimated number of chapels built in Wales up to 1915.

9 – Percent of people who attended a place of worship in Wales went to an Anglican Church. (1851 Census)

87 – Percent of people who attended a place of worship in Wales went to Nonconformist Chapels. (1851 Census)

33 – Is the percentage of the population of Wales who attended either Chapel or Church, in 1851.

47 – Is the number of Baptist Chapels built in the Cynon Valley, (30 Welsh, 17 English). 26% of the total of 180 built.

43 – The number of Independent Congregational Chapels built in the Cynon Valley, (35 Welsh, 8 English). 24% of the total built.

38 – The number of Methodist Chapels built in the Cynon Valley, (24 Welsh, 14 English). 21% of the total built.

(v) A Fond Farewell to the Chapels of Yesteryear

"Alas, we must now say farewell to too many of these fallen Temples, and we turn away from their decaying former stout walls with longing and sadness. May they never be destroyed! Stand firmly and upright in your old age you grey tired walls, like the greying heads of the devout stalwarts of the past. May the birds nest and keep you company in your crumbled old ruins, and the gentle breeze of summer and winter sing among your remains as once the strains of familiar hymns were lovingly heard with fond emotion. May nature's green moss thrive and spread on your fallen walls like a warm blanket, and let the sprawling ivy and thick brambles of the ages cosset you and make protective forts around you. The murmuring sounds of the fussy little brook nearby, rambling its crooked course to join the Afon Cynon will greet you and awaken you each morning, and young saplings will embrace you and grow near and around you and give strength and support to your ailing foundations. Let the rains from Heaven above clean and freshen your ruined dusty weak walls, and may you stand proudly while you are able in your greying creaking years until at the last hour you fall together with your old cousins and neighbours – the lost Stately Homes and Mansions of the Valley; in the day when all things visible and tangible will cease to exist, and all that remains are the distant happy memories faintly echoing from the decaying timbers and broken walls that once shook with passion, and trembled with the sweet harmonious strains of song and glorious praise!"

Alan Vernon Jones
Autumn 2004.
(With undertones of "Glanffrwd").

APPENDIX A

MAP OF CYNON VALLEY.

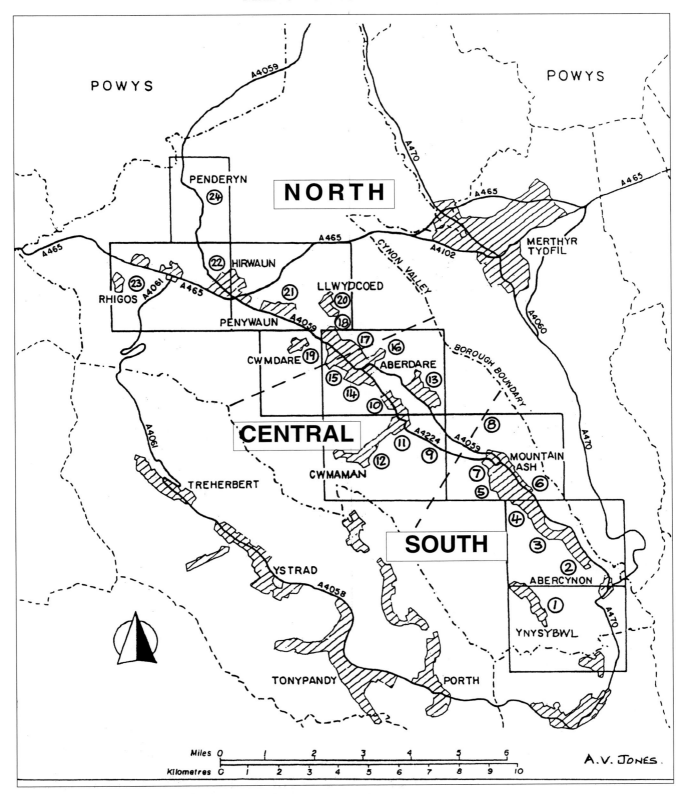

A.V. JONES.

APPENDIX B

SCHEDULE OF LOCATIONS AND TOWNS
AS SHOWN ON MAP OF CYNON VALLEY.

Region.	Location Reference.	Town	Number of Chapels.	Total
SOUTH	1	Ynysybwl	11	
	2	Abercynon	11	
	3	Ynysboeth	4	
	4	Penrhiwceiber	9	69
	5	Miskin	11	
	6	Newtown	2	
	7	Mountain Ash	19	
	8	Cefnpennar	2	
CENTRAL	9	Abercwmboi	3	
	10	Aberaman	16	
	11	Godreaman	6	
	12	Cwmaman	7	
	13	Cwmbach	10	66
	14	Aberdare	18	
	15	Gadlys	3	
	16	Abernant	3	
NORTH	17	Robertstown	2	
	18	Trecynon	12	
	19	Cwmdare	5	
	20	Llwydcoed	3	45
	21	Penywaun	2	
	22	Hirwaun	13	
	23	Rhigos	3	
	24	Penderyn	5	

TOTAL NUMBER OF CHAPELS & OTHER PLACES OF NON-CONFORMIST RELIGIOUS WORSHIP IN THE CYNON VALLEY BOROUGH – 180.

APPENDIX C

THE 180 CHAPELS IN ALPHABETICAL ORDER.

NAME OF CHAPEL	LOCALITY	CHAPEL REF. NO.	PAGE NO.	DENOMINATION
Abernant-y-Groes Uchaf	Cwmbach	94	86	Un.
Aberdare Kingdom Hall	Cwmbach	95	88	J.W.
Apostolic (Christian Centre)	Trecynon	123	120	A.C.
Apostolic Church	Penrhiwceiber	26	24	A.C.
Apostolic Church	Aberaman	172	162	A.C.
Apostolic Church	Cwmbach	173	162	A.C.
Apostolic Church	Abernant	174	162	A.C.
Apostolic Church	Mountain Ash	175	162	A.C.
Apostolic Church	Hirwaun	176	162	A.C.
Bethania	Abercynon	11	13	W.I.
Bethania	Mountain Ash	48	44	W.I.
Bethania	Cwmbach	96	88	W.B.
Bethania	Aberdare	103	94	C.M
Bethany	Godreaman	84	76	E.C.
Bethel	Ynysybwl	1	3	C.M.
Bethel	Penrhiwceiber	27	25	W.W.M.
Bethel	Miskin	35	33	W.I.
Bethel	Cwmaman	89	81	P.M.
Bethel	Gadlys	117	112	W.Cong.
Bethel	Abernant	120	116	W.B.
Bethel	Penywaun	142	143	P.C.
Bethel (Old)	Hirwaun	144	144	W.C.M.
Bethel (New)	Hirwaun	145	146	W.C.M.
Bethel	Rhigos	156	156	W.M.
Bethel (Old)	Penderyn	158	158	W.B.
Bethel (New)	Penderyn	159	158	W.B.
Bethesda	Penrhiwceiber	28	26	E.B.
Bethesda	Miskin	36	34	E.M.
Bethesda	Abercwmboi	68	60	W.B.
Bethesda	Abernant	121	117	W.I.
Bethesda	Hirwaun	146	146	A.C.
Bethlehem	Mountain Ash	49	45	C.M.
Bethlehem	Abercwmboi	69	62	W.I.
Beulah	Aberaman	71	63	E.B.
Brethren Meeting Room	Trecynon	179	164	B.M.R.
Brotherhood	Mountain Ash	50	46	L..C.
Bryngolwg (Mission Hall)	Miskin	37	35	E.F.C.
Bryn Moriah, Ysgoldy	Cwmaman	170	162	W.I.
Bryn Seion	Mountain Ash	51	46	W.W.M.

NAME OF CHAPEL	LOCALITY	CHAPEL REF. NO.	PAGE NO.	DENOMINATION
Bryn Seion (Welsh)	Cwmbach	97	89	W.I.
Bryn Seion (English)	Cwmbach	98	91	E.C.
Bryn Seion (Ysgoldy)	Cwmbach	99	91	W.B.
Bryn Sion (Now Carmel E.B.)	Trecynon	124	121	E.B.
Calfaria	Rhigos	157	157	W.I.
Calvaria	Abercynon	12	14	W.B.
Calvaria	Aberdare	104	95	W.B.
Cana	Penywaun	143	143	W.I.
Canaan	Miskin	38	36	E.C.
Capel Bryn Moriah	Cefnpennar	67	60	W.Cong.
Carmel	Abercynon	13	15	W.W.M.
Carmel	Ynysboeth	22	23	E.M.
Carmel	Penrhiwceiber	29	27	W.I.
Carmel	Aberdare	105	97	E.B.
Carmel	Trecynon	125	122	C.M.
Carmel (Ysgol Sabbothol)	Cwmbach	100	92	W.I.
Central Forward Movement	Abercynon	14	16	F.M.
Christadelphian Hall	Miskin	39	37	C.H.
Christadelphian Hall	Aberaman	163	162	C.H.
Christadelphian Hall	Aberdare	164	162	C.H.
Christ Church	Gadlys	118	114	E.B.
Church of Christ	Godreaman	180	164	E.B.
Cwmdare Mission Hall	Cwmdare	134	135	M.H.
Ebenezer	Ynysybwl	2	4	W.W.M.
Ebenezer	Mountain Ash	52	47	P.M.
Ebenezer	Cwmbach	101	92	C.M.
Ebenezer	Trecynon	127	125	W.I.
Elim	Aberdare	106	99	P.C.
Elim	Cwmdare	135	136	W.Cong.
Emmanuel	Trecynon	126	124	E.F.C.
English C.M.	Mountain Ash	53	48	E.C.M.
English Cong.	Ynysybwl	3	5	E.C.
English Cong.	Abercynon	15	17	E.C.
English Baptist	Cefnpennar	66	59	E.B
English Wesleyan.	Abercynon	16	18	E.W.M.
English Wesleyan.	Mountain Ash	54	49	E.W.M.
English Wesleyan.	Aberaman	72	64	E.W.M.
English Wesleyan.	Aberdare	107	100	E.W.M.
English Wesleyan.	Trecynon	128	127	E.W.M.
English Wesleyan.	Hirwaun	147	146	E.W.M.
Ffrwd	Mountain Ash	55	50	W.B.
Ffrwd Ysgoldy	Mountain Ash	56	51	W.B.M.R.

NAME OF CHAPEL	LOCALITY	CHAPEL REF. NO.	PAGE NO.	DENOMINATION
Gadlys W. B.	Gadlys	119	115	W.B.
Gospel Hall.	Ynysybwl	4	5	G.H.
Gospel Hall.	Miskin	40	38	G.H.
Graig Street Methodist	Abercwmboi	70	63	E.M.
Gwawr.	Aberaman	73	66	W.B.
Gwawr (was Hebron C.M.)	Godreaman	85	77	W.B.
Hebron	Ynysboeth	23	23	W. Cong.
Hen-Dy-Cwrdd	Trecynon	129	128	Un.
Heol-Y-Felin	Trecynon	130	130	W.B.
Hermon	Penrhiwceiber	30	29	W.C.M.
Highland Place	Aberdare	108	101	Un.
Hope	Penrhiwceiber	31	30	P.M.
Hope Sunday School	Cwmdare	136	137	W.B.
Horeb	Llwydcoed	139	140	W.I.
Islamic Centre	Robertstown	171	162	IS.
Jerusalem	Ynysybwl	5	7	W.P.
Jerusalem	Penrhiwceiber	32	31	W.B.
Jerusalem	Penderyn	160	159	W.C.M.
Jewish Synagogue	Aberdare	178	164	J.S.
Libanus	Aberaman	74	67	W.C.M.
Miskin Baptist.	Miskin	41	38	E.B.
Methodist Chapel (Elim).	Miskin (Perthcelyn)	42	38	E.W.M.
Mission Room	Hirwaun	148	147	M.R.
Moriah	Abercynon	17	19	E.B.
Moriah	Penrhiwceiber	33	32	C.M.
Moriah	Llwydcoed	140	141	W.C.M
Moriah Aman	Cwmaman	90	82	W.I.
Mormon Church	Hirwaun Aberdare Cwmbach	177	162	M.
Mortuary Chapel	Aberdare	109	103	E.C./ D.C.
Mortuary Chapel	Mountain Ash	57	51	M.C.
Mount Pisgah	Miskin	43	40	E.B.
Mount Pleasant	Hirwaun	149	148	E.C.
Mount Zion	Abercynon	18	20	E.B.
Nazareth	Mountain Ash	58	52	E.B
Nazareth	Abercynon	19	20	W.B.
Nazareth	Aberdare	110	103	W.C.M

NAME OF CHAPEL	LOCALITY	CHAPEL REF. NO.	PAGE NO.	DENOMINATION
Nebo (old)	Cwmdare	137	138	W.B.
Nebo Newydd ("new") was Gobaith CM.	Cwmdare	138	138	W.B.
Nebo	Hirwaun	150	149	W.I.
Noddfa	Ynysybwl	6	8	W.B.
Noddfa (Elim)	Mountain Ash	59	53	P.C.
Noddfa	Godreaman	86	78	W.I.
Noddfa	Trecynon	131	131	W.B.
Pentecostal	Godreaman	87	80	P.C.
Pentecostal Church	Aberaman	75	68	P.C.
Pentwyn Gospel Hall	Trecynon	132	132	G.H.
Penuel	Penrhiwceiber	34	32	E.P.
Penuel (Ysgol Beddyddwr)	Cwmbach	102	93	W.B.
Presbyterian Church	Ynysybwl	7	9	E.P.
Providence	Mountain Ash	60	54	E.C.
Ramoth	Hirwaun	151	150	W.B.
Rhos	Mountain Ash	61	55	W.B.
Saint David's	Aberdare	111	105	E.P.
Salem	Godreaman	88	80	W.B.
Salem	Robertstown	122	118	W.Cong.
Salvation Army Hall	Mountain Ash	62	56	S.A.
Salvation Army Hall	Aberdare	165	162	S.A.
Salvation Army Hall	Aberaman	166	162	S.A.
Salvation Army Hall	Rhigos	167	162	S.A.
Salvation Army Hall	Cwmaman	168	162	S.A.
Salvation Army Hall	Ynysybwl	169	162	S.A.
Saron Ysgoldy	Aberaman	76	69	W.I.
Saron	Aberaman	77	70	W.I.
School Room	Miskin	44	41	W.I.
Seiloh	Aberaman	78	71	C.M.
Siloa	Aberaman	79	72	E.W.M.
Siloa	Aberdare	113	106	W.Cong.
Siloam	Penderyn	161	160	W.B.
Siloh	Aberaman	80	73	A.C.
Siloh	Trecynon	133	133	W.I.
Sion	Cwmaman	91	83	W.B.
Sion	Aberdare	112	106	E.W.M.
Soar	Mountain Ash	63	57	W.I.
Soar	Cwmaman	92	84	W.C.M.
Soar	Aberdare	114	108	W.M.

NAME OF CHAPEL	LOCALITY	CHAPEL REF. NO.	PAGE NO.	DENOMINATION
Soar	Llwydcoed	141	142	W.B.
Soar	Hirwaun	152	152	W.W.M.
Soar	Penderyn	162	161	W.I.
Sunday School	Abercynon	20	21	W.C.M.
Sunday School	Miskin	45	41	E.B.
St. John's	Mountain Ash	64	58	S.C./ G.H.
Sunday School	Mountain Ash	65	59	P.C.
St. Margaret's	Aberaman	81	73	E.B.
Tabernacle	Ynysybwl	8	10	W.I.
Tabernacle	Abercynon	21	22	W.C.M.
Tabernacle	Ynysboeth	24	23	E.B.
Tabernacle	Aberaman	82	73	E.M.
Tabernacle	Aberdare	115	109	E.C.
Tabernacle	Hirwaun	153	153	W.I.
Trinity	Cwmaman	93	85	E.B.
Trinity	Aberdare	116	110	W.P.
Welsh Baptist	Newtown	46	42	W.B.
Wesleyan	Ynysybwl	9	11	E.W.M.
Ynysboeth Welsh Baptist	Ynysboeth	25	24	W.B.
Ynyslwyd	Aberaman	83	74	W.B.
Zion	Ynysybwl	10	12	E.B.
Zion	Newtown	47	43	P.M.
Zion (Old)	Hirwaun	154	155	E.B.
Zion (New)	Hirwaun	155	155	E.B.

APPENDIX D

SCHEDULE OF CHAPELS IN EACH TOWN AS SHOWN ON THE KEY MAP

SOUTH

REF.NO.	NAME	LOCATION & NO.	PAGE NO.
1	BETHEL	YNYSYBWL (1)	3
2	EBENEZER	"	4
3	ENGLISH CONG.	"	5
4	GOSPEL HALL	"	5
5	JERUSALEM	"	7
6	NODDFA	"	8
7	PRESBYTERIAN	"	9
169	SALVATION ARMY	"	162
8	TABERNACLE	"	10
9	WESLEYAN	"	11
10	ZION	"	12
11	BETHANIA	ABERCYNON (2)	13
12	CALVARIA	"	14
13	CARMEL	"	15
14	CENTRAL F.M.	"	16
15	ENGLISH CONG.	"	17
16	ENG. WESLEYAN	"	18
17	MORIAH	"	19
18	MOUNT ZION	"	20
19	NAZARETH	"	20
20	SUNDAY SCHOOL.	"	21
21	TABERNACLE	"	22
22	CARMEL	YNYSYBOETH (3)	23
23	HEBRON	"	23
24	TABERNACLE	"	23
25	YNYSYBOETH CHAPEL	"	24
26	APOSTOLIC CHURCH	PENRHIWCEIBER (4)	24
27	BETHEL	"	25
28	BETHESDA	"	26
29	CARMEL	"	27
30	HERMON	"	29
31	HOPE	"	30
32	JERUSALEM	"	31
33	MORIAH	"	32
34	PENUEL	"	32
35	BETHEL	MISKIN (5)	33
36	BETHESDA	"	34
37	BRYNGOLWG	"	35
38	CANAAN	"	36
39	CHRISTADELPHIAN	"	37
40	GOSPEL HALL	"	38
41	MISKIN BAPTIST	"	38
42	METHODIST CHAPEL	MISKIN (PERTHCELYN)	38
43	MOUNT PISGAH	MISKIN	40
44	SCHOOL ROOM	"	41
45	SUNDAY SCHOOL	"	41

REF.NO.	NAME	LOCATION & NO.	PAGE NO.
46	WELSH BAPTIST	NEWTOWN (6)	42
47	ZION	"	43
175	APOSTOLIC CHURCH	MOUNTAIN ASH (7)	162
48	BETHANIA	"	44
49	BETHLEHEM	"	45
50	BROTHERHOOD	"	46
51	BRYN SEION	"	46
52	EBENEZER	"	47
53	ENGLISH CALVINISTIC METHODIST	"	48
54	ENGLISH WESLEYAN	"	49
55	FFRWD	"	50
56	FFRWD YSGOLDY	"	51
57	MORTUARY CHAPEL	"	51
58	NAZARETH	"	52
59	NODDFA (ELIM)	"	53
60	PROVIDENCE	"	54
61	RHOS	"	55
62	SALVATION ARMY	"	56
63	SOAR	"	57
64	SAINT JOHN'S	"	58
65	SUNDAY SCHOOL	"	59
66	ENGLISH BAPTIST	CEFN PENNAR (8)	59
67	CAPEL BRYN MORIAH	"	60

CENTRAL

REF.NO.	NAME	LOCATION & NO.	PAGE NO.
68	BETHESDA	ABERCWMBOI (9)	60
69	BETHLEHEM	"	62
70	GRAIG ST. METHODIST	"	63
172	APOSTOLIC CHURCH	ABERAMAN (10)	162
71	BEULAH	"	63
163	CHRISTADELPHIAN	"	162
72	ENGLISH WESLEYAN	"	64
73	GWAWR	"	66
74	LIBANUS	"	67
75	PENTECOSTAL	"	68
166	SALVATION ARMY	"	162
76	SARON YSGOLDY	"	69
77	SARON	"	70
78	SEILOH	"	71
79	SILOA	"	72
80	SILOH	"	73
81	ST. MARGARET'S	"	73
82	TABERNACLE	"	73
83	YNYSLWYD	"	74
84	BETHANY	GODREAMAN (11)	76
180	CHURCH OF CHRIST	"	164
85	GWAWR	"	77
86	NODDFA	"	78
87	PENTECOSTAL	"	80
88	SALEM	"	80

REF.NO.	NAME	LOCATION & NO.	PAGE NO.
89	BETHEL	CWMAMAN (12)	81
170	BRYN MORIAH YSGOLDY	"	162
90	MORIAH AMAN	"	82
168	SALVATION ARMY	"	162
91	SION	"	83
92	SOAR	"	84
93	TRINITY	"	85
94	ABERNANT-Y-GROES	CWMBACH (13)	86
95	ABERDARE KINGDOM HALL	"	88
173	APOSTOLIC CHURCH	"	162
96	BETHANIA	"	88
97	BRYN SEION (WELSH)	"	89
98	BRYN SEION (ENGLISH)	"	91
99	BRYN SEION (YSGOLDY)	"	91
100	CARMEL YSGOL SABBATHOL	"	92
101	EBENEZER	"	92
102	PENUEL YSGOLDY BEDDYDDWR	"	93
103	BETHANIA	ABERDARE (14)	94
104	CALVARIA	"	95
105	CARMEL	"	97
164	CHRISTADELPHIAN	"	162
106	ELIM	"	99
107	ENGLISH WESLEYAN	"	100
178	JEWISH SYNAGOGUE	"	164
108	HIGHLAND PLACE	"	101
177	MORMON CHURCH	"	162
109	MORTUARY CHAPEL	"	103
110	NAZARETH	"	103
111	SAINT DAVID'S	"	105
165	SALVATION ARMY	"	162
112	SION	"	106
113	SILOA	"	106
114	SOAR	"	108
115	TABERNACLE	"	108
116	TRINITY	"	110
117	BETHEL	GADLYS (15)	112
118	CHRISTCHURCH	"	114
119	GADLYS	"	115
120	BETHEL	ABERNANT (16)	116
121	BETHESDA	"	117
174	APOSTOLIC CHURCH	"	162

NORTH

REF.NO.	NAME	LOCATION & NO.	PAGE NO.
122	SALEM	ROBERTSTOWN (17)	118
171	ISLAMIC CENTRE	"	162

REF.NO.	NAME	LOCATION & NO.	PAGE NO.
123	APOSTOLIC	TRECYNON (18)	120
179	BRETHREN MEETING ROOM	"	164
124	BRYN SION (CARMEL)	"	121
125	CARMEL	"	122
126	EMMANUEL	"	124
127	EBENEZER	"	125
128	ENGLISH WESLEYAN	"	127
129	HEN-DY-CWRDD	"	128
130	HEOL-Y-FELIN	"	130
131	NODDFA	"	131
132	PENTWYN GOSPEL HALL	"	132
133	SILOH	"	133
134	CWMDARE MISSION	CWMDARE (19)	135
135	ELIM	"	136
136	HOPE SUNDAY SCHOOL	"	137
137	NEBO (OLD)	"	138
138	NEBO NEWYDD	"	138
139	HOREB	LLWYDCOED (20)	140
140	MORIAH	"	141
141	SOAR	"	142
142	BETHEL	PENWAUN (21)	143
143	CANA	"	143
176	APOSTOLIC CHURCH	HIRWAUN (22)	162
144	BETHEL (OLD)	"	144
145	BETHEL (NEW)	"	146
146	BETHESDA	"	146
147	ENGLISH WESLEYAN	"	146
148	MISSION ROOM	"	147
149	MOUNT PLEASANT	"	148
150	NEBO	"	149
151	RAMOTH	"	150
152	SOAR	"	152
153	TABERNACLE	"	153
154	ZION (OLD)	"	155
155	ZION (NEW)	"	155
156	BETHEL	RHIGOS (23)	156
167	SALVATION ARMY	"	162
157	CALFARIA	"	157
158	BETHEL (OLD)	PENDERYN (24)	158
159	BETHEL (NEW)	"	158
160	JERUSALEM	"	159
161	SILOAM	"	160
162	SOAR	"	161

180 CHAPELS IN TOTAL.

APPENDIX E

ABBREVIATIONS USED TO DENOTE DENOMINATIONS

Apostolic Church	**A.C**
Baptist	**B.**
Brethren Meeting Room	**B.M.R.**
Congregational Chapel	**C.C.**
Calvinistic Methodist	**C.M.**
Christadelphian Hall	**C.H.**
English Baptist	**E.B.**
English Congregational	**E.C.**
English Calvinistic Methodist	**E.C.M.**
Episcopal Chapel / Dissenter's Chapel	**E.C./ D.C.**
Evangelical Free Church	**E.F.C.**
English Independent	**E.I.**
English Methodist	**E.M.**
English Presbyterian	**E.P.**
English Wesleyan Methodist	**E.W.M.**
Forward Movement	**F.M.**
Gospel Hall	**G.H.**
Islamic	**IS.**
Jehovah's Witness	**J.W.**
Jewish Synagogue	**J.S.**
Labour Church	**L.C.**
Mission Hall	**M.H.**
Mission Room	**M.R.**
Mormon	**M.**
Mortuary Chapel	**M.C.**
Pentecostal Church	**P.C.**
Primitive Methodist	**P.M.**
Salvation Army	**S.A.**
Spiritual Chapel / Gospel Hall	**S.C./ G.H.**
Unitarian	**Un.**
United Reformed Church	**U.R.C.**
Welsh Baptist	**W.B.**
Welsh Baptist Meeting Room	**W.B.M.R**
Welsh Calvinistic Methodist	**W.C.M.**
Welsh Congregational	**W.Cong.**
Welsh Independent	**W.I.**
Wesleyan Methodist	**W.M.**
Welsh Presbyterian	**W.P.**
Welsh Wesleyan Methodist	**W.W.M.**

APPENDIX F

RELIGIOUS DENOMINATIONS – A BRIEF DESCRIPTION

"There is only one religion though there are a hundred versions of it."

George Bernard Shaw
From "Arms and The Man", 1894

Apostolic

Relating to, deriving from or contemporary with the Apostles, or relating to the teachings of practice of the Apostles.

Baptist (Welsh or English)

A member of any of various Christian sects that affirm the necessity of baptism, usually of adults and by immersion, following a personal profession of the Christian faith. Mainly derived from early seventeenth century England and Wales. Proclaims the doctrine of adult or believing baptism as the condition of church membership, as opposed to infant baptism in which a child is made a church member by an adult on his behalf.

Brethren (Plymouth Brethren)

A Fundamental Religious Christian Protestant sect, characterised by extreme simplicity of belief, founded in Dublin in 1827 by Rev. John Nelson Darby (1800-1882). Strongly puritanical in outlook and prohibiting many secular occupations for its members. No ordained Priesthood. Three basic divisions. In 1848 a split occurred into open and closed Brethren

Open Brethren - restricts members' contacts with those outside the sect.

Closed Brethren – refuses communion with those not of their persuasion

Exclusive Brethren – strict rules regarding dress and conduct.

All have a common belief in future millennium following the second coming of Christ during which He will reign on earth in peace. Autonomy of each local church. (See also Chapel Ref. 125A) Note also "Plymouth Colony" – the puritan colony founded by the Pilgrim Fathers in S.E. Massachusetts in 1620, sailing from Plymouth in the ship "The Mayflower", taking 66 days, and carrying 100 passengers.

Calvinistic Methodist (Welsh and English)

Calvinism – the theological system of John Calvin (1509-64) and his followers, characterised by emphasis on the doctrines of predestination, the irresistibility of grace and justification by faith. John Calvin founded the Reform Church at Geneva in 1541.

Christadelphian

Member of Christian sect founded by John Thomas (1805-71) in the United States in 1848, holding that only the just will enter eternal life, that the wicked will be annihilated, and that the ignorant and unconverted will not be raised from the dead. Teaches a return to primitive Christianity and that Christ will soon come again to establish a theocracy lasting for a millennium. Christadelphians are congregational in organisation, and there are no ordained ministers. The name also means "Brothers of Christ". See also Chapel Ref. 39 – "General Notes on The Christadelphians".

Congregational (Independent) Welsh and English)

Individual congregations manage their own affairs with church government (The Congregational Union), exercising moral authority. Maintains the right of each gathered community of Christians to govern its own affairs and choose its own minister, independent of outside control. Congregations are governed by principles of congregationalism. System of doctrines and ecclesiastical government in which each congregation is autonomous and self-governing, and maintains bonds of faith with other similar local congregations. In the seventeenth century were known as Independents.

Episcopal Church (Dissenters' Chapel)

An autonomous branch of the Anglican Communion in Scotland and the United States. Advocates the principle of church government by Bishops. The Anglican Church in the U.S.A. was formerly established in 1784 after the War of Independence.

Evangelical Free Church
Based upon, or following from, the Gospels. Denoting or relating to any of certain Protestant sects or parties, which emphasize the importance of personal conversion and faith in atonement through the death of Christ as a means of salvation. To spread or preach the Christian Gospel. The Evangelical movement in Britain was a nineteenth Century group that stressed basic Protestant beliefs and the message of the four Gospels. Associated with Charles Simeon (1783-1836).

Forward Movement
A Home Missionary Movement establishing churches in the Cynon Valley in the early 1900's, formed by Rev. Dr. John Pugh (1846-1907) of Cardiff, (See Chapel Ref. 14).

Gospel Halls
Refer to chapel Ref. No. 4 (Ynysybwl) and No. 40 (Miskin).
An assembly of Christian Brethren holding Gospel meetings and services. Members preach the Good News of Salvation in Jesus Christ.

Independents (Welsh and English)
See under "Congregationalists".

Jehovah's Witness
Members of a Christian Church of American origin, the followers of which believe that the end of the world is near, that all war in unlawful, and that the civil law must be resisted whenever it conflicts with their Church's own religious principles. "Jehovah" – the personal name of God, revealed to Moses on Mount Horeb (Exodus 3, ch.16). (Definition by Collins English Dictionary). A millenarian movement organised in the U.S.A. in 1872 under Charles Taze Russell (1852-1916) They adopted the name "Jehovah's Witness" in 1931. Previously called "Millennial Dawnists" and "International Bible Students". They interpret the Bible literally. Belief in the imminent second coming of Christ. They publish "The Watchtower", and meet in Kingdom Halls, and all witness through regular house-to-house preaching. They numbered some 6 million in 2002 and are now an international movement. There are no clergy. Rejection of obligations such as military service, have often brought them into conflict with authority. See Chapel Ref. 38 and 95.

Labour Church
Founded in Cynon Valley in 1912 by Rev. George Neighbour. Also referred to as "Brotherhood Labour Church". See Chapel Ref. 50.

Latter Day Saints
See under the "Mormon Church".

Methodists
The systems and practices of the Methodist Church developed by John Wesley (1703-91) and his followers and founded in 1739. A member of any of the Nonconformist denominations that derive from the system of faith and practice initiated by John Wesley and his followers. Became a separate body away from the Church of England in 1795. Methodist doctrines are contained in Wesley's sermons and "Notes on The New Testament". See also under "Wesleyan Methodists" (Welsh & English).

Mission Halls/Rooms
Refer to Chapel Ref. 148

Mormon Church
Refer to Chapel Ref. 177 under – "A Brief History of The Mormon Church – Worldwide". Members of a Christian sect known as "The Church of Latter Day Saints", founded in Fayette, New York in 1830 by Joseph Smith (1805-1844).

Pentecostals
Relating to any of the various Christian groups that emphasize the charismatic aspects of Christianity and adopt a fundamental influence of The Holy Ghost, and attitude to the Bible. The Movement began in 1901 at Topeka, Kansas, U.S.A. and became organised in 1905 at Los Angeles. Characterised by a literal interpretation of the Bible. It represents a reaction against the rigid theology and formal worship of the traditional churches and chapels. Note also the "Assemblies of God" movement. See Chapel Ref. 75 and 86.

Presbyterians (Welsh and English)

Formerly known as Calvinistic Methodists. Congregations are governed by Elders of equal rank. In England, and where in Wales English is the medium of worship, the Presbyterians and Congregationalists combined in 1972 to form the United Reform Church (U.R.C.). Of or relating to any of various Protestant churches governed by Presbyters or Lay Elders, and adhering to various modified forms of Calvinism. The original Puritans proclaiming a system of Church Government headed by a body of Elders or Presbyters. A Protestant sect established in 1560 by John Knox (1513-72).

Primitive Methodists

Definition, Protestant Theology – Relating to or associated with a minority group that breaks away from a sect, denomination, or church in order to return to what is regarded as the original simplicity of the Gospels. An offshoot of Wesleyan Methodism that emerged in 1811. In 1932 The Primitive Methodist became a constituent of a United Methodist Church.

Protestantism

The religion or religious system, originating from the sixteenth Century Reformation, of any of the Churches of Western Christendom that are separated from the Roman Catholic Church and adhere substantially to principles established by Luther, Zwingli, and Calvin etc., in the Reformation.

Salvation Army

A Christian body founded in the East End of London in 1865 by William Booth, and organized on quasi-military lines for evangelism and social work among the poor. Its members, both men and women, wear distinctive uniform. It is now established in over 80 countries. Originally called The Christian Revival Association, but since 1878 has been know as The Salvation Army. Renowned for its brass bands and its weekly journal "The War Cry". See Chapel Ref. 62.

Unitarians

As the name implies, Unitarians believe that God is not a Trinity but in one person. They claim belief in only one God and deny the divinity of Christ. They believe that God is one being and reject the doctrine of the Trinity which is the Union of three persons – Father, Son, and Holy Ghost in one God head. As an organised group it dates back to the sixteenth century Protestant Reformation, first in parts of Southern Europe and from the eighteenth century in Britain and America. Note also "Arianism" which is a system of Christian theology that denies the complete divinity of Jesus. Some seventeenth and eighteenth century theologians held Arian views akin to those of Unitarianism. Note – Arius (c. 250-336) was founder of Arianism, born in Libya. Through the Toleration Act of 1689, Presbyterianism was recognised as the official religion of Scotland. However, the law did not tolerate the Unitarians until much later in 1813, because the 1689 Act only applied to those dissenters who subscribed to the Triniterian Creed – (The Trinity).

United Reform Church

In England and Wales, a Protestant denomination formed from the union of the Presbyterian and Congregational Churches in 1972. The Presbyterian Church in England, like its counterpart the Congregational Union of Scotland, has no control over individual churches but is simply consultative. Its basis and structure are set out in the revised Scheme of Union, and its legal standing was confirmed by the passing of The United Reformed Church Act of 1981.

Wesleyan Methodists (Welsh & English)

Relating to or deriving from the English preacher John Wesley (1703-91), the founder of Methodism. See also under "Methodists". Relating to Methodism in its original forms or upheld by the branch of the Methodist Church known as Wesleyan Methodists. John Wesley founded the first Methodist Chapel in Bristol in 1739.

References with courtesy of the following:-
- The Hutchinson Encyclopaedia, 1998. Helicon Publishing Ltd., Oxford.
- The New Penguin Encyclopaedia, 2002. Penguin Books, London.
- The Collins English Dictionary, 1998. William Collins Sons & Co. Ltd. London & Glasgow.

APPENDIX G.

BIBLIOGRAPHY AND FURTHER RECOMMENDED READING

Aberdare Central Library, *Numerous Chapel Centenary History Booklets.*

Kevin Adams, *A Diary of Revival (The 1904 Welsh Awakening).* 2004

D.T. Alexander, *Glamorgan Reminiscences,* 1915, Reprinted 1973.

William Alexander, *Fitting up of Meeting Houses for Public Worship,* 1820.

William Alexander, *Meeting Houses.*

Almanacks, *Aberdare and Mountain Ash,* 1888 to 1906.

Anon, *The Parish of Mountain Ash and Its Churches,* 1973.

Ivor Astle, *Aberdare at The Dawn of the 19th Century,* 1901.

Bernard Baldwin, *Mountain Ash Remembered,* 1984.

Bernard Baldwin, *Mountain Ash and Penrhiwceiber Remembered in Pictures,* 1986.

Bernard Baldwin & Harry Rogers, *Mountain Ash, Penrhiwceiber and Abercynon in Pictures,* 1994.

David A. Barton, *Chapels & Meeting Houses,* 1975.

Peter Benes, *New England Meeting House and Church, 1630-1850.* 1979.

John Betjeman, *First and Last Loves,* 1952, 1969.

William Bevan, *Hanes Aberpennar – (History of Mountain Ash),* 1896.

Marcus Binney & Peter Burman, *Churches & Chapels, "Who Cares".* 1977.

Blaengwawr Comprehensive School, *The Way We Were. Book 1 –* 1987; *Book 2 –* 1988.

Elwyn Bowen, *Vaynor. A Study of The Welsh Countryside,* 1992.

Martin Briggs, *Puritan Architecture and Its Future,* 1946.

CADW (Welsh Historic Monuments), *Chapels in Wales – Conservation and Conversion,* 1999.

Celtic Press Newspapers, *Aberdare Times,* 1862-1902.

Celtic Press Newspapers, *Aberdare and Mountain Ash Leaders,* From 1902.

Cubitt, *Church Designs for Congregations,* 1880.

Cynon Valley History Society (Founded 1971), *Old Aberdare Volumes 1-9,* (1976-2003).

C.V.H.S., *Aberdare Pictures From The Past Vol. 1-1986; Vol. 2-1992.*

C.V.H.S., *Cynon Coal,* 2001.

Cynon Valley Museum, *Chapel Histories, Photographs and Memorabilia.*

David Davies ('Dewi Cynon') *–Hanes Plwyf Penderyn – 1905, 1924.*

D.L. Davies, *Translation (1982) of Aberdare in 1853 by Thomas Dafydd Llewellyn,* 1854.

John Davies, *History of Wales,* 1990.

A.H. Dodd, *Life in Wales (p.132-159).* 1972.

George Dolby, *The Architectural Expression of Methodism,* 1964.

Hywel Teifi Edwards, *Cwm Cynon,* (in Welsh) 1997.

Alice Thomas Ellis, *Wales – An Anthology,* 1989.

David Evans, *Wales In Modern Times.* 1979.

Eifion Evans, *The Welsh Revival of 1904.* 1969. Bryntirion Press.

Geoffrey Evans, A *History of St. John's Church, Aberdare,* 1982.

Thomas Evans, *The Story of Abercynon,* 1944.

Thomas Evans, *The History of Miskin Higher,* 1946.

"Glanffrwd" – (Rev. William Thomas), *Hanes Plwyf Llanwynno (History of Llanwonno),* 1888.

Raymond K.J. Grant, *How They Lived Then. Aberdare in The 1850's,* 1978.

Raymond K.J. Grant, *On The Parish,* 1988.

Edward Greening, *A History of The Cynon Valley (Typed manuscript),* 1967.

John Harvey, *Image of the Invisible: The Visualization of Religion in the Welsh Nonconformist Tradition,* (Welsh and English), 1999.

John Harvey, *The Art of Piety – The Visual Culture of Welsh Nonconformity,* 1995.

John Hilling, *Architecture in Glamorgan. Glamorgan County History, Ch. xix Glamorgan Society 1780-1980 Vol. vi p.409-410.*

John Hilling, *The Architecture of The Welsh Chapel. – Lecture Notes p.132-156. Reprinted from The Transactions of The Honourable Society of Cymmrodorin,* 1983.

John Hilling, *The Historic Architecture of Wales,* 1975.

John Hilling, *Cardiff and The Valleys,* 1973.

F.J. Jobson, *Chapel and School Architecture,* 1850.

Jean & Russell John, *Llwydcoed in Old Photographs.* 1997.

Jean John, *Grey Trees, - Childhood Memories of Llwydcoed,* 1996.

Alan Vernon Jones, *History of a Nonconformist Chapel in Mountain Ash – "Providence" (1869 – 1987).* 1987

Alan Vernon Jones, *Chapels of The Cynon Valley –Photographs and Plans in Three Volumes, (Unpublished, private collection),* 1985-2004.

Alan Vernon Jones, *History of Mountain Ash (Translation from The Welsh) with Additional Notes and Illustrations, 1990.*

Anthony Jones, *Nonconformist Chapel Architecture in Merthyr Tydfil, 1962.*

Anthony Jones, *Welsh Chapels,* 1984.

Anthony Jones, *Welsh Chapels,* 1996.

D. Parry-Jones, *Welsh Country Characters,* 1952, 1973.

David Watkin Jones, ("Dafydd Morganwg"), *Hanes Morganwg, 1874.*

J. Graham Jones, *The History of Wales, 1990, 1998.*

Penri Jones, *Capeli Cymru, 1980.*

Ronald P. Jones, *Nonconformist Church Architecture,* 1914.

William Rhys Jones ("Mab-Y-Mynydd"), *History of Cwmaman – The Religion of The Community. - Unpublished Typed Manuscript,* 1946.

Rev. H. Elvet Lewis, *With Christ Among The Miners* (1904-05 Welsh Revival), Pub. 1906.

Tom Lewis, *The History of the Hen Dy Cwrdd, Cefn Coed Y Cymmer, 1947.*

Kenneth Lindley, *Chapels and Meeting Houses,* 1969.

Michael Llewellyn, *The Sand In The Glass,* 1943.

Thomas Dafydd Llewelyn, *Aberdare in 1853 (Old Aberdare Vol.2). Translated by D.L. Davies 1982.* 1854.

D. Lloyd, *History of Cwmaman (Trans.).*

John Mear, *Aberdare – The Railways and Tram roads,* 1999.

John Mear, *The Story of Cwmdare,* 1991.

Merthyr Teachers' Centre Group, *Merthyr Tydfil – A Valley Community,* 1981.

Mid. Glamorgan County Council (Education Department), *Environmental Studies in The Cynon Valley,* 1980.

Ivor Morgan, *Saint Elvan's – Parish History and Churches,* 1995.

Rev. J Vyrnwy Morgan, *The Welsh Religious Revival 1904-05. A Retrospect and a Criticism,* 1909.

Morgannwg, *Vol. xxi.* 1997.

David Morganwg, *Hanes Morganwg (Including a Brief History of Mountain Ash),* 1874.

Morris & Morris, *Dictionary of Biblical Terms,* 1952.

John Newman, *The Buildings of Wales – Glamorgan,* 1995.

Ivor Parry, *History of Aberdare. Chapters 13-22, Nonconformity, P. 46-76. Unpublished Typed Manuscript,* 1965.

Ivor Parry, *Research Collection – Aberdare Central Library.*

Ivor Parry, *Sidelights on Aberdare, (Glamorgan Historian, Vol. 10),* 1974.

Ivor Parry and Tom Whitney, *Old Aberdare in Photographs,* 1976.

Rowland Parry, *Abercynon – Past and Present, In Photographs,* 1996.

Perkins & Hearne, *The Methodist Church Builds Again,* 1946.

Rev. D.M. Phillips, *Evan Roberts – The Great Welsh Revivalist and His Work,* 1906.

W.W. Price, *Biographical Index –* Aberdare Central Library.

W.W. Price, *Research Collection – All Religious Denominations in the Cynon Valley –* Aberdare Central Library.

Helen Prince, *Social Conditions in The Cynon Valley and The Place of The Nonconformist Religion. (B. Ed. Thesis).* 1981

Beddoe Rees, *Chapel Building: Hints and Suggestions.* 1905

D. Ben Rees, *Chapels in The Valley.* 1975

D. Ben Rees, *Wales: The Cultural Heritage.* 1981

D.J. Rees, *In The Footsteps of Glanffrwd.* 1994

D.J. Rees, *Pontypridd with Ynysybwl (Photographs).* 1990

Rev. R.M. Rees, *Hanes Hirwaun.*

Thomas Rees, *History of Protestant Nonconformity in Wales.* 1883

Thomas Rees, *Hanes Eglwysi Annibynol Cymru – Vol. 2.* 1872

D.M. Richards, *Aberdare in 1837 (Old Aberdare Vol. 1)*. 1897

Nansi Selwood, *A History of The Villages of Hirwaun and Rhigos*. 1997

Nansi Selwood, *Penderyn – A History*. 1990

Gilbert Scott, *Domestic and Secular Architecture*. 1858

Jane Shaw and Alan Kreider, *Culture and the Nonconformist Tradition*. 1999

Dai Smith, *Wales! Wales?* 1984

"The Builder", *Periodical Magazines (Chapel Architecture & Plans).19th.& 20th.Century.*

John Thomas, *Hanes Eglwysi Annibynon Cymru – Vol. 5*. 1891

Rev. William Thomas ("Glanffrwd"), *History of Llanwonno*. 1888

Ruth Thomas, *South Wales*. 1977

Stephen Thomas, *A Pictorial History of Ynysybwl Vol. 1, - 1995; Vol. 2, -1997.*

Wynford Vaughan-Thomas, *Wales – A History*. 1885

Welsh Arts Council, *Recording Wales 2: Chapels*. 1969

Western Mail, *Pamphlets 1-6; The Welsh Revival 1904-05.*

James F. White, *Protestant Worship and Church Architecture*. 1964

Glanmor Williams, *The Welsh and Their Religion*. 1991

Gwyn Williams, *When Was Wales?* 1985

Stewart Williams, *Old Pontypridd and District in Photographs*. 1977, 82, 85

Note – Reference is made to numerous Chapel Centenary or Jubilee History Booklets throughout Chapter One.

INDEX

A.

Aberaman Colliery 63, 78
Aberaman Hotel 80
Aberaman Lesser Hotel 163
Abercynon Girls' School 20
Aberdare Canal, Boat trips & the building of the canal 128, 352
Aberdare Cemetery 243, 340
Aberdare & Hirwaun Tramway 153
Aberdare Leader 289, 311, 316, 317, 336, 348, 358
Aberdare, Lord 243, 353
Aberdare Mountain (Mynydd Aberdar) 181
Aberdare Times 234, 263-265, 282, 284, 285, 353, 354
Aberffrwd Cemetery, Mountain Ash 55,56
Abergwawr Farm, Aberaman 70
Act of Uniformity (1662) 188
Alberti, Leon Battista 94,196,197
Alternative use of vacant chapel sites 361
Albion Hotel (Lodging House), Aberaman 74
American G.I. soldiers 39, 52, 289, 290
Anthony, Rev. David John 12, 274
Anthony, Thomas (Engineer) 84
Architects & Designers 196, 198-200
Architects Fees 199, 396
Architectural Association 198
Architecture, Development in the locality 192-198
Arianism 184
Armenianism 185, 186
Armenians 184, 185
Arnold, Mrs. A.S. (Organist) 9
Arnold, John Beale 127
Art Nouveau style of chapel design 19, 131, 198
Articles, (the thirty nine) of the Church of England 189
Assembly Rooms, Aberdare 37
Attendance, Chapel 282, 283

B.

Baby Boom, The 290
Bachelors' Knife & Fork Teas 338, 339
Baileys Arms, Miskin 33, 40, 54
Band of Hope 283, 336, 338, 343, 344, 367, 372, 394
Barn-Type Chapels 183, 185, 192, 193, 204
Baroque style chapel design 198
Barracks, The 56, 57, 69
Bazaars, Sale of Works, Jumble Sales 256, 345, 346
Beaufort Arms public house, Aberaman 64
Beddgelert Revival (Gwynedd) 294
Beeching Report (1963) 348
Beehive Inn, Hirwaun 148, 155
Belgian Refugees 289
Belle Vue Inn, Hirwaun 148
Bethel Cottages, Ynysybwl 3
Bethlehem C.M. Chapel, Mountain Ash (Religious Revival 1904-05) 45, 46, 299, 308,310
Bevan, David. (Coal owner) 84
Bevan, William 231, 284, 298, 352

Bible Classes 347, 348
Bibliography 414-416
Bill of Rights (1689) 183, 189
Bird in Hand (Public house), Aberdare 384
Black Lion Hotel, Aberdare 94, 97, 105
Blackouts (during war) 290
Blaencanaid Conventicle 181, 182
Blaenannerch (1904-5 Revival) 300,301
Blaengwawr Inn, Aberaman 37
Blaengwawr School, Aberaman 17
Bloody Acre, Bloody Spot, Cwmaman 83, 336
Blue Books, Royal Commission on The State of Education in Wales (Report 1847) 189,190
Board of Education 343
Board of Guardians 261
Board Meetings 285
Board Schools 77
Boat Trips (Aberdare Canal) 43, 352
Bodwigiad Estate 146
Bodie, Dr. Walford 316
Bomb Damage 48, 88, 277
Book of Common Prayer 188
Boom in chapel building work 195
Boot Hotel, Aberdare 100, 106, 123
Bowen, Rev. Glaslyn Desmond 111, 123, 267, 387
'Bowler Hat Brigade' 60
Box-type pews 223
Brakes, Horse Drawn 348, 350, 351
Brewster, Percy 53
Brick Yard Farm, Cefn Rhigos 156
British Legion 88
British Schools 37, 70, 71, 117, 118, 138, 140, 148, 260
Broniestyn Lane Meeting Room 124
Brothers of Christ 37
Bruce Arms, Mountain Ash 52, 187
Bruce, Henry Austin M.P. 297
Brunel, Isambard Kingdom 198, 384
Bryn Seion C.M. (Carmel E.B.), Trecynon (1904-05 Revival) 299, 303, 304, 308
Brynteg Chapel, Loughor. (1904-05 Revival) 303
Building activity 308, 357-359
Building funds 198
Building & Demolition of chapels 356-360
Builders of chapels 201, 202
'Buona Vista' Liner 163
Burial Grounds 242, 243, 340
Burton's Clothiers shop 37
Bwllfa Colliery 144, 382

C.

CADW (Welsh Historic Monuments) 202, 362, 363
Calon Lan 45, 340
Calvin, John 411
Calvinistic Methodists 411
Calvinists, Calvinism 184, 186
Cambrian Lamp Works 101

Canal House, Cwmbach 92
Candle King, Grocers shop, Mountain Ash 37
Capel, The Chapels Heritage Society 363
Capel Bricks 91
Capel Groes Wen (near Caerphilly) 183
Capel Harris 144, 149
Capel Lletty Shiencyn 92, 385
Capel Pen-Rhiw 183, 193
Capel-Y-Comin 157
Capel-Y-Drindod 153
Caradog's Choir 274, 341
Caretakers, Chapel 280
Carne Park Hotel, Carnetown, Abercynon 15, 18
Castle Inn, Aberaman 68
Catholicism 189, 261
Catholic rule 189
Cefn Pennar House 60
Ceiling design & roses 205, 206, 211-219, 225, 244, 245,
    248, 250
Cemeteries 58, 242, 243, 340
Census, (1851) 357
Certificate of Merit 334, 344, 367, 368
Chairs (Commemorative & Memorial) 232
Chapel design phases 204
Chapel Ghosts 358
Chapel names and their meanings 237-240
Charabanc outings 350, 351
Charles 1, King 181
Charles11, King 183, 188
Chartered Surveyors (R.I.C.S.) 362
Chartist Riots 358
China ware 234, 259, 321, 322, 324, 331-333
Cholera Epidemic 89, 149-151, 243, 359, 396
Cholera Revival 294, 295
Choral societies 339
Christadelphians (Ecclesia) 37, 38, 279, 411
Church Rate (1860) 191
Cistercian Monks 384
Civic Sunday 65
Clarendon Code (1662) 183; (1661-1665) 188
Classic phase of chapel design 196-198
Clift, Austin, (Treasurer) 54
Clocks, makers & suppliers 231, 258, 321-323, 329, 330
Coleman, David Edward ('Eos Hefin') 45, 340, 341
Cole's Bazaar Stores 99, 120
Collier, George (Choir), Aberaman 147
Colliers Arms, Mountain Ash 340
Colliery winding engine houses 194
Composers of the Cynon Valley 339, 340
Conductors, Choirmasters & Precentors of Cynon Valley
    340, 341
Conventicle Act (1664) 182, 188
Conventicle period 192, 204
Conventiclers 187
Conversion (of vacant chapels) 361, 362
Converted, quotes from the (Religious Revival) 313, 314
Co-operative Stores, Cwmaman 81; Cwmbach 91
Corinthian capitals (column supports) 224

Corporation Act (1661) 188
Cory, Richard 26, 31
Coughing in Chapel 282
Crawshay Arms public house, Hirwaun 149, 151
Crawshay Bailey Estate 67
Cribinddu Farm, Ynysybwl 7, 12
Critics; Criticism; Chapel (Ministers & Sermons) 263,
    264
Cromwell, Oliver 181
Crystal Palace, London 45, 274, 341
Cunnick, Rev. John (Vicar) 190, 191
Cwm, The (Cwm Clydach) 353
Cwmaman Coal Company 81
Cwmaman Colliery 313
Cwmaman Hall & Institute 82, 84, 85
Cwmdare Farm, Duffryn Dar 125
Cwmdare Primary School 135
Cwmneol Colliery, Cwmaman 82
Cwmneol Waun Fawr Field, Cwmaman 84
Cwm-Y-Glo Chapel 128, 181-186
Cynon Valley Museum 199, 232, 363

D.

'D-Day' (1944) 39
Darby, Rev. John Nelson 124
Dare Fychan Foundry   106, 131
Dare Inn, Cwmdare 125, 138
Dare Valley Country Park 13, 123, 240
Davies, Rev. Aeron 109
Davies, Miss Annie (Evangelist) 302
Davies, Rev. Bleddyn Cynwyn 270
Davies, Byron. (Organist) 101
Davies, Rev. D.M. 90
Davies, Rev. D. Herbert 96, 269
Davies, Rev. David Jacob 102, 129, 268, 276
Davies, Rev. David Owen ('D.O'), (Elim, Cwmdare)
    137, 266
Davies, Rev. David Owen (Old Bethel, Ynysfelin, near
    Penderyn) 158
Davies, Rev. David Teify 145, 270, 273
Davies, Rev. E. R. 109, 270
Davies, Evan Thomas 339
Davies, Father David (St. John's) 298
Davies, Gomer Lloyd (Organist) 54, 62, 385
Davies, Handel (Organist) 28, 396
Davies, Rev. Haydn 45
Davies, Rev. Henry Aeron 79, 82
Davies, Rev. J. Sulgwyn 134
Davies, Rev. Jonah 62
Davies, Rev. John 109
Davies, John ('Pen-Dar') 115, 230, 274
Davies, Rev. John Bowen (Davis Bach) 62
Davies, Lord 10
Davies, Rev. Luther 64, 85 - 86
Davies Nev Lukey 54
Davies, Miss Rosina (Evangelist) 7
Davies, Tom (Organist) 67
Davies, Rev. Thomas 66

Davies, Rev. William Samlet 140, 268, 395
Davis, David (Blaengwawr) 152, 191, 297, 311
Davis, David (Maesyffynon) 62, 108, 311, 386
Day Schools 42, 260
Deacons, Chapel 11, 27, 161, 266, 270 – 277, 280, 342
Debain, Alexande. F. 227
Debasement Phase (chapel design) 197, 204
Decadent Phase (chapel design) 197
Declarations of Indulgence (1672) 188; (1687-88) 189
Decline in Chapels 357, 360, 362 - 364
Deep Duffryn Colliery, Mountain Ash 44, 298, 299
Demolished Chapels (numbers of) 360, 363, 395, 396
Dennis, Rev. E.R. 128, 266, 271
Denomination, Religious, Abbreviations 410
Diaconate 271
Disestablishment (Royal Assent 1914) 191
Dissenters 183, 184, 187 - 189, 192
Domestic, Long Wall Façade 193
Drama 339
Drama Group, Ebenezer, Trecynon 343
Drawings, original colour-washed 39, 41, 47, 199, 208, 209
Duffryn Boys' Infant School 46, 48
Duffryn Aman Ambulance Centre, Aberaman 73
Duffryn Dar (Cwmdare Farm) 125
Dunning, Arthur 86
Dyffryn (or Duffryn) House 233, 353

E.
Early Chapel interiors and layouts 222
Early Classic Phase of Chapel Design 194, 195, 204
Early Dissent 181-187
Early Nonconformist Chapels of the Cynon Valley 186, 187
Early Religious Revivals, (1620 to 1884) 292-295
Ebenezer W. I., Trecynon, (1859 and 1904-05 Religious Revivals) 297, 303, 304, 309
'Eccentric' Style/Years of Chapel Design 197, 198
Ecclesia (Christadelphians) 37, 38
Education Act (Foster's Act 1870) 260
Education Act (1902) 191
Edward IV, King 243
Edwards, Rev. J. 155
Edwards, Rev. William 126, 240, 262, 269, 297
Eisteddfodau 260
Elias, John 257, 293, 294, 357, 358
Ellis, Hugh 341
Episcopal Church (Dissenters' Chapel) 411
Episcopal Church, New York State 295
Evacuees 6, 52, 79, 290
Evans, Rev. Ben ('Telynfab') 115
Evans, Rev. Christmas, (Calvaria, Aberdare) 95
Evans, Rev. Christmas, (Llandysul) 294
Evans, David 339
Evans, Rev. David Silyn, Siloa, Aberdare 107, 267, 298, 309, 324, 339, 395
Evans, Edward (Ton Coch) 87, 128, 129
Evans, Miss Florrie (Religious Revival 1904-05) 308

Evans, Mrs. Heulwen (Organist) 70
Evans, Rev. Idris 36, 54
Evans, Ivor 107, 340
Evans, Rhys (Ton Coch) 87
Evans, Sydney (1904-05 Revivalist) 300, 302
Evans, Ted (Organist) 126
Evans, Thomas ('Tomos Glyn Cothi') 128, 186, 293, 384
Evans, William John (Organist, Conductor, Choir Master) 107, 267, 276, 340
External Memorial and Foundation Stones 240

F.
Facts 'Figure It Out' 395, 397
'Fairfield House', Aberdare 101, 135
Fanhaulog Seat, Ynysybwl 193
Fanheulog ('Vanhayly') Chapel, Ynysybwl 3
Farmers Arms Public House, Aberdare 96
Fforchneol Arms Public House, Godreaman 80
Final Phase of Chapel Design, 204; of building, 357
Fire Watches; Fire Guards and Lectures (War Time) 290
Five Mile Act, (1665) 188
Floors 224
Foel Quarry, Penderyn 159
Forward, Brother James 120
Foster's Education Act, (1870) 260
Fothergill, Richard 117, 241
French Revolution 293, 384
Friendly Societies 261, 369

G.
Gabriel, W.H. (Organist) 19
Gadlys Central School 114
Gadlys Uchaf Estate 115
Gadlys Uchaf Farm ('Tir-Yr-Neathe') 118, 186
Galleries 214, 217, 223, 224, 248
Gardd Aberdar 340
Gas Works 231
Gelli Wrgan Farm, Llanwonno 8, 54, 353, 383
General Strike (1926) and The Depression Years 68, 76, 288
George, David Lloyd 191, 291
George, Rev. John Joseph 102
George, Sheridan (Organist) 101
George, Miss. Sophia (Organist) 102
German Town (Perthcelyn) 39, 358
G.I.'s, American Soldiers 39, 52, 290
'Gin Palace', (Prince of Wales Public House), Aberaman 68
Glog Seat, Ynysybwl 193
Glamorgan Family History Society 243
Glamorgan Record Office 3, 23, 26, 363
Glamorganshire Canal 352
Glancynon Inn, Hirwaun 162
Glancynon Inn, Mountain Ash 44
Glandover Inn, Gadlys 115
'Glanffrwd', (Rev. William Thomas) 3, 186, 192, 193, 382, 386, 395
Glan Rhondda (Hymn Tune) 340

Glorious Revolution, (1688) 183
Gold Medal/Temperance Movement 334
Golden Age of Classicism 196, 204
Golden Lion Public House, Trecynon 120
Goldie, Richard 37
Good Templars 283
Gothic, Perpendicular 10, 17, 51, 54, 55, 81, 101, 105, 109, 149, 197, 198, 225
Gothic Windows 55, 225
Grade Two Listed Chapel Buildings 202, 203, 362, 396
Graig School House, Newtown 42
Grand Bazaars, stalls etc. 256, 345, 346
Grand Classical Style of Chapel Design 196-198
Grange, The, Aberdare 384
Grave Yards 242, 243
Great Western Railway 81, 352
Green Fach 386
Griffin Inn, Aberaman 66
Griffiths, Rev. David 137
Griffiths, Evan (Junior), Architect, Aberdare 128, 186, 200
Griffiths, Evan ('Ty Mawr') 128, 145, 186, 200
Griffiths, Rev. James 96, 268, 275, 309
Griffiths, Jessie Millicent (Organist) 121, 124
Griffiths, Rev. (Father/Vicar) John 190, 242, 267, 298
Guilds; Groups; Clubs 280, 347
Gwalia Hall, Penrhiwceiber 36
Gwrandawyr (Listeners, hearers in the congregation) 261, 298
'Gwyrosydd' (Daniel James) 45, 340
Gymanfa Ganu 7, 45, 95, 260, 285, 298, 339, 340, 341, 343

H.
Halo Arch 196, 225
Hann, E.M. 78
Harmonium Organs; Manufacturers and Suppliers 220, 226, 228, 229, 230, 253, 254, 256
Harmston, A.E. (Organist) 101
Harmston & Co., Organ & Piano Merchants, Aberdare 229, 230, 253
Harp Inn, Mountain Ash 340
Harries, Rev. William 130
Harris, Howell (Revivalist) 3, 293, 382
Harris, Rev. Mary Constance 102
Harris, Owen 131, 328
Harrison, Rev. Joseph 119, 126, 149, 153, 262, 263, 265
Harrison, Rev. William 112
Heating and Lighting of Chapels 230, 231
Henchman, William 162
Hen-Dy-Cwrdd (Presbyterian), Cefn Coed-Y-Cymmer 185
Hen-Dy-Cwrdd, (Unitarian), Trecynon 128, 129, 185, 186
Hen Wlad Fy Nhadau 340
Hinchcliffe, Rev. George 86
Hippodrome, (Now The Palladium), Aberdare 297
Hodge, William 100

Hodges, William and Sons, Clothiers, Aberdare 100
Hollyman, Rev. James Ashford 54
Hopkins, Rev. D. 131
Horse and Groom Inn, Aberdare 97
Howells, Rev. John 52
H.T.V. Documentary 33
Hughes, Rev. Efonwy 274
Hughes, Rev. Evan John 150, 160
Hughes, Rev. Hugh ('Huw Tegai') 112, 137, 385
Hughes, John 45, 340
Hughes, Rev. John Richard (Revivalist, Anglesey) 295
Hughes, Rev. T.T. 56
Humphreys, Rev. Thomas 81, 84, 266
Hwyl 262, 339
Hyde, Edward (Earl of Clarendon) 188
Hymn Writers of The Cynon Valley 339, 340
Hypnotism (Religious Revival, 1904-05) 316, 317

I.
Illuminated Address 5, 27, 365
Iron Foundries (Local) 241
Iron Work, Art in 205, 217, 220, 241
Iron Works, Aberdare, Gadlys, Llwydcoed 149, 241
Iron Works, Hirwaun 145, 149, 150, 241
Italian Plasterers 225
Italian Renaissance Period, and Architects 196, 197

J.
James, Daniel ('Gwyrosydd,) 45, 340
James, James ('Iago Ap Ieuan') 340
James II, King 183, 189
James, Rev. William 94
Jeffreys, Rev. T.M. 109, 270
Jenkins, Canon-Vicar 260
Jenkins, Captain D. (Hensol) 184
Jenkins, Rev. H.P. 70, 269
Jenkins, Rev. Joseph, Newquay, (Revivalist) 301
Jenkins, Rev. Matthias 61
Jenkins, Rev. Morgan 17,
Job Creation Project 2
John, Daffydd 287, 341
John, Rev. Thomas ('Twrfab') 75
John, W.H. (Precentor, Conductor and Organist) 81, 341
Jones, Mrs. Afonwy (Precentor and Organist) 79
Jones, Alan Vernon (Organist) 54
Jones, Rev. Arfon 77
Jones, Rev. Cefni 155
Jones, Rev. Dafydd 126
Jones, Dan (Captain) 162
Jones, Rev. Daniel, (Rhos W.B., Mountain Ash) 56
Jones, Rev. Daniel, (Soar W.B., Llwydcoed) 142
Jones, David Watkin ('Dafydd Morgannwg') 184
Jones, Mrs. Florrie (Organist) 32
Jones, Rev. Glannant 70, 269
Jones, Griffith (Revivalist) 293
Jones, Griffith Rhys ('Caradog') 129, 271, 341
Jones, Humphrey (Revivalist) 295, 296
Jones, Rev. J. Eric 102, 129

Jones, Rev. J. Francis 52
Jones, Rev. J. Grawys 126, 143, 144, 268, 287
Jones, Rev. James 289
Jones, Rev. John (Talysarn) 294
Jones, Rev. Josiah Thomas 191
Jones, Llangollen 384
Jones, Rev. M 46
Jones, Miss. M.S. 19, 396
Jones, Rev. Margam 141, 268
Jones, Rev. Owen (Dowlais) 298
Jones, Rev. Rees Jenkin 128, 266
Jones, Rev. Thomas 97
Jones, Titus 386
Jones, Tom (Professor) 341
Jones, Rev. William (Ton Pentre) 198
Jones, Rev. William Aerwyn ('Jones-Nebo') 138, 268
Jones, Rev. William-Barker 269
Jones, Rev. W. Christmas 80
Joseph, Thomas (Colliery Engineer) 95

K.

Keesey of Birmingham, (Sunday School Banners) 96, 233
Keyboard Manuals (Organs) 227, 229, 230
King William Inn, Aberaman 66

L.

Labour Church 46
Lady Windsor Colliery, Ynysybwl 7, 9
Lamb and Flag Inn, Cardiff Road, Aberaman 57
Lamb Hotel, Penderyn 161
Lamp Works, Graig Street 101
Lan Farm, Perthcelyn 35, 353
Langley, Lionel (Organist) 101
Large, Rev. Percy 39, 49
Largest chapels in The Cynon Valley 203, 297, 396
Leach (Brother) Tom 120
Leading Denominations (Welsh and English) 359, 397
Lee Hotel, Penrhiwceiber 358
Lee, Major V.H. 26, 358
Lectures, Talks and Debates 337
Lewis, Rev. Benjamin 269
Lewis, Rev. D.M. 148
Lewis, Rev. (Vicar) Evan 191
Lewis, Rev Howell 182
Lewis, Rev. John 77
Lewis, Rev. Morgan 89
Lewis, Rev. P.H. 11
Lewis, Mr. & Mrs. Penn (Leicester) 305
Lewis, Tom ('Mab-Y-Mynydd') 185
Lewis, Rev. William 88
Licensed Places for Worship 189
Life Boat Public House, Cwmbach 93
Lindsay Constitutional Club, Abercynon 16
Listed Building Status 202, 203, 362
Llanfaches, Monmouthshire 181, 182
Llangeitho (Religious Revival 1735 and 1762-63) 293
Llanwenarth Chapel, Govilon, Mon. 183

Llanwonno Parish Church 242
Lletty Turner Fields 39, 289, 290
Llewellyn, Rev. Arthur G. 61
Llewellyn, D.R. ('Fairfield') 135
Llewellyn, Sion 185
Llewellyn, Rev. Thomas 45
Llewellyn, Thomas Dafydd ('Llewellyn Alaw') 129, 271, 340
Lloyd, Henry ('Ap Hefin') 340
Llwydcoed Brass Band 140
Llwyn Onn Reservoir 158
Llyfr Tonau (Book of Hymn Tunes) 340
Local Health Boards 199, 231, 242, 265, 284
Local School Boards 260
Local Vernacular Style (Architecture) 194
London Missionary Society 90
Long Wall Façade Design 123, 193, 204, 222
Lougher (1904-05 Religious Revival) 122, 292, 299, 301-303, 307, 308-310
Lower Duffryn Colliery (Lower Pit) Cefnpennar 60

M.

Mackworth Arms Hotel, Gadlys 122
Maesgwyn Estate, Cwmdare 135
Maesyrarian Cemetery, Mountain Ash 58, 243
Maesyronnen Chapel, Hay on Wye 183, 192
Magic Lantern Slide Shows 337
Manpower Services Commission 2
Map of Cynon Valley 399
Marches, Sunday School 232-234, 354, 355
Market House, Aberdare 96
Marquis of Bute 157
Marshall, John 37
Mary II, Queen 183, 189
Mathias, Rev. J.L. 7
Meadon, S. (Treasurer) 155
Memorial and Foundation Stone (External) 165, 166, 240
Merthyr Independents 185
Merthyr to Hirwaun Railway Line 141
Mid Glamorgan County Council 2
Mid Glamorgan County Council (Planning Dept.) 3, 362
Millar, Tom. W. (Architect), Mountain Ash 200
Mills, Rev. John 116
Miners' Institute, 'The Square', Trecynon 133
Miner's Lamp Factory 37
Ministers; Preaching; Sermons; Salaries 262-265
Monk Street, Aberdare 384
Moody, Dwight Lyman 286
Moose Hall, Aberdare 88
Morgan, Rev, David (Dafydd-'Ysbyty-Ystwyth', Revivalist) 121, 295, 296
Morgan, Rev. Daniel Stanley 54
Morgan, Edward (Revivalist) 309
Morgan and Elford (Architects), Aberdare 200
Morgan, Rev. John 303
Morgan, Rev. Jonah 89, 268
Morgan, Pamela ('Mother Shepherd') 120, 132, 135, 265, 309, 310

Morgannwg, Dafydd 184
Moriah Chapel, Loughor (1904-05 Revival) 301-303
Morley, Samuel, M.P. 198, 234
Mormon Church 109, 162-164, 359, 382, 412
Morris, Rev. W.D. 85
Morse, Rev. William 126
Mortuary Chapel, Aberdare, 103; Mountain Ash 51
Moses, Edward (Organist) 109, 341, 395
Moss House, Abernant, Aberdare 100
Mother Shepherd (Pamela Morgan) 120, 132, 135, 265,
     309, 310
Mountain Ash Coffee Tavern 48, 187
Mountain Ash Male Voice Choir 341
Mountain Ash Temperance Football Club 315
Museum of Welsh Life, St Fagans 183, 193
Music and Singing in Chapel 285, 286, 339, 343
Mutual Improvement Society 343
Mynachdy Farm, Old Ynysybwl 5, 383
Mynachdy Seat, Ynysybwl 193
Mynydd Aberdar (Aberdare Mountain) 181

N.

Name Plaques (Stone, External) 165, 166, 169, 235-237
Nant Clydach 353
Nant Melyn Colliery, Cwmdare , 110, 138; (Religious
     Revival 1904-05), 311, 312
Napiers Public House, Mountain Ash 58
National Eisteddfod (1905, Mountain Ash) 316
National Library of Wales, Aberystwyth 307, 363
National Museum of Wales, Cardiff 363
Neighbour, Rev. George 40, 46
Neo-Classical Architectural Features 196, 198
Newcastle Emlyn (School) 300, 301
New Inn, Aberdare 109
New Inn, Abercynon 14
New Organ Funds 228
New Theatre, Aberdare 297
New Quay, Cardiganshire, (1904-05 Revival), 301, 302
Nici-Naci Pit, Aberaman 69, 359
Nixon, John 42
Nonconformity and Dissent in The Cynon Valley 181-
     191
Number of Chapels built (1751-2004) 358, 359

O.

Old Duffryn Colliery 163
Oliver, David 128, 187
'On The Chapel Trail', (1995 HTV Documentary) 33,
     360
Orgapian (Wind Organ/Piano) 13, 230, 286
Organs 220, 226-230, 251-254
Organ Builders and Manufacturers 229, 230
Organ Recitals 228
Organ Specification 228
Orchestra, Ebenezer Chapel, Trecynon 286, 287
Outings to the Countryside 353
Overton, George 144, 150, 187
Owen, Rev. Morfydd Llwyn (Hymnist) 32

Owen, Rev. Rees 86
Owen, Richard (Revivalist, Anglesey) 295
Owen, Mrs. Valerie (Organist and Secretary) 160

P.

Palace Cinema, Hirwaun 153
Palladian Composition 28
Palladio, Andrea 196
Palladium Cinema, Aberdare 37, 297
Parades, Sunday School 65, 232-234, 354, 355
Park School, (Ysgol-Y-Comin) 120, 134
Park View Inn, Trecynon 359
Parry, Dr. Joseph 298
Parry, Rev. R. Ivor 107, 182, 186, 189, 266, 268, 363,
     395
Patagonia, Welsh Settlement 137
Patriot Arms Public House, Hirwaun 162
Pawn Shop, Mountain Ash 56, 358
Peace Meetings (1939-45 War), 290
Peace Park, Mountain Ash 289
Peg-legged preacher, The 388
'Pendar' (John Davies) 115, 230, 274
Pen Pews 223
Penny Bun Collections 337
Penny Readings 337
Pen Pont Farmhouse, Cwm Taf 158
Penpound Welsh Baptist Chapel 96, 97
Penrhiwceiber Colliery 27
Pentwyn Bach 121, 123, 127, 132, 133, 145, 187
Penywaun Welfare Hall 143
Perpendicular, Gothic style of Architecture 10, 17, 51,
     54, 55, 81, 101, 105, 109, 149, 197, 198, 225
Persecution & Suppression of Dissent (The Acts) 187-
     189
Persecution of the Nonconformists 189
Pews, Arrangements & layouts 216, 223, 244, 249
Pew Rents 223
Phillips, Ben 230
Phillips, Rev. John 45
Pit Horses (Religious Revival, underground services) 313
Pickering, William 335, 336
Plasdraw, Site of 353, 384
Pledges of Abstinence 314, 334, 343
Plymouth Brethren 124, 411
Poems 389-394
Police Court 109
Police Records 315
Poor Children's Boot Fund 289
Poor Law 261
Poplar's Field, Mountain Ash 53
Post Classical period of chapel design 204, 357
Powell Duffryn Steam Coal Company 63, 76
Powell, Rev. Thomas 139
Powell, Vavasour 183
Powell's No.1 Pit, Cwmbach 163
Prayer Meetings, (Religious Revivals) 307
Preaching 262-265
Preaching Tubs 222

Presbyterianism 183, 184, 413
Present position of chapels (number of) 360
Presentation Trowels 234, 320
Press (newspapers) Role of the 317, 318
Price, Rev. Dr. David 107, 117, 267
Price, Rev. Morgan 62
Price, Rev. Peter (Dowlais) 305
Price, Rev. Dr. Thomas 96, 97, 116, 121, 130, 190, 191
Price, William Watkin (WWP., Local Historian) 129, 132, 231, 242, 271, 363
Primitive phase of chapel design 192, 204
Prince of Wales Public House, Aberaman – 'The Gin Palace' 68
Prosser, David 54, 267, 353, 383
Pryce, Hon. John Bruce (Lord Aberdare) 243
Public Cemeteries 243
Puddlers Arms Public House, Hirwaun 151
Pugh, Rev. Ebenezer 265
Pugh, Rev. Dr. John 16
Pugh, Brother William 37
Pulpits 206-07, 210-12, 214-18, 222, 223, 247
Puritan Revolution (1660), 188
Pwll Bara Menyn (Williams' Pit, Nici-Naci Pit), Aberaman 69

Q.

Quakers 188
Queens Hotel, Aberdare 37

R.

Rammell Report (1853) 243
Reading Rooms 264
Redevelopment of sites after demolition 361
Reed Organs 227
Rees, Rev. Dr. Ben 22, 29
Rees, Glyn (Treasurer) 156
Rees, Mrs. Mary Gwen 156
Rees, Rev. J.D. 119
Rees, Joseph 26, 341
Rees, Rev. Owen 128, 186
Rees, Rev. Dr. Thomas 126, 385
Refugees, Belgian 289
Relations between the Established Church & Nonconformity 189-191
Relief of Tramps 261
Religious Census (1877), 359
Religious Mania 316
Religious Revival (1859) 195, 196, 223, 295-298, 307, 309, 311
Religious Revival (1904-05) 197, 300-317
Religious Revival in the Cynon Valley 307-311
Religious Revivals (1620-1884) 292-295
Religious Revivals, effects on various addictions & secular attractions 314-316
Renowden's Boot Repair Shop, Hirwaun 152
Revolution, French 293, 384
Rex Cinema, Aberdare 57
Rhyd-Y-Gwreiddyn Farm Cottage, Ynysybwl 3, 193, 395

Rhys, Rhys Hopkin 102, 129, 271
Richard, Henry M.P. 191
Richards, Richard 128, 186
Richards, Theophilus 128, 186
Richards, Thomas Glyndwr 45, 341
Riley, E & Co. Banners (Leeds) 233
Rivalry and competition between denominations 195
Roberts Arms public house, Aberdare 109
Roberts, Dan (Revivalist) 302, 310
Roberts, Evan (Revivalist) 292, 295, 299-311, 317, 318
Roberts, Rev. Huw 269
Roberts, John ('Ieuan Gwyllt') 340
Robertstown Hotel, Ynysybwl 8, 9, 12
Roderick, Thomas (Architect), Aberdare 200
Roger, Rev. R.S. 56
Roll of Honour, (1914-18 War) 325
Roman Catholics 188, 189, 261
Rowland, Daniel (Revivalist) 293
Rowlands, Rev. R 70, 269
Royal Albert Hall (organ) 228, 396
Royal Commission on the Ancient and Historical Monuments of Wales (RCAHMW) 363
Royal Commission on the State of Education in Wales (Report, 1847) ('The Blue Books') 189, 190
Royal Institute of British Architects 198
Royal Institution of Chartered Surveyors 362
Royal National Eisteddfod of Wales (Mountain Ash 1905) 316
Rudge, John 281
Rule, George 81
Rule, Pastor Haydn 136
Rules, Discipline & Procedures (Chapel) 281-283
Runge, (Jewellers) 132

S.

Saint John's Parish Church, Aberdare 128, 185, 242
Salvation Army 57, 295, 358, 413
San Andrea Church, Mantua, Italy 94, 196, 197
Sankey, Ira David 286
School of Commerce, Aberdare 37
Seaside Trips 39, 348, 349, 387
Secretaries, Chapel 277
Secretary of State for Wales 202
Secular attractions 336
Separation (split) from Cwm-Y-Glo Chapel 185, 186
Sermons; Criticism, Advice 262-265
Services held below ground (Religious Revivals) 311-313
Sêt Fawr ('Big Seat') 222
Shepherd, Rev. David (Welsh Evangelist) 136
Shepherd's Pit, Cwmaman 84
Singing Festivals 285, 286
Sister-hood 280
Sleeping in Chapel 281, 286
Smith, Joseph 163
Soiree 289
Soup Kitchens 288, 289, 396
South Wales Choral Union 45